SECULAR ANNOTATIONS

ON

SCRIPTURE TEXTS.

Scripture Texts Illustrated

BY

GENERAL LITERATURE.

BY THE

REV. FRANCIS JACOX, B.A.

NEW YORK: THOMAS NELSON & SONS,
42, BLEECKER STREET.
1871.

Issued in this country by special arrangement with Messrs.
Hodder & Stoughton, *of London, England.*

CONTENTS.

SECULAR ANNOTATIONS

ON

SCRIPTURE TEXTS.

FELLOWSHIP IN ACHAN'S FALL.

JOSHUA xxii. 20.

WHEN Achan the son of Zerah committed a trespass in the accursed thing, wrath fell not alone upon Achan, but upon all the congregation of Israel; "and that man perished not alone in his iniquity." The text is one to arrest the thoughtless, and to suggest even to the most thoughtful matter for very serious consideration.

"Should one man sin, and would God be wroth with all the congregation?" That deprecatory question had been put twenty years before Achan's trespass, by the congregation of Israel, in the matter of Korah, when they fell upon their faces and pleaded with God, the God of the spirits of all flesh. And some centuries later the confession of King David in time of pestilence took this form: that he had sinned and done wickedly; but those sheep—those subjects of his, involved in the penalty of his transgression, and dying off like sheep in a flock to the right and left of him, seventy thousand of them from morning to evening, from Dan even to Beersheba,—what had they done?

If, indeed, says Dr. South, a man could be wicked and a villain to himself alone, the mischief would be so much the more tolerable. But the case, as he goes on to show, is much otherwise: the guilt of the crime lights upon one, but the example of it sways a multitude; especially if the criminal be of any note or eminence in the world. "For the fall of such a one by any temptation (be it never so plausible) is like that of a principal stone or stately pillar, tumbling from a lofty edifice into the deep mire of the street; it does not only plunge and sink into the black dirt itself, but also dashes or bespatters all that are about it or near it when it falls." It is by no very subtle and far-fetched reasoning that a living divine essays to show that we may sin in the persons of other men, and so may sin in other countries which we never saw, and in years after we are in our graves. For may we not, he asks, be partakers in other men's sins of which at their commission we knew not, indeed at whose commission we would shudder? May we not in the moral world sometimes set the great stone rolling down the hill, with little thought of the ruin it may deal below? "Ah, you may live after you are dead, to do mischief; live in the evil thoughts you instilled, the false doctrines you taught, the perverted character you helped to form." And just as a righteous exemplar, "being dead, yet speaketh," and is a living means of good ages after he has been in his grave, "so may you, insignificant though you be, have left some impress of yourself upon minds more powerful than your own, and so be exercising a power to do harm to people you have never heard of, years after you are dead." Thus it is that far down into unknown time, and far away into the unknown distance, the moral contagion of our sin may be proved to spread; so that we may still be incurring guilt after the green turf is over us, and in lands which we have never seen and shall never see. "The evil principle we instilled, the evil example we set, may ripen into bitter fruit in the murderous blow which shall be dealt a century hence upon Australian plains!" Well may the note of exclamation follow: how strange, yet how inevitable, the tie which may link our uneventful life with the stormy passions of numbers far away! More wonderful than even the Atlantic cable is declared to be that unknown fibre, along which, from other men's sins, responsibility may thrill even to our departed souls: "a chain whose links are formed perhaps of idle words, of forgotten looks, of phrases of double meaning, of bad advice, of cynical sentiment hardly seriously meant; yet carried on through life after life, through soul after soul, till the little seed of evil sown by you has developed into some deed of guilt at which you shudder, but from participation in responsibility for which you cannot clear yourself." Every sin, we are in fine reminded, may waken its echo; every sin is reduplicated and reiterated in other souls and lives.

A distinguished French preacher, of the Reformed faith, has a striking discourse on what he entitles the *solidarity* of evil; and he too dilates upon the mysterious links which connect together persons and acts that appear to have nothing in common,—suggesting melancholy examples of the contagion of guilt and its consequences, of the expansive power of corruption and its almost boundless results.

Our most powerful female writer of fiction has emphatically taught, if a striking story can teach, that there is no sort of wrong deed of which a man can bear the punishment alone; you can't isolate yourself, and say that the evil which is in you shall not spread. Men's lives are as thoroughly blended with each other as the air they breathe; evil spreads as necessarily as disease. "I know, I feel the terrible extent of suffering this sin of Arthur's has caused to others,"—so the good rector tells one who cherishes vengeance on the wrong-doer; "but so does every sin cause suffering to others besides those who commit it." The problem how far a man is to be held responsible for the unforeseen consequences of his own deed this speaker pronounces to be one that might well make us tremble to look into it; the evil consequences that may lie folded in a single act of selfish indulgence being a thought so awful that it ought surely to awaken some feeling less presumptuous than a rash and vindictive desire to punish.

In another of her books the same authoress takes pains to prove how deeply inherent it is in this life of ours that men have to suffer for each other's sins; so inevitably diffusive is human suffering that we can conceive no retribution which does not spread beyond its mark in pulsations of unmerited pain.

There is a passage in one of Madame de Charrière's letters in which, avowing her full recognition of the fact that she must pay in person for the costly experience of life, she expresses the futile wish that others might not have to share in the costs, but owns with a sigh that the wish *is* futile, for one does nothing absolutely alone she says, and nothing so happens to us as to entirely exclude the participation of others: "*On ne fait rien tout seul, et il ne nous arrive rien à nous seuls.*" We are taught by modern science that the slightest movement, of the smallest body, in the remotest region, produces results which are perpetual, which diffuse themselves through all space, and which, though they may be metamorphosed, cannot be destroyed.* Or again, as Mrs. Browning reminds us,—

> "Each creature holds an insular point in space :
> Yet what man stirs a finger, breathes a sound,
> But all the multitudinous beings round,
> In all the countless worlds, with time and place
> For their conditions, down to the central base,
> Thrill, haply, in vibration and rebound,
> Life answering life across the vast profound,
> In full antiphony. . . ."

If no good work that a man does is lost—the smallest useful work, as an octogenarian essayist assures us, continuing to be useful long after the man is dead and forgotten, so neither do bad actions die with the doer. "Future generations suffer for the sin of their ancestors, and one great crime or act of folly causes the misery of unborn millions." So all things, it is added, hang together in one unbroken chain, of which we see a few links, but the beginning and the end we see not and never shall see.

Seneca was writing for all time when he said that no man's error is confined to himself, but affects all around him, whether by example, or consequences, or both: "*nemo errat uni sibi.*" A latter-day philosopher assigns to a place among the most

* "Wave your hand; the motion which has apparently ceased is taken up by the air, from the air by the walls of the room, etc., and so by direct and re-acting waves, continually comminuted, but never destroyed."—*Grove's Correlation of Physical Forces.*

insoluble riddles propounded to mortal comprehension what he calls the fatal decree by which every crime is made to be the agony of many innocent persons as well as of the single guilty one. "Ah!" exclaims Hilda to guilty Miriam, in the story of "Transformation,"—"now I understand how the sins of generations past have created an atmosphere of sin for those that follow. While there is a single guilty person in the universe, each innocent one must feel his innocence tortured by that guilt. Your deed, Miriam, has darkened the whole sky!" To apply the lines of a reflective poet,—

> "'Tis not their own crimes only, men commit;
> They harrow them into another's breast,
> And they shall reap the growth with bitter pain."

Very forcibly Mr. Isaac Taylor warns us that in almost every event of life the remote consequences vastly outweigh the proximate in actual amount of importance; and he undertakes to show, on principles even of mathematical calculation, that each individual of the human family holds in his hand the centre lines of an interminable web-work, on which are sustained the fortunes of multitudes of his successors; the implicated consequences, if summed together, making up therefore a weight of human weal or woe that is reflected back with an incalculable momentum upon the lot of each. The practical conclusion is that every one is bound to remember that the personal sufferings or peculiar vicissitudes or toils through which he is called to pass are to be estimated and explained only in an immeasurably small proportion if his single welfare is regarded, while their "full price and value are not to be computed unless the drops of the morning dew could be numbered." So the most popular of domestic story-tellers expatiates in an early work on the impossibility of wiping off from us, as with a wet cloth, the stains left by the fault of those who are near to us. Another of the tribe, but more "sensational" in subject and style, is keen to show how the influence of a man's evil deed slowly percolates through insidious channels of which he never dreams; how the deed of folly or of guilt is still active for evil when the sinner who committed it has forgotten his wickedness. "Who shall say where or when the results of one man's evil-doing shall cease? The seed of sin engenders no common root, shooting straight upwards through the earth, and bearing a given crop. It is the germ of a foul running weed, whose straggling suckers travel underground beyond the ken of mortal eye, beyond the power of mortal calculation." And so again the caustic showman of "Vanity Fair," in his last completed work, paused to explain how a culprit's evil behaviour of five and twenty years back, brought present grief and loss of rest to three unoffending persons; and he characteristically utters the wistful wish that we "could all take the punishment for our individual crimes on our individual shoulders," but laments the futility of any such wish, recognising as he does so plainly that when the culprit is condemned to hang, it is those connected with him who have to weep and suffer, and wear piteous mourning in their hearts long after he has jumped off the Tyburn ladder.

We conclude with a suggestive stanza of Mr. Robert Browning's, worth learning by heart in more senses than one: he is speaking of the soul declaring itself by its fruit—the thing it does:—

> "Be Hate that fruit, or Love that fruit,
> It forwards the general deed of Man;
> And each of the many helps to recruit
> The life of the race by a general plan,
> Each living his own, to boot."

——o——

SILENT SYMPATHY.

JOB ii. 13.

JOB'S friends have long since been a sort of bye-word. But be it not forgotten that the friendship of Eliphaz, Bildad, and Zophar, to the ruined and desolate man of Uz, evidences itself as very genuine in one or two salient points, before it came to be, what it is apt to be now exclusively considered, all talk. Before the talk there was prolonged silence; and before the silence there was lamentation of undoubted earnest. Coming from afar to mourn with him, and to comfort him, from afar off they caught sight of him, but so altered—*heu, quantum mutatus!*—that they lifted up their voice and wept; and they rent each one his mantle, and sprinkled dust upon their heads towards heaven. And then they "sat down with him upon the ground seven days and seven nights, *and none spake a word unto him;* for they saw that his grief was very great."

The sonnet of a Quaker poet has thus far vindicated the sincerity of their friendship, and on the ground of their silent sympathy:

"However ye might err in after-speech,
The mute expression of that voicelesss woe
Whereby ye sought your sympathy to show
With him of Uz, doth eloquently preach,—
Teaching a lesson it were well to teach
Some comforters, of utterance less slow,
Prone to believe that they more promptly know
Grief's mighty depths, and by their words can reach.
Seven days and nights, in stillness as profound
As that of chaos, patiently ye sate
By the heart-stricken and the desolate.
And though your sympathy might fail to sound
The fathomless depth of his dark spirit's wound,
Not less your silence was sublimely great."

In his vivid picture of the desolation of a bereaved husband, Sir Richard Steele goes on to say, "I knew consolation would now be impertinent; and therefore contented myself to sit by him, and condole with him in silence." "*Les consolations indiscrètes,*" says Rousseau, "*ne font qu'aigrir les violentes afflictions. L'indifférence et la froideur trouvent aisément des paroles, mais la tristesse et* LE SILENCE *sont alors le vrai langage de l'amitié.*" Gray writes to Mason, while yet uncertain whether the latter is already a widower or not,—"If the last struggle be over . . . allow me (at least in idea, for what could I do were I present more than this,) to sit by you in silence, and pity from my heart, not her who is at rest, but you who lose her." So it happened that Mason received this little billet at almost the precise moment when it would be most affecting.

Horace Walpole, again, writes to an afflicted correspondent, —"I say no more, for time only, not words, can soften such afflictions, nor can any consolations be suggested, that do not more immediately occur to the persons afflicted. To moralize can comfort those only who do not want to be comforted." So Marcia replies to Lucia, in Addison's tragedy:

> "*Lucia.* What can I think or say to give thee comfort?
> *Marcia.* Talk not of comfort, 'tis for lighter ills."

Words are words, says Shakspeare's Brabantio, and never yet heard he that the bruised heart was relieved through the ear. When, towards the close of Campbell's metrical tale of fair Wyoming, on Susquehanna's side, "prone to the dust, afflicted Waldegrave hid his face on earth, him watched, in gloomy ruth, his woodland guide; but words had none to soothe the grief that knows not consolation's name." But the Oneyda chief was not on that account Waldegrave's least efficient comforter. What though others around him, less reticent, and more demonstrative, found utterance easy, and shaped their kind common-place meaning into kind common-place words? "Of them that stood encircling his despair, he heard some friendly words, but knew not what they were." Wise-hearted, too, was Southey's young Arabian, in watching silently the frantic grief of the newly childless old diviner: in pitying silence Thalaba stood by, and gazed, and listened: "not with the officious hand of consolation, fretting the sore wound he could not hope to heal." It has been called the last triumph of affection and magnanimity, when a loving heart can respect the suffering silence of its beloved, and allow that lonely liberty in which alone some natures can find comfort. A late author portrayed in one of his tales a dull, common-place fellow enough, of limited intellect and attainments, whose, however, was one of those kind and honest natures fortunately endowed with subtle powers of perception that lie deeper than the head. Accordingly he is described, in the capacity of an unofficious condoler, as appreciating perfectly the grief of his friend; at his side throughout the day, but never obtruding himself, never attempting jarring platitudes of condolence: "in a word he fully understood the deep and beautiful sympathy of silence." So with Adela and Caroline in *The Bertrams*,—interchanging those pressures of the hand, those mute marks of fellow-feeling, "which we all know so well how to give when we long to lighten the sorrows which are too deep to be probed by words." But though we all may know so well how to give these mute marks, we do not all and always practice what we know. 'Tis true, 'tis pity; pity 'tis 'tis true.

Adam Bede's outburst of maddened feelings, uttered in tones of appealing anguish, when the loss of Hetty is first made clear to him, is noted in silence by the discreet rector, who is too wise to utter soothing words at present, as he watches in Adam that look of sudden age which sometimes comes over a young face in moments of terrible emotion. As Bartle Massey elsewhere describes this silent sympathizer, "Ay, he's good metal; . . . says no more than 's needful. He's not one of those that think they can comfort you with chattering, as if folks who stand by and look on knew a deal better what the trouble was than those who have to bear it."

Madame de Sévigné frankly deposes of her capacity as regards wordy consolation: "*Pour moi, je ne sais point de paroles dans une telle occasion.*" Mr. Tennyson submits what is applicable to any *telle occasion*,

> "That only silence suiteth best.
> Words weaker than your grief would make
> Grief more. 'Twere better I should cease."

Miss Procter sings the praises of a true comforter in little Effie,—"just I think that she does not try,—only looks with a wistful wonder why grown people should ever cry." It is such a comfort to be able to cry in peace, adds that sweet singer (with *larmes dans la voix*):

> "And my comforter knows a lesson
>   Wiser, truer than all the rest:—
> That to help and to heal a sorrow,
>   Love and silence are always best."

THE TEMPTER'S "IT IS WRITTEN."

MATTHEW iv. 6.

"IT is written," said the Tempter, quoting Scripture for his purpose, when it was his hour and the power of darkness, in the day of temptation in the wilderness. The quotation was refuted on the spot, and the Tempter was foiled. But his failure has not deterred mankind, at sundry times and in divers manners, from venturing on the same appeal, with no very unlike design. The wise as serpents (there was a serpent in Eden) who are not also harmless as doves, have now and then essayed to round a sophistic period, or clench an immoral argument, with an *It is written.*

Among the crowd of pilgrims who throng the pages of his allegory, Bunyan depicts one Mr. Selfwill, who holds that a man may follow the vices as well as the virtues of pilgrims; and that if he does both, he shall certainly be saved. But what ground has he for so saying? is Mr. Greatheart's query. And old Mr. Honesty replies, "Why, he said he had Scripture for his warrant." He could cite David's practice in one bad direction, and Sarah's lying in another, and Jacob's dissimulation in a third. And what they did, he might do too. "I have heard him plead for it, bring Scripture for it, bring arguments for it," etc., quoth old Honesty with a degree of indignation that does credit to his name.

"The devil can quote Scripture for his purpose.
An evil soul, producing holy witness,
Is like a villain with a smiling cheek,
A goodly apple rotten at the core."

Such is Antonio's stricture on Shylock's appeal to Jacob's practice, "When Jacob grazed his uncle Laban's sheep"; and there is a parallel passage in the next act, where Bassanio is the speaker:—

"In religion,
What damnèd error but some sober brow
Will bless it and approve it with a text,
Hiding the grossness with fair ornament?"

Against divines, indeed, of every school and age, the reproach of citing a text in support of doctrine or practice the reverse of divine, has been freely cast, with more or less of reason. Orthodox and heterodox, each has flung against the other his retort uncourteous.

> "Have not all heretics the same pretence
> To plead the Scriptures in their own defence?
> How did the Nicene Council then decide
> That strong debate? Was it by Scripture tried?
> No, sure; to that the rebel would not yield:
> Squadrons of texts *he* marshall'd in the field.
> * * * * *
> With texts point-blank and plain he faced the foe;
> And did not Satan tempt our Saviour so?"

A Dublin synod of the Irish Roman Catholic bishops, a few years since, which distinguished itself by its enthusiasm for Pope Pius IX., against the King of Italy, and by its arrogation of a divine right of practical monopoly in overseeing the schools and colleges of Ireland, was made the theme of comment by unsympathetic British critics; who remarked that when the question of education is stirred in such quarters, the dullest heretic can divine that the national system is to be denounced; and that it is easy to guess at the text of Scripture to be quoted in support of the pretensions of the Church. "The command to 'go and teach all nations' vested in the successors of the Apostles a rightful monopoly of instruction in Greek, mathematics, and civil engineering." According to the same elastic authority, the "Puritans," we are reminded, were justified in shooting and hanging their enemies, because Samuel hewed Agag in pieces, or because Phineas arose and executed judgment. "There never was a proposition which could not be proved by a text; and perhaps the effect is more complete when the citation is taken from the Vulgate." Gray's malicious lines against Lord Sandwich, a notorious evil-liver, as candidate for the High Stewardship in the University of Cambridge, include this stanza, supposed to be uttered by a representative

D.D., of the old port-wine school, and a staunch supporter of his profligate lordship :

"Did not Israel filch from th' Egyptians of old
Their jewels of silver and jewels of gold ?
The prophet of Bethel, we read, told a lie ;
He * drinks—so did Noah :—he swears—so do I."

Gray's *jeu d'esprit* was, throughout, not in the best of taste; but it was vastly relished at the time, as an election squib. The reference to spoiling the Egyptians is a well worked one in the history of quotations. Coleridge has a story of a Mameluke Bey, whose "precious logic" extorted a large contribution from the Egyptian Jews. "These books, the Pentateuch, are authentic?" "Yes." "Well, the debt then is acknowledged : and now the receipt, or the money, or your heads! The Jews borrowed a large treasure from the Egyptians; but you are the Jews, and on you, therefore, I call for the repayment." Such conclusions, from such premises, and backed by such vouchers, are open to logicians of every order, sacred and profane.

"Hence comment after comment, spun as fine
As bloated spiders draw the flimsy line ;
Hence the same word that bids our lusts obey,
Is misapplied to sanctify their sway.
If stubborn Greek refuse to be his friend,
Hebrew or Syriac shall be forced to bend :
If languages and copies all cry, No!
Somebody proved it centuries ago."

Burns was never any too backward in having his fling at a "minister"; and there is exceptional (and perhaps exceptionable) gusto in his averment that,

"E'en ministers, they have been kenn'd,
In holy rapture,
A rousing *whid*, at times, to vend,
And nail't wi' Scripture."

There was a time in the life of Diderot when that freest of free-thinkers made a living, such as it was, by writing sermons

* The Candidate, Lord Sandwich.

to order—half a dozen of them, for instance, a missionary bespoke for the Portuguese colonies, and is said to have paid for them very handsomely at fifty crowns each. Mr. Carlyle is caustic in his commemoration of this incident in Denis Diderot's career. "Further, he made sermons, to order; as the Devil is said to quote Scripture." In Mr. Carlyle's latest and longest history, we find once and again the like allusion. Frederick William, and his advisers, bent on a certain match for the Princess Wilhelmina, which the queen, her mother, as steadfastly opposed, took to quoting Scripture by way of subduing her majesty's resistance. "There was much discourse, suasive, argumentative. Grumkow quoting Scripture on her majesty, as the devil can on occasion," says Wilhelmina. "Express scriptures, 'Wives, be obedient to your husbands,' and the like texts; but her majesty, on the Scripture side, too, gave him as much as he brought." And at a later stage of the negotiation, the same Grumkow appears again, citing the Vulgate to a confidential correspondent, in reference to their political schemings. "But '*Si Deus est nobiscum*'—'If God be for us, who can be against us?' For the Grumkow can quote Scripture; nay, solaces himself with it, which is a feat beyond what the devil is competent to." Shakespeare embodies in Richard of Gloster a type of the political intriguer of this complexion; as where that usurper thus answers the gulled associates who urge him to be avenged on the opposite faction:

"But then I sigh, and with a piece of Scripture,
Tell them, that God bids us do good for evil.
And thus I clothe my naked villany
With old odd ends, stolen forth of holy writ;
And seem a saint when most I play the devil."

An unmitigated scoundrel in one of Mr. Dickens's books is represented as overtly grudging his old father the scant remnant of his days, and citing holy writ for sanction of his complaint. "Why, a man of any feeling ought to be ashamed of being eighty—let alone any more. Where's his religion, I should like to know, when he goes flying in the face of the Bible like that? Threescore and ten's the mark; and no man with a conscience, and a proper sense of what's expected of him, has any business to live longer." Whereupon the author interposes this parenthetical comment, and highly characteristic it is: "Is any one surprised at Mr. Jonas making such a reference to such a book for such a purpose? Does any one doubt the old saw that the devil . . . quotes Scripture for his own ends? If he will take the trouble to look about him, he may find a greater number of confirmations of the fact in the occurrences of a single day than the steam-gun can discharge balls in a minute." Fiction would supply us with abundant illustrations—fiction in general, and Sir Walter Scott in particular. As where Simon of Hackburn, the martial borderer, backs his hot appeal to arms, for the avenging a deed of wrong, by an equivocal reference to holy writ. "Let women sit and greet at hame, men must do as they have been done by; it is the Scripture says it." "Haud your tongue, sir," exclaims one of the seniors, sternly; "dinna abuse the Word that gate; ye dinna ken what ye speak about." Or as where the Templar essays to corrupt the Jewess by citing the examples of David and Solomon: "If thou readest the Scriptures," retorts Rebecca, "and the lives of the saints, only to justify thine own licence and profligacy, thy crime is like that of him who extracteth poison from the most healthful and necessary herbs." One other example. Undy Scott, that plausible scamp of Mr. Trollope's making, propounds an immoral paradox, to the scope of which one of his dupes is bold enough to object. But how is the objector disposed of? "'Judge not, and ye shall not be judged,' said Undy, quoting Scripture, as the devil did before him." Dupes can quote Scripture, too, and perhaps that is more demoralizing still. For Cowper did not rhyme without reason when he declared, that

> "Of all the arts sagacious dupes invent,
> To cheat themselves, and gain the world's assent,
> The worst is—Scripture warped from its intent."

——o——

ROYALTY REMINDED OF THE POOR.

DANIEL iv. 27.

GREAT was Nebuchadnezzar king of Babylon, even as the tree that he saw in his dream; for, by the avowal of the Hebrew prophet who interpreted that dream, the king was indeed become strong, and his greatness was grown, and reached unto the heaven, and his dominion unto the ends of the earth. But sentence had gone forth, as against the tree, so against the king. Nebuchadnezzar was to be degraded; despoiled of his kingdom, cast down from his throne, and driven from men, to eat grass as oxen. This counsel, however, the prophet urged upon the sovran, that he should break off his sins by righteousness, and his "iniquities by showing mercy to the poor"; if it might be a lengthening of his tranquillity, or a healing of his error.

What error? That of which ex-king Lear accused himself, when he owned, amid words of frenzy, all however with more or less of tragic significance in them, that he had taken too little care of *this*,—of sympathy with desolate indigence, and of readiness to relieve the sufferings of the destitute and forlorn.

The storm is raging on the heath, and faithful Kent implores his aged master to take shelter, such as it is, within a hovel hard by; some friendship will it lend him against the tempest; the tyranny of the open night's too rough for nature to endure. But Lear would be let alone. "Wilt break my heart?" he exclaims, in answer to Kent's fresh entreaty: Kent had rather break his own. Again the drenched, discrowned old man is urged to enter the hovel on the heath. But he stays outside, to reason on his past and present, till reason gives way. Kent may think it a matter of moment that this contentious storm invades them to the skin; and so it is to him. But Lear has deeper griefs to shatter him; and "where the greater malady is fixed, the lesser is scarce felt." Let Kent go in, by all means: the king enjoins it—at least the ex-king desires it: let Kent seek his own ease—and perhaps Lear will follow him in. Meanwhile, in draggling robes, drenched to the skin, chilled to the heart, Lear's thoughts perforce are turned to "houseless poverty," to the indigent and vagrant creatures once, and so lately, his subjects, equally exposed to the downpour of the wrathful skies, of whom he had seldom, if ever, thought till now. Poor naked wretches, he apostrophises them, wheresoever they are, that bide the pelting of this pitiless storm,—how shall their houseless heads, and unfed sides, their looped and windowed raggedness, defend them from seasons such as these? And then, in an outburst of repentant self-reproach, he that had been King of Britain breaks forth into the avowal,

> "O, I have ta'en
> Too little care of this! Take physic, pomp;
> Expose thyself to feel what wretches feel;
> That thou mayst shake the superflux to them,
> And show the heavens more just."

Between the history of Lear and that of Gloster, in the same play, there is a curious and significant parallel maintained throughout. And it is observable that when Gloster too, another duped and outcast father, is wandering in his turn on the same heath, and is accosted by "poor mad Tom,"—the sightless, miserable father thus addresses the "naked fellow" whose identity he so little suspects:

> "Here, take this purse, thou whom the heaven's plagues
> Have humbled to all strokes: that I am wretched,
> Makes thee the happier:—Heavens, deal so still!
> Let the superfluous and lust-dieted man,
> That slaves your ordinance, that will not see
> Because he doth not feel, feel your power quickly;
> So distribution should undo the excess,
> And each man have enough."

Strictly a parallel passage to the one just cited from the lips of Lear, even as the disastrous personal experiences of King of Britain and Duke of Gloster were along parallel lines, as we have said.

The words of Amos, the herdman of Tekoa, include a denunciation of woe to them that lie upon beds of ivory, and eat the lambs out of the flock, and the calves out of the midst of the stall, and drink wine in bowls, and anoint themselves with costly ointments, and chant to the sound of the viol,—but are not grieved for the affliction of Joseph. As the minor prophet with his woe to them that are thus at ease in Zion, so a major prophet declares this to have been the iniquity of a doomed race—pride, fulness of bread, and abundance of idleness, with disregard of all means to strengthen the hand of the poor and needy. Lazarus the beggar was, as some scholars interpret the passage, "content to be fed" on the crumbs which fell from the rich man's table; in which case he would not appear to have been refused the crumbs: indeed, had this been the case, it would scarcely, they contend, have been omitted in the rebuke of Abraham. "The rich man's sins were ravenousness and negligence rather than inhumanity." * He took too little care of this—that beggary lay in helpless prostration before his doorway, the while he clothed himself in purple and fine linen, and fared sumptuously every day.

La Bruyère observes that "la santé et les richesses ôtent aux hommes l'expérience du mal, leur inspirent la dureté pour leurs semblables;" and adds, that "les gens déjà chargés de leur propre misère sont ceux qui entrent davantage, par leur compassion, dans celle d'autrui." If these by comparison become wondrous kind, it is their fellow-feeling that makes them so. *Haud ignari mali, miseris succurrere discunt.* In another chapter of his "Characters," La Bruyère sketches the portrait of one he styles Champagne, who "au sortir d'un long dîner qui lui enfle l'estomac, et dans les douces fumées d'un vin d'Avenay ou de Sillery, signe un ordre qu'on lui présente, qui ôterait le pain à toute une province, si l'on n'y remédiait: il est excusable. Quel moyen de comprendre, dans la première heure de la digestion, qu'on puisse quelque part mourir de faim?" *Il est excusable,* on the principle of Horace Walpole's similar plea, or apology, for unheeding royalty. He writes to

* See on the scope of the words *ἐπιθυμῶν χορτασθῆναι* (St. Luke xvi. 21), *Analecta Theologica* (Rev. W. Trollope's) *in loc.*

Miss Hannah More that he used to hate that king and t'other prince—but that on reflection he found the censure ought to fall on human nature in general. "They are made of the same stuff as we, and dare we say what we should be in their situation? Poor creatures! think how they are educated, or rather corrupted, early, how flattered! To be educated properly, they should be led through hovels [as Lear was on the heath—somewhat late in life], and hospitals, and prisons. Instead of being reprimanded (and perhaps immediately afterwards *sugar-plum'd*) for not learning their Latin or French grammar, they now and then should be kept fasting; and, if they cut their finger, should have no plaster till it festered. No part of a royal brat's memory, which is good enough, should be burthened but with the remembrance of human suffering." "*Il y a une espèce de honte d'être heureux à la vue de certaines misères*," writes La Bruyère again. Adam Smith, however, made a dead set against what he calls those "whining and melancholy moralists," who he complains, are perpetually reproaching us with our happiness, while so many of our brethren are in misery, who regard as impious the natural joy of prosperity, which does not think of the many wretches that are at every instant labouring under all sorts of calamities, in the languor of poverty, in the agony of disease, etc. "Commiseration for those miseries which we never saw, which we never heard of, but which we may be assured are at all times infesting such numbers of our fellow-creatures, ought, they think, to damp the pleasures of the fortunate, and to render a certain melancholy dejection habitual to all men." Adam Smith opposes this "extreme sympathy" as altogether absurd and unreasonable; as unattainable too, so that a certain affected and sentimental sadness is the nearest approach that can be made to it; and he further declares that this disposition of mind, though it could be attained, would be perfectly useless, and could serve no other purpose than to render miserable the person who possessed it. This, of course, is assuming the wretchedness in question to be beyond the sympathiser's relief.

Dr. Smith may be supposed to have had in view Thomson's celebrated passage :

"Ah ! little think the gay licentious proud,
Whom pleasure, power, and affluence surround ;
They, who their thoughtless hours in giddy mirth,
And wanton, often cruel, riot waste ;
Ah ! little think they, while they dance along,
How many feel this very moment death
And all the sad variety of pain."

Many variations on that theme of sad variety the poet sings : moving accidents by flood and fire,—pining want, and dungeon glooms,—the many who drink the cup of baleful grief, or eat the bitter bread of misery—sore pierced by wintry winds, how many shrink into the sordid hut of cheerless poverty (the hovel on the heath again), etc., etc., etc.

"Thought fond man
Of these, and all the thousand nameless ills
That one incessant struggle render life
One scene of toil, of suffering, and of fate,
Vice in his high career would stand appalled,
And heedless rambling impulse learn to think ;
The conscious heart of charity would warm,
And her wide wish benevolence dilate ;
The social tear would rise, the social sigh,
And into clear perfection, gradual bliss,
Refining still, the social passions work."

This may, perhaps, said Baron Alderson, in winding up a charge to a grand jury, whom he exhorted at that winter season to show sympathy and kindness to the distressed,—this, perhaps, may be one of the objects for which God sends suffering, that it may tend to re-unite those whom prosperity has severed. So Burns—

"O ye who, sunk in beds of down,
Feel not a want but what yourselves create,
Think for a moment on his wretched fate
  Whom friends and fortune quite disown.
Ill-satisfied keen nature's clam'rous call,
  Stretch'd on his straw he lays himself to sleep,
While through the ragged roof and chinky wall,
  Chill, o'er his slumbers, piles the drifty heap.

* * * * *

> Affliction's sons are brothers in distress :
> A brother to relieve, how exquisite the bliss !"

Again and again the question recurs, to quote from an able casuist on casual charity, why one man should be literally dying of want, whilst another is able to send him a cheque for £100 without thinking about it, or knowing that the money is gone? If Dives, it is asked, feels bound to give Lazarus so much, where does he draw the line? If the demand upon the superfluities of the rich is to be measured by the wants of the poor, why stop at £100 rather than £1000 or £10,000 or £100,000? "This is the question which lies at the root of half the melancholy sarcasms and still more melancholy wit of the present day. The writings of such men as Hood are little more than embodiments of it in a variety of forms, ludicrous or pathetic. It forms the burden of a whole class of literature, not the less influential because it is somewhat vague in its doctrines, and rests rather on sentiments than on dogmas." Now this writer believes it to be always the best to look such questions in the face, and to attempt at least to give the true answer to them. And the answer, at least in part, in this instance, he takes to be that the antithesis is only sentimental, and not logical. The poverty of the very poor is not, he contends, either a cause or an effect of the riches of the very rich, nor would it be relieved by their permanent impoverishment. "That it is not a cause of their riches, is obvious from the fact that if by any change pauperism and misery were suddenly abolished, the rich would be all the richer." But not to follow out a line of argument that would take us too far afield, we may advert to a corresponding essay, in the same *Review*, if not by the same contributor,—in which a picture is drawn of a rich man at church, who hears some stray verses in the second lesson, or some eloquent menace from the pulpit, which makes him very uncomfortable about the contrast between his own easy life and the massive wretchedness of Spitalfields or Poplar. The uneasiness is supposed to rankle in him for some time, spoiling his digestion, and making him very cross to his wife and daughters. Not that he "for a moment dreams of literally obeying the texts in the New Testament that have hit him hard; for he has a shrewd notion that they imply a very different state of society from the busy nineteenth century. He feels that he has no time for visiting the sick, and that if he had, the sick would think him a great nuisance; and he knows that when he got to the bedside, he would probably be at his wits' ends for anything to say, and would end by twisting his watch-chain, and remarking that it was a cold day." The practical inference is, that if he is to do any of the corporal works of mercy, he must do them by commission;—and so, at last, the irritation in his conscience throws itself out in the form of a liberal cheque upon his bankers. *He*, at least, will vindicate himself, so far as that vicarious beneficence may avail, from any possible charge of branded fellowship with such as the poet of the Seasons depicts, in

> "The cruel wretch
> Who, all day long in sordid pleasure rolled,
> Himself a useless load, has squandered vile
> Upon his scoundrel train, what might have cheered
> A drooping family of modest worth."

Horace Walpole, on being complimented by letter on the patience with which he bore an acute attack of his chronic malady, replies: "If people of easy fortunes cannot bear illness with temper, what are the poor to do, who have none of our comforts and alleviations? The affluent, I fear, do not consider what a benefit-ticket has fallen to their lot out of millions not so fortunate; yet less do they reflect that chance, not merit, drew the prize out of the wheel." Crabbe portrays this non-reflecting complacency in one of his metrical tales:

> "Month after month was passed, and all were spent
> In quiet comfort and in rich content:
> Miseries there were, and woes, the world around,
> But these had not her pleasant dwelling found;
> She knew that mothers grieved, and widows wept,
> And she was sorry, said her prayers, and slept.
> Thus passed the seasons, and to Dinah's board
> Gave what the seasons to the rich afford;
> For she indulged," etc.

Not so serenely does Bishop Jeremy Taylor imagine a gazer from the skies to look down on the sorrows of this earth of ours, in the celebrated paragraph beginning, "But if we could from one of the battlements of heaven espy how many men and women lie fainting and dying," etc. And, by the way, there is another of Crabbe's Tales, in which, too late, a self-upbraiding spirit thus accuses itself for neglecting a ruined wrong-doer, whose death she has just discovered:

"To have this money in my purse—to know
What grief was his, and what to grief we owe;
To see him often, always to conceive
How he must pine and languish, groan and grieve;*
And every day in ease and peace to dine,
And rest in comfort!—what a heart is mine!"

Richard Savage, as Mr. Whitehead pictures him, bitterly conversant with cold and hunger, a houseless vagrant through the streets by night, and a famishing lounger in them by day, apostrophises Mr. Overseer in his pursy prosperity, much as (*mutatis mutandis*) Lear apostrophises pomp. "Turn out, fat man of substance, and bob for wisdom and charity on the banks of Southwark. They are best taken at night, when God only sees you—when the east wind is abroad, making you shake like the sinner who was hanged for breaking into your dwelling-house. 'The air bites shrewdly, it is very cold,' sayest thou? It is so. But tell me whether, on the fourth night, when thou liest stretched on thy blessed bed, thy heart is not warmer than it was wont to be—whether thou dost not pray prayers of long omission—whether thou wilt not, in the morning, bethink thee of the poor, and relieve them out of thy abundance? Sayest thou, no? God help thee!" As Van den Bosch tells the big-wigs of Ghent,

* Earlier in the tale there is a touch to remind us of Lear on the heath:

"'Know you his conduct?' 'Yes, indeed, I know,
And how he wanders in the wind and snow;
Safe in our rooms the threatening storm we hear,
But he feels strongly what we faintly fear.'"

"Ah, sirs, you know not, you, who lies afield
When nights are cold, with frogs for bedfellows;
You know not, you, who fights and sheds his blood,
And fasts and fills his belly with the east wind."

Diderot rose one Shrove Tuesday morning, and groping in his pocket, found nothing wherewith to dine that day—which he spent in wandering about Paris and its precincts. He was ill when he got back to his quarters, went to bed, and was treated by his landlady to a little toast and wine. "That day," he often told a friend, in after life, "I swore that, if ever I came to have anything, I would never in my life refuse a poor man help, never condemn my fellow-creature to a day as painful." As the sailor says, after the wreck, in one of Mr. Roscoe's tragedies: "We may be wrecked a dozen times, for what our betters care; but being aboard themselves, they see some spice of danger in it, and that breeds a fellow-feeling." And, proverbially, a fellow-feeling makes us wondrous kind.

Mr. Ruskin demands whether, even supposing it guiltless, luxury would be desired by any of us, if we saw clearly at our sides the suffering which accompanies it in the world. "Luxury is indeed possible in the future—innocent and exquisite; luxury for all, and by the help of all; but luxury at present can only be enjoyed by the ignorant; the cruelest man living could not sit at his feast, unless he sat blindfold."

Gibbon records to the honour of at least one Pontiff's temporal government of Rome, that he—Gregory the Great—relieved by the bounty of each day, and of every hour, the instant distress of the sick and needy—his treasurers being continually summoned to satisfy, in his name, the requirements of indigence and merit. "Nor would the pontiff indulge himself in a frugal repast, till he had sent the dishes from his own table to some objects deserving of his compassion." A *non possumus* this, in its beneficent *nisi prius* scope, more appreciable by Protestants at least than that of some other Holy Fathers. A sovran's interest in the sufferings of his or her subjects is always of exceptional interest in the eyes of fellow-subjects. Leigh Hunt knew this, when he pictured, in her early happy wifehood, our Sovran Lady the Queen of these realms,

> "Too generous-happy to endure
> The thought of all the woful poor
> Who that same night lay down their heads
> In mockeries of starving beds,
> In cold, in wet, disease, despair,
> In madness that will say no prayer;
> With wailing infants some; and some
> By whom the little clay lies dumb;
> And some, whom feeble love's excess,
> Through terror, tempts to murderousness.
> And at that thought the big drops rose
> In pity for her people's woes;
> And this glad mother and great queen
> Weeping for the poor was seen,
> And vowing in her princely will
> That they should thrive and bless her still."

Madame de Chevreuse, in a popular French romance, is made to say to, and *at*, Anne of Austria, that kings are so far removed from other people, from the "vulgar herd," that they forget that others ever stand in need of the bare necessaries of life. She likens them to the dweller on African mountains, who, gazing from the verdant table-land, refreshed by the rills of melted snow, cannot comprehend that the dwellers in the plains below him are perishing from hunger and thirst in the midst of their lands, burnt up by the heat of the sun. When, in the same romance—by courtesy historical; only the proportion of history to romance in it is much about that of Falstaff's bread bill to his running account for sack—one of Anne of Austria's sons, the reigning king, young Lewis the Fourteenth, is substituted in the Bastille for his ill-starred brother, and so comes to taste of suffering *in propriâ personâ*,—the royal prisoner tries to remember at what hour the first repast is served to the captives in that fortress—but his ignorance of this detail occasions a feeling of remorse that smites him like the keen thrust of a dagger: "that he should have lived for five and twenty years a king, and in the enjoyment of every happiness, without having bestowed a moment's thought

[O, I have ta'en too little thought of this !]

on the misery of those who had been unjustly deprived of their liberty. The king blushed for very shame. He felt that Heaven, in permitting this fearful humiliation, did no more than render to the man the same torture as was inflicted by that man upon so many others."—It is in a glowing description of one of the great fêtes at Versailles under the auspices of this, the Grand Monarque, that M. Arsène Houssaye delivers himself of this pensive aside : "Et la musique de Lulli achève d'enivrer tout ce beau monde, qui ne pense pas un seul instant que près de là, à la grille même du château des merveilles, une pauvre femme prie et pleure, tout affamée, pour ses enfants. Qu'importe ! passe ton chemin, et reviens plus tard. Comment t'appelles-tu, bonne femme ?—Je m'appelle la France : *je reviendrai.*"

Part of the education of the royal heir-apparent of the Incas consisted in a course of gymnastic training, with competitive trials of skill—during which, for a period of thirty days, "the royal neophyte fared no better than his comrades, sleeping on the bare ground, going unshod, and wearing a mean attire, —a mode of life, it was supposed, which might tend to inspire him with more sympathy with the destitute." It is to royalty that Jeanie Deans is pleading, when she exclaims, "Alas ! it is not when we sleep soft and wake merrily ourselves, that we think on other people's sufferings. Our hearts are waxed light within us then. . . . But when the hour of trouble comes—and seldom may it visit your leddyship—and when the hour of death comes, that comes to high and low—lang and late may it be yours—O my leddy, then it isna what we hae dune for oursells, but what we hae dune for others, that we think on maist pleasantly." An English traveller in Russia, discussing the difficulty with which news of starving peasants reaches the ears of the czar, and tracing the roundabout track by which, at last, when many have died, and many more are dying, a stifled wail penetrates through the "official cotton-stuffed ears of district police auditoria, district chambers of domains, military chiefs of governments, and imperial chancelleries without number," and comes soughing into the private cabinet of the czar at the Winter Palace or Peterhoff, —goes on to say: "The empress, good soul, sheds tears when she hears of the dreadful sufferings of the poor people so many hundred versts off. The imperial children, I have no doubt, wonder why, if the peasants have no bread to eat, they don't take to plum-cake; the Emperor is affected, but goes to work," etc. Which last expression, by the way, reminds us of a *quasi* quotation by Mr. Carlyle of Shakespeare's text in juxtaposition with mention of the greatest of czars: "Descend, O Donothing Pomp; quit thy down-cushions; expose thyself to learn what wretches feel, and how to cure it! The czar of Russia became a dusty toiling shipwright; . . . and his aim was small to thine." There was a miserable day in the Highland wanderings of Prince Charles when, with Ned Burke and Donald Macleod for companions, after roving about all night, excessively faint for want of food, he was obliged to subsist on meal stirred in brine—there being no fresh water within reach. The prince is said to have expressed himself thankful for even this nauseous food—"salt-water drammock"—and to have declared, on the occasion, that if ever he mounted a throne, he should not fail to remember "those who dined with him to-day." When Flora Macdonald and Lady Clanranald, not long afterwards, came to the royal outcast,—on entering the hut they found him engaged in roasting the heart and liver of a sheep on a wooden spit; a sight at which some of the party could not help shedding tears. "Charles, always the least concerned at his distressing circumstances, though never forgetting the hopes inspired by his birth, jocularly observed that it would be well perhaps for all kings if they had to come through such a fiery ordeal as he was enduring." At a subsequent period we find him living for days together on a few handfuls of oatmeal and about a pound of butter—referring to which he afterwards told a Highland gentleman that he had come to know what a quarter of a peck of meal was, having once subsisted on such a quantity for the better part of a week. Another time we find him spending the night in an open cave, on the top of a high hill between the Braes of Glenmorriston and Strathglass,—a cave too narrow to let him stretch himself, and in which he lay drenched to the skin, with no possibility of getting a fire to dry him. "Without food, and deprived of sleep by the narrowness and hardness of his bed, the only comfort he could obtain was the miserable one of smoking a pipe." Hardly was Lear himself more thoroughly exposed to feel what wretches feel, on that night beside the hovel on the heath.

In that paradoxical essay of his, on saying grace before meat, Charles Lamb remarks that the indigent man, who hardly knows whether he shall have a meal the next day or not, sits down to his fare with a present sense of the blessing, which can be but feebly acted by the rich, into whose minds the conception of wanting a dinner could never, but by some extreme theory, have entered. According to the essayist, the heats of epicurism put out the gentle flame of devotion : the incense which rises round is pagan, and the belly-god intercepts it for his own. "The very excess of the provision beyond the needs, takes away all sense of proportion between the end and means. The Giver is veiled by his gifts. You are startled at the injustice of returning thanks—for what?—for having so much, while so many starve. It is to praise the gods amiss."

Taking for his text the apprenticeship of good Abbot Samson at St. Edmund's shrine, Mr. Carlyle moralises on how much would many a Serene Highness have learnt, had he travelled through the world with water-jug and empty wallet, *sine omni expensâ*, and returned only to sit down at the foot of St. Edmund's shrine to shackles and bread and water. Patriotism itself, a political economist has remarked, can never be generated by a passive enjoyment of good; the evil tendency of which he bids us see by merely looking to a city like London; where the rich who live together in streets of fine houses many miles long, and have every comfort provided for them without their interference, and need nothing from the poor but what they buy for money, and conclude that the same State which cares for them will care equally for the poor,—such rich men, it is alleged, have every inducement to become isolated from all but the few with whom it is pleasant to live. We may choose, says Professor Kingsley, to look at the masses in the gross as subjects for statistics—and of course, where possible, for profits. "There is One above who knows every thirst, and ache, and sorrow, and temptation of each slattern, and gin-drinker, and street boy. The day will come when He will require an account of these neglects of ours—not in the gross." Mrs. Gaskell ably describes the fear of Margaret Hale, in "North and South," lest, in her West-end ease, she should become sleepily deadened into forgetfulness of anything beyond the life that was lapping her round with luxury. "There might be toilers and moilers there in London, but she never saw them; the very servants lived in an underground world of their own, of which she knew neither the hopes nor the fears; they only seemed to start into existence when some want or whim of their master and mistress needed them." Mr. Thackeray presents Ethel Newcome in the fairest light when he shows her studious to become acquainted with her indigent neighbours—giving much time to them and thought; visiting from house to house without ostentation; awe-stricken by that spectacle of poverty which we have with us always, of which the sight rebukes our selfish griefs into silence, the thought compels us to charity, humility, and devotion. "Death never dying out; hunger always crying; and children born to it day after day,—our young London lady, flying from the splendours and follies in which her life had been passed, found herself in the presence of these; threading darkling alleys which swarmed with wretched life; sitting by naked beds, whither by God's blessing she was sometimes enabled to carry a little comfort and consolation; or whence she came heart-stricken by the overpowering misery, or touched by the patient resignation, of the new friends to whom fate had directed her." No longer *ignara mali, miseris succurrere discit.* An essayist of Mr. Thackeray's school, on the topic of parliamentary trains, breaks out, or off, into the apostrophe: "Ah, judges of Amontillado sherry; crushers of walnuts with silver crackers; connoisseurs who prefer French to Spanish olives, and are curious about the yellow seal; gay riders in padded chariots; proud cavaliers of blood-horses,—you don't know how painfully and slowly, almost agonisingly, the poor have to scrape and save, and deny themselves the necessaries of life, to gather together the penny-a-mile fare." Lord Jeffrey eagerly asserted the even painful interest with which one of Mr. Dickens's Christmas books affected him: "sanative, I dare say, to the spirit, but making us despise and loathe ourselves for passing our days in luxury, while better and gentler creatures are living such lives as make us wonder that such things can be in a society of human beings, or even in the world of a good God." Lord Lytton has compared the stray glimpses one gets of want and misery, to looking through a solar microscope at the monsters in a drop of water, when the gazer wonders how things so terrible have hitherto been unknown to him: "Lapped in your sleek comforts, and lolling on the sofa of your patent conscience . . . you are startled and dismayed" at the sight: you say within yourself, "Can such things be? I never dreamed of this before! I thought what was invisible to me was non-existent in itself—I will remember this dread experiment." The like is the moral of Hood's poem of the Lady's Dream. From grief exempt, she had never dreamt of such a world of woe as appals her in apocalyptic visions of the night; never dreamt till now of the hearts that daily break, and the tears that hourly fall, and the many, many troubles of life that grieve this earthly ball—disease, and hunger, and pain, and want; but now she dreams of them all—of the naked she might have clad, the famished she might have fed, the sorrowing she might have solaced; of each pleading that, long ago, she scanned with a heedless eye.

"I drank the richest draughts;
And ate whatever is good—
Fish, and flesh, and fowl, and fruit
Supplied my hungry mood;

But I never remembered the wretched ones
  That starve for want of food.

I dressed as the noble dress,
  In cloth of silver and gold,
With silk, and satin, and costly furs,
  In many an ample fold;
But I never remembered the naked limbs
  That froze with winter's cold.

The wounds I might have healed!
  The human sorrow and smart!
And yet it never was in my soul
  To play so ill a part:
But evil is wrought by want of Thought
[So Lear's "O, I have ta'en *too little thought* of this!"]
  As well as want of Heart!

She clasped her fervent hands,
  And the tears began to stream;
Large, and bitter, and fast they fell,
  Remorse was so extreme;
And yet, O yet, that many a dame
  Would dream the Lady's Dream!"

An *Edinburgh* Reviewer of mortality in trades and professions, dwelling on the fatal conditions under which very many classes earn their daily bread, and sometimes not so much as that,—observes that the great middle and upper classes, accustomed to be furnished with all the appliances of easy life and luxury, seldom give a thought as to the manner in which their wants are supplied. "Accustomed to sip the honey, it never strikes us that perhaps its product involves in some cases the life of the working-bee. The lady, who, from the silken ease of her fauteuil, surveys her drawing-room, may learn a lesson of compassion for the poor workmen in nearly every article that lies before her." To take one example out of the many upon which Dr. Wynter dilates—the case of the silverer of looking-glasses: "If the charming belle, as she surveys her beauty in the glass, could but for a moment see reflected this poor shattered human creature, with trembling muscles, brown visage, and blackened teeth, she would doubtless start with horror; but, as it is, the slaves of luxury and vanity drop out of life unobserved and uncared for, as the stream of travellers disappeared one by one through the bridge of Mirza."

"O let those cities that of plenty's cup,
And her prosperities, so largely taste,
With their superfluous riots, hear these tears!
The misery of Tharsus may be theirs."

The moral of the eastern tale of Nourjahad is practical and pertinent. He delivers himself up to luxury and riot. He forgets that there are wants and distresses among his fellow-creatures. He lives only for himself, and his heart becomes as hard as the coffers which hold his misapplied treasures. But before it is too late he is awakened to remorse, and looks back with shame and horror on his past life. What shall he do to expiate his offences? One thing at least is within his power, and that will he do at once: expend his riches in the relief of want—nor rest until he has found out every family in Ormuz whom calamity has overtaken, that he may restore them to prosperity. Henceforth he spends his days in his closet, laying plans for the benefit of his fellow-creatures. Ben Jonson's Sordido promises the like amendment:—

"Pardon me, gentle friends, I'll make fair 'mends
For my foul errors past. . . .
My barns and garners shall stand open still
To all the poor that come, and my best grain
Be made alms-bread, to feed half-famished mouths.
Though hitherto amongst you I have lived
Like an unsavoury muck-hill to myself,
Yet now my gathered heaps, being spread abroad,
Shall turn to better and more fruitful uses.
. . . . . O how deeply
The bitter curses of the poor do pierce!
I am by wonder changed; come in with me
And witness my repentance: now I prove
No life is blest that is not graced with love."

So again with the rich man in one of Crabbe's Borough sketches from life; that rich man, to wit, who

"built a house, both large and high,
And entered in and set him down to sigh;

And planted ample woods and gardens fair,
And walked with anguish and compunction there;
The rich man's pines to every friend a treat,
He saw with pain and *he* refused to eat;
His daintiest food, his richest wines, were all
Turned by remorse to vinegar and gall:
The softest down by living body pressed
The rich man bought, and tried to take his rest;
But care had thorns upon his pillow spread,
And scattered sand and nettles in his bed:
Nervous he grew—would often sigh and groan,—
He talked but little, and he walked alone;
Till by his priest convinced, that from one deed
Of genuine love would joy and health proceed,
He from that time with care and zeal began
To seek and soothe the grievous ills of man;
And as his hands their aid to grief apply,
He learns to smile and he forgets to sigh.
Now he can drink his wine and taste his food,
And feel the blessings Heaven has dealt are good;
And since the suffering seek the rich man's door,
He sleeps as soundly as when young and poor."

——o——

WIND, EARTHQUAKE, FIRE, AND STILL SMALL VOICE.

1 KINGS xix. 11, 12.

WHILE Elijah stood upon the mount before the Lord, there arose a great and strong wind that rent the mountains, and brake in pieces the rocks; but the Lord was not in the wind: and after the wind an earthquake; but the Lord was not in the earthquake: and after the earthquake a fire; but the Lord was not in the fire: and after the fire a still small voice. We are not told that the Lord was not in the still small voice. We find that He was. And with that voice He addressed Elijah, reasoned with him, admonished, sustained, and directed him. May it not be said, in applying and adapting the narrative, which things are an allegory? The import of the narrative sublimely anticipates the homely fable of sun and wind. Wind, earthquake, and fire, are mighty agents; but they may pass by without tangible result as regards real influence on the spirit of man; whereas the gentle influence of a still small voice speaks home to it at once, and it responds to the strain, and is subdued by the spell.

The drift of the present annotations, in their applied sense, finds expression in Ben Jonson's reminder:

> "There is
> A way of working more by love than fear:
> Fear works on servile natures, not the free."

In Landor's Parable of Asabel, the angel's gentleness wrought upon that turbulent, refractory spirit, "even as the quiet and silent water wins itself an entrance where tempest and fire pass over." It is written that other angels did look up with loving and admiration into the visage of this angel on his return; and he told the younger and more zealous of them, that whenever they would descend into the gloomy vortex of the human heart, under the softness and serenity of their voice and countenance its turbulence would subside.

Plutarch tells us of Fabius Maximus, that he thought it hard that, while those who breed dogs and horses soften their stubborn tempers, and bring down their fierce spirits by care and kindness, rather than with whips and chains, he who has the command of men should not endeavour to correct their errors by gentleness and goodness, but treat them in even a harsher and more violent manner than gardeners do the wild fig-trees, pears, and olives, whose nature they subdue by cultivation, and which by that means they bring to produce very agreeable fruit.*

* Plentiful illustrations might be drawn from Plutarch to the same effect. There is Mutius Scævola, for instance, addressing Porsenna: "Your threatenings I regarded not, but am subdued by your generosity." There is Porsenna himself, who, as Publicola found, could not be quelled by dint of arms, but whom he converted into a friend to Rome, by "the gentle arts of persuasion." There is young Alexander, afterwards to be, or to be called, the Great, whose astute father saw that he did not easily submit to authority, because he would not be forced to anything, but that he might be led to his duty by the gentler hand of reason; and therefore, as

We read of the distinguished Spanish author and statesman, Fermin Caballero, that while under the care of a kind and judicious instructor, he, as a boy, made rapid advance in the study of classical literature; but that on being removed from this tutor, and subjected to harsh and grinding discipline, he lapsed into idleness and obstinacy beyond all control. Not the least wise of the maxims to be culled from the pages of Terence is that in which *satius esse credit Pudore et liberalitate liberos retinere, quam metu.* Southey insists that no man was ever more thoroughly ignorant of the nature of children than John Wesley, as when he enjoins: "Let a child from a year old be taught to fear the rod, and to cry softly; from that age make him do as he is bid, if you whip him ten times running to effect it." If Wesley had been a father himself, urges that tenderest of fathers, Robert the Rhymer, "he would have known that children are more easily governed by love than by fear." And as with children, so with men, who are but children of a larger growth; and especially so with women, if we may take the word of one of Shakspeare's most winsome women for it:

> "You may ride us
> With one soft kiss a thousand furlongs, ere
> With spur we heat an acre."

---

a wise father, who knew his own son, Philip took the method of persuasion rather than of command.

What Plutarch says of the gentler hand of reason, reminds us of Swift's account of the *Houyhnhnms*, that "they have no conception how a rational creature can be compelled, but only advised or exhorted." And by the way, Swift remarks in a letter on England's harsh rule over the Irish, "Supposing even the size of a native's understanding just equal to that of a dog or a horse, I have often seen these two animals civilized by rewards at least as much as by punishments."

But to return to Plutarch. There is his Flaminius, again, whose appointment to the command in the war with Macedon, he calls very fortunate for Rome, since what was required was "a general who did not want to do everything by force and violence, but rather by gentleness and persuasion." As Claudian says, *Peragit tranquilla potestas quod violenta nequit.*

Fear, observes Adam Smith, is in almost all cases a wretched instrument of government, and ought in particular never to be employed against any order of men who have the smallest pretensions to independency. "To attempt to terrify them, serves only to irritate their bad humours, and to confirm them in an opposition which more gentle usage perhaps might easily induce them, either to soften, or to lay aside altogether."

So with Landor's Filippa, on whom harsh treatment and compulsory measures are simply thrown away :

> "Rudeness can neither move nor discompose her :
> A word, a look, of kindness, instantly
> Opens her heart and brings her cheek upon you."

And as with men and women, so with peoples, who are made up of men and women. And yet, although, as the author of the "Wealth of Nations" expresses it, management and persuasion are always the easiest and safest instruments of government, as force and violence are the worst and most dangerous ; such, it seems, is the natural insolence of man, that he almost always disdains to use the good instrument, except when he cannot or dare not use the bad one. Not that nations are without diversities of character, and so of susceptibility to diverse modes of government. Gibbon apologises, as it were, for Diocletian's utter destruction of those proud cities, Busiris and Coptos, and for his severe treatment of Egypt in general, by the remark, that the character of the Egyptian nation, insensible to kindness, but extremely susceptible to fear, could alone justify this excessive rigour. The tone is that of the courtier Crispe, to Phocas, in Corneille's "Heraclius :"

> "Il faut agir de force avec de tels esprits . . .
> La violence est juste où la douceur est vaine."

And Coke maintains that if they are the best whom love induces, they are the most whom fear restrains : *Si meliores sunt quos ducit amor, plures sunt quos corrigit timor.* La Fontaine's fable of the fishes and the flute-playing shepherd, intimates the sheer futility of wasting sweet sounds on ears not to be so caught. There are men, sententiously quoth Dr. Tempest, in the "Last Chronicle of Barset," who are deaf as adders to courtesy, but who are compelled to obedience at once by ill-usage.

Educationists must provide for the contingency of having to deal with abnormal natures of this crabbed and distorted kind. But as exceptions only. The Jesuits are confessedly masters of the arts of education ; and the rule of the Jesuits is to lead not to drive, their pupils; to allure and win, not to coerce and constrain them. Winsome womankind is mistress of the like arts. Those of the sex who *are* winsome, it has been said, with their plastic manners and non-aggressive force, always have their own way in the end. "They coax and flatter for their rights, and consequently they are given privileges in excess of their rights; whereas the women who take their rights, as things to which they are entitled without favour, lose them and their privileges together." Kitely's advice is good, in "Every Man in his Humour," and of general application:

> "But rather use the soft persuading way,
> Whose powers will work more gently, and compose
> The imperfect thoughts you labour to reclaim;
> More winning, than enforcing the consent."

The first bishop sent from Iona for the Northumbrian Church was Corman, a man described by Dean Milman as of austere and inflexible character, who, finding more resistance than he expected to his doctrines, in a full assembly of the nation sternly reproached the Northumbrians for their obstinacy, and declared that he would no longer waste his labours on so irreclaimable a race. A gentle voice was heard: "Brother, have you not been too harsh with your unlearned hearers? Should you not, like the apostles, have fed them with the milk of Christian doctrine, till they could receive the full feast of our sublimer truths?" All eyes, it is added, were turned on Aidan, a humble but devout monk; and by general acclamation that discreet and gentle teacher was saluted as bishop. The same historian describes Aldhelm of Malmesbury, in minstrel's garb, arresting the careless crowd of church-goers on a bridge they must pass, and having fully enthralled their attention by the sweetness of his song, anon introducing into it some of the solemn truths of religion; thus succeeding in winning to the faith many hearts, which he would have attempted in vain to move by severer language, or even by the awful excommunication of the Church.* When Fenelon was

* The history of Latin Christianity supplies abundant examples, more or

intrusted by Lewis the Fourteenth with a mission to Poitou, to convert the Protestants, he refused the aid of dragoons, and resorted to suavity of persuasion alone as an instrument of conversion. Of the Protestant missions in the west of Ireland, complaint has been made of their being conducted too offensively, like raids upon heathendom: the Romanist, who might possibly open his bosom to the warm rays of charity, only folds the cloak of his hereditary faith more closely round him, when assailed by the bitter wind of a propagandism which seeks its way to the heart by violence and insult.*

It is at once, on the one part pleasant, on the other painful, to find the Lord Treasurer Burleigh, who had ever been the fast friend of Whitgift, frequently expressing his disapprobation of the primate's severity against non-conformists, and his wish "that the spirit of gentleness might win, rather than severity." And being here on Elizabethan ground, let us

less pertinent. Columban and his disciples are characterized as having had little of the gentle and winning perseverance of missionaries: they had been accustomed to dictate to trembling sovereigns; and their haughty and violent demeanour provoked the pagans, instead of weaning them from their idolatries (iii. 106). So of Boniface (v. 167): it was in the tone of a master that he commanded the world to peace, a tone which provoked resistance. "It was not by persuasive influence, which might lull the conflicting passions of men, and enlighten them as to their real interests." Contrast with these the temper and policy of Pope Eugenius III. (iii. 407), whose "skilful and well-timed use of means more becoming the head of Christendom than arms and excommunications, wrought wonders in his favour;" and who, by his gentleness and charity, gradually supplanted the senate in the attachment of the Roman people: "the fierce and intractable people were yielding to this gentler influence." On a later page we come across the able portraiture of our Henry II., as drawn by a churchman who was warning Becket as to the formidable adversary he had undertaken to oppose: "He will sometimes be softened by humility and patience, but will never submit to compulsion," etc. Ariste *a raison* when he counsels Geronte, in Gresset's "Le Méchant," as the *bien plus sage* course of dealing with a difficult subject,

"Que vous le rameniez par raison, par douceur,
Que d'aller opposer la colère à l'humeur."

* "Such access as Protestantism has gained to the minds of the Catholics in Ireland, it owes, not to the thunders of any missionary Boanerges, but to men like the [late] Archbishop of Dublin [Whately], and the Dean of Elphin, who have taken a very different course, and presented Protestant Christianity to their neighbours in a very different form."—*Saturday Review*, xi. 71.

note Mr. Froude's reference to the diverse procedure of Cecil and Throgmorton in their several dealings with the queen,—she being one of the many strong-willed people, on whom menaces and reproaches operate only as a spur. Cecil understood best Elizabeth's disposition. "By 'practices,' by 'bye-ways,' as he afterwards described it, by affecting to humour what he was passionately anxious to prevent, he was holding his mistress under delicate control; and he dreaded lest his light leading-strings should be broken by a ruder touch." As with the queen, so with her people. When Catherine de Medici expressed astonishment to Sir Thomas Smith, at a certain deference paid by his sovereign to the nation she ruled, "Madam," he replied, "her people be not like your people; they must be trained by *douceur* and persuasion, not by rigour and violence." The greatest of Russian empresses emulated in this respect the greatest of English queens. Indeed, her tendency to indulgence was imputed to Catharine II. as a fault, advantage being taken of her constant reluctance to punish. But how far greater things did she, on the whole, achieve with her subjects, exclaims Mr. Herman Merivale, "thus gently led, than those of her predecessors and successors who employed on them in such abundance the more forcible methods of government!"

Mr. Freeman, in the course of showing that Harold's way of bringing in the proud Danes of the North to his obedience was not exactly the same as William's way, describes him as determining, with that noble and generous daring which is sometimes the highest prudence, to trust himself in the hands of the people who refused to acknowledge him. "These his enemies, who would not that he should reign over them, instead of being brought and slain before him, were to be won over by the magic of his personal presence in their own land." To apply what the Gaulish ambassador says of a great Roman in Jonson's tragedy,

> "This magistrate hath struck an awe into me,
> And by his sweetness won a more regard
> Unto his place, than all the boisterous moods

> That ignorant greatness practiseth, to fill
> The large, unfit authority it wears."

The Antwerp authorities had reason and experience on their side when they sought to persuade the Prince of Parma, in 1585, that the hearts of, not the Antwerpers only, but of the Hollanders and Zealanders, were easily to be won at that moment: give them religious liberty, and "govern them by gentleness rather than by Spanish grandees," and a reconciliation would speedily be ensured. Two years later, but then two years too late, we find the prince averring that he liked "to proceed rather by the ways of love than of rigour and effusion of blood." This was in answer to Queen Elizabeth, who, at a previous juncture, angrily derided any "slight and mild kind of dealing with a people so ingrate," and was all for corrosives instead of lenitives for such festering wounds. Rulers, who fail to secure what they wish by gentle means, are apt very soon to resort to the less excellent way; like Chilperic, the "Nero of France," coaxing the Jew Priscus to turn Christian; first employing argument, then trying blandishments, and anon taking to more powerful reasoning by throwing the Jew into prison. Tytler remarks of the "violent instructions" enforced by Henry VIII. on his envoy to James V., that had the overbearing Tudor adopted a suaver tone, a favourable impression might have been made; but the King o' Scots was "not to be threatened into a compliance with a line of policy which, if suggested in a tone of conciliation, his judgment might have approved," and his unwounded sense of self-respect have consented to carry into effect.

Simon the glover, in Scott's story of mediæval Perth, is well described as watchful over the tactics his daughter employs towards Henry Smith, "whom he knew to be as ductile, when influenced by his affections, as he was fierce and intractable when assailed by hostile remonstrances or threats." *Par un chemin plus doux*, says a shrewd counsellor in Racine, *vous pourrez le ramener;* whereas *les menaces le rendront plus farouche.* Archbishop Whately deprecates the bullying and browbeating system in vogue with certain barristers, and declares it to be a mistake as a means of eliciting truth: he cites his own observation of the marked success of the opposite mode of questioning, and maintains that, generally speaking, a quiet, gentle, and straightforward examination will be the most adapted to elicit truth; the browbeating and blustering which are likeliest to confuse an honest, simple-minded witness, being just what the dishonest one is the best prepared for. "The more the storm blusters, the more carefully he wraps round him the cloak which a warm sunshine will often induce him to throw off."

We are told of Dr. Beattie, in his relations as a professor with his class, that his sway was absolute, because it was founded in reason and affection; that he never employed a harsh epithet in finding fault with any of his pupils; and that when, instead of a rebuke, which they were conscious they deserved, they met merely with a mild reproof, it was conveyed in such a manner as to throw, not only the delinquent, but sometimes the whole class into tears. Fielding's boy-hero is at once in tears when the kind squire takes him in hand, instead of the harsh tutor; his "guilt now flew in his face more than any severity could make it. He could more easily bear the lashes of Thwackum than the generosity of Allworthy." Mrs. Fry used to bear eager record of the docility she had found, and the gratitude she had experienced, from female prisoners, though the most abandoned of their sex: kind treatment, even with restraint obviously for their good, was so new to them, that it called forth, as Sir Samuel Romilly says, "even in the most depraved, grateful and generous feelings." True to the life is the picture Mr. Reade has drawn of the effect on the actress, of a young wife coming to her as a supplicant, instead of inveighing against her,—coming with faith in her goodness, and sobbing to her for pity: "a big tear rolled down her cheek, and proved her something more than an actress." In another of his books he illustrates the truth that men can resist the remonstrances that wound them, and so irritate them, better than they can those gentle appeals which rouse no anger, but soften the whole heart. "The old people stung him; but Mercy, without design, took a surer way. She never said a word; but sometimes, when the discussions were at their height, she turned her dove-like eyes on him, with a look so loving, so humbly inquiring, so timidly imploring, that his heart melted within him." So with Janet Dempster, in George Eliot's story of clerical life, who "was not to be made meek by cruelty; she would repent of nothing in the face of injustice, though she was subdued in a moment by a word or a look that recalled the old days of fondness." In fine, we may conclude with the conclusion of old Master Knowell, in the Elizabethan play:

> "There is a way of winning more by love,
> And urging of the modesty, than fear:
> Force works on servile natures, not the free.
> He that 's compelled to goodness, may be good,
> But 'tis but for that fit; where others, drawn
> By softness and example, get a habit."

——o——

HAMAN HANGED ON HIS OWN GALLOWS.

ESTHER vii. 10.

HARBONAH was one of the chamberlains of that king Ahasuerus, who reigned from India even unto Ethiopia, over an hundred and seven and twenty provinces. And Harbonah it was that said before the king,—when Haman, the son of Hammedatha the Agagite, the Jews' enemy, had gone one step too far in his enmity to the Jews, and had let his vaulting ambition overleap itself in his insolent confidence in royal favour,—Harbonah it was that prompted royal vengeance with the suggestive reminder,—"Behold also, the gallows fifty cubits high, which Haman had made for Mordecai, who had spoken good for the king, standeth in the house of Haman." Then the king said—catching at once at the chamberlain's suggestion—"Hang him thereon." "So they hanged Haman on the gallows that he had prepared for Mordecai."

Somewhat musty is the adage that no law is more equitable than that by which the deviser of death perishes by his own device: *nec lex est æquior ulla, quam necis artificem arte perire suâ.* Musty it might be even in Harbonah's days; but the chamberlain, in the excitement of so signal an example, would feel that time cannot stale, nor custom wither, the force and import of that retributive law.

Mr. de Quincey, in his memorable narrative of the revolt of the Tartars, or flight of the Kalmuck Khan and his people from the Russian territories to the frontiers of China (1771), relates in conclusion how Zebek-Dorchi, the author and originator of this great Tartar *exodus*, perished after a manner specially gratifying to those who compassed his ruin; the Chinese morality being exactly of that kind which approves in everything the *lex talionis*. "Finally, Zebek-Dorchi was invited to the imperial lodge, together with all his accomplices; and under the skilful management of the Chinese nobles in the emperor's establishment, the murderous artifices of these Tartar chieftains were made to recoil upon themselves, and the whole of them perished by assassination at a great imperial banquet." Iterated and reiterated in holy writ is the retributive law that the wicked shall fall by his own wickedness; that transgressors shall be taken in their own naughtiness; that he that seeketh mischief it shall come unto him. The presidents and princes under King Darius, who sought occasion against Daniel, and persuaded their reluctant sovereign to cast the prophet into the den of lions, who however wrought him no manner of hurt,—upon *them* the *lex talionis* vindicated its literal severity when they in their turn were cast into the lions' den, and the lions had the mastery of them, and brake all their bones in pieces or ever they came at the bottom of the den.

The early ballads of almost every literature delight in these retributive surprises. Genuine was the zest of our fathers for such a retort as that of William of Cloudesly on the Justice who is having him measured for his grave:—

"'I have seen as great a marvel,' said Cloudesly,
'As between this and prime
He that maketh a grave for me
Himself may lie therein.'"

So fond is popular history of teaching this sort of philosophy by examples, that examples to the purpose are widely accepted which are yet not historical. Cardinal Balue, under Louis XI., is pointed out in his iron cage, as a malignant inventor punished in and through his own invention; but Michelet has exposed the fallacy of supposing Balue the inventor of those iron cages which had long been known in Italy. Still he had the "merit" of being their importer into France; and the *lex talionis* has its application to him. One remembers of course the Regent Morton hugged to death by the "maiden" he had been the means of introducing into Scotland. The French doctor, Guillotin, is even now not uncommonly believed to have perished in the reign of terror by the instrument invented by and named after him; whereas he quietly died in his bed, many, many years later than that. But the Revolution history is well stored with instances like that of Châlier, condemned to death by the criminal tribunal at Lyons,—the guillotine, which he had sent for from Paris to destroy his enemies, being first destined to sever his own head from his body. A bungling executioner prolonged the last agonies of this man, who in fact was hacked to death, not decapitated. He tasted slowly, as Lamartine says, of the death, a thirst for which he had so often sought to excite in the people; "he was glutted with blood, but it was his own." Alison recognises in the death of Murat a memorable instance of the moral retribution which often attends upon "great deeds of iniquity, and by the instrumentality of the very acts which appeared to place them beyond its reach." He underwent in 1815 the very fate to which, seven years before, he had consigned a hundred Spaniards at Madrid, guilty of no other crime than that of defending their country; and this, as Sir Archibald adds, "by the application of a law to his own case, which he himself had introduced, to check the attempts of the Bourbons to regain a throne which he had usurped." No man, Lord Macaulay affirms, ever made a more unscrupulous use of the legislative power for the destruction of his enemies than Thomas Cromwell; and it was by an unscrupulous use of the legislative power that he was himself destroyed. Those who tauntingly reminded Fenwick, when attainted in 1696, that he had supported the bill which attainted Monmouth, were warned that they might perhaps themselves be tauntingly reminded in some dark and terrible hour, that they had supported the bill which attainted Fenwick. "God forbid that our tyrants should ever be able to plead, in justification of the worst that they can inflict upon us, precedents furnished by ourselves!" Again, it is in recording how, late in life, a horrible calumny settled upon Cicero, that Mr. de Quincey, without lending a moment's credit to the foul insinuation, nevertheless is free to recognise the equity of this retribution revolving upon one who, he asserts, had so often slandered others in the same malicious way. "At last the poisoned chalice came round to his own lips, and at a moment when it wounded the most acutely." *Sæpe*, as Seneca has it, *in magistrum scelera redierunt sua.*

For

> "in these cases
> We still have judgment here; that we but teach
> Bloody instructions, which, being taught, return
> To plague the inventor : this even-handed justice
> Commends the ingredients of our poisoned chalice
> To our own lips."

Plutarch rejoices in showing in Hercules an avenger who adapted the special mode of vengeance to the distinctive deserts of the wrong-doer. He punished with the very mode of punishment devised by those who were now made to suffer it. Antæus he killed in wrestling, and Termerus by breaking his skull,—it being the *specialité* of Termerus to destroy the passengers he met by dashing his head against theirs. Theseus was the imitator of Hercules in this retributive system; he punished Sinis, a bandit,—who used to kill travellers by binding them to the boughs of two pine-trees, which were then allowed to swing back and separate—by making an end of him in the self-same way; Procrustes again he stretched on his own bed. Phalaris, the tyrant of Agrigentum, infamous for his cruelty, and specially for the device devised for him by Perillus of a brazen bull in which he burnt his victims—this Phalaris first tried the device on this Perillus; and when Phalaris was deposed an indignant mob practised upon *him* the self-same torture to which he had subjected so many. And ever memorable among other tales of antiquity,—old wives' fables if you will, but then have not all fables a moral?—is that of Diomedes, who was devoured by the horses he had himself taught to feed on the flesh and blood of men. "Ashes always fly back in the face of him that throws them," is a proverb in the Yoruba language, quoted by Archbishop Trench as equivalent to our "Harm watch, harm catch," and perhaps to the Spanish, "He that sows thorns, let him not walk barefoot." An overruling Power disposes of what the malignity of man proposes, and

> "Thus doth it force the swords of wicked men
> To turn their own points on their masters' bosoms."

The psalmist felt that he was praying in accordance with the Divine will, when he prayed that the ungodly might fall into their own nets together, while he ever escaped them. So again with his prayer that the mischief of their own lips might fall upon the heads of them that compassed him about. For it was a matter at once of faith and of experience with the psalmist, that the evil deviser and evil-doer, travailing with mischief, conceiving sorrow, and bringing forth ungodliness, who had graven and digged up a pit, was apt to fall himself into the destruction that he made for other. "For his travail shall come upon his own head, and his wickedness shall fall on his own pate." Owen Feltham delights to recall, from the stores of ancient and mediæval story, how Bagoas, a Persian nobleman, having poisoned Artaxerxes and Artamenes, was detected by Darius, and forced to drink poison himself; how Diomedes, as we have already seen, for the beasts he had fed on human flesh was by Hercules made food; and how Pope Alexander VI., having designed the poisoning of his friend Cardinal Adrian, by his cup-bearer's mistake of the bottle, took the draught himself, "and so died by the same engine which he himself had appointed to kill another"—a sort of enginery glanced at in Ben Jonson :—

"I have you in a purse-net,
Good master Picklock, with your worming brain,
And wriggling engine-head"

too clever by half. Luther, in his Table-talk, welcomes the import of the Jewish story of Og, king of Bashan, who they say had lifted a great rock to throw at his enemies, "but God made a hole in the middle, so that it slipped down upon the giant's neck, and he could never rid himself of it." The fourth book of Southey's "Thalaba" closes with a shriek from Lobaba the sorcerer, which this final stanza sufficiently explains :—

"What, wretch, and hast thou raised
The rushing terrors of the wilderness,
To fall on thine own head?
Death! death! inevitable death!
Driven by the breath of God,
A column of the desert met his way."

Nor, among the lyrical pieces of the same poet, be forgotten that ballad of the Inchcape rock, which tells how the bell put up by the abbot of Aberbrothok to warn ships of their peril, was taken down by a sea pirate, Sir Ralph the Rover, who in the words of an old Scottish topographer, "a yeare thereafter perished upon the same rocke, with ship and goodes, in the righteous judgment of God." Many and many

"stories have been told of men whose lives
Were infamous, and so their end. I mean
That the red murderer has himself been murdered;
The traitor struck with treason; he who let
The orphan perish came himself to want:
Thus justice and great God have ordered it!
So that the scene of evil has been turned
Against the actor; pain paid back with pain;
And poison given for poison."

Prescott's narrative of the decline and fall of Luna, minister under John II. of Castile, is pointed with this moral to adorn the tale; that "by one of those dispensations of Providence which often confound the plans of the wisest, the column which the minister had so artfully raised for his support served only to crush him." *Sæpe intereunt aliis meditantes necem;* and that by the very means mediated.

> "For 'tis the sport, to have the engineer
> Hoist with his own petard,"

says Hamlet, in vindictive anticipation of such an issue, or rather upshot. The guilty king, his uncle, suggests misgivings lest his arrows, by a certain mischance, might

> "have reverted to my bow again,
> And not where I had aimed them;"

and arrows, so returning, are by poetical justice apt to do the foiled bowman a mischief. That king's fellow-conspirator, Laertes, is thus punished, and owns it:—

> "*Osric.* How is't, Laertes?
> *Laertes.* Why as a woodcock to my own springe, Osric;
> I am justly killed with mine own treachery."

And so is the king himself; and he, Laertes testifies,—

> "is justly served:
> It is a poison tempered by himself"

for Hamlet, which Claudius has just drank of, and drinking died. The tragedy of the prince of Denmark does indeed abound in instances of what Horatio calls

> "Accidental judgments, casual slaughters,
> And deaths put on by cunning and forced cause;
> And, in this upshot, purposes mistook
> Fallen on the inventors' heads."

——o——

TO-DAY'S SUFFICING EVIL, AND TO-MORROW'S FORECAST CARE.

St. Matthew vi. 34.

WITH a divine calm fall those words from the Sermon of the Mount—spoken as never man spake—which bid us take "no thought for the morrow; for the morrow shall take thought for the things of itself. Sufficient unto the day is the evil thereof."

Pagan philosophy had, and natural theism has, its approximation to the same point of view. Horace is all for letting the mind enjoy the enjoyable present, and for leaving no room or resting-place for the sole of the foot of Black Care, raven and unclean bird that she is. The morrow may be hers, but to-day at least is his, and the morrow shall take care for the things of itself:

> "Lætus in præsens animus quod ultra est
> Oderit curare."

David Hume, again, meets the doctrine that we should always have before our eyes, death, disease, poverty, blindness, calumny, and the like, as ills which are incident to human nature, and which may befall us to-morrow,—by the answer, that if we confine ourselves to a general and distant reflection on the ills of human life, such a vague procedure can have no effect to prepare us for them; and that if, on the other hand, by close and intense meditation we render them present and intimate to us, we realise the true secret for poisoning all our pleasures, and rendering us perpetually miserable. He grieves more than need be, who begins to grieve before he need, is one of Seneca's sententious sayings: *Plus dolet quam necesse est, qui ante dolet quam necesse est.* One of Mrs. Gore's women of the world—who might probably be counted by the hundred—is sprightly and smart in her rebuke of her husband and his sister for their delight in perplexing the brightest moments of existence by all the agonies of second sight, and whom she represents as quite indignant when they find her sympathy waiting the actual occurrence of evil. "I hate," she says, "to turn back my head towards the dark shadow that follows me, or direct my telescope towards a coming storm." And herein was she wise, if not with all the wisdom of those Christian morals, of which we have so impressive an expositor in Sir Thomas Browne. "Leave future occurrences to their uncertainties," writes the fine old physician, Religiosus Medicus, "think that which is present thy own; and, since 'tis easier to foretell an eclipse than a foul day at some distance, look for little regular below. Attend with patience the uncertainty of things, and what lieth yet unexerted in the chaos of futurity." Shakspeare's noble Roman, at the dawn of the day of battle on which so much depends, is natural man enough to utter the aspiration :

> "O, that a man might know
> The end of this day's business, ere it come!"

But he is also stoic philosopher enough to check that prospective yearning, with the reflection,

> "But it sufficeth that the day will end,
> And then the end is known."

Swift opens his Birthday Address to Stella with the assurance,

> "This day, whate'er the fates decree,
> Shall still be kept with joy by me :
> This day, then, let us not be told,
> That you are sick and I grown old;
> Nor think on our approaching ills,
> And talk of spectacles and pills;
> To-morrow will be time enough
> To hear such mortifying stuff."

For once, however, it is only in the opening verses that the dean is jocose; and he soon turns aside from his strain of levity to bid Stella accept some serious lines "from not the gravest of divines." Schleiermacher, in one of his rather gushing letters, —for he, too, though nothing of a Swift, and though of real weight in divinity, was not in all senses the gravest of divines, —implores his "dearest Jette" not to look so much into the future. He cannot beg this too earnestly and too often, he says, —so depressed is Jette apt to be by anticipation of things to come, and from a perverse habit of condensing advent difficulties. "It is easy to see through *one* pane of glass, but through ten placed one upon another we cannot see. Does this prove that each one is not transparent? or are we ever called upon to look through more than one at a time? Double panes we only have recourse to for warmth; and just so it is with life. We have but to live *one* moment at a time. Keep each one isolated, and you will easily see your way through them." So again writes good Frederick Perthes to his wife, whose fearful and hopeful longings, he tells her, are indeed guarantees for the great future beyond the grave, but whom he urges to bear in mind that a vigorous grasp of the present is our duty so long as we are upon earth. It is the present moment, he reminds her, that supplies the energy and decision that fit us for life; retrospect brings sadness, and the dark future excites fears, so that we should be crippled in our exertions were we not to lay a vigorous grasp upon the present. And

"Labour with what zeal you will,
Something still remains undone;
Something uncompleted still
Waits the rising of the sun.

By the bedside, on the stair,
At the threshold, near the gates,
With its menace or its prayer,
Like a mendicant it waits;

Waits, and will not go away;
Waits, and will not be gainsaid:
By the cares of yesterday
Each to-day is heavier made;

Till at length the burden seems
Greater than our strength can bear;
Heavy as the weight of dreams
Pressing on us everywhere.

And we stand from day to day,
Like the dwarfs of times gone by,
Who, as Northern legends say,
On their shoulders held the sky."

Quite exceptional is the temperament impersonated by Wordsworth in one who seemed a man of cheerful yesterdays and confident to-morrows.

Longfellow has his midnight reflection on To-morrow; himself a watcher and contemplative, his little ones asleep: and thus the *pensées* end:

"To-morrow! the mysterious, unknown guest,
Who cries to me, 'Remember Barmecide,
And tremble to be happy with the rest.'
And I make answer, 'I am satisfied;
I dare not ask; I know not what is best;
God hath already said what shall betide.'"

There is never, observes Madame d'Arblay, in her diary, such a superfluity of actual happiness as to make it either rational or justifiable to feed upon *expected* misery. "That portion of philosophy which belongs to making the most of the present day, grows upon me strongly; and, as I have suffered infinitely from its neglect, it is what I most encourage, and, indeed, require." Kindly ordained, she takes it, is the concealment of

"the day of sorrow;
And enough is the present tense of toil—
For this world, to all, is a stiffish soil—
And the mind flies back with a glad recoil
From the debts not due till to-morrow."

It is one of Scott's young heroes who opens a letter of troublous tidings with the confession that, until now, he had rarely known what it was to sustain a moment's real sorrow; what he called such was, he now felt assured, only the weariness of mind which, having nothing actually present to complain of, turns upon itself, and becomes anxious about the future—disregarding the Scriptural monition that sufficient unto the day is the evil thereof. Is there, Armstrong asks,

"an evil worse than fear itself?
And what avails it that indulgent Heaven
From mortal eyes has wrapt the woes to come,
If we, ingenious to torment ourselves,
Grow pale at hideous fictions of our own?
Enjoy the present; nor, with needless cares
Of what may spring from blind misfortune's womb,
Appal the surest hours that life bestows:
Serene, and master of yourself, prepare
For what may come; and leave the rest to Heaven."

Prevision and imagination, as Rousseau says, multiply the evils of our lot: "*Pour moi,*" he professes—however the profession may have squared with the practice—"*j'ai beau savoir que je souffrirai demain, il me suffit de ne pas souffrir aujourd'hui pour être tranquille.*" It is certainly a frenzy, quoth old Montaigne, to go now and whip yourself, because it may so fall out that fortune may one day decree you a whipping, and to put on your furred gown at Midsummer, because you will stand in need of it at Christmas. It was one of Madame de Sévigné's maxims in life to "regarder l'avenir comme une obscurité, dont il peut arriver des biens et des clartés à quoi l'on ne s'attend pas." Milton's Adam laments the mournful privilege of "visions ill foreseen." Better had he lived ignorant of future! so had borne his part of evil only, each day's lot enough to bear. So again, in Milton's Masque, the elder brother bids the younger be not over-exquisite to cast the fashion of uncertain evils :

"For grant they be so, while they rest unknown,
What need a man forestall his date of grief,
And run to meet what he would most avoid?"

And once more, Milton himself, in one of those Sonnets which stand in the like relation of merit to his great epic that Shakspeare's do to his great dramas, admonishes his scholar, Cyriack Skinner, that heaven disproves the care,

"though wise in show,
That with superfluous burden loads the day,
And when God sends a cheerful hour, refrains."

"Melancholy commonly flies to the future for its aliment," says Sydney Smith, "and it must be encountered," he adds, "by diminishing the range of our views." The great remedy for melancholy, he insists in another place, is to "take short views of life." Are you happy now? Then why destroy present happiness by a distant misery, which may never come at all? For "every substantial grief has twenty shadows, and most of them shadows of your own making." One of his correspondents he emphatically counsels to dispel that prophetic gloom which dives into futurity, to extract sorrow from days and years to come, and which considers its own unhappy visions as the decrees of Providence. "We know nothing of to-morrow, our business is to be good and happy to day." In effect, like Maucroix,

"Il rit de ces prudents qui, par trop de sagesse,
S'en vont dans l'avenir chercher de la tristesse
Et des soucis cuisants."

Once and again in his autobiography does the most influential, perhaps, of French philosophers avow his resolve *á vivre désormais au jour la journée*, to take short views of life, and regard distant objects as at once illusive and elusory. "Usons de chaque jour sans trop de prévoyance du lendemain," says another. And it was an old French poet, fourscore and upwards, who in 1700 wrote the four verses which since then have been often cited:

> "Chaque jour est un bien que du ciel je reçois,
> Je jouis aujourd'hui de celui qu'il me donne;
> Il n' appartient pas plus aux jeunes gens qu'a moi,
> Et celui de demain n'appartient a personne."

Dr. Boyd recognises as sound philosophy in Sydney Smith, the advising us, whether physically or morally, to "take short views." One of his illustrations to the purpose is, that it would knock you up at once if, when the railway carriage moved out of the station at Edinburgh, you began to trace in your mind's eye the whole route to London. Never do that, he says; think first of Dunbar, then of Newcastle, then of York, and, putting the thing thus, you will get over the distance without fatigue of mind. What little child, he asks, would have heart to begin the alphabet, if, before he did so, you put clearly before him all the school and college work of which it is the beginning? "The poor little thing would knock up at once, wearied out by your want of skill in putting things. And so it is that Providence, kindly and gradually putting things, whiles us onward, still keeping hope and heart, through the trials and cares of life." Every dog has its day, quaintly observes A. H. K. B. on another occasion; but the day of the rational dog is overclouded in a fashion unknown to his inferior fellow-creatures; it is overclouded by the anticipation of the coming day which will not be his. And the essayist reminds us accordingly how "that great though morbid man, John Foster," could not heartily enjoy the summer weather, for thinking how every sunny day that shone upon him was a downward step towards the winter gloom—each indication that the season was advancing, though only to greater beauty, filling him with a sort of forecast regret. "I have seen a fearful sight to-day," he would say, "I have seen a buttercup." And we know, of course, adds his critic, "that in his case there was nothing like affectation; it was only that, unhappily for himself, the bent of his mind was so onward-looking, that he saw only a premonition of December in the roses of June." Waife, in Lord Lytton's story, checks his grandchild's query when, happy, and unaccustomed to happiness, and therefore distrusting its continuance, she wistfully exclaims, "It cannot last, can it?" "'Tis no use in this life, my dear," Waife tells her, "no use at all disturbing present happiness by asking, 'Can it last?' To-day is man's, to-morrow his Maker's." Life being a succession of stages, urges another practical philosopher, we should think of one stage at a time. Most people, he judiciously reminds us, can bear one day's evil; what breaks men down is the trying to bear on one day the evil of two days, twenty days, a hundred days. "We can bear a day of pain, followed by a night of pain, and that again by a day of pain, and thus onward. But we can bear each day and night of pain, only by taking each by itself. We can break each rod, but not the bundle." And the sufferer, in real great suffering, is well described as turning to the wall in blank despair, when he looks too far on. To cite another illustration of A. K. H. B.'s, we should, for certain purposes, look not at the entire chain, but at each successive link of it; we know, of course, that each link will be succeeded by the next; but we should think of them one at a time.

Do not say, *wait the end*, is a maxim of Paul Louis Courier's, who declares that, saving the respect due to the ancients, nothing is more false than that rule. "The evil of to-morrow shall never deprive me of the good of to-day," is one of the brilliant Frenchman's resolves. Another brilliant but highly bilious Frenchman testifies from observation and experience to the necessity, in the long run, of living from day to day, without indulgence either in unavailing regrets or anxious forecast, "on s'aperçoit qu'il faut vivre au jour le jour, oublier beaucoup, enfin éponger la vie à mésure qu'elle s'écoule." But it may too truly be said of this philosopher that he wrote, and lived, as one having no hope, and without God in the world.

Horace was in his placid *Il Penseroso* mood when he counselled the acceptance of each new-born day as possibly one's last, and appropriating it accordingly :

> "Inter spem curamque, timores inter et iras,
> Omnem crede diem tibi diluxisse supremum :
> Grata superveniet quæ non sperabitur hora."

We might suggest suggestive parallels by the score, as this from a play of Leigh Hunt's,

> "One day—could you not try one day and then
> Enjoy or fear another as it suited ?
> Ay, one—one—one. Try but one day, and then
> Trust me if one day would not give you strength,"

for morrows in store. Or this, from a poem of Owen Meredith's :

> "Be quiet ! Take things as they come ;
> Each hour will draw out some surprise.
> With blessing let the days go home :
> Thou shalt have thanks from evening skies."

——o——

MEDICAMENTAL MUSIC.

I SAMUEL xvi. 23.

IN the days when Saul loved David greatly, and found comfort in the constant presence of his favourite, it sometimes "came to pass that when the evil spirit from God was upon Saul, that David took an harp, and played with his hand : so Saul was refreshed, and was well, and the evil spirit departed from him."

That there is something more than ordinary in music, Bishop Beveridge, in his "Private Thoughts," infers from this fact—that David made use of the harp for driving away the evil spirit from Saul, as well as for bringing the good spirit upon himself. The gentle prelate therefore recognises in music a sort of secret and charming power, such as naturally dispels "those black humours which the evil spirit is apt to brood upon," and such too as composes the mind into a more regular, sweet, and docile disposition, thereby rendering it "the fitter for the Holy

Spirit to work upon, the more susceptive of Divine grace, and more faithful messenger to convey truth to the understanding." And he cites his personal experience—*experto crede*—in favour of this view.

Anatomizing melancholy, old Burton adds to the instance of David that of Elisha, who when he was troubled by importunate kings, called for a minstrel, "and when he played, the hand of the Lord came upon him." Of course the erudite anatomist heaps up corroborative instances of all kinds and ages, mythological, classical, mediæval; and he quotes many of those obscure and obsolete authorities whom it has been the cheap policy of many a bookmaker to cite from Burton's *thesaurus* second-hand.

Spenser opens a canto of his "Faerie Queene" with a tribute to the powers of minstrelsy as exercised by Orpheus,—

> "Or such as that celestial psalmist was,
> That when the wicked fiend his lord tormented,
> With heavenly notes, that did all others pass,
> The outrage of his furious fit relented."

Or again, to quote a parallel passage from a later poet of the didactic school, whom, perhaps simply because he (Dr. Armstrong) was didactic, some people think as essentially prosy as Spenser is on all sides allowed to be quintessentially poetical:—

> "Such was the bard, whose heavenly strains of old
> Appeased the fiend of melancholy Saul."

Buretti declares music to have the power of so affecting the whole nervous system as to give sensible ease in a large variety of disorders, and in some cases a radical cure, Particularly he instances sciatica as capable of being relieved by this agency. Theophrastus is mentioned by Pliny as recommending it for the hip gout; and there are references on record by old Cato and Varro to the same effect. Æsculapius figures in Pindar as healing acute disorders with soothing songs.

> "Music exalts each joy, allays each grief,
> Expels diseases, softens every pain,

> Subdues the rage of poison and of plague :
> And hence the wise of ancient days adored
> One power of Physic, Melody, and Song."

Over Luther, as Sir James Stephen has remarked, there brooded a constitutional melancholy, sometimes engendering sadness, but more often giving birth to dreams so wild that, if vivified by the imagination of Dante, they might have passed into visions as awful and majestic as those of the "Inferno." Various were the spells to which Luther had recourse, to cast out the demons that haunted him; and of these remedial agencies the most potent perhaps was music. "He had ascertained and taught that the spirit of darkness abhors sweet sounds not less than light itself; for music (he says), while it chases away the evil suggestions, effectually baffles the wiles of the tempter. His lute, and hand, and voice, accompanying his own solemn melodies, were therefore raised to repel the vehement aggressions of the enemy of mankind."

A story is told of Farinelli, the famous singer, being sent for express to Madrid, to try the effect of his magical voice on the king of Spain, who was then buried in the profoundest melancholy—proof against every appeal to exertion, living without signs of life in a darkened chamber, the unresisting prey of dejection beyond relief. But relief came with Farinelli. The vocalist was desired by the physicians to sing in an outer room, which for a day or two he did, without any apparent effect upon the royal patient. But at length it was noticed that the king seemed partially roused from his stupor, and became an evident listener; next day tears were seen starting from his eyes; the day after he ordered the door of his chamber to be left open; and at last "the perturbed spirit entirely left our modern Saul, and the medicinal voice of Farinelli effected what no other medicine could." Well known in modern verse is the poet's picture of a despairing sufferer, whom nought avails to move until—

> "At last a slave bethought her of a harp :
> The harper came, and tuned his instrument ;
> At the first notes, irregular and sharp,
> On him her flashing eyes a moment bent,

> Then to the wall she turned as if to warp
> Her thoughts from sorrow through her heart re-sent.
> *   *   *   *   *
> Anon her thin wan fingers beat the wall
> In time to his old tune . . .
> . . . And in a gushing stream
> The tears rushed forth from her o'erclouded brain,
> Like mountain mists at length dissolved in rain."

Nor be forgotten the impressive instance of Schiller's Wallenstein, in his hour of darkness, tranquillised by Thekla's voice and lute :—

> "Come here, my girl. Seat thee by me,
> For there is a good spirit on thy lips.
> Thy mother praised to me thy ready skill ;
> She says a voice of melody dwells in thee,
> Which doth enchant the soul. Now such a voice
> Will drive away from me the evil demon
> That beats his black wings close above my head."

William Godwin makes his savage Tyrell amenable to well warbled melody. Readers of Scott will remember how a frenzied Highlander is soothed into self restraint by the minstrelsy of Annot Lyle. Goethe makes the first bar of an air by Gretchen suffice to lull the sorrows of young Werter, who protests that " instantly the gloom and madness which hang over me are dispersed, and I breathe freely again." Another Charlotte—our English Richardson's—is less successful in her manipulation of medicinal melody, when essaying to subdue an angry spirit by the spells of song : " I go to my harpsichord ; music enrages him. He is worse than Saul ; for Saul could be gloomily pleased with the music even of the man he hated," But this is antedating Saul's aversion ; in those days Saul loved David greatly.

Dr. Croly, in an eloquent paragraph of his elaborate eastern romance, records how carefully music, " of all pleasures the most intellectual, that glorious painting to the ear, that rich mastery of the gloomier emotions of our nature," was studied by the Jewish priesthood, and with a skill that influenced the habits of the country. " How often," exclaims Salathiel, "have my fiercest perturbations sunk, at the sounds that once filled the breezes of Judæa! How often, when my brain was burning, and the blood ran through my veins like molten brass, have I been softened down to painless tears by the chorus from our hills, the mellow harmony of harp and horn, blending with the voices of the youths and maidens of Israel!"

It is characteristic, as Herr Kohl observes, of music-loving Bohemia, that in the lunatic asylum of its capital, music should be considered one of the chief aids and appliances for the improvement of the patients. In addition to the garden concerts, in which all assist who can, there is chamber music—quartets, trios, etc.,—every morning and evening in the wards; and a musical director takes high rank in the official staff of the establishment.

Elizabeth Charlotte of Orleans, mother of the Regent, describes in one of her letters a Madame de Persillie, well born and well bred, but a dangerous lunatic; who however, if you could but slip a guitar into her hand when the fury-fit came on, would become calm again as soon as she began to play. "I pity her greatly," writes the good-natured duchess (whose homely German nature never became properly assimilated to the French court); "she was very fond of me, and used to address me as *Mon aimable;* but whenever she came to see me I always had a guitar quite ready for her." It was but common prudence to be thus prepared for the worst; and when the worst came to the worst, then a guitar was best.

Schleiermacher exclaims in one of his letters, "Surely, if there was any good in Saul's innermost soul it must have been an *adagio* that exorcised the evil spirit." The evil spirit in question is introduced by name, Malzah, in a recent Canadian drama, and is made to avow the accomplished fact of exorcism in the following strain:—

"Music, music hath its sway:
Music's order I obey,
I have unwound myself at sound
From off Saul's heart, where coiled I lay."

Which snaky or serpentine similitude is akin to a passage in

Mr. Browning's "Paracelsus"—distant as the kinship between the two poems may be in other respects :

> "My heart ! they loose my heart, those simple words ;
> Its darkness passes, which nought else could touch ;
> Like some dank snake that force may not expel,
> Which glideth out to music sweet and low."

Again and again in Shakspeare is the remedial agency of music resorted to by afflicted royalty. At one time it is Queen Katharine, fading and heartsore, who bids one of her women cease working, and sing—

> "Take thy lute, wench ; my soul grows sad with troubles ;
> Sing, and disperse them if thou canst."

And the singer's theme is how "in sweet music is such art, killing care and grief at heart." At another time it is dying Harry IV., who prays his attendants, as they bear him to an inner room—

> "Let there be no noise made, my gentle friends !
> Unless some dull* and favourable hand
> Will whisper music to my weary spirit."

And once more, we have Lear's physician prescribing music for the safer awakening of the distraught old man from that long sleep which was only not his last.

——o——

FREE FROM RIGHTEOUSNESS.

ROMANS vi. 20.

IN being, and so long as they continued, slaves of sin (δοῦλοι τῆς ἁμαρτίας), the recipients of St. Paul's epistle to the Romans are forcibly described by him as having been, *ipso facto*, free from righteousness (ἐλεύθεροι τῇ δικαιοσύνῃ). But what fruit had they in the freedom of which they were now ashamed?

* Gently soothing.

"He is the freeman whom the truth makes free,
And all are slaves beside."

They knew that to whom men yield themselves servants to obey, his servants they are to whom they are obedient, whether of sin unto death, or of loyal service unto righteousness. There is a freedom from righteousness, which is servitude to sin; and there is that service of God which, though a service, or rather because a service, is perfect freedom.

Gray, in the best known of his odes (best known by heart) devises this expressive phrase,—

"Constraint, that sweetens liberty."

It refers to schoolboys, enjoying all the more their playground freedom for the previous and succeeding restraints and constraints of the schoolroom. All work and no play makes a dull boy; but so does all play and no work. In this sense, as in so many others, does the paradox hold good that half is more than the whole (πλέον ἥμισυ παντός); and even a schoolboy can find by experience that a half holiday may be more than a whole one.

Wordsworth sounds the depths of this philosophy in his magnificent Ode to Duty. He is fatigued by freedom; he would be no longer the sport of every random gust; he would no longer stray in smooth walks, but would serve Duty more strictly if he might:—

"Through no disturbance of my soul,
Or strong compunction in me wrought,
I supplicate for thy control;
But in the quietness of thought:
Me this uncharted freedom tires;
I feel the weight of chance desires;
My hopes no more must change their name,
I long for a repose that ever is the same."

Whose service is perfect freedom—that is God's service only. The true character of that service (in Greek Testament phrase, *slavery*) is aptly indicated by St. Paul to the Ephesians, where he speaks of *with good will doing service*—μετ' εὐνοίας ΔΟΥΛΕΥΟΝΤΕΣ, ὡς τῷ Κυρίῳ καὶ οὐκ ἀνθρώποις. The law of the Spirit of life makes free from the law of sin and death, that the righteousness of spiritual law may be fulfilled in those who sometime were free from righteousness. Freedom from righteousness is, in fact, identical with that bondage of corruption from which they are delivered into the glorious liberty of the children of God. He that is so called, being free, is yet Christ's servant, δοῦλος. And, as a servant, whatsoever he doeth he is to do heartily, as to the Lord, and not to men—τῷ γὰρ Κυρίῳ Χριστῷ ΔΟΥΛΕΥΕΙ. Goethe's biographer tells us how he would assert, against the encyclopedists, that "whatever frees the intellect, without at the same time giving us command over ourselves, is pernicious;" or would utter one of his profound and pregnant γνῶμαι such as *Nur das Gesetz kann uns die Freiheit geben*, i.e., only within the circle of law can there be true freedom. "We are not free when we acknowledge no higher power, but when we acknowledge it, and in reverence raise ourselves by proving that a Higher lives in us." We may wrest to our purpose the lines of Schiller, in *Wallensteins Tod:*

> "Nay, let it not afflict you that your power
> Is circumscribed. Much liberty, much error!
> The narrow path of duty is securest."

Liberty of will is likened by Jeremy Taylor to the motion of a magnetic needle towards the north, full of trembling and uncertainty till it be fixed in the beloved point: "it wavers as long as it is free, and is at rest when it can choose no more." What is liberty? asks M. Jules Simon; and answers, The power of doing or not doing. But, he proceeds to inquire, can this liberty exist independent of law?—*cette liberté peut-elle subsister sans règle?* Nay, liberty without rule, or law, so far from ennobling him who possesses it, degrades him. Liberty is not given to us to withdraw us from the authority of law, but that we may obey it in recognising its great First Cause. Unrestrained liberty is our ruin; liberty subjected to law, and that an immovable law, is the instrument and the token of our true greatness. Wordsworth philosophically affirms that "all men may find cause, when life is at a weary pause, and they have panted up the hill of duty with reluctant will," to

> "Be thankful, even though tired and faint,
> For the rich bounties of constraint;
> Whence oft invigorating transports flow,
> That choice lacked courage to bestow."

The truth admits of exemplification in a thousand minor details of every-day life. Mrs. Gaskell relates how she heard Charlotte Brontë declare, in reference to the "exact punctuality and obedience to the laws of time and place" enforced by her somewhat despotic aunt on the motherless family at Haworth parsonage, that no one but themselves could tell the value of this control in after life: "with their impulsive natures it was positive repose to have learnt obedience to external laws." In the last of her own fictions—and, though unfinished, the ripest and best—Mrs. Gaskell herself suggestively observes of a patient who, when a medical adviser is at length called in, finds it a great relief to be told what to do, what to eat, drink, and avoid, that "such decisions *ab extra* are sometimes a wonderful relief to those whose habit has been to decide, not only for themselves, but for every one else;" and that occasionally the relaxation of the strain which a character for infallible wisdom brings with it does much to restore health. M. de Vigny, in one of his highly finished *historiettes*, speculates on the nature and power of the instinct which seems to urge mankind, as by a kind of necessity, to seek pleasure in obedience, and to feel a desire to depose, as it were, their free agency and consequent responsibility in other hands; as if thereby a burden was laid down, too weighty to be voluntarily supported; and how this sensation of relief seems to give a secret feeling of complacency, and a freedom to the act of obedience, which reconcile it to the pride of human nature. Soldiers, observes Sir Walter Scott, are always most pleased when they are best in order for performing their military service; and licence or inactivity, however acceptable at times, are not, when continued, so agreeable to men of the camp as strict discipline and a prospect of employment. "I have heard men talk of the blessings of freedom," says Wamba to himself, when suddenly freed from sharing the captivity of his master; "but I wish any wise man would teach me what use to make of it now that I have it." So Elia, in his essay on The Superannuated Man, to whom life being now one long holiday has no holiday henceforth; where he expatiates on the sight of "busy faces to recreate the idle man, who contemplates them ever passing by—the very face of business a charm by contrast to his relaxation from it." Many an individual experience can put its own private interpretation on the averment of one of Rousseau's correspondents—*Ce lien si redouté me delivre d'une servitude beaucoup plus redoubtable.*

Of significant application again is De Quincey's denial of the truth of Lessing's æsthetical assertion, that the sense of necessary and absolute limitation is banished from the idea of a fine art. On the contrary, he maintains this sense is indispensable as a means of resisting (and therefore realizing) the sense of freedom: "the freedom of a fine art is found not in the absence of restraint, but in the conflict with it." So in literature. That certain rules of composition sustain themselves at all is due, according to Mr. W. Caldwell Roscoe, to the fact that creative genius of a high order is not impatient of forms, but rather loves, on the contrary, to have certain limits defined for it, and to be freed to some extent from "the weight of too much liberty." Shakspeare, he adds, did not fret because tragedies are limited to five acts, nor Milton quarrel with the formal conditions of an epic poem. Here again shall we find in Wordsworth a passage to the point:—

"In truth the prison, unto which we doom
Ourselves, no prison is: and hence for me,
In sundry moods, 'twas pastime to be bound
Within the Sonnet's scanty plot of ground;
Pleased, if some souls (for such there needs must be),
Who have felt the weight of too much liberty,
Should find brief solace there, as I have found."

The biographer of Edward Irving tells us how deeply he was affected when the decision of the presbytery against him removed him from the range of their control, so that, "notwithstanding all his independence, the profound loyalty of his soul was henceforth baulked of its healthful necessities." He felt himself with a pang to be cast unnaturally free of restraint—"that lawful, sweet restraint, . . . to which the tender dutifulness so seldom wanting to great genius naturally clings."* Habits of instant and mechanical obedience are affirmed by Sir Henry Taylor to be those that give rest to the child, and spare its health and temper. Men are but children of a larger growth; and though as regards obedience to a Father which is in heaven, "mechanical" obedience may not be the word, yet is cheerfully implicit obedience the thing; obedience is the privilege of the child.

> "For obedience is nobler than freedom. What's free?
> The vexed straw on the wind, the frothed spume on the sea.

---

* Another type of mind, deficient in the higher attributes of independence, is often feverishly eager to sink its sense of individual responsibility by seeking what is called "rest in the Church." Dr. Bungener represents his Julian, when committed to the Bastile, as rather rejoicing at than terrified by the despotism of the hand laid upon him; and in the same way, on taking holy orders, he, being "subdued in heart, enslaved in mind, tired of being his own master, only to create his own torments," flatters himself that he gives the Church complete power over his faculties at the same time that he gives her plenary power over his actions.

To the baser sort, remarks Sir James Stephen, no yoke is so galling as that of self control, no deliverance so welcome as that of being handsomely rid of free agency. "With such men mental slavery readily becomes a habit, a fashion, and a pride. To the abject many the abdication of self-government is a willing sacrifice."

One of our acutest essayists on social subjects comments on the readiness of a man to exult in the fact that he has done something which he cannot undo, and has pledged himself to a course from which he cannot draw back, as more commonly the sign of a weak than of a strong nature. "The comfort of plunging right into the stream is unspeakable to anybody who has been accustomed to stand shivering and irresolute on the bank." When a person of this sort, it is justly observed, has brought himself to take the plunge, his exultation and fearlessness are wonderful: the knowledge that the Rubicon is crossed, and the die cast, seems to relieve him from the necessity of further resolution. "He has set in motion a machine which will of itself wind off results and consequences for him without more ado on his own part; and this is an order of release from the demands of circumstances upon his will, for which he cannot be too thankful."

The great ocean itself, as it rolls and it swells,
In the bonds of a boundless obedience dwells."

The next section takes up the same theme under another heading, and with a fresh set of variations.

——o——

THE SERVICE OF FREEDOM.

ST. MATTHEW xi. 29, 30.

IT is in tones of winning promise and invitation that men are offered the wearing of Christ's yoke. Let all who are weary and heavy laden come to Him: come, that they may take His yoke upon them. There is a seeming paradox in the invitation. Should not the weary be invited by promised freedom from all yoke-bearing? Should not the heavy-laden be attracted by a pledge of entire immunity from burdens grievous to be borne, whether heavy or light? Not so. Christ's yoke is easy, but it is a yoke. The burden he imposes is light, but a burden of some sort He does impose. Being made free from sin, men become the servants—servitors, slaves even, δοῦλοι, of righteousness. But in so being made free from sin, and becoming servants, δοῦλοι, to God, they have their fruit unto holiness, and the end everlasting life. And the yoke of privilege promised by Christ differs from the irksome bonds and rigid constraint of scribes and rabbis; a yoke which, says St. Peter, neither we nor our fathers were able to bear, inasmuch as it implies and involves a purely spiritual service—that we should serve (δουλεύειν) in newness of spirit, and not in the oldness of the letter. "If the Son therefore shall make you free, ye shall be free indeed."

Keble says of men, in the "Christian Year," that,

"Freely they own, or heedless prove,
The curse of lawless hearts, the joy of self-control."

The joy of self-control. For what Wordsworth expressively calls "unchartered freedom," as revelled in by those who ignore a holy and happy-making law of duty, is not in the long run, a boon, but a bane. True, that, as Cowper has it,

> "'Tis liberty alone that gives the flower
> Of fleeting life its lustre and perfume,
> And we are weeds without it. All constraint,
> Except what wisdom lays on evil men,
> Is evil."

But the constraint that sweetens liberty is excepted; the control that enfranchises from servitude to self, and exalts to a liberty which monarchs cannot grant: "'Tis liberty of heart, derived from Heaven," "and held by charter;" "a clean escape from tyrannizing lust." "Grace makes the slave a freeman;" for "He is the freeman whom the truth makes free, and all are slaves beside." Byron was drawing on his own bitter experience when he wrote the lines,

> "Lord of himself—that heritage of woe,
> That fearful empire which the human breast
> But holds to rob the heart within of rest."

Imlac, the sage, describes, in "Rasselas" the placid flow of life enjoyed by a devout brotherhood, whose "time is regularly distributed; one duty succeeds another, so that they are not left open to the distraction of unguided choice, nor lost in the shades of listless inactivity. There is a certain task to be performed at an appropriated hour," and the constraint is to them a pledge of happiness, hallowed as it is with a Divine sanction, and promissory of "an ampler ether, a diviner air" to come, in which they shall breathe more freely, and inhale more deeply, the breath of life.

Freedom is not the being free to do nothing, or to do just what one likes, and when, and how, without why or wherefore. *La liberté n'est pas oisiveté*, says La Bruyère; and then he proceeds to say what liberty is: "C'est le choix de travail et de l'exercice: être libre, en un mot, n'est pas ne rien faire, c'est être seul arbitre de ce qu'on fait, ou de ce qu'on ne fait point. Quel bien en ce sens que la liberté!" But how much worthier of that note of admiration the gospel definitions, explicit or implicit, of *ce que c'est la liberté!*

F 2

There is a touching suggestiveness in what Frederick Perthes says in a letter after the death of his wife. All his doings and plannings for four and twenty years past had been solely, he declares, in reference to her. "But now all this is over. I am no longer bound; I can do what I will, and next to the yearning after her, I am most oppressed in my solitude by the consciousness of freedom." Fain would he be in those dear bonds again; to apply a passage in one of Shakspeare's minor poems, he

"In her fillet still would bide,
And, true to bondage, would not break from thence."

Or as Ferdinand says of Miranda, in the "Tempest,"

"All corners else o' the earth
Let liberty make use of; space enough
Have I in such a prison."

In this sense may be applied in earnest what Butler writes in sport, of an independent spirit who

"Disdains control, and yet can be
Nowhere, but in a prison, free."

So the sculptor in Hawthorne's tale of "Transformation," intent on winning winsome Hilda for his own, "would try if it were possible to take this shy, yet frank and innocently fearless creature captive, and imprison her in his heart, and make her sensible of a larger freedom there than in all the world besides." "I have read somewhere," says a simple maiden in one of Lord Lytton's fictions, "that the slave is gay in his holiday from toil; if you free him, the gaiety vanishes, and he cares no more for the dance under the palm-tree." Don Alphonse, in Madame de Rémusat's "Lettres Espagnoles," writes to his sister an account of the courtiers' embarrassment on being released by the king from ceremonial attendance, and allowed to do each one as he liked. "L'improvisation en tout est chose assez difficile, et particulièrement celle de la liberté. Il faut que je confesse que nous n'avons su que faire de la nôtre." The moral of the fable may be read in Landor's lines, supposed to be indited by the caged nightingales so tenderly tended by Agapenthe, and brought to Athens for her from Thessaly, and who bid the reader think not

> "That we would gladly fly again
> To gloomy wood or windy plain.
> Certain we are we ne'er should find
> A care so provident, so kind. . . .
> O may you prove, as well as we,
> That e'en in Athens there may be
> A sweeter thing than liberty."

Apply, again, to the general subject the special fact, by way of illustration, that restrictions and shackles are essential to rhythmic writing, and voluntary thraldom the natural condition of poetry. The Chevalier de la Faye, in his "Apology" for the supposed difficulties of rhyme in our Cisalpine dialects (one Italian poet being "distinguishable among his fellow-captives by the light aërial nature of his fetters,") suggests an ingenious parallel to the *jets d'eau* that ornament the gardens of the Tuileries, Versailles, and St. Cloud, in a copy of verses which have been thus Englished by Father Prout:—

> "From the rhyme's restrictive rigour
> Thought derives its impulse oft,
> Genius draws new strength and vigour,
> Fancy springs and shoots aloft.
> So, in leaden conduits pent,
> Mounts the liquid element,
> By pressure forced to climb:
> And he who feared the rule's restraint
> Finds but a friendly ministrant
> In Reason's helpmate, Rhyme."

Pithy and pertinent too are Mr. Coventry Patmore's lines on those who

> "Live by law, not like the fool,
> But like the bard, who freely sings
> In strictest bonds of rhyme and rule,
> And finds in them, not bonds, but wings."

They who so live are in every sense the happier, without an

"except these bonds," but because of them. They find in them not bonds, but wings; and thenceforth have free course, and go on their way rejoicing. They, like the repentant rebels in Shakspeare's "King John," and by the same river metaphor,

> "Leaving their rankness and irregular course,
> Stoop low within those bounds they had o'erlook'd,
> And calmly run on in obedience."

What they are no longer free to do, is to do ill. And that freedom is as perfect servitude as the service of God is perfect freedom. In fine, and in the words (but expanding the meaning) of one of Samuel Butler's metrical reflections :—

> "Law does not put the least restraint
> Upon our freedom, but maintain't;
> Or if it does, 'tis for our good,
> To give us freer latitude;
> For wholesome laws preserve us free
> By stinting of our liberty."

——o——

THE DISCREET SILENCE OF FOLLY.

PROVERBS xvii. 28.

IT is written among the Proverbs of Solomon, that "Even a fool, when he holdeth his peace, is counted wise." Even the fool that shutteth his lips is esteemed a man of understanding. The wise king declares in another place, that a fool's mouth is his destruction, and that his lips are the snare of his soul. Let him keep his mouth closed, and his folly is an unknown quantity; out of sight, out of mind. Let him keep his lips shut, and wisdom shall be imputed unto him. Of him lookers-on will say, a discreet man that. For they are only lookers-on, not listeners. To listen would break the spell. As it is, they are apt to count him as deep as he is still. Do not still waters run deep?

Sir Thomas Browne—himself a silent man, but no fool; quite the other way—bids us, in one of his stately sentences, think not silence the wisdom of fools; but if rightly timed, the honour of wise men, who have not the infirmity, but the virtue of taciturnity, and speak not out of the abundance, but the well-weighed thoughts of the heart. "Such silence may be eloquence, and speak thy worth above the power of words." Would the author of "Vulgar Errors," however, have sanctioned for one moment the reference of the proverb on reticent foolishness to that limbo? On the contrary, the drift of his argument is wholly in favour of the proverb; for, if the silence of the wise is wisdom, as he contends, much more is a tongue-tied condition expedient in the fool.

Stultitiam dissimulare non potes nisi taciturnitate, says the Latin adage: there is no way to conceal folly but by holding your tongue.

There is something at once of pathos and almost of humorous reproach, in the appeal of the Man of Uz, in his extremity, to his too didactic and complacently dogmatical friends: "Oh that ye would altogether hold your peace! and it should be your wisdom."

Montaigne exclaims, "To how many blockheads of my time has a cold and taciturn demeanour procured the credit of prudence and capacity!" Note the counsel of Carlo to Sogliardo, in one of Ben Jonson's heaviest comedies: "When anything is propounded above your capacity, smile at it, make two or three faces, and 'tis excellent; they'll think you've travelled; though you argue a whole day in silence thus, and discourse in nothing but laughter, 'twill pass." Elsewhere rare Ben cites approvingly the "witty saying," about one who was taken for a great and weighty man so long as he held his peace: "This man might have been a counsellor of state, till he spoke; but having spoken, not the beadle of the ward." Denouncing in his strong dialect the vapid verbiage of shallow praters, Mr. Carlyle exclaims, "Even Triviality, Imbecility, that can sit silent, how respectable is it in comparison!" Michelet says of the Spanish grandees of Charles the Fifth's time, that the haughty silence they maintained, scarce deigning even a syllable of reply, served them admirably to conceal their dearth of ideas. Silence and imperturbability, according to the author of "The Gentle Life," are the two requisites for a man to get on in the world.

If there are two things not to be hidden—love and a cough—there is a third, contends Nello, the barber of Florence, and that is ignorance, when once a man is obliged to do something besides wagging his head. Charles Lamb shrewdly observes that a man may do very well with a very little knowledge, and scarce be found out, in a mixed company; everybody being so much more ready to produce his own than to call for a display of your acquisitions. But in a *tête-à-tête*, he adds, there is no shuffling; the truth will out.

The Abbé de Choisy hugged himself on the success of a discreet silence during his residence in Batavia, where he had special reasons to beware of committing, and of exposing, himself. "Often when I utter not a word, they suppose it is because I don't choose to talk; whereas the real motive for my silence is a profound ignorance, such as it is best to keep concealed from the gaze of mortals." Molière's sprightly chevalier, Dorante, counsels a fatuous marquis not to talk of what he knows nothing at all about—bidding him hope that in virtue of a scrupulously observed silence, he and the like of him may haply come to be regarded as clever fellows. "Et songez qu'en ne disant mot, on croira peut-être que vous êtes d'habiles gens." A story is told of Zeuxis, how he reproved a certain Megabyzus, high priest of great Diana of the Ephesians, who discoursed of pictures in the painter's studio with so reckless an audacity of ignorance, that the very lads who were grinding colours there could not refrain from giggling; whereupon quoth Zeuxis to his too-eloquent friend, "As long as you kept from talking, you were the admiration of these boys, who were all wonder at your rich attire, and the number of your servants; but now that you have ventured to expatiate upon the arts, of which you know simply nothing, they are laughing at you outright." Plutarch tells the same story of Apelles. Again to draw upon Molière: a fool who keeps his folly tongue-tied, is not to be distinguished from a savant who hold his peace:

> "Un sot qui ne dit mot ne se distingue pas
> D'un savant qui se tait."

Not to be distinguished, possibly, from a savant who talks, and talks to the purpose too.

There are two opposite ways, on Washington Irving's showing, by which some men get into notice—one by talking a vast deal and thinking a little, and the other by holding their tongues and not thinking at all. By the first, he says, many a vapouring, superficial pretender acquires the reputation of a man of quick parts; by the other, many a vacant dunder-pate, like the owl, the stupidest of birds, comes to be complimented, by a discerning world, with all the attributes of wisdom. Silent, quiet people, as Miss Jewsbury incidentally remarks, have a charmed mystery about them which gives them a great advantage over more demonstrative mortals; "nobody knows exactly what they think, nor the impression made on them by anything; all within them has the prestige of an oracle; the extent of what they indicate is unknown; and what little is uttered goes so far." The best, perhaps, as well as the best-known of all stories illustrative of our theme, is that of Coleridge admiring a certain dinner-guest, so impregnable in his sublime reserve, so inexorably proof against every temptation to join in the table-talk, such a model (in appearance) of dignified superiority—until there was carried in that unlucky dish of apple-dumplings, the very first glance at which roused Sir Oracle to the enthusiastic outburst, "Them are the jockeys for me!" Goldsmith had, long before, recorded a somewhat parallel passage of disenchantment. His travelled Chinese, Lien Chi Altangi, is present at a dinner-party of dignitaries and dons in whose company and from whose converse he expects to find a feast of reason as well as turtle, and a flow of soul as well as claret. Their silence before dinner is served, rather puzzles and disappoints the eager expectant; who, however, accounts for and excuses it by the reflection, that men of wisdom are ever slow of speech, and deliver nothing unadvisedly. "Silence," says Confucius, "is a friend that will never betray." The dons and dignitaries were now by the mandarin's surmise, inventing maxims, or hard sayings, for their mutual instruction, when some one should think proper to begin. "My curiosity was now wrought up to the highest pitch; I impatiently looked round to see if any were going to interrupt the mighty pause; when at last one of the company declared that there was a sow in his neighbourhood that farrowed fifteen pigs at a litter." Broken at once was the spell, and disillusion was the Chinaman's doom.

Pope, being satirist of the first class, as well as poet of (say) the second, took care, in his imitative stanzas on Silence, not to be all sentiment and rhapsodical rapture on that subject. Hence, one of his stanzas begins, "Silence, the knave's repute;" and another declares Dulness to be her bosom-friend:

> "And in thy bosom lurks in Thought's disguise;
> Thou varnisher of fools, and cheat of all the wise."

The moral of one of Gay's fables is to the purpose—that one, namely, in which a young dog, ignorant of game, gives tongue as lustily as if he knew all about it, and gets well lashed for his pains. To the astounded puppy's remonstrance the whip-bearing huntsman replies:—

> "Had not thy forward noisy tongue
> Proclaim'd thee always in the wrong,
> Thou might'st have mingled with the rest,
> And ne'er thy foolish nose confess'd;
> But fools, to talking ever prone,
> Are sure to make their follies known."

So a French satirist of the last century bids *le sot* remember, that by simply holding his tongue, he will acquire not a little respect—hopeless as the reminder in such a case may be; for you might as well counsel the coward not to tremble, as the fool not to expose himself in words, words, words:

> "Souvenez-vous qu'un sot doit garder le silence,
> Il serait respecté beaucoup plus qu'il ne pense;
> Mais vouloir le contraindre à ne jamais parler,
> C'est, sans espoir, défendre au poltron ne trembler."

Could it but be enforced, the one injunction to be laid upon the fool might be condensed into an applied line from Molière, where Orgon bids Dorine hold her tongue, and regard that as a standing order :—

"Taisez-vous. C'est le mot qu'il vous faut toujours dire."

All silent people, Lord Lytton affirms, can seem conventionally elegant. And he tells the story of a groom married to a rich lady, and in consequent trepidation as to the probability of being ridiculed by the guests in his new home and her old one, to whom an Oxford clergyman gave this bit of advice : "Wear a black coat, and hold your tongue." The groom took the hint, and, we are assured, was always considered the most gentlemanly man in the county. Elsewhere, again, the same author relates his meeting with a diplomatist of weighty name, a stock example of political success, but of whom he could make nothing whatever, except indeed that he was a preposterous numskull. When, therefore, the Prime Minister, some days later, spoke to our author of this "superior man," he got for a reply, "Well, I don't think much of him. I spent the other day with him, and found him insufferably dull." "Indeed !" said the minister, with something of horror in his tone ; "why then, I see how it is. Lord ——— has been positively talking to you !" Had he but altogether held his peace, it had been his wisdom.

According to La Bruyère, everything tells in favour of the man who talks but little ; the presumption is that he is a superior man ; and if, in point of fact, he is not a sheer blockhead, the presumption then is that he is very superior indeed. His comparative freedom from folly is positively presumed to exist in the superlative degree. In another place the same observant philosopher describes in his best style the sort of people who, by a grand talent for silence, win golden opinions from all sorts of men ; they look wise, and now and then enforce and re-enforce the look by a timely shrug of the shoulders, or significant shake of the head ; but the assumed depth of wisdom don't really go two inches down ; scratch the surface, and you come to the bottom at once.

For, as Shakspeare has it,

> "There are a sort of men whose visages
> Do cream and mantle like a standing pond ;
> And do a wilful stillness entertain,
> With purpose to be dress'd in an opinion
> Of wisdom, gravity, profound conceit.
> * * * *
> O, my Antonio, I do know of those,
> That therefore only are reputed wise,
> For saying nothing ; who, I am very sure,
> If they should speak, would——"

not be reputed wise, but the uttermost opposite, whatever that may be called.

——o——

PENAL PREVISION.

I SAMUEL xxvii. 19, 20.

WHY had Saul disquieted Samuel, to bring him up from the place of the dead, by the midnight agency of the "wise woman" of Endor? Because he would fain pry into futurity, and learn from supernatural sources his coming fate. The desired foresight was vouchsafed him. By to-morrow he and his sons were to be with the dead-and-gone seer, whose spirit he had rashly invoked. The prevision had its present penalty. "Then Saul fell straightway all along on the earth, and was sore afraid, because of the words of Samuel." The secret things belong unto the Lord our God, and only those things which are revealed belong unto us and to our children. The tree of fore-knowledge of good and evil may offer fruit that is pleasant to the sight, and seemingly to be desired to make one wise; but it is fatal food, not to be eaten of, nor to be touched, by any but the venturesome profane.

Indulged to his cost with previsions of what should befall his posterity, Milton's Adam, at sight of the Flood and its ravages, breaks out into the exclamation,

> "O visions ill foreseen! Better had I
> Lived ignorant of future! so had borne

My part of evil only, each day's lot
Enough to bear."

Warned by so distressful an experience, he would have no man seek henceforth to be foretold what shall befall him or his children; "evil he may be sure, which neither his foreknowing can prevent; and he the future evil shall, no less in apprehension than in substance, feel grievous to bear." It has been asked what would become of men, were their future absolutely foreknown by them: would they not become in imagination, and therefore in reality, the passive slaves of an inevitable fate, with all hope extinguished, all fear intensified, awaiting in terror the foreseen evil, and looking with indifference on the promised good, darkened as it would be by the shadow of intervening calamities, and stripped of the bright colouring of hope? And yet,

"With eager search to dart the soul,
Curiously vain, from pole to pole,
And from the planets' wandering spheres
To extort the number of our years,
And whether all those years shall flow
Serenely smooth, and free from woe,
Or rude misfortune shall deform
Our life with one continual storm;
Or if the scene shall motley be
Alternate joy and misery,—
Is a desire which, more or less,
All men feel, though few confess."

So at least affirms the author of the "Rosciad,"—who in another of his writings puts the query:

"Tell me, philosopher, is it a crime
To pry into the secret womb of time;
Or, born in ignorance, must we despair
To reach events, and read the future there?"

Assuredly, says Cicero, the ignorance of evils to come is of more advantage than the knowledge of them: *certe ignoratio futurorum malorum utilior est quam scientia.* And Horace, in a celebrated passage:

"Prudens futuri temporis exitum
Caliginosâ nocte premit Deus:
Ridetque, si mortalis ultra
Fas trepidat." . . .

Caliginosa nox forms a thick black curtain.

"What hangs behind that curtain?—would'st thou learn?
If thou art wise, thou would'st not."

A thoughtful mind, sententiously observes Miss Clarissa Harlowe, is not a blessing to be coveted, unless it has such a happy vivacity with it as her friend Miss Howe's: a vivacity which enables one to enjoy the present, without being anxious about the future. It is, according to Goldsmith, the happy confidence in bright illusions that gives life its true relish, and keeps up our spirits amidst every distress and disappointment. "How much less would be done, if a man knew how little he can do! How wretched a creature would he be, if he saw the end as well as the beginning of his projects! He would have nothing left but to sit down in torpid despair, and exchange enjoyment for actual calamity." The warrior in Mr. Roscoe's tragedy argues judiciously when he says,

"What is't to me, that I should vex my soul
In dim forebodings of what is to be?
It is enough I know, and ache to know,
What on this bridge of time I have to do,
Not overlook the abysm till my head fail."

Fortunately for us mortals, Mr. Froude says, necessary as any future may be, and inevitable as by our own actions we may have made it, it is kindly kept from us wrapt up in clouds, and we are not made wretched about it by anticipation. "O my fortune," prays Agrippina, in one of Jonson's Roman tragedies, "let it be sudden thou preparest against me; strike all my powers of understanding blind, and ignorant of destiny to come!"

Seek to know no more, is in vain the joint appeal of the three witches to Macbeth, beside the magic caldron in the cave; but as to the future of Banquo's issue he *will* be satisfied. Cranmer, predicting a glorious reign for the infant Elizabeth, parenthesises a sigh on the common lot—

"Would I had known no more! but she must die."

Shakspeare's King Henry the Fourth, again, in one place utters the aspiration, "O Heaven! that one might read the book of fate!" Hardly an aspiration, however, as the context shows; a privilege to be deprecated rather; for could there be foreseen all the changes and chances of one's mortal life, "how chances mock, and changes fill the cup of alteration with divers liquors,"

> "O, if this were seen,
> The happiest youth,—viewing his progress through,
> What perils past, what crosses to ensue,—
> Would shut the book, and sit him down and die."

Mr. de Quincey describes an Installation of the Knights of St. Patrick at which he was present, during the Lord-Lieutenancy of Lord Cornwallis—the narrator's companions on that occasion being Lord and Lady Castlereagh, who "were both young at this time, and both wore an impressive appearance of youthful happiness; neither, happily for their peace of mind, able to pierce that cloud of years, not much more than twenty, which divided them from the day destined in one hour to wreck the happiness of both." Vision ill foreseen it were to know the times and the seasons, the manner how, and the place where.

> "O tell me, cried Ereenia, for from thee
> Nought can be hidden, when the end will be.
> Seek not to know, old Casyapa replied,
> What pleaseth Heaven to hide.
> Dark is the abyss of Time.
> But light enough to guide your steps is given;
> Whatever weal or woe betide,
> Turn never from the way of truth aside,
> And leave the event, in holy hope, to Heaven."

The hermit in Scott's "Talisman," who, after failing to read aright the fate of others, has to own himself uncertain whether he may not have miscalculated his own,—withdraws from the action of the story with the reflection that God will not have us break into His council-house, or spy out His hidden mysteries. "We must wait His time with watching and prayer—with fear and with hope. I came hither the stern seer—the proud prophet, skilled, as I thought, to instruct princes, and gifted even with supernatural powers, but burdened with a weight which I deemed no shoulders but mine could have borne. But my bands have been broken! I go hence humble in mine ignorance," etc. In Scott's other and less popular Tale of the Crusaders, Eveline deprecates the Lady of Baldringham's offer to show her niece how the balance of fate inclines, and shrinks from the asserted privilege "enjoyed" by their house of looking forward beyond the points of present time, and seeing in the very bud the thorns or flowers which are one day to encircle their head. "For my own sake, noble kinswoman," answered Eveline, "I would decline such foreknowledge, even were it possible to acquire it without transgressing the rules of the Church. Could I have foreseen what has befallen me within these last unhappy days, I had lost the enjoyment of every happy moment before that time." So again reasons the Italian adept, Baptista Damiotti, in one of Sir Walter's shorter tales, when dismissing the two agitated ladies who have been consulting his magic mirror. "Few," he added, in a melancholy tone, "leave this house as well in health as they entered it. Such being the consequence of seeking knowledge by mysterious means, I leave you to judge of the condition of those who have the power of gratifying such irregular curiosity." Cowper observes in one of his letters that man often prophesies without knowing it; but that did he foresee, what is always foreseen by him who dictates what he supposes to be his own, he would suffer by anticipation as well as by consequence; and wish perhaps as ardently for the happy ignorance to which he is at present so much indebted, as some have foolishly and inconsiderately done, for a knowledge that would be but another name for misery. Even in the ecstasy of rapturous foresight the Seer exclaims,

> "Visions of glory, spare my aching sight,
> Ye unborn ages, crowd not on my soul!"

When Harold and Haco, "pale king and dark youth," in

Lord Lytton's historical novel, would read the riddle of the future, and "climb to heaven through the mysteries of hell," the witch bids them—poor "worms"—crawl back to the clay—to the earth: "One such night as the hag ye despise enjoys as her sport and her glee, would freeze your veins, and sear the life in your eyeballs," etc., etc. What says the wizard, again, in Tasso?

> "But that I should the sure events unfold
> Of things to come, or destinies foretel,
> Too rash is your desire, your wish too bold."

Cagliostro, professing to foresee the fate of La Perouse, is importunately asked by his fellow-guests at that memorable dinner-party commemorated by M. Dumas, why then he did not forewarn and save that brave man before setting out. At the very least, why not have told him to "beware of unknown isles"—that he might at any rate have had the chance of avoiding them? But, "I assure you no, count," is the mystic's reply; "and, if he had believed me, it would only have been the more horrible, for the unfortunate man would have seen himself approaching those isles destined to be fatal to him, without the power to escape from them. Therefore he would have died, not one, but a hundred deaths, for he would have gone through it all by anticipation. Hope, of which I should have deprived him, is what best sustains a man under all trials." "Yes," says Condorcet, the sceptical and sententious, "the veil which hides from us our future, is the only real good which God has vouchsafed to man." And what again, to the same purport, says the Hermit Monk to Alpine's Lord:—

> "Roderick, it is a fearful strife
> For man endowed with mortal life,
> Whose shroud of sentient clay can still
> Feel feverish pang and fainting chill, . . .
> 'Tis hard for such to view, unfurl'd,
> The curtain of the future world.
> Yet witness every quaking limb,
> My sunken pulse, mine eyeballs dim,
> My soul with harrowing anguish torn,—
> This for my chieftain have I borne!"

And therefore, says Sir Thomas Browne, in his moralisings on the undesirableness of all such foresight, "and therefore the wisdom of astrologers, who speak of future things, hath wisely softened the severity of their doctrines; and even in their sad predictions, while they tell us of inclination not coaction from the stars, they kill us not with Stygian oaths and merciless necessity, but leave us hopes of evasion." *Tant mieux* for those who, like Hudibras,

> . . . "still gape to anticipate
> The cabinet-designs of fate,
> Apply to wizards to foresee
> What shall, and what shall never be;"

like Hudibras, bursting with the wish,

> "Oh, that I could enucleate
> And solve the problem of my fate;
> Or find, by necromantic art,
> How far the destinies take my part!"

Vanity and vexation of spirit, these visionary previsions all. Sacred, therefore, be, in Thomson's phrase, the veil that kindly clouds a light too keen for mortals,

> . . . "for those that here in dust
> Must cheerful toil out their appointed years."

In a feeling paragraph on the pains of a first separation, Miss Ferrier observes, or rather asks, if in the long and dreary interval that ensues, it were foreseen what griefs were to be borne, what ties severed, what hearts seared or broken—"who of woman born could bear the sight and live? But 'tis in mercy these things are hidden from our eyes." Looking back upon a certain year's accumulated troubles, Mrs. Gaskell's Margaret Hale "wondered how they had been borne. If she could have anticipated them, how she would have shrunk away and hid herself from the coming time!" And yet day by day, it is explained, had of itself, and by itself, been very endurable—small, keen, bright little spots of positive enjoyment having come sparkling into the very middle of sorrows.

Margaret Hale does but exemplify in prose what Home's Lady Randolph enunciates in sonorous verse:

"Had some good angel oped to me the book
Of Providence, and let me read my life,
My heart had broke when I beheld the sum
Of ills which one by one I have endured."

Whereupon the lady's faithful Anna remarks:

"That God, whose ministers good angels are,
Hath shut the book, in mercy to mankind."

Not but that this doctrine has found special recusants, if too generally taken, or, in their own instance, too particularly applied. "I have somewhere read," says Caleb Williams, "that Heaven in mercy hides from us the future incidents of our life. My own experience does not well accord with this assertion." And mentioning one critical occasion, he adds, that this once at least he should have been saved from insupportable labour and indescribable anguish, could he have foreseen what was then impending.—Sometimes the natural complaint is like that of Duke Ferdinand in John Webster's tragedy:

"Oh, most imperfect light of human reason,
That mak'st us so unhappy to foresee
What we can least prevent!"

Sometimes a solace is found in such a reflection as this:

"Then did I see how that presentient shroud
Of grief, which raiseth many a fond complaint
In mortal bosoms, is a friendly cloud.
Storms fall less heavily which men fore-paint.
And the struck spirit utterly would faint,
Hurl'd from full joy."

To be ignorant of evils to come, as well as forgetful of past, Sir Thomas Browne hails as a merciful provision of nature, "whereby we digest the mixture of our few and evil days." In another of his works the fine old physician would have us, in the heyday of prosperity, "think of sullen vicissitudes," but beat not our brains to foreknow them. "Be armed against such obscurities, rather by submission than fore-knowledge. The knowledge of future evils modifies present felicities, and there is more content in the uncertainty or ignorance of them. This favour our Saviour vouchsafed unto Peter, when he foretold not his death in plain terms, and so by an ambiguous and cloudy delivery damped not the spirit of His disciples. But in the assured fore-knowledge of the deluge, Noah lived many years under the affliction of a flood, and Jerusalem was taken unto Jeremy before it was besieged." Holy George Herbert is scarcely more quaint in verse than Sir Thomas Browne in prose:

"Only the present is thy part and fee.
And happy thou,
If, though thou didst not beat thy future brow,
Thou couldst well see
What present things required of thee.

They ask enough; why shouldst thou further go?
Raise not the mud
Of future depths, but drink the clear and good.
Dig not for woe
In times to come; for it will grow.

Man and the present fit; if he *provide*
He breaks the square.
This hour is mine: if for the next I care,
I grow too wide,
And do crusade upon death's side:

For death each hour environs and surrounds.
He that would know
And care for future chances, cannot go
Unto those grounds,
But thro' a churchyard which them bounds."

The assured knowledge of the exact minute of one's death may be treated religiously as a privilege, after the manner of appeals by gaol-chaplains to condemned-cell criminals; as where the clergyman of the Tolbooth Church bade Wilson and Robertson, convicted Porteous rioters, not despair on account of the suddenness of the summons, "but rather to feel this comfort in their misery, that, though all who now [in that church] lifted the voice, or bent the knee in conjunction with them, lay under the same sentence of certain death, *they* only had the advantage of knowing the precise moment at which it should be executed upon them." But how does Professor Henry Rogers treat the question, in its practical aspect, in his so-called "Vision about Prevision"? The seer, or foreseer, in that *fantasiestück*, when asked, concerning those who consult him as to the future, whether some at least do not wish to know the hour of their death—that they may duly prepare for it? answers, "That least of all. Not a soul will hear his tale told to the end; they won't let us unveil to them the hour or the mode of their dissolution. . . . They prefer having a veil thrown over the closing scene of their life. Like other play-goers, they do not like death to be actually exhibited on the stage, and willingly let the curtain fall ere the catastrophe." Well, but the seer himself: he at any rate is above that weakness: he at any rate has inquired into the secret of his end? "For what purpose?" is his reply: is not that knowledge the very misery of prisoners in the condemned cell? are they not accounted miserable precisely because they are to die just that day month? will not hundreds, who pity them for that very circumstance, in fact die before them? and yet are not these accounted happy in comparison, because they know it not?

> "E'en the great shadow, Death, lost half its gloom
> In kind oblivion of impending doom,"

says one philosophical poet. Another, and a greater, in a poem on presentiments, has this among many stanzas addressed to them:

> "'Tis said, that warnings ye dispense,
> Emboldened by a keener sense;
>   That men have lived for whom,
> With dread precision, ye made clear
> The hour that in a distant year
>   Should knell them to the tomb.
> Unwelcome insight!"——

that is the comment, that the note of exclamation, with which Wordsworth commences the stanza next ensuing. When death has invaded the quiet rectory in Miss Tytler's Huguenot story, we have each servant mysteriously and fanatically delivering her experience in the matter of corpse-candles, death-spells, death-watches, etc., so that one might have learned for all one's life afterwards to look on one's death as a dark fate, haunting and hovering over one's own person and those of beloved friends, from which there is no escape, not even by prayer and fasting; might have learned to "look out for it in dim prognostications, to watch for it, and anticipate its cruel blows in incipient madness.—'Our Bibles say we know not the day nor the hour,' said Grand'mère; 'but He knows—that is enough.'" One of La Bruyère's *pensées sur la mort* is, that "ce qu'il y a de certain dans la mort, est un peu adouci par ce qui est incertain: c'est un indéfini dans le tems, qui tient quelque chose de l'infini, et de ce qu'on appelle éternité." Byron indeed utters the remonstrant query,

"Ah! why do darkening shades conceal
The hour when man must cease to be?"

But his sigh was little in the spirit of the Psalmist's prayer to be made to know his end, and the measure of his days, what it was.

——o——

BEATIFIC VISION AND OVERSHADOWING CLOUD.

St. Luke ix. 34.

TO the three favoured apostles it was granted by their Master to be eye-witnesses of His majesty, when they were with Him on the holy mount. They saw the fashion of His countenance altered, and His raiment become white and glistering. They saw with Him in glory Moses, whose burial-place no man knew, and Elijah, who was translated that he should not see death. And Peter said it was good to be there, and he desired to make that mount of transfiguration a dwelling-place, and to prolong the splendours of that beatific vision. Three tabernacles he proposed to rear, in that eager impetuosity which so often marked his character;

at present scarcely knowing what he said, but conscious of a privileged apocalypse, and deprecating its speedy withdrawal. But "while he thus spake, there came a cloud, and overshadowed them; and they feared as they entered into the cloud."

So it was again at a later day, and upon another mount, when the risen Master was asked by His assembled apostles would He at this time restore again the kingdom to Israel? Brief was the reply, and no sooner uttered than, while they beheld—gazed wistfully, hopingly, longingly, on the Presence they had so lately lost, and were now eager to retain—while they beheld, "He was taken up, and a cloud received Him out of their sight."

The overshadowing cloud to mar the sunshine is one of the commonest of common-places in man's experience. Perpetually being verified in prosaic reality, all too real, is the poet's image—

> "Across the sunbeam, with a sudden gloom,
> A ghostly shadow flitted."

Medio de fonte leporum surgit amari aliquid. The very exuberance of human happiness tends to suggest its opposite.

Gibbon felt simply as a man when he felt what he has described in a memorable passage relating to his sense of gratified triumph at the conclusion of his *magnum opus.* It was between the hours of eleven and twelve, he records, on a calm night in June, that he wrote the last lines of his last page in a summer-house in his garden at Lausanne. After laying down his pen, he took several turns in a covered walk of acacias, which commanded a prospect of the country, the lake, and the mountains. The air was temperate, the sky was serene, the silver orb of the moon was reflected from the waters, and all nature was silent. "I will not dissemble the first emotions of joy on the recovery of my freedom, and, perhaps, the establishment of my fame. But my pride was soon humbled, and a sober melancholy was spread over my mind, by the idea that I had taken an everlasting leave of an old and agreeable companion, and that whatsoever might be the future date of my history the life of the historian must be short and precarious." It is the common lot. It is but another reading of the complaint in Prior's pastorals—

> "Yet thus beloved, thus loving to excess,
> Yet thus receiving and returning bliss,
> In this great moment, in this golden Now,
> * * * * *
> A melancholy tear afflicts my eye,
> And my heart labours with a sudden sigh;
> Invading fears repel my coward joy,
> And ills foreseen the present bliss destroy."

Or as elsewhere the same poet gloomily exclaims, and fruitlessly supplicates—

> "O impotent estate of human life,
> Where hope and fear maintain eternal strife!
> Where fleeting joy does lasting doubt inspire,
> And most we question what we most desire!
> Amongst Thy various gifts, great Heaven, bestow
> Our cup of love unmixed; forbear to throw
> Bitter ingredients in; nor pall the draught
> With nauseous grief."

Hardly can it be called, though the author of "The Ring and the Book" does call it,—

> . . . "strange how, even when most secure
> In our domestic peace, a certain dim
> And flitting shade can sadden all; it seems
> A restlessness of heart, a silent yearning,
> A sense of something wanting, incomplete."

A thought comes over us sometimes in our career of pleasure, Lord Lytton remarks, or in the exultation of our ambitious pursuits, a thought comes over us like a cloud, that around us and about us Death, Shame, Crime, Despair, are busy at their work. He tells us what he has read somewhere of an enchanted land where the inmates walked along voluptuous gardens, and built palaces, and heard music, and made merry; while around and within the land were deep caverns, where the gnomes and the fiends dwelt; and ever and anon their groans and laughter, and the sounds of their unutterable toils or ghastly revels, travelled to the upper air, mixing in an awful strangeness with the summer festivity and buoyant occupation of those above. And this he claims to be a picture of human life.

Always there is a black spot in our sunshine, exclaims Mr. Carlyle; and he tells us what it is, "the shadow of ourselves."

At a seeming crisis of assured prosperity the heroine of a French *roman* is made to exclaim, "The future is all our own—the radiant future, without cloud or obstacle, pure in the immensity of its horizon, and extending beyond the reach of sight." But while she thus speaks her features suddenly assume an expression of touching melancholy, as she adds, in a voice of profound emotion, "And yet—at this very hour—so many unfortunate creatures are suffering pain!" So with the young hero in one of Mr. Hannay's fictions: "In that moment he felt that he had attained a new stage of life; yet, an instant's reaction seized him, as in every fruition through one's progress in time comes that curious moment's speck, the touch of an unseen hand, that seems to tell you, 'Too much joy is not for you here.' It passed away, having just dashed his triumph as it always does." At a later stage in this adventurer's career the ebb of his spirits is made the text of a paragraph comparing them to a ship in the tropics, where a light wind comes, and dies again, and leaves you becalmed, or the horizon blackens suddenly and death seems impending in the unhealthy air. "Few things are more touching than that peculiar melancholy which sometimes comes over one in theatres or at feasts, and reminds us of the dark element in nature and the heart . . . which chills the philosopher and the pleasure-taker. . . . When the light southerner of old got a glimpse of it he called for his lyre and his garlands; but roses will not charm it away from the deep heart of the child of the Teuton, and he sees its awful shadow trembling in the wine." The English Opium-eater somewhere professes to derive from the spectacle of dancing, where the motion is continuous and the music not of a trivial character but charged with the spirit of festal pleasure, "the very grandest form of passionate sadness which can belong to any spectacle whatever." Wordsworth is treating of presentiments when he says that—

> "The laughter of the Christmas hearth
> With sighs of self-exhausted mirth
> They feelingly reprove."

And of such is Currer Bell too treating in a passage that tells of the writer's fancy budding fresh and her heart basking in sunshine; only these feelings "were well kept in check by the secret but ceaseless consciousness of anxiety lying in wait on enjoyment, like a tiger crouched in a jungle. The breathing of that beast of prey was in my ear always." Ἐξ ἡδονῆς γὰρ φύεται τὸ δυστυχεῖν.

> "Who knows what that low sullen murmur means,
> The river's fall sends up to blast life's fairest scenes?"

The happiest, as Pope's Homer has it, "taste not happiness sincere, but find the cordial draught is dashed with care." What biography of successful ambition but has its parallel passage to one in Prescott's history of the conqueror of Peru: "Amidst this burst of adulation the cup of joy commended to Pizarro's lips had one drop of bitterness in it that gave its flavour to all the rest"! As M. Ampére's Cleopatra owns,—

> "Oui, parmi les plaisirs, la joie et les festins,
> Je médite du sort les arrêts incertains."

How apt, at a bright banquet, is the thought of death to flash across the mind, is trite among the truisms of experience. It was at Belshazzar's feast, while they drank wine out of the golden vessels of the temple, and praised the gods of gold, and of silver, of brass, of iron, of wood, and of stone, when the revelry was at its height and the revellers at their best, that in the same hour there came forth fingers of a man's hand, and wrote over against the candlestick upon the plaster of the wall of the king's palace; and then was king Belshazzar greatly troubled, and his countenance was changed in him, and his lords were astounded. In Hawthorne's allegory of the Maypole at Merry Mount, the lord and lady of the May are abruptly overcome with a shadow of sadness, just when the minstrelsy of pipe, cittern, and viola is pealing forth in such a mirthful cadence that the boughs of the maypole quiver to the sound; and just then too, as if a spell had loosened them, down comes a little shower of withering roseleaves from the maypole. There is sometimes, says Fielding, a little speck of black in the brightest and gayest colours of fortune, which contaminates and deadens the whole.

> "In every joy there lurks
> An impulse of decay;
> With silent speed it works,
> While all without is gay:"

—with silent speed, like the worm at Jonah's gourd. "Fleurs, vous aussi," so Béranger apostrophizes them,

> . . . "vous avez vos souffrances.
> Le ver est là; le vent peut accourir."

Le ver, as the worm prepared for Jonah's gourd; *le vent*, as the vehement east wind to wither Jonah's strength.

> "While blooming love assures us golden fruit,
> Some inborn poison taints the secret root;
> Soon fall the flowers of joy."

But Jonah's gourd must have a section apart.

——o——

THE SPREADING GOURD AND THE SPEEDING WORM.

JONAH iv. 6–8.

AS Elijah the Tishbite sat down in the wilderness under a juniper-tree, heavy-hearted, and fleeing for his life from the grasp of Jezebel, yet requesting for himself that he might die; as he said, "It is enough; now, O Lord, take away my life," yet anon found rest and refreshment under the juniper-tree, and did eat and drink, and lay down again, and went in the strength of that rest and that meat, forty days and forty nights, unto Horeb the mount of God; so Jonah the son of Amittai, displeased exceedingly, and very angry, prayed in bitterness the same prayer, "O Lord, take, I beseech thee, my life from me; for it is better for me to die than to live." Did he well to be angry? Did Elijah well to despair? Under a juniper-tree Elijah recovered strength, took heart, and became of good courage. For Jonah there was preparing a gourd. A gourd; and a worm to make short work of the gourd.

Jonah left the city in wrath, and made him a booth, and sat under it in the shadow, till he might see what would become of the city—the city which he had doomed and God had spared. Under the burning sun he awaited the judgment of Nineveh. "And the Lord God prepared a gourd, and made it to come up over Jonah, that it might be a shadow over his head, to deliver him from his grief. So Jonah was exceeding glad of the gourd.

"But God prepared a worm when the morning rose the next day, and it smote the gourd that it withered."

And when the sun arose, there arose too another thing of God's preparing. As He had prepared the gourd, and prepared the worm to smite the gourd, so, at sunrise, "God prepared a vehement east wind; and the sun beat upon the head of Jonah, that he fainted, and wished in himself to die." And not only so, but again expressed the wish, with the old bitterness and even increasing wrath. Did he well to be angry for the gourd? "I do well to be angry, even unto death," he exclaimed. The gourd was so gladdening a creation, it made even that morose spirit exceeding glad. But scarcely had he time to congratulate himself on this relief, in complacent assurance of its continuance, when the sheltering gourd was eaten to the heart by a speeding worm, and what came up in a night, perished in a night; and this also was vanity, vanity and vexation of spirit.

A perverse fate seems to lie in wait for man,

> "And though he in a fertile climate dwell,
> Plague him with flies: though that his joy be joy,

Yet throw such charges of vexation on't,
As it may lose some colour."

In the words of another of Shakspeare's dramas, "joy cannot show itself modest enough without a badge of bitterness." *Inter delicias semper aliquid sævi nos strangulat*, says the Latin adage; the *aliquid sævi* answering to the *aliquid amari* of Lucretius, *quod in ipsis floribus angat;* or again to the *aliquid solliciti* of Ovid,

. . . "Nulla est sincera voluptas;
Sollicitique aliquid lætis intervenit."

Why, Byron asks himself, in his diary (at Ravenna), why, at the very height of desire and human pleasure, does there mingle a certain sense of doubt and sorrow—a fear of what is to come—a doubt of what *is*—a retrospect of the past, leading to a prognostication of the future? Mrs. Browning has penned a suggestive sonnet to which the title is superscribed of Pain in Pleasure:

"A thought lay like a flower upon my heart,
And drew around it other thoughts like bees
For multitude and thirst of sweetnesses,—
Whereat rejoicing, I desired the art
Of the Greek whistler, who to wharf and mart
Could lure those insect swarms from orange-trees,
That I might hive me with such thoughts, and please
My soul so, always. Foolish counterpart
Of a weak man's vain wishes! While I spake,
The thought I called a flower, grew nettle-rough—
The thoughts called bees, stung me to festering,
Oh, entertain (cried reason, as she woke,)
Your best and gladdest thoughts but long enough,
And they will all prove sad enough to sting."

As Shakspeare words it in one of *his* sonnets,

"Roses have thorns, and silver fountains mud;
Clouds and eclipses stain both moon and sun,
And loathsome canker lives in sweetest bud,"

and every gourd has its worm. So again Cowper:

"Here every drop of honey hides a sting;
Worms wind themselves into our sweetest flowers."

On the same text moralizes the meditative sire of the Cid, in Corneille's tragedy :

> "Jamais nous ne goûtons de parfaite allégresse :
> Nos plus heureux succès sont mêlés de tristesse ;
> Toujours quelques soucis en ces événements
> Troublent la pureté de nos contentements."

Semper amari aliquid. It is like Johnson's reflections on his first transports at Ranelagh. When first he entered those festive gardens, it gave, he tells Boswell, an expansion and gay sensation to his mind, such as he never experienced anywhere else. But, as Xerxes wept when he reviewed his immense army, and considered that not one of that great multitude would be alive a hundred years afterwards, so it went to the doctor's heart to consider that there was not one in all that brilliant circle but was afraid to go home and think ; that "the thoughts of each individual there would be distressing when alone." Boswell approves the reflection as "experimentally just," and appends a commonplace of his own, upon the feeling of langour, which succeeds the animation of gaiety, being itself a very severe pain.

It was in the mid hey-day of military triumph that Paulus Æmilius astonished his encircling admirers by, first, a prolonged silence, and next, a sombre homily on the vicissitudes of fortune, and of human affairs. What time for confidence can there be to man, he asked, when in the very instant of victory he must necessarily dread the power of fortune, and the very joy of success must be mingled with anxiety—*aliquid solliciti*—from a reflection on the course of unsparing fate, which humbles one man to-day, and to-morrow another! Gladdening is the gourd, with its pleasant promise of protection against the arrow that flieth by day from a burning sun ; but only him can it make, like Jonah, exceeding glad, who knows not, or makes a point of forgetting, what a worm can do, between a setting and a rising sun.

The night thoughts of man in general are one with the Night Thoughts of Young in particular, when he exclaims,

"How sad a sight is human happiness
To those whose thoughts can pierce beyond an hour!
—Know, smiler! at thy peril thou art pleased:
Thy pleasure is the promise of thy pain."

This is the state of man, by the experience of Shakspeare's Wolsey: to-day he puts forth the tender leaves of hope; to-morrow blossoms, and bears his blushing honours thick upon him. He is exceeding glad, even as the prophet of his gourd; but a worm is preparing, or if not, a frost; and next day, or at latest

"The third day, comes a frost, a killing frost;
And,—when he thinks, good easy man, full surely
His greatness is a ripening,—nips his root,
And then he falls."

The worm may speed in its mission, or otherwise; but the fulfilment of its mission is only a question of time. There is a

. . . "little rift within the lute,
That by-and-by will make the music mute,
And ever widening slowly silence all.

"The little rift within the lover's lute
Or little pitted speck in garner'd fruit,
That rotting onward slowly moulders all."

Slowly, sometimes, but surely. Not so slowly as surely.

Remembering both the "foolish pride" of Jonah in his gourd, and his "impious discontentment" at the decree which smote it, which of us but might, for ourselves, do worse than adopt the words and the spirit of one verse at least of Pope's Universal Prayer,

"Save me alike from foolish pride
And impious discontent
At aught Thy wisdom hath denied,
Or aught Thy bounty lent."

——o——

SELF-PRAISE.

PROVERBS xxvii. 2.

"LET another man praise thee, and not thine own mouth; a stranger, and not thine own lips." Our English adage, "Self-praise is no recommendation," has its analogue in the Latin: *Laus in proprio ore sordescit*—"A man's own laudation of himself is unseemly." Another bit of good old Latin admonition is, to enlarge rather upon the praises of one's friends, than upon one's own: *Amicorum, magis quàm tuam ipsius laudem, prædica;* which seems to be, however, but a literal transcript of the second line in a couplet from the Greek Anthology:

Ὑπὲρ σεαυτοῦ μὴ φράσῃς ἐγκώμια·
Φίλων ἔπαινον μᾶλλον ἢ σαυτοῦ λέγε.

Syrus, again, utters the caution, "That whoso praiseth himself will soon find some one to laugh at him"—*Qui seipsum laudat, cito derisorem inveniet.* It was Æsop's derisive counsel to an unreadable author, who did all his own praising and puffing, and therefore did it well—well, at least, in quantity, if not in quality—to stick by all manner of means to that home-brewed system; for it was the poor creature's only chance of ever tasting the sweets of praise at all.

"Ego, quod te laudas, vehementer probo,
Namque hoc ab alio nunquam continget tibi."

In one of the wordy encounters between Shakspeare's Beatrice and Benedick, the lady imputes signal unwisdom to the signor, when she tells him "There's not one wise man in twenty that will praise himself." Benedick scouts this as an old, old apophthegm, quite out of date; for, says he, "if a man do not erect in this age his own tomb ere he dies, he shall live no longer in monument than the bell rings, and the widow weeps." And how long is *that?* Why, an hour in clamour (the bell), and (the widow) a quarter in rheum. Therefore, he infers, "it is most expedient for the wise to be the trumpeter of his own virtues, as I am to myself. So much for praising myself (who, I myself will bear witness, is praiseworthy)." Shakspeare often expatiates, with dramatic diversities of phase and aspect, of character and incident, upon this worldly-wise theme, by the worldly-wise held worthy of all acceptation, of every man his own trumpeter. To a few examples out of these many we may recur anon.

Swift is writing after his own humour when he says, in the work he seems to have admired the most of his voluminous *opera omnia*, but to which some refer as the distinct cause of his never getting a bishopric—"That as for the liberty he has thought fit to take of praising himself upon some occasions or none, he is sure it will need no excuse, if a multitude of great examples be allowed sufficient authority; for it is to be noted," he goes on to say, that praise was originally a pension paid by the world; but the moderns, finding the trouble and charge too great in collecting it, "have lately bought out the fee simple; since which time the right of presentation is wholly in ourselves." But it is in the simpler states and stages of society, according to a latter-day essayist on social subjects, that the man who values himself highly has little scruple in confessing as much. "Savages have no more reticence in parading their good points than peacocks." North American Indians, and the like, sublimely ignore any such courses of conduct as that, Not he that approveth himself is commended. Their faith and practice run counter to this kind of self-discipline. Chateaubriand gives an example of the style of chant in which a jubilant warrior, Sioux or Iroquois, proclaims his doughty prestige:—"Brave and renowned were my forefathers. My grandsire was the wisdom of his tribe, and the thunder of war. My father was a pine-tree in strength. My great-grandmother gave birth to five men of war; my grandmother was alone worth a council of sachems; my mother makes first-rate soup. As for myself, I am stronger and wiser than all my ancestors." Later Americans, *not* of the redskin family, are charged with a scarcely inferior knack of extolling themselves in all the simplicity of an ignorance which knows nothing higher or better, and with being frankly astonished at their own successes. Among them, it is alleged by caustic Cis-atlantic criticism, nobody is thought the worse of for praising himself; whereas among ourselves, "the practice is out of date; a man cannot here puff himself off with impunity—without in fact, being taken for a fool; and therefore, if he have ordinary sagacity, he will keep within bounds." But not the less, it is allowed, must the thought of the heart find some outlet; men draw wide distinctions between pride and vanity, but both have at least this in common, that they like to feel and be acknowledged "first;" and both, it is added, "agree in the instinct to gain their end by a side-wind—to boast themselves by implication, if circumstances will not permit the more agreeable incense of positive praise and adulation."

Plutarch does not blame Cato (the elder) for perpetually boasting and exalting himself, although the old censor somewhere pronounces it absurd for a man either to praise or to disparage himself. But Plutarch *does* "think the man who is often praising himself, not so complete in virtue as the modest man, who does not even want others to praise him." He takes frequent note of the habit of self-commendation in some of his heroes, and of the absence of it in others. Cato, "who was never sparing in his own praises, and thought boasting a natural attendant on great actions," was nothing like so grievous an offender in this respect, to Plutarch's thinking, as Cicero, whose writings, says he, "were so interlarded with encomiums on himself that, although his style was elegant and delightful, his discourses were disgusting and nauseous to the reader; for the blemish stuck to him like an incurable disease." Comparing this greatest of Roman orators with the greatest of the Greek, Plutarch observes of their respective writings, that Demosthenes, when he touches on his own praise does it with an inoffensive delicacy, never, indeed, giving way to it at all unless he has some important matter in view; whereas Cicero, habitually and systematically, "speaks in such high terms of himself that it is plain he had a most intemperate vanity." Modern critics not a few, German,

English, and French, have made the most—not to say made the best—of this foible of Cicero's. In particular, Mr. de Quincey makes merry over it, without mercy, at the father of his country's expense.

Isaac Barrow points the moral of the text which these heterogeneous annotations are meant to illustrate, with a special warning against Cicero's infirmity. "If a man have worthy qualities and do great deeds, let them speak for him," urges that masterly divine; they will of themselves extort commendation; his silence about them, his seeming to neglect them, will enhance their worth in the opinion of men. "Prating about them, obtruding them upon men, will mar their credit, inducing men to think them done, not out of love to virtue, but for a vain-glorious design. Thus did Cicero, thus have many others, blasted the glory of their virtuous deeds." It is quaintly said by Owen Feltham, that whoso makes boast of the good he truly has, obscures much of his own worth, in drawing it up by so unseemly a bucket as his own tongue. "Though the vaunts be true, they do but awaken scoffs; and instead of a clapping hand, they find a look of scorn." When a soldier bragged too much of a great scar in his forehead, he was asked by Augustus if he did not get it when he turned his back on the enemy. So, "If I have done anything well"—this is one of Feltham's "Resolves,"—"I will never think it worth while to tell the world of it."

> "O sir, to such as boasting show their scars,
> A mock is due,"

says Shakspeare's Troilus to Ulysses—modest, valiant Trojan, to shrewd, circumspect Greek. So another Trojan to another Greek, in the same play—which Coleridge reckoned almost the most wonderful of Shakspeare's all—Æneas, namely, to Agamemnon; or rather, indeed, Æneas to himself, in Agamemnon's hearing:—

> . . . "But peace, Æneas,
> Peace Trojan; lay thy finger on thy lips!
> The worthiness of praise disdains his worth,
> If that the praised himself bring the praise forth:

H 2

> But what the repining enemy commends,
> That breath fame follows ; that praise, sole pure, transcends."

And in yet another scene, Agamemnon, King of Men, pithily and pointedly tells that stalwart dullard—big, blustering, boisterous Ajax—who, for the life of him, cannot see the pith or point of it, that "whatever praises itself but in the deed, devours the deed in the praise." Ajax suspects not the general to mean that *he*, son of Telamon, is his own praise, his own chronicle.

One more excerpt from our myriad-minded poet :—"Then we wound our modesty, and make foul the clearness of our deservings, when of ourselves we publish them." The wise saw drops from the sententious lips of the sage old steward of the Countess of Roussillon in what is probably as little read and slightly relished as any of Shakspeare's plays.

Years ago there used to perambulate the streets of London, a prodigy of a hat, some seven feet high, the trade-mark advertisement of a hatter in the Strand. This gigantic puff Mr. Carlyle once made the text for some characteristic strictures on the puffery of the age. Every man his own trumpeter : that he alleged was, to an alarming extent, the accepted rule. "Make loudest possible proclamation of your hat." Against which doctrine our strenuous *censor morum* objected, that nature requires no man to make proclamation of his doings and hat-makings ; but, on the contrary, forbids all men to make such. There is not, he contends, a man, or hat-maker born into the world but feels, or has felt, that he is degrading himself if he speak of his excellences, and prowesses, and supremacy in his craft. His inmost heart says to him, "Leave thy friends to speak of these : if possible, thy enemies to speak of these ; but at all events, thy friends."

——o——

PAINTED FACE, TIRED HEAD, & EXPOSED SKULL.

2 KINGS ix. 30, 35.

JEZEBEL'S painting her face and tiring her head, is so immediately followed, in the narrative of her death and non-burial, by there being found no more of her left than the skull, besides the feet and the palms of the hands, that the connection is grimly suggestive of certain stanzas in the "Vision of Sin:"

> "You are bones, and what of that?
> Every face, however full,
> Padded round with flesh and fat,
> Is but modell'd on a skull.
>
> "Death is king, and Vivat Rex!
> Tread a measure on the stones,
> Madam—if I know your sex
> From the fashion of your bones."

Byron muses on a skull* from among scattered heaps, as now a shattered cell which even the worm disdains; he ponders on its broken arch, its ruined wall, its chambers desolate, and portals foul; yet,

> . . . "this was once Ambition's airy hall,
> The dome of Thought, the palace of the Soul:
> Behold through each lack-lustre, eyeless hole,
> The gay recess of Wisdom and of Wit
> And Passion's host, that never brook'd control."

It is Yorick's skull that Hamlet is apostrophizing when he says, "Now get you to my lady's chamber, and tell her, let her paint an inch thick, to *this* favour she must come." *Tôt ou tard*, as *le bon réligieux* in "Atala" reminds his fair young listener, *quelle qu'eût été votre felicité, ce beau visage se fût changé en cette figure uniforme que le sépulcre donne à la famille*

* When at Bologna he used to visit the Campo Santo, the sexton of which was a favourite of his, and the "beautiful and innocent face" of whose daughter of fifteen, he used to contrast with the skulls that peopled several cells there—and particularly with that of one skull dated 1766, "which was once covered (the tradition goes) by the most lovely features of Bologna—noble and rich."

d'Adam. The good king Réné had painted on the walls of one of the rooms in the Celestine monastery at Avignon, a skeleton—it was that of a once surpassing beauty who had won his heart. How would the moral have lost its point had the head of the skeleton been replaced, like that in the painter's room in the Strada Vecchia of Rome, so graphically described in "Dutch Pictures," by a mask, or cardboard "dummy" of a superlatively inane cast of beauty—the blue eyes and symmeterical lips (curved into an unmeaning and eternal simper), the pink cheeks, and silken doll's tresses, "contrasting strangely with the terribly matter-of-fact bones and ligaments beneath—the moral to my lady's looking-glass." Gwillim, the Pursuivant, as quoted, not approvingly, in Southey's "Doctor," counsels all gentlewomen that are proud of their beauty to consider that they "carry on their shoulders nothing but a skull wrapt in skin, which one day will be loathsome to be looked on." The old French poet Villon, *aux charniers des Innocents*, speculates in a manner that to one critic recalls the graveyard scene in "Hamlet," on the destiny of *corps féminin, qui tant est tendre, poli, suave, gracieux*—for how can he help his thoughts running thitherward "quand il considère ces têtes entassées en ces charniers"? Who, indeed, as Keats once asked,

"Who hath not loiter'd in a green churchyard,
  And let his spirit, like a demon mole,
Work through the clayey soil and gravel hard,
  To see skull, coffin'd bones, and funeral stole;
Pitying each form that hungry Death has marr'd,
  And filling it once more with human soul?"

In such a spot Blair lingers, to apostrophize beauty, as a pretty plaything, a dear deceit, which the grave discredits. The charms expunged, the roses faded, and the lilies soiled, what has beauty more to boast of? Will the lovers of it flock round it now, to gaze and do it homage?

"Methinks I see thee with thy head low laid,
While, surfeited upon thy damask cheek,
The high-fed worm, in lazy volumes roll'd,
Riots unscared. For this was all thy caution?
For this thy painful labours at the glass,

> T' improve those charms, and keep them in repair,
> For which the spoiler thanks thee not?"

So that much less known, but much more powerful, writer, Thomas Lovell Beddoes, muses in Death's cabinet, the Campo Santo of Ferrara, on the "unfashionable worm," respectless of, alike, the crown-illumined brow and the cheek's bewitchment, as he creeps to his repast—on what? "No matter how clad or nicknamed it might strut above, what age or sex,—it is his dinner-time." The final residuum of such repasts becomes an unrecognisable skull, about which some chance possessor of it shall, in after days, perhaps, indulge in cynical conjectures and speculations in a tone and to a tune like this:

> "Did she live yesterday, or ages back?
> What colour were the eyes when bright and waking?
> And were your ringlets fair, or brown, or black,
> Poor little head! that long has done with aching?"

Mercury, in Lucian's dialogue, shows Menippus the skulls of several world-famous beauties; and the philosopher falls to moralizing upon that of Helen. "Was it for this,"* he exclaims, "that a thousand ships sailed from Greece, so many brave men died, and so many cities were destroyed?" Menippus was so far of the Ralph Nickleby type, "not a man to be moved by a pretty face," with a grinning skull beneath it: men like him profess to look and work below the surface, and so to see the skull, and not its delicate covering.

Where, asks the author of "Esmond," are those jewels now that beamed under Cleopatra's forehead, or shone in the sockets of Helen? With Mr. Thackeray in another place, again, we take the skull up, and think of the glances that allured, the tears that melted, of the bright eyes that shone in those vacant sockets, and cheeks dimpling with smiles that once covered that ghastly yellow framework. "They used to call those teeth pearls once. See! there's the cup

* Not to be forgotten, however, is the suggestive rejoinder of Mercury, that Menippus would have been as easily fooled as the rest of them, had he but seen, not that grinning skull, but the living face that once concealed it.

she drank from, the gold chain she wore on her neck, the vase which held the rouge for her cheeks, her looking-glass, and the harp she used to dance to. Instead of a feast we find a gravestone, and in place of a mistress, a few bones." And has not Macaulay his "Sermon in a Churchyard"? wherein one practical improvement of the subject, as conventional pulpiteers phrase it, runs thus :—

> "Dost thou beneath the smile or frown
> Of some vain woman bend thy knee?
> Here take thy stand, and trample down
> Things that were once as fair as she.
> Here rave of her ten thousand graces,
> Bosom, and lip, and eye, and chin,
> While, as in scorn, the fleshless faces
> Of Hamiltons and Waldegraves grin."

——o——

THE CARCASE OF JEZEBEL ON THE FACE OF THE FIELD.

2 KINGS ix. 37.

IN the portion of Jezreel—by a retributive local coincidence—were to lie the mangled remains of Jezebel—what the dogs should leave of her. "And the carcase of Jezebel shall be as dung upon the face of the field in the portion of Jezreel; so that they shall not say, This is Jezebel." *This*, Jezebel? how could *this* be identified with the superb wife and superior of the king of Israel, as she was in her prime of life and pride of place? or even with the faded form of her that, newly a widow, but energetic and manœuvring to the last, and defiant in her fall, painted her face, and tired her head, and looked out at the window as Jehu entered in at the gate? Imperious Jezebel, thrice puissant and insatiably presuming, transformed into a heap of bone dust—reduced to her lowest terms as mere organic matter—resolved into just so much manure upon the face of the field.

> "Imperious Cæsar, dead, and turn'd to clay,
> Might stop a hole to keep the wind away:
> O that the earth which kept the world in awe
> Should patch a wall to expel the winter's flaw."

So muses and speculates Hamlet, on the theme of "to what base uses we may return, Horatio," when his imagination traces the noble dust of Alexander, till he find it stopping a bunghole. 'Twere to consider too curiously to consider so, Horatio may object. Not a jot, is Hamlet's answer to the objection; for look you, Alexander died, was buried, was resolved into dust; the dust is earth; of earth we make loam. "And why of that loam, whereto he was converted, might they not stop a beer barrel?" *Quod erat demonstrandum.*

The Prince of Denmark was in the like mood when, in other company, he talked, to the same purpose, of how a man may fish with the worm* that hath eat of a king; and eat of the fish that hath fed of that worm.

Well may Juvenal bid the meditative moralist, *expende Annibalem*, and expound the text that *Mors sola fatetur quantula sint hominum corpuscula.* But it needs a Shakspeare to reduce these to their lowest terms, in the style of Hamlet with imperious Cæsar,—a *reductis ad absurdum* indeed.

Sydney Smith somewhere girds at the idea of doctrinaire legislators making irrevocable laws for men who toss their remains about with spades, "and use the relics of these legislators, to give breadth to brocoli, and to aid the vernal eruption of asparagus." Hawthorne once designed a symbolical tale of a young man being slain and buried in the flower garden of his betrothed, and the earth levelled over him. That particular spot, which she happens to plant with some peculiar variety of flowers, produces them of admirable splendour, beauty, and perfume; and thus the classic fantasy is realized, of dead people transformed to flowers.

* In the book called "God's Acre; or, Historical Notices relating to Churchyards," there is a loathsome story of a Mr. Thompson, of Worcester, who baited his angling-hook with part of the corrupted form of King John, and carried the fish he caught with it in triumph through the streets.

Sir Thomas Browne—how pregnant his hints are!—touches on Mummy as having become merchandize: Mizraim curing wounds, and Pharaoh being sold for balsams.

The heroic dust, as Chateaubriand calls it, of the heart of Duguesclin, stolen during the Revolution, was on the point of being pounded up by a glazier to mix his paints. So again we read of the slaughtered hosts during the retreat from Moscow: "Some industrial companies have transported themselves into the desert with their furnaces and their caldrons; the bones have been converted into animal black; whether it come from the dog or from the man, the varnish is equally valuable, and is as brilliant when drawn from obscurity as from glory." Cornelia Knight mentions a Parmese canon, who one day, while the French were in occupation of Piacenza, found the church in possession of three surgeons, or surgeons' mates, of that army, "busily skinning" the dead body of a French soldier. "Horrified at the sight, he asked the meaning of this ghastly proceeding, and was told that some scientific men had discovered that the human skin made excellent leather," and that it had been therefore ordered that all dead bodies should be skinned, for the purpose of providing boots and shoes for the soldiers. Ziska's skin-deep drum-destiny was at least a seeming nobler, if not essentially a more useful one.

Xenophon makes his pattern-prince desirous of having his body turned to beneficial uses after death, by being incorporated with mother earth; positively enjoining his sons not to enshrine it in gold or silver, but to bury it in the ground as soon as the life was gone out of it. Little would trouble him the anticipated contingency of such a *peut-être* as Burns surmises, in the case of a recently deceased acquaintance —like Xenophon, a sportsman to the core:—

> "There low he lies, in lasting rest;
> Perhaps, upon his mould'ring breast
> Some spitefu' moorfowl bigs her nest,
> To hatch and breed."

Cyrus, like the essentially practical statesman in Mrs. Gore's tale, would presumably have detected no irony in Hamlet's assignment of purpose to the ashes of imperious Cæsar: "It seemed a relief to his mind that emperors, when turned to clay, could be turned to account." No more objection to that, than to such a circumstance as "The Traveller" deplores, that

> . . "in those domes where Cæsar once bore sway,
> Defaced by time, and tottering in decay,
> There in the ruin, heedless of the dead,
> The shelter-seeking peasant builds his shed."

Have we not heard Liebig indignantly complain of our importing immense quantities of bones from abroad, thereby draining the fair foreign fields of their very life-blood—scouring as we are said to do foreign battle-plains, that the bony reliques of warriors who fought a good fight in their day, may now be of further avail to make our bread? An English satirist of German sentimentalism pictures a contemplative young Teuton, at dinner time, pausing over his *sauer kraut*, as he calls to mind that the churchyard wherein his ancestor was decently deposited, has been converted into a kitchen garden; and the conviction flashes upon him that what was a distinguished man is now on the table in the form of cabbage.

Have we not, again, heard Monseigneur Dupanloup, Bishop of Orleans, indignantly brand, as the outcome of current materialism, such a "practical suggestion" as that of a certain M. Moleschott, that, in the interest of humanity, "the honour of the dead should be abolished," and all cemeteries desecrated after being used a twelvemonth, that the bones contained in them may "supply to plants the power of creating fresh men"?

It is, I think, in one of Mr. Dicey's letters from the East that mention is made of the writer's seeing at Sakhara a half score of camels pacing down from the mummy pits to the bank of the river, laden with nets in which were human bones, some two hundredweight in each net on each side of the camel; while among the pits were to be seen people busily engaged in searching out, sifting, and sorting the bones with which the ground is almost encrusted. The cargoes were to be sent on to Alexandria, and thence shipped to manure manufacturers in England. It is a strange fate, as the tourist reflects, to preserve one's skeleton for thousands of years in order that there may be fine Southdowns and Cheviots in a distant land; and he stops to muse on the idea of a *gigot* that consists in great part of the dwellers in Memphis.

That is a graphic picture the historian of the United Netherlands paints, of the artificial earthworks devised in extremity during the siege of Ostend, in 1604, when there was no earth left for the defenders to use, nearly everything solid having been scooped away in the perpetual delving. The very sea-dykes had been robbed of their material, so that the coming winter might find besiegers and besieged all washed together into the German Ocean, and it was hard digging and grubbing among the scanty cellarages of the dilapidated houses. But there were plenty of graves, Mr. Motley proceeds to relate; and now, not only were all the cemeteries within the precincts shovelled and carted in mass to the inner fortifications, but rewards being offered of ten stivers for each dead body, great heaps of disinterred soldiers were piled into the new ramparts. "Thus these warriors, after laying down their lives for the cause of freedom, were made to do duty after death."

Who, exclaims Owen Feltham, would have thought when Scanderbeg was laid in his tomb, that the Turks would afterwards break into it, and wear his bones for jewels? But *telle est la vie*—or rather, in such a connection, *la mort.*

The Rev. John Eagles, avowing an inclination to join in Shakspeare's anathema on the movers of bones, adverts incidentally to the alleged fact of Swift's larynx having been stolen, and being now in possession of the purloiner in America,—of an itinerant phrenologist now hawking about Pope's skull,—and of Mathews's thigh-bone circulating from house to house.

Coupling such corporeal vicissitudes *post mortem* with the

text with which we started, of Jezebel's scattered remains on the face of the field, we call to mind Ben Jonson's description (only too historically true) of the dispersed fragments of him that the other day had been virtually master of Rome, and so of the wide world. Contending hands have appropriated all that is left of him: some have ravished an arm, others a thigh; this spoiler has the hands, and that the feet; "these fingers, and these toes; that hath his liver, he his heart. . . .

> "The whole, and all of what was great Sejanus,
> And, next to Cæsar, did possess the world,
> Now torn and scatter'd, as he needs no grave;
> Each little dust covers a little part;
> So lies he nowhere, and yet often buried."

"CONSIDER THE LILIES."

St. Matthew vi. 28.

VULGAR utilitarianism—for there is a vulgar and shallow phase of it, as well as a scientific and a misrepresented one—can surely find little to its fancy (but then it has no fancy) the invitation, or monition, even though uttered in the Sermon on the Mount, of "Consider the lilies." Why consider them, it would fain object, seeing that they toil not, neither do they spin? But that is the very reason for considering them. They are clothed from above with surpassing beauty, without taking thought for themselves; so clothed, not for utilitarian ends, except in the large sense that the *dulce* too is *utile*, that a thing of beauty is a joy for ever; and *that* is undeniably to be of some "use" in the world.

Herein lies the simple answer to the query in the laureate's poem,—

> "Oh, to what uses shall we put the wildweed flower that simply blows?
> And is there any moral shut within the bosom of the rose?
> But any man that walks the mead, in bud, or blade, or bloom, may find,
> According as his humours lead, a meaning suited to his mind."

And liberal applications lie in art as nature. The Warwickshire justice tells Shakspeare, after hearing him recite his stanzas on a sweetbriar, "Thou mightest have added some moral about life and beauty: poets never handle roses without one." But then Justice Shallow is the critic. The author of the "Citation and Examination" in which the criticism is uttered, has an imaginary dialogue between Vittoria Colonna and Michel Angelo—the former of whom defines the difference betwixt poetry and all other arts, all other kinds of composition, to be this: in them, utility comes before delight; in this, delight before utility. Buonarotti submits that in some pleasing poems there is nothing whatsoever of the useful. But Vittoria thinks he is mistaken: an obvious moral is indeed a heavy protuberance, which injures the gracefulness of a poem; but there is wisdom of one kind or other, she alleges, in every sentence of a really good composition, and it produces its effect in various ways. "The beautiful in itself is useful by awakening our finer sensibilities, which it must be our own fault if we do not often carry with us into action." Leigh Hunt, in his "Song of the Flowers," makes them exult in the fact, by their mere existence demonstrated, that heaven loves colour; that great Nature clearly joys in red and green: "What sweet thoughts she thinks of violets, and pinks, and a thousand flashing hues, made solely to be seen:"

"Uselessness divinest
Of a use the finest
Painteth us, the teachers of the end of use;
Travellers weary eyed
Bless us far and wide;
Unto sick and prison'd thoughts we give sudden truce;
Not a poor town window
Loves its sickliest planting,
But its wall speaks loftier truth than Babylon's whole vaunting."

So again Mr. Procter apostrophizes Nature in his "Song of the Snowdrop," as having surely sent it forth alone to the cold and sullen season, like a thought at random thrown,—"sent it thus for some grave reason.

"If 'twere but to pierce the mind
With a single gentle thought,
Who shall deem thee hard or blind,
Who, that thou hast vainly wrought?"

Bishop Copleston, in his plea for a free cultivation of the poetic faculty, contends that its being entirely neglected must prove an irreparable injury to young minds—losing as they do that intellectual charm from which life borrows its loveliest graces: hence he takes exception to Locke's expression, that educators should beware of making "anything a boy's business but downright virtue." Surely, argues his critic, the improvement of the faculties which God has implanted in us is itself a virtue: our attention may be given in undue measure to one, and so may violate that just harmony without which nothing is virtuous, nothing lovely. The faculty itself, which the philosopher seems to condemn, the divine claims to be one of the kindest gifts of heaven. And why, then, it is asked, should man be niggardly where Providence has been bountiful? "Why should he think scorn of that pleasant land, and undervalue those fair possessions, which were not thought beneath the care of the Almighty?" In the garden of Eden, we are reminded, was made to grow, not only what was good for food, but every tree also that was pleasant to the sight: and in that garden man was placed, to keep it, and to dress it.

It is, as Isaac Taylor remarks, by her diversities,—her gay adornments, her copious fund of forms, and her sportive freaks of shape and colour, that Nature allures the eye of man, while she draws him on toward the more arduous, but more noble pursuit of her hidden analogies. An insensible process goes on, the effect of which is gradually to invest general truths with a sort of majesty, as well as beauty; so that, at length, this new charm is found to prevail over the graces and attractions of the exterior diversity of things.

Even philosophy, however, has been said to teach us that nature scatters the lavish beauties of form and colour not always with a utilitarian purpose; or rather, that beauty—merely to display beauty—is often, as in birds and flowers and shells and crystals, the object of material organization. "There is no special use in the metallic lustre on the plumage of the humming-bird, and tropical blossoms blaze for the mere sake of being splendid." Yet is it owned to be noticeable that only in the lower ranks of the kingdom of being is nature lavish of beauty for the mere sake of the beautiful; and that as we advance upward in the scale of created things, a certain severity and reserve seem to grow upon nature itself.

Shenstone—a now all but forgotten poet—in a now quite forgotten ode, asserts, as in duty bound, the uses beyond use of Nature's fancy work:

"Search but the garden or the wood,
Let yon admired carnation own
Not all was meant for raiment, or for food,
Not all for needful use alone;
There while the seeds of future blossoms dwell,
'Tis colour'd for the sight, perfumed to please the smell.

"Why knows the nightingale to sing?
Why flows the pine's nectareous juice?
Why shines with paint the linnet's wing?
For sustenance alone? for use?
For preservation?" . . .

An art-poet significantly and suggestively writes, in lines to which the contributory reader, must, on his part, supply readings as it were between the lines:

"This wild white rose-bud in my hand hath meanings meant for me alone,
Which no one else can understand: to you it breathes with altered tone;
How shall I class its properties for you? or its wise whisperings
Interpret? Other eyes and ears it teaches many other things."

The dull of hearing and seeing, it teaches very little. Josiah the curate, in Colonel Hamley's tale, finds nothing suggestive in a rose in a buttonhole—not that he lacks interest in the flower in what he thinks its proper place. He never, he owns, could see any possible affinity between flowers and broadcloth; and why people should pluck blossoms from the stems and leaves that harmonize so well with them, to stick them into a dingy produce of the loom, he holds to be one of the puzzles of humanity. But Josiah is indulgent to that sister Rosa of his, who confessedly resembles the lilies in so far that she toils not, neither does she spin; and who, idle child, seems to think human beings ought to be content with merely blooming.

We like our churches to be beautiful, and our temples, and our whole symbolic creations, Mr. Hannay somewhere observes; their beauty represents the general beauty of the universe, and that is one of the modes by which God is pleased to appeal to our faculties of love and wonder and admiration. "The Romanists call the Virgin Mary a 'mystical rose,' and a beautiful woman is a mystical rose; attractive, and yet, at the same time, a religious symbol—an object which keeps alive in you the sense of wonder and love of beauty, and thankfulness to the Supreme for the glories of His creation."

It has been said by an art-poet already quoted, that "the girl who twines in her soft hair the orange-flower, with love's devotion, by the mere act of being fair, sets countless laws of life in motion." Dr. Croly, in his "Salathiel," pleading for the *right* of beauty to have a natural power over the heart, urges, for instance, that all that overcomes selfishness—the besetting sin of the world—is an instrument of good; and goes on to say that beauty is but melody of a higher kind—both alike softening the troubled and hard nature of man. "Even if we looked on a lovely woman but as on a rose, an exquisite production of the summer hours of life, it would be idle to deny her influence in making even those summer hours sweeter." We may apply the suggestion in one of Mrs. Browning's last poems—

"What if God has set her here
Less for action than for Being?—
For the eye and for the ear.

"Just to show what beauty may,
Just to prove what music can."
* * * *

——o——

A HISTRIONIC ASPECT OF LIFE.

1 CORINTHIANS vii. 31.

THE apostle would have his brethren so to use this world, as not abusing it; and for this reason, that "the fashion of this world passeth away." In the original the phrase runs: *παράγει γὰρ τὸ* ΣΧΗΜΑ *τοῦ κόσμου τούτου.* The expression is said by Grotius and others to be borrowed from the theatre, and to refer to the scene-shifting of the stage. Life here below has verily its histrionic aspects; the fashion of it passeth away much as do the scene-painter's creations, the stage-carpenter's framework, the spectacular effects and dissolving views, nay the very actors themselves. For, all the world is in some sense a stage, and all the men and women merely players—

> "They have their exits and their entrances;
> And one man in his time plays many parts,
> His acts being seven ages."

Considering his own profession, the figure is one that must often have crossed and occupied Shakspeare's mind—at once so keenly observing and so profoundly meditative. Not that he harps much upon it, so much as might, perhaps, have been expected, in his plays. Still he does now and then recur to the histrionic metaphor. And it is in his graver mood, not his lighter, that he does so; in sober sadness, not with gibing glee. As where Lear, in the extremity of his distraction, intent on preaching to Gloster, takes for his text the wail of infancy, crying, the first time that it smells the air: for

> "When we are born, we cry, that we are come
> To this great stage of fools."

Or again, as where Antonio, the care-fraught merchant of Venice, assured by a friend that he is looking far from well, indeed "marvellously changed," and remonstrated with for not taking life more easily, replies:

> "I hold the world but as the world, Gratiano,
> A stage where every man must play a part,
> And mine a sad one."

Mundus universus exercet histrioniam,—the saw is Petronius Arbiter's. There is an obverse reading, by some other old Eminent Hand: *Totum mundum agit histrio.* If all the world's a play, so again there's not in all the world a character the player won't act. Lucretius had the stage simile of life in his mind's eye, when he said of those who hide certain of their doings, *vitæ post-scenia celant,*—the *post-scenium* being what we call "behind the scenes," where the actors dress and "make up" for their parts. And what says a distich in the Greek Anthology:

> "Σκηνὴ πᾶς ὁ βίος, καὶ παίγνιον· ἢ μάθε παίζειν,
> Τὴν σπουδὴν μεταθείς, ἢ φέρε τὰς ὀδύνας."

> "Life is a stage, a play: so learn thy part,
> All cares removed, or rend with grief thy heart."

Sir Thomas Browne professes, in his large utterance and stately style: "The world to me is but a dream or mock show, and we all therein but pantaloons and anticks, to my severer contemplations." To the same effect, though not in the same spirit, Wordsworth's recluse avows himself tired

> "Of the ostentatious world—a swelling stage
> With empty actions and vain passions stuffed."

When both Swift and Bolingbroke had closed the tenth lustre of their years, his cynical lordship wrote from Brussels to the cynical dean, that he thought it high time to determine how they should "play the last act of the farce. Might not my life," adds accomplished St. John, "be entitled much more properly a what-d'ye-call-it than a farce? Some comedy, a great deal of tragedy, and the whole interspersed with scenes of Harlequin, Scaramouch, and Dr. Baloardo." Accomplished St. John was always, and to the last an accomplished actor. As for Dr. Swift, he expanded the histrionic similitude of life into some eighteen stanzas on the puppet-show—which record how wit, "the life of man to represent, and turn it all to ridicule, did once a puppet-show invent, where the chief actor is a fool"—and of which, perhaps, the gravest runs thus:

"This fleeting scene is but a stage
Where various images appear;
In different parts of youth and age,
Alike the prince and peasant share."

Don Quixote tells Sancho Panza how like human life is to a play. One takes the part of a ruffian, another of a liar, a third of a merchant, a fourth of a soldier. This man is for the occasion the lover; that man is the judicious friend. At last the play is ended. Each takes off the clothes which belong to his part, and the players remain equal. So it is in the comedy of this world, says Don Quixote. There are emperors and popes, and all the characters that can be introduced into a play; but it is played out, death takes away the outward trappings which made them seem to differ, and they remain equal in the tomb.

Where, is the author of the Complaint's complaining query, or querulous plaint,

"Where, the prime actors of the last year's scene;
Their port so proud, their buskin, and their plume?"

It is a trite topic, indeed, with Dr. Young,—that of "Life's gay stage, one inch above the grave," whereon those strut and fret their hour, that shall soon be seen no more for ever. All, merely players.

"Each, in his turn, some tragic story tells,
With now and then a wretched farce between."

Dr. Maginn takes note of the frequency with which Lucian compares life to a theatrical procession, in which magnificent parts are assigned to some, who pass before the eyes of the spectators clothed in costly garments, and bedecked with glittering jewels; but, the moment the show is over, are reduced to their original nothingness, no longer kings and heroes, but poor players whose hour has been strutted out.

No wonder that the master Showman of Vanity Fair should pen an *envoi* after this fashion:

"The play is done; the curtain drops,
Slow falling to the prompter's bell:

A moment yet the actor stops,
And looks around, to say farewell.
It is an irksome word and task;
And when he's laughed and said his say,
He shows, as he removes the mask,
A face that's anything but gay."

Horace Walpole will be found iterating and reiterating in his letters a favourite apophthegm of his—that the world is a comedy to those who think, a tragedy to those who feel.

One might safely assume beforehand that a people of so histrionic a turn as the French would make good use of the histrionic metaphor of life, in their *belles lettres*, of whatever date. And in point of fact the figure is a well-worked one in French literature. Now it is a Cardinal de Retz, who, on being named coadjutor to his uncle, the Archbishop of Paris, describes himself as thereupon ceasing to be "in the pit, or at best in the orchestra, playing and funning with the fiddles," but mounting thence to the stage itself. Indeed, a modern critic has remarked that Retz is perpetually making use of these expressions and images of *théâtre* and *comédie*. He was an accomplished actor from first to last—not above the line of low comedy now and then, and quite an adept in the Cloak-and-Sword business. Now again it is his contemporary, Madame de Motteville, who so frequently represents herself as an occupant of one of the best boxes, intent on diverting herself with the *belle comédie* that was being played under her eyes. "Les cabinets des rois," says Madame—who ought to know—are theatres in which pieces of universal interest are for ever being played : some simply comic; others decidedly tragical, though so frequently occasioned by the merest trifles. So, again, Madame des Ursins (the Princess Orsino), another *habituée* behind the scenes, and herself a star of the first magnitude in any working company, describes the world as *une comédie où il y avait souvent de bien mauvais acteurs.*

Then, too, we have the Abbé Chaulieu, when dancing attendance on the Duke of Vendôme, and assisting at all the fêtes and galas got up in that prince's honour, writing in a sort of apologetic strain to his sister-in-law, that since all the world's a stage, one must just be content to don cap and bells with the rest*—for if all your men and women are merely players, motley's your only wear.

Of another *spirituel*, and very unspiritual, abbé of that period, Choisy, it has been observed, that his life resembled a comedy, rife with all that is most various and most improbable: his career of fourscore years composed a complete masquerade; for

"this man in his time play'd many parts,"

and in each of them he seems to have acted with professional aptitude, facility, and zest.

Such another actor, with a difference, was Voltaire. As Voltaire himself said of the Duchess of Maine, "Elle aimera la comédie jusqu'au dernier moment, et, quand elle sera malade, je vous conseille de lui administrer quelque belle pièce," etc., etc.,—so of the mocking philosopher of Ferney, playing his many parts, it has been said, that he had a genius for transformations, having always more than one *rôle* to play in the comedy of life—which diversity of *rôles* jumped with his humour, and just hit the mobile preferences of a man who so early in his existence turned player. The life of Voltaire is a comedy, says Sainte-Beuve: his correspondence with D'Alembert shows us the coulisses and background—and lets us in to damaging and disenchanting revelations behind the scenes. Elsewhere he may be seen to fret and strut his hour upon the stage, carefully made up, and all in point device costume; but here we have him in undress, and by dusty daylight, and off his guard.

Tous les comédiens ne sont pas du théâtre, is rightly reckoned one of the prettiest *provèrbes* of M. Théodore Leclerc. In the Proverbe which bears that pregnant title, a nephew incidentally tells his uncle, "Vous qui êtes un homme du monde, vous appelez cela l'esprit du monde; moi qui suis un comédien, j'appelle cela de la comédie. C'est toujours la même chose,

* "Et puisque le monde n'est qu'une comédie, il faut prendre la queue lapin et l'épée de bois comme les autres."—Lettres de Chaulieu, ed. 1850.

sous un nom différent." The salon and the stage are on a level. To be a real man of the world, is to be an actor of the first class.

M. Scribe puts the proverb as a practical epigram into the mouth of old Michonnet, when trying to soothe and inspirit his pet pupil for the stage : "Calme toi et étudie; . . . il y a dans le monde de plus grands comédiens que nous!"

Indeed, according to Chamfort, there is no choice in the matter; every man, however wise and unsophisticated and open-hearted, must, sooner or later, turn actor, on this great stage of fools. For, "la fortune et le costume qui l'entourent font de la vie une représentation au milieu de laquelle il faut qu'à la longue l'homme le plus honnête devienne comédien malgré lui." We are all actors and actresses, says one of Miss Eden's characters, and "none of us quite up to our parts, though we act all day long." Not that every one plays just the part he or she would have chosen. The distribution of *rôles* would seem often to make this a mad world, my masters.

> "Le monde, à mon avis, est comme un grand théâtre,
> Où chacun en public, l'un par l'autre abusé,
> Souvent à ce qu'il est, joue un rôle opposé."

This, one might almost paraphrase in the words of John Webster's wobegone Duchess Mariana :

> "I account this world a tedious theatre,
> For I do play a part in't 'gainst my will."

By way of introducing his elaborate narrative of Darnley's fate, Mr. Froude tells us of Mary Stuart, that on the political stage she was "a great actress. The 'woman' had a drama of her own going on behind the scenes; the theatre caught fire; the mock heroics of the Catholic crusade burnt into ashes; and a tremendous domestic tragedy was revealed before the astonished eyes of Europe." And later again, describing Mary's caressing wiles to beguile and tranquilise her doomed husband, on the eve of the catastrophe, the same historian employs the same histrionic figure: "Mary Stuart was an admirable actress; rarely, perhaps, on the world's stage has there been a more skilful player." But the part, he adds, was a difficult one; she had still some natural compunction; and the performance was not quite perfect.

Most of our business is farce, writes old Montaigne: *Mundus universus exercet histrioniam* (which the old French essayist's old English translator renders, "All the world 's a stage, and all the men and women merely players"). We must play our part well, he adds, but withal as the part of a borrowed personage; we must not make a real essence of a mask and outward appearance, etc. So it is one of Ben Jonson's "Discoveries," "de vitâ humanâ," that our whole life is like a play—wherein every man, forgetful of himself, is in travail with expression of another. In one of his comedies, rare Ben makes a sham inn-keeper, taking his ease in his own inn, and following his own fancies there, "imagine all the world 's a play:—

> "The state, and men's affairs, all passages
> Of life, to spring new scenes; come in, go out,
> And shift, and vanish. . . . I have got
> A seat to sit at ease here, in mine inn,
> To see the comedy; and laugh, and chuck
> At the variety and throng of humours
> And dispositions, that come justling in
> And out still, as they one drove hence another."

For every man, in the play of this world, says pious Master Feltham, is not only an actor, but is a spectator, too: "At the beginning (that is, in his youth) it promises so much that he is loth to leave it; when it grows towards the middle (the act of virility), then he sees the scenes grow thick, and fill, and would gladly understand the end: but, when that draws near, and he finds what it will be, he is then content to depart and leave his room to others."

Fielding's philosopher asks if the actor is esteemed happier to whose lot it falls to play the principal part, than he who plays the lowest? and yet the drama may run twenty nights together, and so outlast our lives; but at the best, says he, "life is only a little longer drama; and the business of the great stage is consequently a little more serious than that which is performed at the theatre-royal."

> "If the world be, indeed, as 'twas said, but a stage,
> The dress only is changed 'twixt the acts of an age.
> From the dark tiring-chamber behind straight reissue
> With new masks the old mummers; the very same tissue
> Of passionate antics that move through the play,
> With new parts to fulfil and new phrases to say."

An old Greek writer, speaking of Alexander of Pheræ, who reigned in Thessaly only ten months, and then was slain, calls him, in derision of his brief lease of power, a theatrical tyrant, a mere stage king, who, as it were, walked on only to walk off again. But the palace of the Cæsars, Plutarch remarks, received four emperors in a less space of time, one entering, and another making his exit, as if to fret and strut each his little hour upon the stage. How soon the stage directions, Enter Galba, enter and exit Otho, enter and exit Vitellius, lapse in *Exeunt omnes!*

In Charles the Sixth's ordinance, authorising the players of the "Mysteries of the Passion" (towards the close of the fourteenth century), that poor crazed monarch styles them his "loved and dear co-mates." And what could be juster? Michelet asks. "A hapless actor himself, a poor player in the grand historic mystery, he went to see his 'co-mates'—saints, angels, and devils, perform their miserable travestie of the Passion. He was not only spectator; he was spectacle as well. His people went to see in him the Passion of royalty."

Players, the abstract and brief chronicles of the time, Hazlitt calls the motley representatives of human nature. They are the only honest hypocrites, he says (and hypocrite, by the way, is classically a correct name for them, though Hazlitt may not have remembered or meant it): their life is a voluntary dream, a studied madness—it being the height of their ambition to be "beside themselves:"—to-day kings, to-morrow beggars, it is only when they are themselves that they are nothing: made up of mimic laughter and tears, they wear the livery of other men's fortunes, till their very thoughts are not their own. "They are, as it were, train-bearers in the pageant of life, and hold a glass up to humanity, frailer than itself. We see ourselves at second-hand in them. . . . The stage is an epitome, a bettered likeness of the world, with the dull part left out: and indeed, with this omission, it is nearly big enough to hold all the rest."

Sir Thomas Overbury had, two centuries before, written characteristically to the same purport. "All men have beene of his occupation," writes the ill-starred knight of a good actor; "and indeed, what hee doth fainedly, that doe others essentially: this day one plays a monarch, the next a private person. Here one acts a tyrant, on the morrow an exile: a parasite this man to-night, to-morrow a precisian," and so of divers others.

> "And why not players strut in courtiers' clothes?
> For these are actors, too, as well as those."

Or, to top (Pope) Alexander the Great with Glorious John (Dryden):

> "Even kings but play, and when their part is done,
> Some other, worse or better, mount the throne."

As we cannot be monarchs, says the Porpora of fiction, we are artists, and have a kingdom of our own: we dress ourselves as kings and great men, we ascend the stage, we seat ourselves upon a fictitious throne, we play a farce, we are actors. The world, he continues, sees us, but understands us not. "It is only when I am at the theatre that I see clearly our true relations to society. The spirit of music unseals my eyes, and I see behind the footlights a true court, real heroes, lofty inspirations; while the wretched dolts who flaunt in the boxes upon velvet couches are the real actors. In truth, the world is a comedy; and we must play our parts in it with gravity and decorum, though conscious of the hollow pageant which compasses us on every side." And Godolphin pronounces life to differ from the play only in this—that it has no plot, all being vague, desultory, unconnected, till the curtain drops with the mystery unsolved.

All this is in Mr. Carlyle's vein—of the *Sartor Resartus* date at least; or as when he depicted the family vagaries of Mirabeaudom, which produced "such astonishing comico-tragical French farces"—with the eight chaotic volumes of family correspondence, wherein the various personages speak their dialogue, unfold their farce-tragedy: "Seen or half seen, it is a stage; as the whole world is. What with personages, what with destinies, no stranger house-drama [than that of the Mirabeau family] was enacting on the earth at that time." The same figure Mr. Carlyle elsewhere applies to our own revolution times, in the century before: "Such is the drama of life, seen in Baillie of Kilwinning; a thing of multifarious tragic and epic meanings, then as now. A many-voiced tragedy and epos, yet with broad-based comic and grotesque accompaniments, done by actors *not* in buskins;—ever replete with elements of guilt and remorse, of pity, instruction, and fear."

ACT WELL YOUR PART:—there all the *moral* lies. Though the world *be* histrionical, and most men live ironically, says Sir Thomas Browne, "yet be thou what thou singly art, and personate only thyself."

It has been sadly and severely said of the Emperor Augustus, who was loved by no one, that if, at the moment of his death, he desired his friends to dismiss him from this world by the common expression of scenical applause (*vos plaudite!*), in that valedictory injunction he expressed inadvertently the true value of his own long life, which, in strict candour, may be pronounced one continued series of histrionic efforts, and of excellent acting, adapted to selfish ends.

L'honnête homme, writes an epigrammatic thinker, *joue son rôle le mieux qu'il peut sans songer à la galerie.*

Remember, says Epictetus, so to act your part upon this stage as to be approved by the master, whether it be a short or a long one that he has given you to perform. If he will have you to represent a beggar, endeavour to act the beggar's part well; and so, a cripple, a prince, or a plebeian. It is your part to perform well what you represent: it is his to choose what that shall be.

Thus spake the stoic philosopher. And how speaks the Christian divine? As the merit of an actor, says Robert Hall, is not estimated by the part which he performs, but solely by the truth and propriety of his representation, and the peasant is often applauded where the monarch is hissed; so when the great drama of life is concluded, He who allots its scenes and determines its period will take an account of His servants, and assign to each his due, in his own proper character.

Since the life of man is likened to a scene, "I had rather," writes John Milton, "that all my entrances and exits might mix with such persons only whose worth erects them and their actions to a grave and tragic deportment, and not to have to do with clowns and vices."

And this, lest such a player have to echo, in spirit, if not to the letter, the bitter conviction of blinded, blundering Leontes —*Io anche*—

> "And I
> Play too; but so disgraced a part, whose issue
> Will hiss me to my grave."

The measure of a happy life, writes Lord Shaftesbury—he of the "Characteristics"—is not from the fewer or more suns we behold, the fewer or more breaths we draw, or meals we repeat; but from the having once lived well, acted our part handsomely, and made our exit cheerfully—or, to print it as he wrote it, for the lovers of old books' sake—"and made our *Exit* cheerfully, and as became us."

It is well remarked by Archbishop Trench that we have forfeited the full force of the statement, "God is no respecter of *persons*," from the fact that "person" does not mean for us now all that it once meant. "Person," from "persona," the mask constantly worn by the actor of antiquity, is by natural transfer the part or *rôle* in the play which each sustains, as *πρόσωπον* is in Greek. "In the great tragi-comedy of life each sustains a 'person;' one that of a king, another that of a hind; one must play Dives, another Lazarus. This 'person' God, for whom the question is not *what* 'person' each sustains, but *how* he sustains it, does not regard."

——o——

PHARAOH'S ALTERNATIONS OF AMENDMENT AND RELAPSE.

EXODUS vii.-x., *passim.*

HIS land of Egypt covered with frogs, Pharaoh was urgent with Moses and Aaron to "intreat the Lord" for him, and with conciliatory proposals in favour of the children of Israel. The plague of the frogs abated accordingly, Pharaoh hardened his heart as soon as he saw that there was respite. So with the plague of flies that came in grievous swarms into the house of Pharaoh, and into his servants' houses, and into all the land of Egypt, so that the land was corrupted by reason of the flies; again Pharaoh besought Hebrew intercession, and pledged himself to acts of clemency; and again no sooner was the plague removed, than Pharaoh hardened his heart at that time also, neither would he let the people go. Plague after plague ensued—the murrain of beasts, the plague of boils and blains, and the plague of hail and fire; and so grievous was the last—smiting all that was in the field, both man and beast, as well as every herb and tree—that Pharaoh once more importuned Moses and Aaron, confessing his sins, imploring forgiveness, and promising amendment. Once and again he was heard and answered. "And when Pharaoh saw that the rain and the hail and the thunders were ceased, he sinned yet more, and hardened his heart . . . neither would he let the children of Israel go." The plague of locusts, destroying all that the hail had left, made him call for the Hebrew brothers again in hottest haste,—entreating forgiveness "only this once," and deliverance "from this death only." But the mighty west wind that swept away the ravagers had no sooner ceased to blow, than the hardening process again set in, and the tyrant revelled as of yore in his accustomed tyranny. How many more plagues might have been added to the ten—decade upon decade—with the like result, each facile amendment merging in a more and more facile relapse, it is superfluous to guess.

We read in Homer, as versified by Pope, that—

> "The weakest atheist-wretch all heaven defies,
> But shrinks and shudders when the thunder flies."

So Boileau satirises the "intrepid" scoffer, who puts off believing in God until fever prostrates him; who is almost as quick as the lightning to lift up his hands to heaven when the lightning glares across it, but laughs at poor feeble humanity as soon as the atmosphere is cleared and the storm quite spent:

> "Attend pour croire en Dieu que la fiévre le presse;
> Et, toujours dans l'orage au ciel levant les mains,
> Dès que l'air est calmé, rit des faibles humains."

Lady Mary Wortley Montagu describes in one of her vivacious letters a stormy passage she has just made from Calais to Dover, and diverts herself not a little, as her ladyship's manner is, at the distress of a fellow-passenger, in alternations of anxiety as to being lost herself and losing her smuggled head-dress. "She was an English lady that I had met at Calais, who desired me to let her go over with me in my cabin. She had brought a fine point-head, which she was contriving to conceal from the custom-house officers. When the wind grew high, and our little vessel cracked, she fell very heartily to her prayers, and thought wholly of her soul. When it seemed to abate, she returned to the worldly care of her head-dress;" and the alternative exclamations of the distracted creature are liberally specified by Lady Mary; who then adds: "This easy transition from her soul to her head-dress, and the alternate agonies that both gave her, made it hard to determine which she thought of greatest value."

Lord Lytton, in one of his fictions, comments on the instinct, as he calls it, of that capricious and fluctuating conscience, belonging to weak minds, "which remains still and drooping and lifeless as a flag on a mast-head during the calm of prosperity, but flutters and flaps and tosses when the wind blows and the wave heaves." And an example to the purpose is given in the case of a selfish uncle, whose orphan nephews are all but coldly discarded until his own son is *in extremis*. "Mr. Beaufort . . . thought very acutely and remorsefully of the condition of the Mortons, during the danger of his own son. So far indeed from his anxiety for Arthur monopolising his care, it only sharpened his charity towards the orphans; for many a man becomes devout and good when he fancies he has an *im-*

mediate interest in appeasing Providence." Such a man, in such a case, becomes at any rate lavish of promises, which perhaps at the moment he even intends to keep. But how are promises of this kind usually kept? Much after the manner predicated of Bajazet, by Acomat, in the French tragedy; a vaguely worded intimation, but definite enough in its scope: only let the pressure that extorts the promise be withdrawn, and gone will be the value of the promise too:

> "Promettez : affranchi du péril qui vous presse,
> Vous verrez de quel poids sera votre promesse."

Pope would consign such trifles light as air to the lunar sphere,

> "Where broken vows and death-bed alms are found,
> And lovers' hearts with ends of ribbon bound,
> The courtier's promises, the sick man's prayers."

Why do these last make so slight an impression on bystanders? Mr. Whitehead says because it is not a living but a dying man that speaks; and a dying man who wants to live. "It is fear that cries out in agony, not penitence that prays." Fielding, in his masterpiece, moralises on the truism that be men ever so much alarmed and frightened when apprehending themselves in danger of dying, yet no sooner are they cleared from this apprehension, than even the fears of it are erased from their minds. It is much later in the same story, that the "hero's" avowed resolution, at a crisis in his fortunes, to sin no more, lest a worse thing happen unto him, is ridiculed by a cynical acquaintance, as the effect merely of low spirits, and confinement—with the quotation of "some witticisms about the devil when he was sick." The epigram in question is a favourite allusion with novelists and moralists of all sorts and sizes. There is a border freebooter of Scott's, who, having recovered from a severe illness, thanks to the medical skill of the Black Dwarf, greets his benefactor, on horseback, all in bandit array, as soon as convalescent. "So," said the dwarf, "rapine and murder once more on horseback!" "On horseback?" said the bandit; "ay, ay, Elshie, your leech-craft has set me on the bonnie bay again." "And all those promises of amendment which you made during your illness forgotten?" continued Elshender. "All clear away, with the water-saps and panada," returned the unabashed convalescent. "Ye ken, Elshie, for they say ye are weel acquent wi' the gentleman,

> "'When the devil was sick, the devil a monk would be;
> When the devil was well, the devil a monk was he.'"

For it is not every vow taken in a panic, to become a monk if spared, that is kept as Luther's was—"devil" though the anti-Lutherans of his day might account and call him. Young Martin saw one of his friends struck dead by his side, by a stroke of lightning, in 1505; and the sight moved him to utter on the instant a vow to St. Anne that he would become a monk if he were himself spared. "The danger passed over, but he did not seek to elude an engagement wrung from him in terror. He solicited no dispensation from his vow." Brother Martin *ipso facto* approved himself no member of the fraternity of what Le Sage calls *vous autres, messieurs les diables*, in a passage that indirectly bears upon our theme, for it refers to the proverbial worthlessness of promises coming from that quarter: "Voilà de belles promesses, répliqua l'Ecolier; mais vous autres, messieurs les diables, on vous accuse de n'être pas fort religieux à tenir ce que vous promettez." The epigram runs, if not rhymes, as well in Latin as in English:

> "Ægrotat dæmon, monachus tunc esse volebat;
> Dæmon convaluit, dæmon ut ante fuit."

Referring to proverbs of this kind it is that Archbishop Trench says, that sometimes an adage, without changing its shape altogether, will yet on the lips of different nations be slightly modified—the modifications, slight as they often are, being not the less eminently characteristic. "Thus in English we say, *The river past, and God forgotten*, to express with how mournful a frequency He whose assistance was invoked, it may have been earnestly, in the moment of peril, is remembered no more, so soon as by His help the danger has been surmounted. The Spaniards have the proverb too; but it is with them: *The* *river past, the saint forgotten:* the saints being in Spain more prominent objects of invocation than God. And the Italian form of it sounds a still sadder depth of ingratitude: *The peril passed, the saint mocked.*" Men indulge in doubts of a Supreme Being, says La Bruyère, when they are lusty and strong; but with sickness comes belief, such as it is. "L'on doute de Dieu dans une pleine santé. . . . Quand on devient malade, et que l'hydropisie est formée . . . l'on croit en Dieu." Believes? As to that, the devils believe, and tremble. But how when the dropsy is relieved and the trembling fit over? Dr. Johnson once adverted in conversation with Seward and Boswell to the evil life he led until sickness wrought a reformation, which, in his case, had been lasting. Mr. Seward thereupon observed: "One should think that sickness, and the view of death, would make more men religious." But Johnson replied to this: "Sir, they do not know how to go about it; they have not the first notion. A man who has never had religion before, no more grows religious when he is sick than a man who has never learnt figures can count when he has need of calculation." * It is to be observed that the doctor claimed for himself a previous regard for religion in quite early life; for some years it had, to use his own phrase, "dropped out of his mind," but "sickness brought it back," and he hoped he had never lost it since.

It is an old, old story, that of the generation which tempted God in the desert, whose days He therefore consumed in vanity, and their years in trouble. When He slew them, then they sought Him; and they returned, and inquired early after God. But it was only to start aside again, like a broken bow.

> "Tamen ad mores natura recurrit
> Damnatos, fixa et mutari nescia."

> "When men in health against physicians rail,"

says Crabbe,

> "They should consider that their nerves may fail;
> Nay, when the world can nothing more produce,
> The priest, the insulted priest, may have his use."

* Boswell's "Life of Johnson," April 29, 1783.

There is a passage in Montesquieu's Persian Letters that reads like a paraphrase and expansion of this: "Quand le médecin est auprès de mon lit, le confesseur me trouve à son avantage. Je sais bien empêcher la religion de m'affliger quand je me porte bien; mais je lui permets de me consoler quand je suis malade: lorsque je n'ai plus rien à espérer d'un côté, la religion se présente, et me gagne," etc. Plutarch tells us of Tullus Hostilius, that he exulted in irreligious opinions while in health, but was frightened into superstition when taken ill. To this passage, one of Plutarch's translators, Dr. Langhorne, appends a footnote, about none being so superstitious in distress as those who, in their prosperity, have laughed at religion; and cites as an instance the famous Canon Vossius, who was "no less remarkable for the greatness of his fears, than he was for the littleness of his faith." Cowper would cite to the same purpose a more distinguished example:

"The Frenchman first in literary fame;
Mention him, if you please. Voltaire? The same.
* * * * *
The Scripture was his jest-book, whence he drew
Bon-mots to gall the Christian and the Jew:
An infidel when well, but what when sick?
Oh, then a text would touch him to the quick."

Swift gives a satirical narrative of "what passed in London during the general consternation of all ranks and degrees of mankind" on account of the predicted destruction of the world by a comet, on a given day. Friday was the declared day; and during Tuesday, Wednesday, and Thursday, public bewilderment and terror are described as extreme—the churches crowded, and thousands praying in the public streets. At length Friday came. But as the day wore on, popular fears began to abate, then lessened every hour; "at night they were almost extinct, till the total darkness that hitherto used to terrify, now comforted every freethinker and atheist. Great numbers went together to the taverns, bespoke suppers, and broke up whole hogsheads for joy. The subject of all wit and conversation was to ridicule the prophecy and rally each other.

All the quality and gentry were perfectly ashamed, nay, some utterly disowned that they had manifested any signs of religion.

"But the next day, even the common people, as well as their betters, appeared in their usual state of indifference. They drank, they swore, they lied, they cheated, they quarrelled, they murdered. In short, the world went on in the old channel."

To apply what Butler says of "saints" in his application of the word, as a cant term then of political significance:

> "For saints in peace degenerate,
> And dwindle down to reprobate; . . .
> And though they've tricks to cast their sins,
> As easy as serpents do their skins,
> That in a while grow out again,
> In peace they turn mere carnal men;
> And from the most refined of saints
> As naturally turn miscreants,*
> As barnacles turn solan geese
> I' th' islands of the Orcades."

That is a fine stroke of nature, in the Knight's Tale (from Chaucer), where Dryden makes Arcite resolve, only when and not until moribund, to avow the wrong he has done to Palamon, and own his fear of repeating it should he recover:

> "When 'twas declared all hope of life was past,
> Conscience (that of all physic works the last)
> Caused him to send for Emily in haste.
> With her, at his desire, came Palamon;"

to whom Arcite owns the faithless part he has played, and desires forgiveness, but at the same time makes this frank avowal:—

> "And much I doubt, should Heaven my life prolong,
> I should return to justify my wrong;
> For while my former flames remain within,
> Repentance is but want of power to sin."

Mr. Tennyson pictures for us a similar instance in Sir Lancelot:

> "Yet the great knight in his mid-sickness made
> Full many a holy vow and pure resolve.

* In the etymological sense, now practically obsolete, of misbeliever.

> These, as but born of sickness, could not live;
> For when the blood ran lustier in him again,
> Full often the sweet image of one face,
> Making a treacherous quiet in his heart,
> Dispersed his resolution like a cloud."

Treating of missions in Abyssinia in the sixteenth century, Gibbon relates how, in a moment of terror, the emperor promised to reconcile himself and his subjects to the Catholic faith. "But the vows," adds the historian, "which pain had extorted, were forsworn on the return of health." Swift again, in his history of England,—for the Dean of St. Patrick wrote one—tells how William Rufus fell dangerously sick at Gloucester, on his return from Scotland, and being moved by the fears of dying, began to discover great marks of repentance, with many promises of amendment and retribution. "But as it is the disposition of men who derive their vices from their complexions, that their passions usually beat strong and weak with their pulses, so it fared with this prince, who, upon recovery of his health, soon forgot the vows he had made in his sickness, relapsing with greater violence into the same irregularities," etc.

Michael Germain—who, however, is allowed to have looked upon the religious observances of Rome with the eye of a French encyclopédiste—makes merry, as one of Mabillon's Italian expedition (in 1685), at the expense of that indolent and hypochondriacal Pope (so Sir James Stephen calls him), Innocent XI. "If I should attempt," writes this French Benedictine, "to give you an exact account of the health of his Holiness, I must begin with Ovid, 'In nova fert animus mutatas dicere formas.' At ten he is sick, at fifteen well again, at eighteen eating as much as four men, at twenty-four dropsical. . . . The worst of it is, that they say he has given up all thoughts of creating new cardinals, forgetting in his restored health the scruples he felt when sick; like other great sinners;" like Louis XV., for instance, at the commencement of whose last illness Mr. Carlyle so vividly depicts the consternation of the infamous Du Barry, lest she should have to take flight, as her predecessors had been constrained to do when the Well-beloved (Bien-aimé) had been sick before. "Should the Most Christian King die, or even get seriously afraid of dying! For, alas! had not the fair, haughty Chateauroux to fly, with wet cheeks and flaming heart, from that fever scene at Metz, long since; driven forth by sour shavelings? She hardly returned, when fever and shavelings were both swept into the background. Pompadour, too, when Damiens wounded Royalty 'slightly, under the fifth rib,' . . . had to pack, and be in readiness; yet did not go, the wound not proving poisoned." His Most Christian Majesty was of no distant kin with that profligate viscount in Mr. Thackeray's story, who used to recount misdeeds "with rueful remorse when he was ill, for the fear of death set him instantly repenting; and with shrieks of laughter when he was well, his lordship having a very great sense of humour." Of the same kindred comes the same author's Miss Crawley, as we see her ill with fright, in her lonely, loveless old age. When in health and good spirits, this venerable inhabitant of Vanity Fair, we are assured, had as free notions about religion and morals as Monsieur de Voltaire himself could desire; but "when illness overtook her, it was aggravated by the most dreadful terrors of death, and an utter cowardice took possession of the prostrate old sinner." Nor be forgotten, as a scion of the same stock, that puffy, pursy, pusillanimous creature, Jos. Sedley, of whom we read that, in the course of his voyage home from Bengal, he disappeared in a panic during a two-days' gale, and remained in his cot reading a religious tract left on board by a missionary's wife; while, "for common reading he had brought a stock of novels and plays," to which of course he would return with all the more zest and devotion when the perils of the gale were past.

Comparing the influence on the mind of danger of death, and of danger from a storm, or from some other external cause than sickness, Archbishop Whately ascribes to the storm a much larger virtue of "wholesome discipline" than to the deadly sickness. He says, "The well-known proverb, 'The devil was sick,' etc., shows how generally it has been observed that people, when they recover, forget the resolutions formed during sickness. One reason of the difference, and perhaps the chief, is, that it is so much easier to *recall* exactly the sensations felt when in perfect health and yet in imminent danger, and to act over again, as it were, in imagination, the whole scene, than to recall fully, when in health, the state of mind during some sickness, which itself so much affects the mind along with the body."

And yet the effects defective of a storm are a commonplace with the satirists. Peter Pindar devotes a "poem" to the subject; and a greater poet—if the said Peter can be called poet at all—has a forcible stanza on the equinoxes, when the Parcæ cut short the further spinning

> "Of seamen's fates, and the loud tempests raise
> The waters, and repentance for past sinning
> In all who o'er the great deep take their ways:
> They vow to amend their lives, and yet they don't;
> Because, if drown'd, they can't—if spar'd, they won't."

—o—

SLEEP AND DEATH.

St. John xi. 11–14.

TO His disciples our Lord spoke of His friend, and theirs, "our friend, Lazarus," as sleeping; intimating at the same time His intention of going on to Bethany, that He might awaken him out of sleep. "Then said His disciples, Lord, if he sleep he shall do well. Howbeit, Jesus spake of his death; but they thought that He had spoken of taking of rest in sleep. Then said Jesus unto them plainly, Lazarus is dead."

The affinity of sleep to death is familiarly recognised in the Old Testament as in the New; indeed, in universal literature of whatever age, sacred and profane. Bathsheba anticipates the day, only too near at hand, when her lord the king "shall sleep with his fathers." Daniel foretells the awaking of many that sleep in the dust of the earth. The psalmist utters a deprecation lest he sleep the sleep of death. Jesus declared the sick maiden to be not dead, but sleeping; and was laughed to scorn by those who *knew* that she was dead. Them that sleep in Jesus, saith the apostle, will God bring with Him. We shall not all sleep, he says elsewhere, but we shall all be changed.

Homer personifies a dualism of "Sleep and Death, two twins of wingèd race, of matchless swiftness, but of silent pace;" and he makes the friends of Sarpedon "his sacred corse bequeath to the soft arms of silent Sleep and Death." He pictures Aphrodite speeding to Lemnos o'er the rolling deep, to "seek the cave of Death's half-brother, Sleep." The dying Gorgias, we are told, being in a slumber, and asked how he did, answered, "Pretty well; only Sleep is commending me to the charge of his brother." Samuel Daniel apostrophizes "Care-charmer Sleep, son of the sable Night, brother to Death, in silent darkness born;" and so too, Beaumont and Fletcher apostrophize him in almost the selfsame words. So again their contemporary, John Webster, "O thou soft natural Death, that art joint twin to sweetest slumber!" Cowley's ode *in memoriam* of William Harvey, begins with sombre commemoration of a dismal and a fearful night, "when sleep, death's image, left his troubled breast, by something liker death possest." And the last verse of Denham's "Song to Morpheus" identifies the twins,—practically makes a hendiadys of them, as grammarians might call it:

> "Sleep, that is thy best repast,
> Yet of death it bears a taste,
> And both are the same thing at last."

Warton's Latin epigram on sleep, as *certissima mortis imago*, has been Englished by Wolcot with a beauty and felicity pronounced by critics to be worthy of the original:

> "Come, gentle sleep! attend thy votary's prayer;
> And, though death's image to my couch repair,
> How sweet, though lifeless, yet with life to lie,
> And, without dying, O how sweet to die!"

Shelley's opening of "Queen Mab" is a stock quotation:

"How wonderful is Death, Death and his brother Sleep! one pale as yonder waning moon, with lips of lurid blue; the other rosy as the morn when, throned on ocean's wave, it blushes o'er the world: yet both so passing wonderful!" But where, asks a prose writer of genius, where, in the sharp lineaments of rigid and unsightly death, is the calm beauty of slumber, telling of rest for the waking hours that are past, and gentle hopes and loves for those which are to come? "Lay death and sleep down, side by side, and say who shall find the two akin." But this is selecting such an aspect of mortality as comes not within the poet's purview. Prosaical in every fibre is Sancho Panza meant to be; yet in his famous invocation of blessings on the invention, or rather on the inventor, of sleep, which, quoth he, "covers a man all over, body and mind, like a cloak"—for Sancho has his poetical moods and tenses after all—he goes on to recognise the affinity which poetry so freely asserts: "It [sleep] has only one fault, as I have heard say, which is, that it looks like death: for between the sleeper and the corpse there is but little to choose." Shakspeare's Iachimo calls sleep the "ape of death." To die, to sleep,—muses Hamlet,—no more; and, by a sleep, to say we end the heart-ache, and the thousand natural ills that flesh is heir to, were a consummation devoutly to be wished. "Thy best of rest is sleep," soliloquizes the duke in "Measure for Measure,"

"And that thou oft provokest; yet grossly fear'st
Thy death, which is no more."

A couplet of Butler's, in a description of nightfall, tells how

. . . "sleep the wearied world relieved,
By counterfeiting death revived."

A Greek proverb designates sleep "the minor mysteries of death"—in allusion to the lesser Eleusinian mysteries as compared with the greater: "*ὕπνος τὰ μικρὰ τõυ θανάτου μυστήρια.*" Sir Thomas Overbury calls sleep, death's picture drawn to the life, or the twilight of life and death. "In sleep we kindly shake death by the hand; but when we are awaked, we will not know him." With the closing clause of this sentence compare the closing lines in the following picture by Byron, of man o'erlaboured with his being's strife, shrinking to "that sweet forgetfulness of life" which sleep induces:

> "There lie love's feverish hope and cunning's guile,
> Hate's working brain, and lull'd ambition's wile;
> O'er each vain eye oblivion's pinions wave,
> And quench'd existence crouches in a grave.
> What better name may slumber's bed become?
> Night's sepulchre, the universal home,
> Where weakness, strength, vice, virtue, sunk supine,
> Alike in naked helplessness recline;
> Glad for awhile to heave unconscious breath,
> Yet wake to wrestle with the dread of death,
> And shun, though day but dawn on ills increast,
> That sleep, the loveliest, since it dreams the least."

We term sleep a death, writes Sir Thomas Browne, and yet it is waking that kills us, and destroys those spirits that are the house of life. "It is that death by which we may be literally said to die daily; a death which Adam died before his mortality; a death whereby we live a middle and moderating point between life and death." And then the golden-tongued physician—in his *Religio Medici*—goes on to say that, in fine, so like death seemed to him sleep, that he dare not trust it without his prayers, and a half adieu to the world; and taking his farewell "in a colloquy with God," that is set in the key of the Evening Hymn, where we pray to be taught to dread the grave as little as our bed. So, in verses of his own weaving, this consummate master of stately rhetorical prose, beseeches God to make his sleep a holy trance:

> "Sleep is a death;—O make me try
> By sleeping, what it is to die!
> And as gently lay my head
> On my grave, as now my bed.
> Howe'er I rest, great God, let me
> Awake again at last with Thee.
> And thus assured, behold I lie
> Securely, or to wake or die.
> These are my drowsy days; in vain
> I do now wake to sleep again:

O come that hour when I shall never
Sleep again, but wake for ever!

"This is the dormitive I take to bedward; I need no other laudanum than this to make me sleep; after which I close my eyes in security, content to take leave of the sun, and sleep unto the resurrection."

George Herbert says, that—

"When boys go first to bed,
They step into their voluntary graves;
Sleep binds them fast; only their breath
Makes them not dead.
Successive nights, like rolling waves,
Convey them quickly, who are bound for death."

Ye children, does death ever alarm you? asks the venerable pastor in Tegner's *Children of the Lord's Supper*: "Death is the brother of Love, twin-brother is he, and is only more austere to behold." Shakspeare's nobleman is gazing with disgust on a sottish sleeper, when he exclaims, "Grim death, how foul and loathsome is thine image!" That image, as embodied in the form of a little child, has often inspired poets to strains of tender admiration. Malaspina, in one of Landor's unacted (not to say, with almost equal truth, unread) plays thus contemplates, and apostrophizes, such an image:—

"And still thou sleepest, my sweet babe! Is death
Like sleep? Ah, who then, who would fear to die?
How beautiful is all serenity!
Sleep, a child's sleep, oh how far more serene,
And oh, how far more beautiful than any!
Whether we breathe so gently, or breathe not,
Slight is the difference."

More familiar to every one in the least conversant with current literature—not ephemeral in its currency, or running so fast as to be, like that which decayeth and waxeth old, ready to vanish away—is Mrs. Browning's poem on a sleeping child—tired out with playing, and slumbering on the floor; the latter portion alone of which may here find room:—

"And God knows, who sees us twain, child at childish leisure,
I am near as tired of pain, as you seem of pleasure;—

Very soon, too, by His grace gently wrapt around me,
Shall I show as calm a face, shall I sleep as soundly!
Differing in this, that you clasp your playthings sleeping,
While my hand shall drop the few given to my keeping.
Differing in this, that I sleeping shall be colder,
And in waking presently, brighter to beholder.
Differing in this beside (sleeper, have you heard me?
Do you move, and open wide eyes of wonder toward me?)—
That while you I thus recall from your sleep,—I solely,—
Me from mine an angel shall, with reveille holy!"

——o——

ELIAB AND DAVID IN THE VALLEY OF ELAH.

I SAMUEL xvii. 28.

WHEN the Spirit of God came upon Saul, so that he prophesied among the company of prophets that met him, all that knew him beforetime asked one another what was this that was come to the son of Kish? was Saul also among the prophets? Insomuch that it became a proverb, "Is Saul also among the prophets?" No prophet is accepted in his own country; *that* is become a proverb too. And as with Saul, a young man among the prophets, so with youthful David among the men of war from their youth. Eliab, his eldest brother, knew, as he thought, the pride and the naughtiness of his heart in coming down to the camp to see the battle; but he knew not what sterling stuff there was in the stripling. *Why* had Jesse's youngest son come down hither? and with whom had he left those few sheep in the wilderness? Eliab's anger was kindled against David for his presumptuous and idle curiosity. His scorn was well-nigh as supreme as that of Goliath himself for the youth,—for he was but a youth, and ruddy, and of a fair countenance. Quit his proper rusticities and retirement for the valley of Elah, that bristled with spear-heads and resounded with the din of battle! a boy like him, that should be feeding his father's sheep at Bethlehem! Was there not a cause? None that Eliab knew of, for one. He had never seen anything in the lad to warrant this forwardness. Not to Eliab or his brethren was it given to foresee in that fresh-coloured shepherd boy the present slayer of Goliath of Gath, and the bosom friend of princely Jonathan, and the paulo-post-future king of Israel, Israel's sweetest singer, and the man after God's own heart.

The adage about unrecognised worth, on the part of kinsfolk and neighbours, the proverb of the prophet without honour in his own country and in his father's house—has its parallel passage in the *Hercules Furens* of Euripides—

> . . . "οὐ γάρ ἐσθ' ὅπου
> Εσθλόν τι δράσας μάρτυρ' ἂν λάβοις πάτραν."

Plutarch adopts it in his treatise on Exile, where he says that you very rarely find a wise man taken for such in his own country: "τῶν φρονιμωτάτων καὶ σοφωτάτων ὀλίγους ἂν εὕροις ἐν ταῖς ἑαυτῶν πατρίσι κεκηδευμένους."

The tradition that Pythagoras borrowed all his learning and philosophy from the East is rejected by modern scholars: could not so great a man, they ask, dispense with foreign teachers? And the answer is, that assuredly he could and did; but his countrymen, it is to be observed, by a very natural process of thought, looked upon his greatness as the result of his Eastern education. "No man is a prophet in his own country, and the imaginative Greeks were peculiarly prone to invest the distant and the foreign with striking attributes;" unable to believe in wisdom springing up from among themselves, they turned to the East as to a vast and unknown region, whence all novelty, even of thought, must come. "Πᾶσι τοῖς φιλοσόφοις," says a Greek philosopher, "ἔδοξε χαλεπὸς ἐν τῇ πατρίδι ὁ βίος."

As the first, so the most arduous conquests of Mohammed were, says Gibbon, those of his wife, his servant, his pupil, and his friend; since he presented himself as a prophet to those who were most conversant with his infirmities as a man. "Thus was Mohammed," writes Dean Milman, after recording the conversion of the child Ali, "the prophet of his household. Slowly however did he win proselytes, even among his own kindred. Three years elapsed before the faith received the accession of Abubeker and of Othman, the future caliphs. Mohammed at length is accepted as the prophet of his family, of the noble and priestly house of Hashem. Abu Talib, his uncle, remains almost alone an unbeliever. And now Mohammed aspires to be the prophet of his *tribe*." But in effect the "false" prophet is an exception to the rule of no prophet accepted in his own house and country. An American commentator on Shakspeare incidentally expounds that rule, in remarking on the degree to which our sense of truth is impeded or impaired by the pressure on our minds of what is actual and visible and present. A faithful painter may, he observes, portray a human face with all its characteristic expression, and in all its true individuality; and yet the nearest relatives are not only the hardest to satisfy, but, by the very nature of their familiarity with the subject, will often be the worst judges of the likeness. We are all of us, he adds, "very apt to fail in appreciating the best and noblest parts in the characters of those whom we know familiarly, for the thousand familiarities of common life interpose; and it is sad to think that often it is not until death has hallowed and idealized the character, that we can do it justice." Envy and jealousy, remarks David Hume in treating of the recognition of real genius, have too much place in a narrow circle, and even familiar acquaintance with the person of one thus gifted may diminish the applause due to his performance—that is, among those of his own age and country. Pindar and Æschylus, we are told, left their country because those who were born their equals could not endure to see them rise their superiors. "What a war against the gods is this!" a heathen admirer is made to exclaim: "it seems as if it were decreed by a public edict that no one shall receive from them any gift beyond a certain value; and that if they do receive it they shall be permitted to return the gods no thanks for it in their native city." There are towns so barbarous, remarks Boccaccio, in Landor's "Pentameron," that they must be informed by strangers of their own great man when they happen to have produced one; and would then detract from his merits, that they might not exhibit their awkwardness in doing him honour, or their shame in withholding it.

Charles IX., on a progress through Provence, sent for Nostradamus, and finding in what slight respect he was held by his countrymen, made a point of publicly declaring, with right royal emphasis, that he should take as a slight to himself the slighting of that philosopher.

In the Journal to Stella, Swift hails with cordiality—for the Dean could be cordial on occasion—the appreciation in polite English circles, by ministers and scholars, of Parnell the poet: "Lord Bolingbroke likes Parnell mightily; and it is pleasant to see that one who hardly passed for anything in Ireland makes his way here with a little friendly forwarding." In no unlike spirit and style writes Horace Walpole to Marshal Conway, then travelling abroad: "The honours you have received, though I have so little taste for such things myself, gave me great satisfaction; and I do not know whether there is not more pleasure in *not* being a prophet in one's own country, when one is almost received like Mohammed in every other. To be an idol at home is no assured touchstone of merit. Stocks and stones have been adored in fifty regions, but do not bear transplanting. The Apollo Belvedere and the Hercules Farnese may lose their temples, but never lose their estimation, by travelling." In another letter we have Walpole exclaiming, "But adieu, retrospect! it is as idle as prophecy, the characteristic of which is never to be believed where alone it could be useful, *i.e.*, in its own country." And once more, in a later epistle, commenting on the darksome aspect of the times: "That the scene grows very serious there is no doubt; nor do I assume vanity from having possessed the spirit of prophecy—a most useless talent, as predictions never serve as warnings. We know prophets are not honoured in their own country: where then should they be honoured? where they are not known? where probably they never are heard of?" But such notes of interrogation might be multiplied *ad libitum.*

It is to a professedly common-place philosopher we owe the remark, that while there are families in which there exists a preposterous over-estimate of the talents and acquirements of their several members, there are other families in which there exists a depressing and unreasonable under-estimate of the same. He speaks to his knowledge of such a thing as a family in which certain boys during their early education had it ceaselessly drilled into them that they were the idlest, stupidest, and most ignorant boys in the world; which boys had no sooner gone to a great public school than like rockets they went up forthwith to the top of their classes, and never lost their places there, and afterwards at the university distinguished themselves pre-eminently in honours: "It will not surprise people who know much of human nature, to be told that through this brilliant career of school and college work the home belief in their idleness and ignorance continued unchanged, and that hardly at its end was the toil-worn senior wrangler regarded as other than an idle and useless blockhead." The writer adds an example of his knowledge of a successful author—to be identified of course by *some* readers, whose relatives never believed, till the reviews assured them of it, that his writings were anything but "contemptible and discreditable trash."

The subject is renewed in the ensuing section, on the text of a prophet's non-acceptance in his own country.

—o—

THE PROPHET IN HIS OWN COUNTRY.

St. Luke iv. 24.

IT was with the emphasis of a "Verily I say unto you," that our Lord prefaced the assurance that no prophet is accepted in his own country. The speaker spoke from bitter experience. For neither did His brethren believe in Him. It was when He was come into His own country, and taught in their synagogues with a wisdom that astonished them, and wrought mighty works of a kind that bewildered them, that His own countrymen set about asking if this was not the carpenter's son? was not His mother the well-known Mary? were not

James, and Joses, and Simon, and Judas, His brethren? and His sisters, were they not all near at hand, and known as such? Whence then had this—οὗτος (indefinitely contemptuous)—all these attributes? And they were offended, scandalized, they found a stumbling-block in the condition of Him and His. A double answer was vouchsafed them: the significant restriction of wonder working, for He did not many mighty works there, because of their unbelief; and the more direct reply, in so many words, that a prophet is not without honour, save in his own country, and in his own house.

Montaigne adverts to this man, or that, having been a miracle to the world, in whom neither his wife nor his servant has ever seen anything remarkable: "Few men have been admired by their own domestics"—a sentence to which point and popularity have been given by the epigrammatic form of it, due to Marshal Catinat. "No one," Montaigne continues, "has been a prophet, not merely in his own house, but in his own country, as the experience of history shows. It is the same in matters of no consequence. . . . In my country of Gascony they look upon it as very droll to see me in print. The farther off I am read from my own home, the better I am esteemed; I am fain to purchase printers in Guienne,—elsewhere they purchase me." Ben Jonson takes note of the greater reverence paid to things remote or strange to us, than to much better, if these be nearer, and fall under our sense. "Men, and almost all sorts of creatures, have their reputation by distance. Rivers, the farther they run, and more from their spring, the broader they are, and greater. And where our original is known, we are the less confident; among strangers we trust fortune." Lord Evandale, in Scott's "Old Mortality," discerns at once the "extraordinary qualities" of Henry Morton, which had escaped the notice of his kinsfolk and friends: "You have not been long in learning all his extraordinary qualities, my lord," says old Major Bellenden. "I, who have known him from boyhood, could, before this affair, have said much of his good principles and good nature; but as to his high talents"—further on *that* head deponent saith not. The opinions of relatives as to a man's power, Dr. Wendell Holmes declares to be very commonly of little value; not so much because they sometimes over-rate their own flesh and blood, as some may suppose; as because, on the contrary, they are quite as likely to underrate those whom they have grown into the habit of considering like themselves. *Vile habetur quod domi est*, Seneca tersely says.

Edmund Burke, in early life, was not happy at home—there being none among the household on Arran Quay to sympathise with his dreams and his aspirations. "He might think himself a genius," says one of his many biographers, "but it was not to be expected that his own relations should yet think him one." Describing his position and influence in Lord Rockingham's administration, Mr. Macknight observes that it is, after all, a man's own relations who generally look with the least confidence on his long wrestle with adversity, and are most astonished when the tide turns, and a great victory succeeds to what had seemed to them a mere hopeless toil. "To some of the Irish Nagles on the Blackwater, the news that Edmund had been taken into the confidence of the great Whig Lord Rockingham, . . . must have seemed as extraordinary as it did to Joseph's brethren that he should have become so great a man in hostile Egypt."

Son pays le crut fou, says La Fontaine, of a Greek sage; *mais quoi! aucun n'est prophète chez soi.* Of Joan of Arc, and her early mental struggles, a French historian writes: "It behoves her to find in the bosom of her family some one who would believe in her: this was the most difficult part of all." Non-recognition, disparagement, cold obstruction. Societies and families, as Goethe says, behave in the same way to their dearest members, towns to their worthiest citizens. Consuelo advising Anzoleto to quit Venice, reminds him that "no person is a prophet in his own country. This is a bad place for one who has been seen running about in rags, and where any one may come to say of you, 'I was his protector, I saw his hidden talent, it was I who recommended him and procured his advance.'" Descartes had to support with philosophic patience the scorn of his family, impatient of a philosopher in it. Jean Bodin, neglected and slighted in his own land, exulted in the welcome accorded to his books in the English Universities, which printed as well as prized them: "il n'est pas rare que nous ayons besoin d'apprendre des étrangers ce que valent nos compatriotes," observes M. Léon Feugère.

Every rule has its exceptions, and most proverbs too. The case of St. Catharine, of Sienna, is cited by a Protestant biographer as "an exception to the rule that excludes a prophet from honour in his own country." The biographer of Edward Irving, recounting with enthusiasm the details of his reception in Annandale in 1828, adds that "for once the proverb seems to have failed. He had honour in his own country, where gentle and simple flocked to hear him,"—neighbouring ministers shutting up their kirks on the Sunday when he preached, and going the "long Sabbath-day's journey" across the Annandale moors to hear him, along with their people. La Bruyère points out on the one side a man recognised by the world at large as a master-mind, honoured and sought after by eager admirers, but at home, of no account at all; *petit dans son domestique et aux yeux de ses proches:* on the other hand, a man who is a prophet in his own house and country, who enjoys a *vogue* that is confined to his immediate surroundings, and who *s'applaudit d'un mérite rare et singulier qui lui est accordé par la famille dont il est l'idole.* But exceptions to a rule are commonly taken in confirmation of it; and the rule as to a prophet's home acceptance is held to be only confirmed, not disproved, by here and there a stray example in history to the contrary; such as Arnold, of Brescia, being rescued from captivity by some of those partisan nobles of Campania by whom he was honoured as a prophet: "Tanquam *prophetam in terrâ suâ* cum omni honore habebant." Or, as the experience, highly exceptional, of young Bernard of Clairvaux, the "strange and irresistible force" of whose character, as the historian of Latin Christianity describes it, enthralled his brothers one after another, and at length his sister. Off to the monastery of Clairvaux they trooped, a complete monastic brotherhood. The youngest boy lingered a short time with his aged father, and then joined the rest. "Even the father died a monk of Clairvaux in the arms of Bernard." But it was not, we are duly reminded, on his own kindred alone that Bernard wrought with this commanding power. "When he was to preach, wives hurried away their husbands, mothers withdrew their sons, friends their friends, from the resistless magic of his eloquence." And those that went—what went they out into the wilderness to hear? A prophet? Yea, and almost more than a prophet, by the verdict of his own country and of his father's house.

——o——

DESIRED BOON: REALIZED BANE.

PSALM cvi. 15; lxxviii. 22 sq.

WE read of those who tempted God in the desert, that He gave them their request, and sent leanness withal into their soul. So they did eat meat and were well filled, for He gave them their own desire; but while their meat was yet in their mouths, His wrath came upon them and slew the fattest of them, and smote down the chosen men of Israel.

A latter-day poetess, almost masculine in genius, as in outspoken vigour of diction, tells us that—

> "God answers sharp and sudden on some prayers,
> And thrusts the thing we have prayed for in our face,—
> A gauntlet with a gift in't,"

and sometimes poison in the gift. Well therefore may the authoress of these lines, which in their original import are scarcely applicable to our theme, make a distressed soul utter a petition that certainly is so:—

> . . . "'tis written in the Book,
> He heareth the young ravens when they cry;
> And yet they cry for carrion. O my God,—
> And we, who make excuses for the rest,
> We do it in our measure. Then I knelt,
> And dropped my head upon the pavement too,
> And prayed, since I was foolish in desire

Like other creatures, craving offal-food,
That He would stop His ears to what I said,
And listen only to the run and beat
Of this poor, passionate, helpless blood. . . ."

Ne mihi contingant quæ volo, sed quæ sunt utilia: the aspiration has been accepted as an adage, worthy of all acceptation, and of acceptation by all.

"Mais, sans cesse ignorants de nos propres besoins,
Nous demandons au ciel ce qu'il nous faut le moins."

To Shakspeare for an illustration. Pompey, not the Great, is anxious for Divine sanction to speed his ambitious resolves to a prosperous issue. If the great gods be just, he assumes, they will assist the deeds of justest men,—and therefore himself, as pre-eminently entitled to that designation. He is impatient, too, for this manifest favour from above; and sage Menecrates takes occasion not only to check his impatience in particular, but to give him a salutary warning on the subject in general:

. . . "We, ignorant of ourselves,
Beg often our own harms, which the wise powers
Deny us for our good; so find we profit
By losing of our prayers."

Xenophon tells us of Socrates, that when he prayed, his petition was only this—that the gods would give to him those things that were good; which he did, forasmuch as they alone knew what was good for man. "But he who should ask for gold or silver, or increase of dominion, acted not, in his opinion, more wisely than one who should pray for the opportunity to fight, or game, or anything of the like nature; the consequence of which, being altogether doubtful, might turn, for aught he knew, not a little to his disadvantage." For,

. . . "why, alas! do mortal men in vain
Of fortune, fate, or Providence complain?
God gives us what He knows our wants require,
And better things than those that we desire:
Some pray for riches; riches they obtain;
But, watched by robbers, for their wealth are slain;
Some pray from prison to be freed; and come,
When guilty of their vows, to fall at home;

> Murdered by those they trusted with their life,
> A favoured servant, or a bosom wife.
> Such dear-bought blessings happen every day,
> Because we know not for what things we pray."

There is a Greek prayer by an unknown poet, but highly commended by the most illustrious of Socrates' disciples: that sovran Jove would grant his subjects good, whether they pray for it or not; and avert from them evil, even though they pray for it.

> *Ζεῦ βασιλεῦ, τὰ μὲν ἐσθλὰ καὶ εὐχομένοις καὶ ἀνεύκτοις*
> *῎Αμμι δίδου· τὰ δὲ δεινὰ καὶ εὐχομένὸις ἀπαλέξοις.*

And it is to Plato's dialogue upon prayer that we owe the instructions imparted by Socrates to Alcibiades, upon which Addison has founded a paper in the *Spectator*. In that dialogue we read how Socrates met Alcibiades going to his devotions, and observing his eyes to be fixed upon the ground with great seriousness and attention—for even that fastest of fast young men could, it seems, be slow enough to say his prayers—told him that he had reason to be thoughtful upon that occasion, since it was possible for a man to bring down evil upon himself by his own supplications, and that those things which the gods sent him in answer to his petitions might turn to his destruction. This, says he, may not only happen when a man prays for what is mischievous in its own nature, as Œdipus implored the gods to sow dissension between his sons; but when he prays for what he believes would be for his good, and against what he believes would be to his detriment. This the philosopher shows must necessarily happen among us, since most men are blinded with ignorance, prejudice, or passion, which hinder them from seeing what things are really eligible for them. And all this, as his manner is, the philosopher teaches by examples.

It seems allowed that Juvenal took the cue of his tenth Satire, as well as Persius of his second, from the Dialogue of Plato aforesaid.

> "Evertêre domos totas, optantibus ipsis,
> Dii faciles. Nocitura togâ, nocitura petuntur
> Militiâ."

Or, as Englished by Mr. Owen of Warrington:

> "Th' indulgent gods whole houses have o'erthrown
> At men's own prayer;—the fatal choice their own.
> In war we ask but woes; in peace but woes," etc.

The Crassi, Pompeii, and the like, are represented as ruined by the assent of Heaven to their ambitious prayers—

> "Magnaque numinibus vota exaudita *malignis*."

Naples to Pompey a kind fever gave, to hide his honours in a welcome grave (the poetry of Parson Owen may pardonably be printed as prose). But public prayers arise: the gods allow the health requested by the erring vow: by Rome's and his cross fate that grave he fled, and lived—to lose his honours and his head.

> . . . "Sed multæ urbes, et publica vota
> Vicerunt. Igitur fortuna ipsius, et urbis,
> Servatum victo caput abstulit."

Juvenal crowds his satire with cases in point, historical and mythological, political and domestic. The sum of the discourse is this: that man should allow the higher powers themselves to determine what may be of advantage to him, and suitable to his real wants,—he being dearer to them than to himself:

> "Permittes ipsis expendere Numinibus quid
> Conveniat nobis, rebusque sit utile nostris:
> Nam pro jocundis aptissima quæque dabunt Dii.
> Carior est illis homo quàm sibi."

Montaigne bethinks him that a foremost proof of our imbecility is, that we cannot, by our own wish and desire, find out what we want. "What plan, how happily soe'er begun, That, when achieved, we do not wish undone?" And he repeats the old-world story of King Midas, who prayed to the gods that all he touched might be turned into gold; and so it was: his bread became gold, his wine gold, the feathers of his bed, his under-clothing and his over-coats, gold all: "so that he found himself overwhelmed with the fruition of his desire, and endowed with a boon so intolerable, that he was fain to unpray his prayers." In another essay Le Sieur Michel tells how severely the gods punished the wicked prayers of Œdipus, in granting them. "He had prayed that his children might amongst themselves determine the succession to his throne by arms: and was so miserable as to see himself taken at his word. We should not pray that all things fall out as our will would have them, but that our will should subserve what is just and right." Owen Feltham records his having observed that what we either desire or fear doth seldom happen—something we think not of, for the most part intervening. How infinitely we should perplex ourselves, he exclaims, if we could obtain whatever we might wish for! "Do we not often desire that, which we afterwards see would be our confusion? . . . Man could not be more miserable, than if left to choose for him self. . . . Nothing brings destruction on him sooner, than when he presumes to part the empire with God." As Aricie warns Theseus in the French tragedy:

> "Craignez, seigneur, craignez que le ciel rigoureux
> Ne vous haïsse assez pour exaucer vos vœux."

And two scenes later Theseus is himself sufficiently of the same mind to exclaim:

> "Ne précipite point tes funestes bienfaits,
> Neptune! j'aime mieux n'être exaucé jamais."

And afterwards again he utters the tristful line:

> "Inexorables dieux! qui m'avez trop servi."

So in a subsequent passage:

> "Je hais jusqu'aux soins dont m'honorent les dieux:
> Et je m'en vais pleurer leurs faveurs meurtrières,
> Sans plus les fatiguer d'inutiles prières.
> Quoi qu'ils fissent pour moi, leur funeste bonté
> Ne me saurait payer de ce qu'ils m'ont ôté."

Madame de Sévigné, in one of her letters to Bussy, moralizes on the superior wisdom of Heaven's disposal to man's proposal; and adds: "C'est ainsi que nous marchons en aveugles, ne sachant où nous allons, prenant pour mauvais ce qui est bon, prenant pour bon ce qui est mauvais, et toujours dans une entière ignorance." The optative mood of yesterday, a past tense, is changed in the present tense of to-day for deprecation and regret.

In one of his many onslaughts against conventionalism, Mr. Emerson says that what we ask daily is to be conventional. "Supply, most kind gods! this defect in my dress, in my form, in my fortunes, which puts me a little out of the ring; supply it, and let me be like the rest whom I admire, and on good terms with them." But the wise gods, according to this essayist, reply, "No, we have better things for thee. By humiliations, by defeats, by loss of sympathy, by gulfs of disparity, learn a wider truth and humanity than that of a fine gentleman,"—a Fifth-Avenue landlord, or a West-End householder, not being Mr. Emerson's ideal of the highest style of man. Æsop, Saadi, Cervantes, Regnard, he adds, have been taken by corsairs, left for dead, sold for slaves, and know the realities of human life.—With Mr. Carlyle, we will not complain, therefore, of Dante's miseries; who, had all gone right with him, as he wished it, might have been Prior, Podestà, or whatsoever they call it, of Florence, well accepted among neighbours,—in which case, the world had wanted one of the most notable works ever spoken or sung. "Florence would have had another prosperous Lord Mayor; and the ten dumb centuries continued voiceless, and the ten other listening centuries (for there will be ten of them and more) had no *Divina Comedia* to hear! We will complain of nothing. A nobler destiny was appointed for this Dante; and he, struggling like a man towards death and crucifixion, could not help fulfilling it. Give *him* the choice of his happiness! He knew not, more than we do, what was really happy, what was really miserable."

Visions, and hopes, and prospects, writes Horace Walpole, are pretty playthings for boys. "It is folly to vex one's self for what cannot last very long. Indeed, what can, even when one is young? Corydon firmly believes he shall be wretched for ever if he does not marry Phyllis. That misery can but last till she has lost her bloom. His eternal woe would vanish if her nose grew red. How often do our griefs become our comforts! I know what I wish to-day; not at all what I shall wish to-morrow. Sixty says, You did not wish for *me*, yet you would like to keep me. Sixty is in the right; and I have not a word more to say." The Strawberry Hill esquire was himself turning the shady side of sixty when he thus wrote. Of quite another school was that gentle and good Q.Q., as she styled herself, once popular, now almost forgotten, who thus moralized her song:

> "How false is found, as on in life we go,
> Our early estimate of bliss or woe!
> —Some sparkling joy attracts us, that we fain
> Would sell a precious birthright to obtain:
> There all our hopes of happiness are placed,
> Life looks without it like a joyless waste;
> No good is prized, no comfort sought beside,
> Prayers, tears implore, and will not be denied:
> Heaven pitying hears th' intemperate, rude appeal,
> And suits its answer to our truest weal.
> The self-sought idol, if at last bestow'd,
> Proves, what our wilfulness required—a goad.
> Ne'er, but as needful chastisement, is given
> The wish thus forced and torn and storm'd from Heaven;
> But if withheld, in pity, from our prayer,
> We rave, awhile, of torment and despair. . . .
> Meantime, Heaven bears the grievous wrong, and waits
> In patient pity till the storm abates . . .
> Deigning, perhaps, to show the mourner soon,
> 'Twas special mercy that denied the boon."

Chateaubriand's most sentimental of melancholy-mad heroes, overwhelmed, as he flatters himself, with imaginary sufferings, offers up a prayer for some real calamity to overtake him; and, to his cost, is taken at his word. "Dans mon délire, j'avais été jusqu'à désirer d'éprouver un malheur, pour avoir du moins un objet réel de souffrance: épouvantable souhait, que Dieu dans sa colère, a trop exaucé!" It is but the Christian (yet not too Christian) expression of the old pagan poet's gloomy verse: *magnaque numinibus vota exaudita malignis.*

There is a sonnet of Filicaja's, of which a good deal is made by Richardson in his History of Sir Charles Grandison,—the concluding lines being an impressive vindication of the ways of Providence to man : *Provvidenza alta infinita,* if it sometimes denies the favours we implore, denies in kindness; and seeming to deny a blessing, grants one in that very refusal : *o negar finge, e nel negar concede.*

William Collins the painter—a loving and lovable man as well as refined artist—in one of his letters home expresses his "decided opinion, that if the Almighty were to give us everything for which we feel desirous, we should as often find it necessary to pray to Him to take away as to grant new favours." And he refers to thousands of cases that he could bring forward in proof of his assertion.

It amounts to a sort of refrain in the melodious rhythm of that fragmentary prose-poem of De Quincey's, "The Daughter of Lebanon,"—the admonition of the prophet to the lovely woman in the Damascus market-place : "Ask what thou wilt—great or small—and through me thou shalt receive it from God. But, my child, ask not amiss. For God is able out of thy own evil asking to weave snares for thy footing. And oftentimes to the lambs whom He loves, He gives by seeming to refuse ; gives in some better sense, or" (and here the prophet's voice swelled into the power of anthems) "in some far happier world." And when the sun is declining to the west on the thirtieth day, the prophet iterates the strain of old : "Lady of Lebanon, the day is already come, and the hour is coming, in which my covenant must be fulfilled with thee. Wilt thou, therefore, being now wiser in thy thoughts, suffer God, thy new Father, to give by seeming to refuse ; to give in some better sense, or in some far happier world?" But the daughter of Lebanon sorrowed at these words; she yearned after her native hills, and the sweet twin-born sister with whom from infant days hand-in-hand she had wandered amongst the everlasting cedars. The delirium of fever, and approaching death, are next described; and again the evangelist sits down by her bedside, and rebukes the clouds that trouble her vision, and bids them stand no more between that dying Magdalen and the forests of Lebanon. Anon, we read how the blue sky parted to the right and to the left, laying bare the infinite revelations that can be made visible only to dying eyes; and how, as the child of Lebanon gazed upon the mighty visions, she saw bending forward from the heavenly host, as if in gratulation to herself, the one countenance for which she hungered and thirsted. "The twin-sister, that should have waited for her in Lebanon, had died of grief, and was waiting for her in Paradise. Immediately in rapture she soared upwards from her couch; immediately in weakness she fell back; and being caught by the evangelist, she flung her arms around his neck; whilst he breathed into her ear his final whisper, 'Wilt thou now suffer that God should give by seem ing to refuse?'—'Oh yes—yes—yes,' was the fervent answer from the daughter of Lebanon." Hitherto she had known not what to ask for as she ought. Hitherto her asking had been amiss: she had asked for she knew not what. But now her vision was purged. Now she had the second-sight that could pierce through and beyond the night-side of nature, and gaze on the land that is very far off. Hitherto she had, at the best, seen through a glass darkly; but now, it might be said, face to face. So that she knew what to ask for, now.

Chactas, the blind old sachem in Chateaubriand's Wertherian romance, is made to bring that once enthusiastically admired story to an end by relating a parable to his woe-fraught young listener. It tells how the Meschacebé, soon after leaving its source among the hills, began to feel weary of being a simple brook; and so asked for snows from the mountains, water from the torrents, rain from the tempests; until, its petitions granted, it burst its bounds, and ravaged its hitherto delightsome banks. At first the proud stream exulted in its force; but seeing ere long that it carried desolation in its flow, that its progress was now doomed to solitude, and that its waters were for ever turbid, it came to regret the humble bed hollowed out for it by nature,—the birds, the flowers, the trees, and the brooks, hitherto the modest companions of its tranquil course.

The moral of the myth of Tithonus is one for all time. Mr. Tennyson has pointed it for ours. He shows us in Tithonus a white-haired shadow roaming like a dream the ever silent spaces of the East; and from this grey shadow, once a man, the wailing utterance of a sad story comes:—

"I ask'd thee, 'Give me immortality.'
Then didst thou grant my asking with a smile,
Like wealthy men who care not how they give.
But thy strong Hours indignant work'd their wills,
And beat me down and marr'd and wasted me,
And tho' they could not end me, left me maim'd
To dwell in presence of immortal youth,
And all I was, in ashes. . . .
. . . Let me go: take back thy gift:
Why should a man desire in any way
To vary from the kindly race of men,
Or pass beyond the goal of ordinance
Where all should pass, as is most meet for all?
* * * * *
Why wilt thou ever scare me with thy tears,
And make me tremble lest a saying learnt,
In days far off, on that dark earth, be true?
'The gods themselves cannot recal their gifts.'"

—o—

"AND HE DIED."

GENESIS v. *passim.*

WELL known is Addison's reference to an eminent man in the Romish Church, who upon reading in the Book of Genesis how that all the days that Adam lived were nine hundred and thirty years, and he died; and all the days of Seth were nine hundred and twelve years, and he died; and all the days of Methuselah were nine hundred and sixty nine years, and he died;—immediately shut himself up in a convent, an absolute recluse from the world, as not thinking anything in this life worth pursuing, which had not regard to another.

What man is he that liveth, and shall not see death?

"Dead!—Man's 'I was,' by God's 'I am'—
All hero-worship comes to that.
High heart, high thought, high fame, as flat
As a gravestone. Bring your *Jacet jam*—
The epitaph's an epigram."

So writes Mrs. Browning. And thus writes Barry Cornwall, on the same trite text; it is the last stanza of the History of a Life, and of a successful one:—

"And then—he died. Behold before ye
Humanity's poor sum and story;
Life—death—and all that is of glory."

And again, in the same poet's chanson of the time of Charlemagne, the stanza that magnifies that hero-king, and tells how he fought and vanquished Lombard, Saxon, Saracen, and ruled every race he conquered with a deep consummate skill—is followed by one beginning,

"But—he died! and he was buried
In his tomb of sculptured stone," etc.

And once again, in one of this author's dramatic fragments is sketched the career of what Mr. Carlyle would call a "foiled potentiality"—of one who, in favourable circumstances, might have been, but who in prosaic reality and the matter-of-fact pressure of this work-a-day world, never actually became, great. Had he but lived under better auspices, he would have been—

B. "A king?
A. A *man!* what else,
King, emperor, tyrant, shah, would matter not.
He would have been—a name; such as of old
Grew into gods!
B. And so he died?
A. He died."

Death stands everywhere in the background, as the elder Schlegel says in his analysis of the elements of tragic poetry, and to it every well or ill-spent moment brings us nearer and closer; and even when a man has been so singularly fortunate as to reach the utmost term of life without any grievous calamity, the inevitable doom still awaits him to leave or to be left by all that is most dear to him on earth. In the words, most musical, most melancholy, of the laureate,

"The woods decay, the woods decay and fall,
The vapours weep their burthen to the ground;

Man comes and tills the field, and lies beneath;
And after many a summer dies the swan."

Addison, in another essay than that already referred to, describes an afternoon he passed in Westminster Abbey, straying through and lingering in the churchyard, the cloisters, and the church, "amusing himself," as the phrase then ran—not quite in our frivolous sense—with the tombstones and the inscriptions that he met with in those several regions of the dead, most of which recorded nothing else of the buried person, but that he was born upon one day, and died upon another; the whole history of his life being comprehended in those two circumstances that are common to all mankind. The "Spectator" could not but look upon these registers of existence, whether of brass or marble, as a kind of satire upon the departed persons, who had left no other memorial of them but that they were born, and that they died. Mr. de Quincey characteristically opened his autobiographic sketches in their original form, with the avowal that nothing makes such dreary and monotonous reading as the old hackneyed roll-call, chronologically arranged, of inevitable facts in a man's life. "One is so certain of the man's having been born, and also of his having died, that it is dismal to be under the necessity of reading it." The man—a man—any man—every man. It is the common lot. And we know what James Montgomery has made of the Common Lot. Here are two or three of the stanzas that are most to the purpose:—

"Once in the flight of ages past,
There lived a man: and who was he?
Mortal! howe'er thy lot be cast,
That man resembled thee.

* * * * *

"He suffered,—but his pangs are o'er;
Enjoy'd,—but his delights are fled;
Had friends,—his friends are now no more;
And foes,—his foes are dead.

* * * * *

"He saw whatever thou hast seen;
Encounter'd all that troubles thee:

He was—whatever thou hast been ;
He is—what thou shalt be.

* * * * *

"The annals of the human race,
Their ruins, since the world began,
Of him, afford no other trace
Than this,—THERE LIVED A MAN !"

There lived a man—lived, and loved, and learned, and laboured—enjoyed the common joys of his kind, endured the common sufferings. AND HE DIED. Old Egeus mooted a veritable truism when moralizing thus, in Chaucer :—

"Yit ither ne lyvede never man, he seyde,
In al this world, that some tyme he ne deyde."

A French historian comments on this characteristic of old cloister chronicles, that the obscurest event of the cloister holds in them as conspicuous a place as the greatest revolutions in history. For instance, in a chronicle cited by him of the year of grace 732, which produced the battle of Poictiers, whereby Charles Martel arrested the vast invasion of Islamism, not a line is vouchsafed to that event. In fact, the year is passed over without notice, as containing nothing really deserving of notice. But beside a date expressly given, we read, "Martin est mort,"—Martin being an unknown monk of the Abbey of Corvey ; and, farther on again, "Charles, maire du palais, est mort." Martin was an unknown monk, and he died. Charles Martel was mayor of the palace, and the conqueror at Poictiers, and he died. Well remarks M. Demogeot, that "tous les hommes deviennent egaux devant la secheresse laconique de ces premiers chroniqueurs." "We must all go, that is certain," writes Mrs. Piozzi to Sir James Fellows, "and 'tis the only thing that *is* certain. Καὶ ἀπεθανε ends all the cases Dr. James quotes from your old friend Hippocrates." All the physician's cases have the same terminal affix, AND HE DIED. Very long-lived some of them may be ; but, as Mr. Browning puts it in his fine poem of "Saul,"

"But the licence of age has its limit ; thou diest at last."

We are told of St. Anschar, whose missionary career in Sweden is commemorated in Milman's "Latin Christianity," that the ardour of youth had begun to relax his strict austerity of monastic discipline, when all at once the world was startled by the tidings of Charlemagne's death. That the mighty sovran of so many kingdoms must suffer the common lot, struck young Anschar as something beyond the common; and from that hour he lived in the world as not of it, and bore on his way through it as verily a stranger and a pilgrim upon earth, with serious work to do, but working in and walking by faith, not sight.

Marcus Antoninus, in his self-communings, bids himself consider how many physicians are dead that used to value themselves upon the cure of their patients, and how many astrologers who thought themselves great men by foretelling the deaths of others; how many warriors, who had knocked out the brains of thousands upon thousands; and how many tyrants who managed the power of life and death with as much rigour as if they had been themselves immortal.

Among the pointed sayings that have been thought worthy of preservation—by Gibbon, for example—of Hormisdas, a fugitive prince of Persia, who was at Rome in the fourth century, is this,—"that one thing only had displeased him, to find that men died at Rome as well as elsewhere." Courtiers have avowed themselves shocked at the non-exception of royalty from the universal doom. A courtly preacher, who had announced the unconditional fact that we are all mortal, is said to have checked himself, on remembering that royalty was present, and to have qualified the assertion by the circumspect salvo, "At least, nearly all." * Lewis the Eleventh was too shrewd a man to give heed to such courtly suggestions; otherwise, if ever there were prince that would fain have believed the fiction, it was he, so abhorrent to his shuddering nature was the imagina-

* Perhaps a better version of perhaps the same story is that of the young Dauphin exclaiming to his right reverend preceptor, when some book mentioned a king as having died, "Quoi donc, les rois meurent-ils?" "Quelquefois, monseigneur," was the reply—ironical, or parasitical, as may be.

tion of his own decease. And Commines relates how physicians combined their remedies with the sacred objects produced from the sanctuary to avert the dread decree, "pour lui allonger la vie. Toutefois le tout n'y fasoit rien; et falloit qu'il passât par là où les autres ont passés." And he died. All stories have the same ending.

> "The Frenchman first in literary fame;
> Mention him, if you please. Voltaire? The same,
> With spirit, genius, eloquence supplied,
> Lived long, wrote much, laughed heartily—and died."

That very old poet, Stephen Hawes, for discovering in whom "one fine line," Warton was called "the indulgent historian of our poetry," tells his own life-story quite to an end, including the particulars of his funeral and epitaph. A finer critic than Warton, or than Warton's critic, bids those who smile at the design dismiss their levity before the poet's utterance:—

> "O! mortal folke, you may beholde and see
> Howe I lye here, sometime a mighty knight.
> The end of joye and prosperitie
> Is death at last thorough his course and might.
> After the day there cometh the dark night,
> For though the day appear ever so long,
> At last the bell ringeth to evensong—"

"Ringeth," says Mrs. Browning, "in our ear with a soft and solemn music, to which the soul is prodigal of echoes."

What—asks the most meditative of Roman emperors, in his Meditations, discussing with himself the ultimate fate, often reluctantly undergone, of certain long-lived persons—what are they more than those who went off in their infancy? What is become of Cæcilianus, Fabius, Julianus, and Lepidus? Their heads are all laid somewhere. They buried a great many; but at last they came to be buried themselves. Mr. Dickens, as well as Hervey, has his meditations among the tombs,—and these are of them in the little hemmed-in churchyards of the city—these, over an old tree at the church window, with no room for its branches, that has seen out generation after generation of civic worthies: "So with the tomb of the old Master of the

M

Company, on which it drips. His son restored it, and died; his daughter restored it, and died; and then he had been remembered long enough, and the tree took possession of him, and his name cracked out." To quote Chaucer again:

> "That is to seyn, in youthe or elles in age,
> He moot ben deed, the kyng as schal a page."

Cranmer's transported prevision, in Shakspeare, of the grand future that awaited the infant princess Elizabeth, is dashed with sadness towards the end—the strain subsiding into a minor key—by the unwelcome but inevitable reflection, "But she must die." So muses and moralises Talbot again, in another of the historical plays:

> "But kings and mightiest potentates must die;
> For that's the end of human misery."

And Warwick, in another of them, finding that, of all his lands, is nothing left him but his body's length, exclaims, as one that at last feels it feelingly,

> "Why, what is pomp, rule, reign, but earth and dust?
> And, live we how we can, yet die we must."

And once more in yet another of them, when King John dies, and Salisbury witnessing the death, exclaims, "But now a king —now thus!" the prince who is to succeed takes home the lesson to himself, and confesses, in diction borrowed from the mere machinery of clockwork,

> "Even so must I run on, and even so stop."

In exhibiting to Odysseus in the shades below a group of the fairest and most famous of women, Homer has been supposed by some of his commentators to have designed a lecture on mortality to the whole sex. Tertullian's trumpet is blown with no uncertain sound when *he* thus addresses the frivolous fair of his day: "I have said, ye are gods, and ye are all the children of the Most High. . . . But, O gods of flesh and blood, O gods of earth and dust, ye shall die like men, and all your glory shall fall to the ground, *veruntamen sicut homines moriemini.*" This is in Tertullian's description of the vain and prodigal and exacting beauty. Suggestive in its way is an anecdote related by Mrs. Thrale about Sir Joshua Reynolds's picture of two fashionable belles, Mrs. Crewe and Mrs. Bouverie, attired as two shepherdesses, and with this motto attached, *Et in Arcadiâ ego.* What could that mean? is Dr. Johnson said to have asked. Reynolds replied that the king could have told him: "*He* saw it yesterday, and said at once, 'Oh, there is a tombstone in the background. Ay, ay, death is even in Arcadia.'" The thought is said to have been borrowed from Poussin—where some gay revellers stumble over a death's head, with a scroll proceeding from its mouth, saying, Et in Arcadiâ *ego.*

Memorable at Saladin's banquet to Richard and his peers—ever memorable among the banners and pennons, the trophies of battles won and kingdoms overthrown, is the long lance displaying a shroud, "the banner of Death, with this impressive inscription—'Saladin, King of Kings—Saladin, Victor of Victors—Saladin must Die.'"

Poet Prior laments with courtly distress the inflexible fact that the British monarch, to whom he is addressing his *carmen seculare* for the year of grace MDCC., must go the way of all flesh:

> "But a relentless destiny
> Urges all that e'er was born:
> Snatch'd from her arms, Britannia once must mourn
> The demi-god; the earthly half must die."

For as Master Matthew puts it in another ode:—

> "Alike must every state and every age
> Sustain the universal tyrant's rage;
> For neither William's power nor Mary's charms
> Could, or repel, or pacify his arms.
> * * * *
> Wisdom and eloquence in vain would plead
> One moment's respite for the learned head:
> Judges of writings and of men have died
> (Mæcenas, Sackville, Socrates, and Hyde);
> And in their various turns their sons must tread
> Those gloomy journeys which their sires have led.

"The ancient sage, who did so long maintain
That bodies die, but souls return again,
With all the births and deaths he had in store
Went out Pythagoras, and came no more.
And modern Asgill,* whose capricious thought
Is yet with stores of wilder notions fraught,
Too soon convinced, shall yield that fleeting breath
Which played so idly with the darts of death."

The truism appears to have been a favourite theme with Prior, who expatiates upon it in a variety of keys. Here is one other specimen from his stores, in octosyllabic metre :—

"All must obey the general doom,
Down from Alcides to Tom Thumb.
Grim Pluto will not be withstood
By force or craft. Tall Robin Hood,
As well as Little John, is dead—
(You see how deeply I am read)."

Does not Cervantes begin the last chapter of his great work with the reflection that, as all human things, especially the lives of men, are transitory, ever advancing to their decline and final termination, so "Don Quixote was favoured by no privilege of exemption from the common fate," for the period of his dissolution came when he least thought of it—and he died.

Death's final conquest is the subject of a fine poem of James Shirley's; the piece by which he is, in every sense, best remembered. How death lays his icy hands on kings, is there told with pitiless candour; and the merry monarch, *par excellence,* Charles the Second, is said to have greatly admired the poetry, if not the candour, of Shirley's strain. Early or late, all stoop to fate; that is the trite topic. But the moral is noble, and nobly expressed. The poet reminds laurelled victors that the garlands are withering on their brow, and that soon upon death's purple altar shall the "victor victim" bleed :—

"All heads must come
To the cold tomb;

* John Asgill distinguished himself by maintaining in a treatise now forgotten, that death is no natural necessity, and that to escape it is within the range of the humanly practicable. But Asgill's biography, like every other, has for a last page the inevitable "And he died."

Only the actions of the just
Smell sweet and blossom in the dust."

The first verse only of George Herbert's "Virtue" is familiar to men; all four have a music and a meaning of their own:—

"Sweet day, so cool, so calm, so bright,
The bridal of the earth and sky,
The dew shall weep thy fall to-night;
For thou must die.

"Sweet rose, whose hue angry and brave
Bids the rash gazer wipe his eye,
Thy root is ever in its grave,
And thou must die.

"Sweet spring, full of sweet days and roses,
A box where sweets compacted lie,
My music shows ye have your closes,
And all must die.

"Only a sweet and virtuous soul,
Like seasoned timber, never gives;
But though the whole world turn to coal,
Then chiefly lives."

——o——

AN ULTRA-PROTESTER.

St. Matthew xxvi. 33–35, 69–75.

TO have written it ultra-Protestant, would mislead into an expectation of polemical matter, offensive to Orangeism, and entirely alien from the purpose. For who is the hyper-protester, not to write it ultra-Protestant, of whom we speak? None other than St. Peter. Nominally the first Pope. But let that pass. Whether technically an ultra-Protestant or not,—let that pass too. It is with his surplusage of protestations, vehemently asserted, and anon ignominiously ignored, that we are at present concerned. Though all men, all, should be offended because of Christ, should stumble and fall because of Him, yet would he never be offended, never stumble, never lose his footing, firm as a rock, firm as his own name, Peter, Cephas; a rock on which the Church was to be built. The protest ofthe apostle won no meed of thanks and assurance of conviction from his Lord. He who needed not that any should testify of man, for He knew what was in man--and knew what was wanting in *this* man,—waved aside, as absolutely worthless, the perfervid protestations of the impulsive son of Jonas. Thrice should Peter deny Him before dawn of another day. Deny Him? Had it come to that? The protester must become ultra in his protests. "Though I should die with Thee, yet will I not deny Thee!" It would be beside the mark here to take into account the other *voces et prœterea nihil*, echoing the same thing—protested notes at the best—for likewise also said all the disciples. Peter is their representative man, and ours.

Gertrude's comment in "Hamlet," on the accumulated asseverations of the stage-queen, "The lady doth protest too much, methinks," has passed into a proverb. "The more vehemently they assert, the less credit they obtain for sincerity," observes Hartley Coleridge, of some examples of impulsive womankind. Racine's Bérénice turns the tables on Titus in this regard, when she tells him,

> "Hé quoi! vous me jurez une éternelle ardeur,
> Et vous me la jurez avec cette froideur!
> Pourquoi même du ciel attester la puissance?
> Faut-il par des serments vaincre ma défiance?
> Mon cœur ne prétend point, seigneur, vous démentir;
> Et je vous en croirai sur un simple soupir."

How fulsome and hollow, exclaims Marcus Antoninus, does that man look who cries, "I'm resolved to deal clearly with you." Hark you, friend, the philosophic emperor addresses him, "what need of all this flourish? let your actions speak." Mr. Disraeli, in his earliest book, has an eloquent paragraph on "that eagerness of protestation which," in the man charged with criminality, "is a sure sign of crime." There is as much of overacting one's part on the great stage of life, as on the mimic boards; and that with graver issues and a drearier fate.

When the subtle and ambitious John of Gischala, pursuing

his own dark course, as it is traced in the "History of the Jews," joined outwardly the party of Ananus, and was active beyond others in council and camp, he yet kept up a secret correspondence with the Zealots, to whom he betrayed all the movements of the assailants. "To conceal this secret he redoubled his assiduities, and became so extravagant in his protestations of fidelity to Ananus and his party, that he completely overacted his part, and incurred suspicion." His intended dupes began gradually, and none too soon, to look with a jealous eye on their too obsequious, most obedient, and most devoted servant.

Describing the ten dreary years during which (A.D. 1198—1208), with but short intervals of truce, Germany was abandoned to all the horrors of civil war, Dean Milman observes that "the repeated protestations" of Pope Innocent III., that *he* was not the cause of these fatal discords, betray the fact that he was accused of the guilt, and that he had to wrestle with his own conscience to acquit himself of the charge. Sir Thomas Overbury suggestively avers that

> "He that says oft that he is not in love,
> By repetition doth himself disprove."

Hawthorne remarks that Italian asseverations of any questionable fact, though uttered with rare earnestness of manner, never vouch for themselves as coming from any depth, like roots drawn out of the substance of the soul, with some of the soil clinging to them. Their energy expends itself in exclamation. The vaulting ambition of their hyperboles overleaps itself, and falls on the other side. Swift refers to oaths in the mouth of a gamester, as ever most used as their truth is most questioned.

> "'Tis not the many oaths that make the truth,
> But the plain single vow, that is vowed true,"

says Shakspeare's Diana of Florence. And though from Shakspeare to Wolcot is a descent indeed, Peter Pindar is for once quotable when he writes,

> "Truth needs not, John, the eloquence of oaths,
> Not more so than a decent suit of clothes

> Requires of broad gold lace the expensive glare,
> That makes the linsey-woolsey million stare;
> Besides, a proverb, suited to my wish,
> Declares that swearing never catches fish."

That scapegrace guardian of George Canning's boyhood, Mr. Reddish, is said to have been significantly fond, on quite trivial occasions, of making affidavits,—"the refuge of base and vulgar minds," Robert Bell calls them,—as if he, Reddish, felt that his word was not to be believed. Cowper is caustic in his application of St. Paul's statement, that oaths terminate all strife, for "some men have surely then a peaceful life!" he infers, in lines that go on to tell how

> "Asseveration blustering in your face
> Makes contradiction such a hopeless case;
> In every tale they tell, or false or true,
> Well-known, or such as no man ever knew,
> They fix attention, heedless of your pain,
> With oaths like rivets forced into the brain;
> And e'en when sober truth prevails throughout,
> They swear it, till affirmance breeds a doubt."

The imprecation of Corneille's Dorante, *Que le foudre à vos yeux m'écrase si je mens!* only evokes from Clarice the contemptuous rebuff, *Un menteur* [which, and more than which, emphatically, Dorante is, for he is *Le Menteur*,] *est toujours prodigue de serments.* So again Racine's Theseus: *Toujours les scélérats ont recours au parjure*,—when Hippolytus begins to call heaven, and earth, and universal nature to witness, etc. So, too, Chamont, in Otway's tragedy: "When a man talks of love, with caution trust him; but if he swears, he'll certainly deceive thee." Indeed, as Owen Feltham has it, wherever there is too much profession, there is cause for suspicion. "Reality cares not to be tricked out with too taking an outside; and deceit, when she intends to cozen, studies disguise. Least o all should we be taken with swearing asseverations. Truth needs not the varnish of an oath to make her plainness credited." Fielding's Pettifogger, on a certain occasion, calling to mind that he had not been sworn, as he usually was, before he gave his evidence, "now bound what he had declared with so many oaths and imprecations, that the landlady's ears were shocked, and she put a stop to his swearing, by assuring him of her belief," inconsiderately enough, as the manner of the man might have proved. Scott's Jorworth, when heaping asseveration on asseveration, is cut short by the honest Fleming he is striving to mislead: "Stop, good Jorworth; thou heapest thine oaths too thickly on each other, for me to value them to the right estimate; that which is so lightly pledged, is sometimes thought not worth redeeming." So again Monkbarns tells the gaberlunzie, after hearing his story of the adept, "I am strongly disposed to believe that you have spoken the truth, the rather, that you have not made any of those obtestations of the superior powers, which I observe you and your comrades always make use of when you mean to deceive folks." The author of "London Labour and the London Poor," recounts the redundance of "Glory be to God! it's the thruth I'm telling of you, sir," etc., etc.; which he had to hear from Irish mendicity, or mendacity, or both. "The dignity of truth is lost with much protesting," the Cicero of Jonson's "Catiline" says.

Take up any ordinary history, and you are but too sure to come across examples enough and to spare, of people who did protest too much, and did not keep their word. Glance at Alison's big book, and on one page you read, of Napper Tandy, for instance, "But the conduct of this leader was far from keeping pace with these vehement protestations; for no sooner did he hear of the reverse sustained by the French corps which had landed in Killala Bay, than he re-embarked on board the French brig *Anacreon*, and got safe across the channel." On another we have Tippoo Saib striving to disarm the suspicions of the British Government by "professions of eternal gratitude and attachment," and considerably overacting his part. On another we have Napoleon bidding Marmont "spare no protestations of assistance to Turkey;" and himself assuring the Turkish ambassador that, "his right hand was not more inseparable from his left, than the Sultan Selim should ever be to him;" in consequence of which protestations, Turkey threw herself into the breach against both Russia and England, only to find the imperial ultra-protester, within one little month from the protestations, arranging for the immediate partition, with the Czar, of the Turkish dominions. Look, again, at Benjamin Constant, launching his vehement philippic against Napoleon, in the *Journal des Débats* on the eve of the Emperor's return from Elba, and declaring, "Never will I crawl, like a base deserter from power to power. Under Louis XVIII. we enjoy a representative government. Under Bonaparte we endured a government of Mamelukes. He is an Attila, a Gengis Khan!" And then we read how, a few days after this fulmination, Constant, the *in*constant, became a councillor of state under this Attila, an active supporter of this Gengis Khan. Another ground of indictment against Napoleon is found by Alison in the eagerness of his protestations to Russia, that he had no way connived at the election of Bernadotte to the throne of Sweden, when next vacant. "The extreme anxiety which Napoleon evinced for some time afterwards to convince the court of St. Petersburg that he had taken no concern in this election, only renders it the more probable that he was in reality at the bottom of the transaction." The asseverations commenced by the younger Pennyboy, in Jonson's "Staple of News," are declined and dismissed, by the elder, who knows their worth, with this summary and suggestive caution:

"No vows, no promises; too much protestation
Makes that suspected oft, we would persuade."

——o——

FLEETING SHADOWS.

JOB xiv. 2.

AS man that is born of a woman is of few days, and full of trouble; as he is said to come forth like a flower, only to be cut down, so is it further said of him, that "he fleeth also as a shadow, and continueth not." His days are like a shadow that declineth. He himself is gone as a shadow that fleeteth away. For man is vanity, his days are as a shadow, saith the psalmist. And the preacher, whose text is vanity of vanities, all is vanity, finds vexation of spirit in meditations on man, all the days of whose vain life he spendeth as a shadow.

What shadows we are, and what shadows we pursue! The exclamation was that of a great statesman, amid the excitement and the contests of public life, when there reached him news of the sudden death of a fellow-candidate and colleague. Shadow-hunted shadows. The pursued and the pursuers—the game and the sportsmen—shadows all. Burke's exclamation was often in the mind of the late Sir James Graham, and, towards the close of his life, not unfrequently on his lips.

"'Ορῶ γὰρ ἡμᾶς οὐδὲν ὄντας ἄλλο, πλὴν
Εἴδωλ', ὅσοιπερ ζῶμεν, ἢ κούφην ΣΚΙΑΝ."

O curas hominum! O quantum est in rebus inane! Men were ever of old, and they are found to be now, the willing victims of illusion in all stages of life: children, youths, adults, and old men, all, as Emerson puts it, are led by one bauble or another. "There are as many pillows of illusion as flakes in a snow-storm. We wake from one dream into another dream. The toys, to be sure, are various, and are graduated in refinement to the quality of the dupe." For instance, the intellectual man requires a fine bait, while the sots are easily amused. "But everybody is drugged with his own frenzy, and the pageant marches at all hours, with music and banner and badge." Shadows before, and shadows behind, and all fleeting. False glozing pleasures, to adopt George Herbert's diction, are the shadowy lure,

. . . "casks of happiness,
Foolish night-fires, women's and children's wishes,
Chases in arras, gilded emptiness,
Shadows well mounted, dreams in a career,
Embroider'd lies, nothing between two dishes,—
These are the pleasures here."

Marcus Antoninus, in his "Meditations," harps on the note of shadow-hunting or shadow-hunted shadows. You will soon be reduced to ashes and a skeleton, he keeps telling himself;

and even if you leave a name,—what is a name? what is in a name? *Vox et præterea nihil.* The shadows you, a shade, pursue, are miserably shadowy. The prizes of life are, he says, so paltry, that to scuffle for them is ridiculous, and puts him in mind of a set of puppies snarling for a bone, or of the contests of children for a toy. Wherever he looks, the wide world over, and in whatever age of its history, he sees abundance of people very busy, and big with their projects, who presently drop off, and moulder to dust and ashes. The freshest laurels wither apace, and the echoes of Fame are soon silenced. The "insect youth" that people the air and make it murmurous with busy life,—is not their close resemblance to the children of men one of poetry's common-places?

"To Contemplation's sober eye,
  Such is the race of man;
And they that creep, and they that fly,
  Shall end where they began.

"Alike the busy and the gay,
But flutter through life's little day,
In fortune's varying colours drest;
  Brushed by the hand of rough Mischance,
  Or chilled by Age, their airy dance
They leave, in dust to rest."

Having asked to be told her fortune by the Wise Wight of Mucklestane Moor, Miss Ildeston, in Scott's story, is told by the cynical recluse, that it is a simple one; an endless chase through life after follies not worth catching, and when caught, successively thrown away—a chase, pursued from the days of tottering infancy to those of old age upon his crutches. "Toys and merry-making in childhood—love and its absurdities in youth—spadille and basto in age, shall succeed each other as objects of pursuit: flowers and butterflies in spring,—butterflies and thistledown in summer,—withered leaves in autumn and winter—all pursued, all caught, all flung aside." *Que vont elles faire de si grand matin*, Cleopas asks his demon-guide, concerning *ces personnes* whose early rising and eager bustle have caught and fixed his attention. "Ce que vous souhaitez de savoir, reprit le Démon, est une chose digne d'être observée. Vous allez voir un tableau des soins, des mouvements, des peines que les pauvres mortels se donnent pendant cette vie, pour remplir, le plus agréablement qu'il leur est possible, ce petit éspace qui est entre leur naissance et leur mort." *Telle est la vie*, as most of us live it.

"Dream after dream ensues,
And still they dream that they shall still succeed,
And still are disappointed,"

writes William Cowper. Not at all in the same measure or manner, but pretty much to the same effect, writes the picturesque poet of Bells and Pomegranates:

"It is but to keep the nerves at strain,
To dry one's eyes and laugh at a fall,
And baffled, get up to begin again,—
So the chase take up one's life, that's all.
While, look but once from your farthest bound,
At me so deep in the dust and dark,
No sooner the old hope drops to ground
Than a new one, straight to the self-same mark
I shape me—ever removed."

There is much that is suggestive in the Abbé Gerbet's discoursings in the Catacombs at Rome. "Ce dernier calque de l'homme," he says, in what has been called a commentary on Bossuet's *mot*, that the corpse of a man becomes a *je ne sais quoi*, for which there is no name in any language—"cette forme si vague, si effacée, à peine empreinte sur une poussière à peu près impalpable, volatile, presque transparente, d'un blanc mat et incertain, est ce qui donne le mieux quelque idée de ce que les anciens appelaient une *ombre*. Cette forme est plus frêle que l'aile d'un papillon, plus prompte à s'evanouir que la goutte de rosée suspendue à un brin d'herbe au soleil; un peu d'air agité par votre main, un souffle, un son deviennent ici des agents puissants qui peuvent anéantir en une seconde ce que dix-sept siècles, peut-être, de destruction ont épargné. Voyez,—vous venez de respirer, et la forme a disparu. Voilà la fin de l'histoire de l'homme en ce monde." What shadows we are! Ashes to ashes ends, even in Westminster Abbey, man's noblest story, and dust to dust concludes his noblest song.

> "O death all-eloquent! you only prove
> What dust we doat on, when 'tis man we love."

Hawthorne's Gervayse Hastings is a type and symbol, when he describes himself as depressed by a haunting perception of unreality; as one to whom all things, all persons, are like shadows flickering on the wall. "Neither have I myself any real existence," he says, "but am a shadow like the rest." And the end—not to say the moral—of his story may serve to remind us of the Abbé Gerbet's words. Gervayse Hastings is seated with other guests at a feast—of very odd fellows—over whom is suspended the skeleton of the oddest of all, the founder of the feast. As the speaker ceased his confession of shadowy experiences, "it so chanced that at this juncture the decayed ligaments of the skeleton gave way, and the dry bones fell together in a heap. . . . The attention of the company being thus diverted for a single instant from Gervayse Hastings, they perceived on turning again towards him, that the old man had undergone a change. His shadow had ceased to flicker on the wall." The woe of this old man was, that to him the world to come was all shadow too.

Mrs. Schimmelpenninck expresses her belief that in youth and middle age there is often a real conviction of the transitory nature of the most established temporal things, but that in old age it is not merely a conviction, but a vivid palpable reality, and that the eternal mountains do then indeed appear near at hand; while all the campaign around seems faded into shadowy distance; and she inclines to say, like the monk, who for forty years had exhibited the picture of the Last Supper, that he had seen so many pass away, that himself and those he spoke to seemed a shadow, while the blessed institution of the Holy Supper stood before him alone a reality. But many are the young hearts that feel as Margaret Hale felt, in Mrs. Gaskell's story, when to her life seemed a vain show, so unsubstantial, and flickering, and fleeting, and when "it was as if from some aërial belfry, high up above the stir and jar of the earth, there was a bell continually tolling, 'All are shadows!—all are passing!—all is past!'"

Le tems même sera detruit, as La Bruyère says: "ce n'est qu'un point dans les espaces immenses de l'éternité, et il sera effacé. Il y a de légères et frivoles circonstances du tems, qui ne sont pas stables, qui passent, et que j'appelle des modes, la grandeur, la faveur, les richesses, la puissance, l'autorité, l'indépendance, le plaisir, les joies, la superfluité. Que deviendront ces modes, quand le tems même aura disparu? La vertu seule, si peu à la mode, va au-delà des tems."

"Between two worlds life hovers like a star
'Twixt night and morn, upon the horizon's verge:
How little do we know that which we are!
How less what we may be! The eternal surge
Of time and tide rolls on, and bears afar
Our bubbles; as the old burst, new emerge,
Lash'd from the foam of ages; while the graves
Of empire heave but like some passing waves."

So writes Byron in the poem that contains perhaps his grandest and most powerful strains, interspersed among his wittiest and most wicked ones. If ever man was haunted by the conviction that we are shadows all, and that shadows are our pursuit, it was he. But with him there was nothing of a "saving faith" in this. As Shakspeare's Prince of Arragon reads on the scroll at Belmont,

"Some there be that shadows kiss;
Such have but a shadow's bliss;"

and of such was Byron. And he knew it. Not more alive to this philosophy was Cowper himself, when he pictured men

"For threescore years employed with ceaseless care
In catching smoke and feeding upon air;"

or when he pointed with this moral his lines on the felled poplars that once lent him a shade, beneath which he had so often been charmed by the blackbird's sweet flowing ditty:

"'Tis a sight to engage me, if anything can,
To muse on the perishing pleasures of man;
Though his life be a dream, his enjoyments, I see,
Have a being less durable even than he."

One great amusement of the household in the Castle of Indolence, on the testimony of its poet-laureate, was,

"In a huge crystal magic globe to spy,
Still as you turned it, all things that do pass
Upon this ant-hill earth; where constantly
Of idly busy men the restless fry
Run bustling to and fro with foolish haste,
In search of pleasures vain that from them fly,
Or which, obtained, the caitiffs no not taste."

If, with Churchill, we stand as

"Spectators only on this bustling stage,
We see what vain designs mankind engage:
Vice after vice with ardour they pursue,
And one old folly brings forth twenty new. . . .
Squirrels for nuts contend, and, wrong or right,
For the world's empire, kings, ambitious, fight.
What odds?—to us 'tis all the selfsame thing,
A nut, a world, a squirrel, and a king."

In other verses, and another measure, the same poet justifies his use of the expression "whatever shadows we pursue," by the interpolated comment,

"For our pursuits, be what they will,
Are little more than shadows still;
Too swift they fly, too swift and strong,
For man to catch or hold them long."

Of world-wide application is what Bernardin de Saint-Pierre said of himself, by way of private interpretation: "Toutes mes idées ne sont que des ombres de la nature, recueillies par une autre ombre." Goldsmith was not altogether in sport when he made Croaker in the comedy pronounce life to be, at the greatest and best, but a froward child, that must be humoured and coaxed a little till it falls asleep, and then all the care is over; while Honeywood assents—Good-natured Man that he is—with a ready "Very true, sir; nothing can exceed the vanity of our existence, but the folly of our pursuits." For Goldsmith was in sad earnest when he wrote of himself as one

"Impelled with steps unceasing to pursue
Some fleeting good that mocks me with the view

> That like the circle bounding earth and skies,
> Allures from far, yet, as I follow, flies."

Shadow-hunted shadows is the very text for Mr. Carlyle. World's memory is very whimsical now and then, he says, in recording the forgotten exploits of Johann, King of Bohemia, "all which have proved voiceless in the World's memory; while the casual Shadow of a Feather he once more has proved vocal there." And a whole chapter is devoted to, and entitled, a Kaiser hunting Shadows,—Kaiser Karl with his Pragmatic Sanction to wit, and similar projects, aims, or hobbies, more or less shadowy and unsubstantial, all. "There was another vast Shadow, or confused high-piled continent of shadows, to which our poor Kaiser held with his customary tenacity. To procure adherences and assurances to this dear Pragmatic Sanction, was even more than the shadow of the Spanish crown," the one grand business of his life henceforth. "Shadow of Pragmatic Sanction, shadow of the Spanish crown,—it was such shadow-huntings of the Kaiser in Vienna" that thwarted the Prussian Double-marriage. Another object which Kaiser Karl pursued with some diligence, and which "likewise proved a shadow," was his Ostend East India Company, which gave much disturbance to mankind. "This was the third grand shadow which the Kaiser chased, shaking all the world, poor crank world, as he strode after it." Foiled in this, as in another and another chase, no wonder he grew more and more saturnine, and "addicted to solid taciturn field-sports. His Political 'Perforce Hunt (*Parforce Jagd*),' with so many two-footed terriers, and legationary beagles, distressing all the world by their baying and their burrowing, had proved to be of Shadows; and melted into thin air, to a very singular degree!" Many chapters later Mr. Carlyle recurs to his picture of the "Kaiser in his Shadow-hunt, coursing the Pragmatic Sanction chiefly, as he has done these twenty years past"—and so begins a chapter entitled, by a mixed metaphor, "Kaiser's Shadow-hunt has caught Fire"—by contact, namely, with inflammable Poland. And a subsequent chapter details the damages the poor Kaiser had to pay for meddling in Polish elections,—"for galloping thither in chase of Shadows. . . . This may be considered as the consummation of the Kaiser's Shadow-hunt; or at least its igniting and exploding point. . . . Shadow-hunt is now all gone to Pragmatic Sanction, as it were: that is now the one thing left in Nature for a Kaiser; and that he will love, and chase, as the summary of all things." From this point we see him go steadily down, and at a rapid rate,—getting into disastrous Turkish wars, "with as little preparation for War or Fact as a life-long Hunt of *Shadows* presupposes."

Or let us take our stand, with the same philosopher, in that *Œil-de-Bœuf*, in the Versailles Palace Gallery—through which what figures have passed, and vanished! "Figures? Men? They are fast-fleeting Shadows; fast chasing each other: it is not a Palace, but a Caravansera."

Macaulay has his Sermon in a Churchyard. To that spot the homilist invites all and sundry, and he takes his standpoint for his text. Come to this school of his, he bids us, with the promise that there we shall learn, "in one short hour of placid thought, a stoicism more deep, more stern, than ever Zeno's porch hath taught:"

"The plots and feats of those that press
To seize on titles, wealth, or power,
Shall seem to thee a game of chess,
Devised to pass a tedious hour.
What matters it to him who fights
For shows of unsubstantial good,
Whether his kings, and queens, and knights,
Be things of flesh, or things of wood?

"We check and take, exult, and fret;
Our plans extend, our passions rise,
Till in our ardour we forget
How worthless is the victor's prize.
Soon fades the spell, soon comes the night:
Say will it not be then the same,
Whether we play the black or white,
Whether we lost or won the game?"

This may remind us of Mrs. Battle's apology for whist, or of the concluding sentence in a characteristic confession by Benjamin Constant—who, by the way, had said of himself in a previous letter, *Je passerai comme une* OMBRE *sur la terre entre le malheur et l'ennui*—he records his *sentiment profond et* (like his name) *constant* of the shortness of life—a sentiment, he says, so deep and so constant that it makes the pen or the book drop from his hand whenever he takes to study: "Nous n'avons pas plus de motifs pour acquérir de la gloire, pour conquérir un empire ou pour faire un bon livre, que n'en avons pour faire une promenade ou une partie de whist." Even so utterly different a man in creed and character as Joseph de Maistre could exclaim, "Ah! le vilain monde! j'ai toujours dit qu'il ne pourrait aller si nous avions le sens commun. . . . C'est notre folie qui fait tout aller." Else when we see—especially when death brings home to us, strikes home to us—what shadows we are, and what shadows we pursue, "en vérité chacun se coucherait et daignerait à peine s'habiller." *N'importe! tout marche et c'est assez.* And readers of M. de Tocqueville's letters will remember how often that philosophic writer confides to his correspondents his conviction that there is no one thing in the world capable of fixing and satisfying him. He had attained a success unhoped for at the beginning of his career, but was far from happy. Often, in imagination, he would fancy himself at the summit of human greatness; and when there, the conviction would force itself irrepressibly upon him, that the same painful sensations would follow him to that sublime altitude.

Succeeding? What is the great use of succeeding? muses the master showman of Vanity Fair. Failing? Where is the great harm? "Psha! These things appear as nought, when Time passes—Time the consoler—Time the anodyne—Time the grey calm satirist, whose sad smile seems to say, Look, O man, at the vanity of the objects you pursue, and of yourself who pursue them!"

"Dust are our frames; and, gilded dust, our pride
Looks only for a moment whole and sound;
Like that long-buried body of the king,

Found lying with his urns and ornaments,
Which at a touch of light, an air of heaven,
Slipt into ashes and was found no more."

The professed cynic, remarks an essayist on the theme of Occasional Cynicism, has reached the delightful conclusion that "the whole thing," by which he means life and all its interests, is a sheer mistake and piece of confusion. And as it presents itself to the grander and loftier type of mind, this difficulty is held by the same writer to be the "starting-point of all systems of religion and philosophy, of which it is the object to show either that aims exist before men's eyes that are solid realities worth pursuing, and not mere shadows, or else that even shadows are better worth pursuing in some one way than in all others."

Jeffrey's earlier letters abound in almost cynical reflections on the folly of ambition and the "ridiculous self-importance" implied in "heroic toils." The whole game of life seemed to him a little childish, "and the puppets that strut and look lofty very nearly as ridiculous as those that value themselves on their airs and graces—poor little bits of rattling timber—to be jostled in a bag as soon as the curtain drops." "God help us! it is a foolish little thing this human life at the best; and it is half ridiculous and half pitiful to see what importance we ascribe to it, and to its little ornaments and distinctions," etc. We are, as a modern poet of name and promise puts it, for ever at hide-and-seek with our souls:

. . . "Not in Hades alone
Doth Sisyphus roll, ever frustrate, the stone,
Do the Danaïds ply, ever vainly, the sieve.
Tasks as futile does earth to its denizens give."

When we reflect on the shortness and uncertainty of life, how despicable, exclaims David Hume, seem all our pursuits of happiness! And even if we would extend our concern beyond our own life, he goes on to say, how frivolous appear our most enlarged and most generous projects, when we consider the incessant changes and revolutions of human affairs, by which laws and learning, books and governments, are hurried away by time, as by a rapid stream, and are lost in the immense ocean of matter. If such a reflection certainly tends to mortify all our passions, does it not, asks the essayist, thereby counterwork the artifice of nature, by which we are "happily deceived into an opinion that human life is of some importance? And may not such a reflection be employed with success by voluptuous reasoners, in order to lead us from the paths of action and virtue into the flowery fields of indolence and pleasure?" The Chinese have been pointed to, by a moral philosopher, to point his moral, which is, the desolating tendency of secularism—they having learnt practically, as well as theoretically, to think of themselves as mere transitory beings, who have no future life to expect, and no present Providence to reverence or fear; and the result he takes to be, that they are the meanest, the most deceitful, and one of the most vicious nations in the world—a people who literally sit in darkness, and whose lives are passed in the shadow of death. "In all the world there is no more terrible or instructive example of the practical results of looking upon men as mere passing shadows, who have no superior and no hereafter." Once succeed, this writer argues, in persuading men that they are mere passing phenomena, possessing no more distinctive qualities than the successive waves of the sea, and the consequence is inevitable. "They will cease—gradually, imperceptibly, and with all sorts of moral, and perhaps religious, reflections on their lips—to care for what is great, permanent, and noble, and they will become, in the fullest sense of the words, beasts that perish."

Many men, says Archdeacon Hare, spend their lives in gazing at their own shadows, and so dwindle away into shadows thereof. And one of his companion guessers at truth remarks, that instead of watching the bird as it flies above our heads, we chase his shadow along the ground; and, finding we cannot grasp it, we conclude it to be nothing.

If a man be a reality, says John Sterling, no empty vision in the dreaming soul of nature, but inwardly substantial and personal, that which he most earnestly desires, which best satisfies his whole being, must be real too. And here is a parallel passage from a later writer:

> "Yes, this life is the war of the False and the True,
> Yet this life is a truth, though so complex to view
> That its latent veracity few of us find. . . .
> Ay, the world but a frivolous phantasm seems,
> And mankind in the mass but as motes in sunbeams;
> But when Fate, from the midst of this frivolous nature,
> Selects for her purpose some frail human creature,
> And the Angel of Sorrow, outstretching a wan
> Forefinger to mark him, strikes down from the man
> The false life that hid him, the man's self appears
> A solemn reality: Him the dread spheres
> Of heaven and hell with their forces dispute,
> And dare we be indifferent? Hence, and be mute,
> Light scoffer, vain trifler! Through all thou discernest
> A Greater than thou is at work, and in earnest;
> And he who dares trifle with man, trifles too
> With man's awful Maker." . . .

——o——

HARAN TAKEN: TERAH LEFT.

GENESIS xi. 28.

THERE is a pathetic significance in what to the unobserving reader might seem a dry record of decease, commonplace among other commonplaces, in the fact mentioned concerning the house of Terah, the father of Abraham,—that "Haran died before his father Terah in the land of his nativity, in Ur of the Chaldees."

It is, as Canon Melvill says, like an inversion of the natural order, when we see parents performing the last office to their children: we feel it natural that children should close the eyes, and shroud the limbs of fathers and mothers, but unnatural that fathers and mothers should perform these sad duties for children. "Haran should have followed Terah, and not Terah Haran."

A great French moralist, in his exposition of the sublime intensity of a father's love, goes on to say of the tie, the *lien*, which unites devoted parent to endeared child, " Et la nature brise ce lien. Elle jette au tombeau cette vie qui commence, et condamne le père à rester vivant." A tender poet of our day was writing from such an experience—not in his case an isolated one—when bewailing the gem of his hearth, his household pride, who, could love have saved from death, would have found a father's love, and a mother's, stronger than death :

" Humbly we bow to Fate's decree ;
Yet had we hoped that Time should see
Thee mourn for us, not us for thee."

Les funérailles des fils, says another French author, *sont toujours contre la nature quand les parents y assistent*. How often Edmund Burke harps on that tremulously vibrating string, in reference to the master-grief which overshadowed his closing period of life ! In a letter to Dr. Lawrence, he expresses his thankfulness to God for dismissing him " so gently from life," and being sent, he adds, " to follow those who in course ought to have followed me." In his famous letter to the Duke of Bedford, the bereaved old man utters the lament : "I live in an inverted order. They who ought to have succeeded me have gone before me. They who should have been to me as posterity, are in the place of ancestors." Shakspeare had anticipated the thought, and the expression of the thought, when he made old Lucretius exclaim :

" If in the child the father's image lies,
Where shall I live, now Lucrece is unlived ?
Thou wast not to this end from me derived.
If children predecease progenitors,
We are their offspring, and they none of ours."

So again he makes Capulet cry out, at the loss of his daughter Juliet, " O thou untaught ! what manners is in this, to press before thy father to a grave ! " Writing to a kinsman on the birth of a son, Burke gives utterance to the wish, " May he live to be the staff of your age, and to close your eyes in peace ; instead of, like me, reversing the order of nature, and having the melancholy office to close *his*." And to his "dear little niece," Mary, he thus writes after the birth of her son (Thomas

Haviland Burke): "May you see your son a support to your old age; . . . and at a very long day may *he* close *your* eyes, not as I have done those of your admirable cousin." His progeny may never be his posterity, muses Sir Thomas Browne, in his meditations on man: "he may go out of the world less related than he came into it; and considering the frequent mortality in friends and relations, in such a term of time, he may pass away divers years in sorrow and black habits, and leave none to mourn for himself; orbity may be his inheritance."

Bitterly Mohammed bewailed the death of his four sons by Kadijah, who died in their infancy; and especially that of one by Maria the Egyptian; for not only was this fatal to his hopes of founding an hereditary religious dynasty, but it affected his claims to pre-eminent favour with God. "Al-as Ebn Wayel, who was so cruel and so daring as to insult him on the loss of his favourite boy, . . . was accursed of heaven, and a special Sura (the 108th) was revealed to console the Prophet." Bitterly Saint Stephen, the first king of Hungary, bewailed the loss of his promising son Emeric—the first of a series of shocks that hastened his own end. Like the desolate sire in Scott's poem who

> . . . "beheld aghast,
> With Wilfrid all his projects pass,
> All turn'd and centred on his son,
> On Wilfrid all—and he was gone.
> 'And I am childless now,' he said."

Réné of Anjou, in surviving his male offspring, was the last representative of his race. Southey observes that *Pauli in domo præter se nemo superest*, is a reflection passing melancholy in the speech of Paulus Æmilius; and applying it to his own emphatically good physician, he says, that the speedy extinction of his family in his own person was often in the Doctor's mind, and that he would sometimes touch upon it, to dear friends, in moods of autumnal feeling.

Michelet's record of the death of Charles le Bel, who leaving only a daughter, was succeeded by a cousin, closes with the reminder, "All that fine family of princes who had sat near their father at the council of Vienne, was extinct. In the popular belief, the curse of Boniface had taken effect." So with Alexander III. of Scotland, whose eldest son died soon after his marriage, leaving no issue, and whose second son died while a boy; other bereavements followed, and the king came to feel in fact as the patriarch felt by anticipation, that to be bereaved of one's children, was bereavement indeed. King James V., in like manner the survivor of both his sons, died a broken-hearted man.

Laelio Torelli, the Florentine statesman and man of letters, survived all his children. Shakspeare lost his only son some twenty years before his own decease. Vincentio Scamozzi, the architect, who died the same year as Shakspeare, caused no little talk at the time, by the very singular will he left, betokening a most extraordinary solicitude for the perpetuation of his name, as he had the grief of outliving his offspring. Sir Francis Vere's three sons and two daughters all died before him. It was accounted a signal calamity in the career of that true nobleman, the Duke of Ormond, that he outlived "the noble-minded Ossory," worthy son of such a sire.

"The feeble wrap the athletic in his shroud; and weeping fathers build their children's tomb." Young's is that truism; and Pope's is the cognate query, "Say, was it virtue, more though Heaven ne'er gave, lamented Digby, sunk thee to the grave?

> "Tell me, if virtue made the son expire,
> Why, full of days and honours, lives the sire?"

Passing in his Meditations from single persons to families, Marcus Antoninus refers to that of the Pompeys, for one instance, as wholly extinct. "This man was the last of his house," he says, is not an uncommon inscription upon a monument. As with Homer's Phænops, in feeble age, who lost his joy and hope in young Xanthus and Thoön:

> "Vast was his wealth, and these the only heirs
> Of all his labours, and a life of cares.
> Cold death o'ertakes them in their blooming years,
> And leaves the father unavailing tears.

> To strangers now descends his heapy store,
> The race forgotten, and the name no more."

Who on his staff is this? we ask with Ossian; who is this whose head is white with age, whose eyes are red with tears, who quakes at every step? "It is thy father, O Morar!" dead and gone Morar: "the father of no son but thee. . . . Weep, thou father of Morar; weep, but thy son heareth thee not. Deep is the sleep of the dead—low their pillow of dust." This flies sure to the old man's heart, says Schiller's Illo of the elder Piccolomini,

> . . . "He has his whole life long
> Fretted and toil'd to raise his ancient house
> From a count's title to the name of prince;
> And now must seek a grave for his only son."

Peter the Great, whether guilty or not of putting to death his elder son, Alexis, was inconsolable for the loss of the only remaining one. It was the fate of Queen Anne to lose, at twelve years of age, the hopeful young prince who alone survived of all her very many children.

Samuel Richardson was the saddened survivor of all his five sons and a daughter. The celebrated Dutch philosopher and mathematician, 'Sgravesande, who, by the way, was born within the same year with Richardson, lost his two sons within eight days of each other, and is honoured for the Christian resignation with which he bore the sharp trial. Sir John Vanbrugh lost his only son at the battle of Tournay. Bishop Warburton died not long after his only son, who was carried off by a decline in the springtide of life. It is of a distinguished Swiss littérateur, who died in his prime, that Sainte-Beuve somewhere says *que sa destinée tranchée avant l'heure a pourtant été complète, si un père octogénaire ne lui survivait.*

> "I ought to have gone before him: I wonder he went so young,"

wails the aged mother in Mr. Tennyson's poem, all whose children have gone before her, she is so old.

The gathering sorrows which clouded the latter years of

Bishop Percy, "after a life in the main prosperous and happy," commenced with the loss of an only son.

Lord Kenyon died in 1802, "sorrow-stricken by the loss of his eldest son, after having accumulated a fortune of £300,000." Lord Stowell lost his son, aged forty-two, about two months only before he too fell on death. Sprengel, the very learned German physician, never recovered the stroke of his son's loss. Cuvier's four children all died before him. "Write ye this man childless:" many a man of genius has felt his heart sink and his strength fail under that blighting sentence. In his sixty-seventh year we find Moore writing, "The last of our five children is now gone, and we are left desolate and alone. Not a single relative have I now left in the world." How Mr. Hallam was successively bereaved of sons so rich in promise, if not in performance, is too well known.

There is a seeming affectation of literary paternity in what Chateaubriand writes of the death of Byron,—as though it were Terah and Haran, with a difference. "I preceded him in life; he preceded me in death. He was summoned before his time. My number came before his, and yet his was drawn first from the urn. It was Childe Harold who ought to have remained."

——o——

THE MOTE AND THE BEAM.

St. Matthew vii. 5.

AS easy is it to discern the mote in a brother's eye as to discern the face of the sky. Hypocrite is the term by which the facile discerner in either case is divinely stigmatised; in the one instance, because with all his discernment he cannot read the signs of the times; in the other, because with all his insight and microscopic nicety of perception, and exceptionally developed faculty of vision, he yet considers not the beam that is in his own eye.

With our Lord's words concerning the mote and the beam, Archbishop Trench bids us compare the Chinese proverb,

"Sweep away the snow from thine own door, and heed not the frost upon thy neighbour's tiles." The Greek and Latin classics are not wanting in various readings of the same theme. Demosthenes meant much the same thing when he said that we must beware of austerely scrutinizing the actions of others, unless first we are conscious of having acquitted ourselves aright: "*οὐ γὰρ ἐστι πικρῶς ἐξετάσαι τι πέπρακται τοῖς ἀλλοῖς, ἀν μὴ παῤ ὑμῶν ἀυτῶν πρῶτον ὑπάρξη τὰ δέοντα.*" "Man is blind to his own faults, but keen-sighted to perceive those of others," is a Latin adage: "Vitiis suis pervidendis cæcus est homo, in alienis perspicax." "Is it never your way to look at yourself when you are abusing another?" is a question in Plautus: "Non soles respicere te, cum dicas injuste alteri?" Cicero pronounces it to be of the nature of folly to see the faults of others, and to forget one's own: "Proprium est stultitiæ aliorum vitia cernere, oblivisci suorum." Horace shrewdly submits that the man who is desirous that his friends should not take offence at his own protuberances, will "ignore" that friend's warts:

> "Qui, ne tuberibus propriis offendat amicum,
> Postulat, ignoscat verrucis illius."

And at least as pointed and piquant is the passage beginning,

> "Quum tua pervideas oculis male lippus inunctis,
> Cur in amicorum vitiis tam cernis acutum," etc.

The query Plautus puts, "How is it that no man tries to search into himself, but each fixes his eyes on the wallet of the one who goes before him?" is in allusion to the fable of Jupiter having loaded men with a couple of wallets; the one, filled with our own vices, being slung at our backs,

> "Propriis repletam vitiis post tergum dedit;"

the other, heavy with our neighbour's faults, hung in front,

> "Alienis ante pectus suspendit gravem."

To pardon those absurdities in ourselves which we cannot suffer in others, is neither better nor worse, says Dean Swift, than to be more willing to be fools ourselves than to have others so. The proverbs of all nations show all nations to be alive to the ridiculous in this respect. The kiln calls the oven, burnt house, says one. In Italy, the pan says to the pot, Keep off, or you 'll smutch me. In Spain, the raven bawls hoarsely to the crow, Get out, blackamoor! (*Quítate allá, negro!*) In Germany, one ass nicknames another, Long-ears. And Dr. Trench is rather taken with a certain originality in the Catalan version of the proverb: "Death said to the man with his throat cut, 'How ugly you look!'" They should be fair, hints Juvenal, who venture to deride the disproportioned leg or sooty hide, *Loripedem rectus derideat, Æthiopem albus.* Yet, as the Ettrick shepherd once sang in his native Doric:—

> "There 's some wi' big scars on their face,
> Point out a prin scart on a frien';
> And some, black as sweeps wi' disgrace,
> Cry out, the whole warld's unclean."

Molière's Chrysale twits her sister Bélise, who is a *femme savante*, with snapping up everybody short who makes a slip with the tongue, while herself liable to graver censure for slips of conduct:—

> "Le moindre solécisme en parlant vous irrite;
> Mais vous en faites, vous, d'étranges en conduite."

Sappho, again, in Mademoiselle de Scudéry's portentous romance—once the rage of readers in France, despite its plurality of volumes, as "Clarissa" was in England, a century later—ridicules the *bizarre* orthography of the fine-ladyism of the day, while amused at the fact that the fine ladies in question, who perpetrated such gross errors in writing, and who lost every particle of wit the moment they took up a pen, would yet make game for days together of some poor foreigner who happened to use one term for another. As if it were less a matter of mirth or marvel for a *grande dame*, claiming to be a woman of wit, too, and a power in society, to commit a thousand blunders in writing her native language, than for a raw foreigner to make a few slips in speaking it.

We every day and every hour, observes Montaigne, say

things of another that we might more properly say of ourselves, could we but revert our observation to our own concerns as well as extend it to others. And the old essayist has his fling at not a few authors of the day who, in this manner, prejudiced their own cause by running headlong upon those they attacked, and darting those shafts against their enemies that might, with much greater propriety and effect, be hurled back at themselves.

A stanza in the most elaborate of Shakspeare's poems that are not plays—for are not all his plays poems?—runs into this eloquence of remonstrant appeal:—

"Think but how vile a spectacle it were
To view thy present trespass in another.
Men's faults do seldom to themselves appear;
Their own transgressions partially they smother:
This guilt would seem death-worthy in thy brother.
O, how are they wrapped in with infamies,
That from their own misdeeds askance their eyes!"

It is of their common friend Breuning that Beethoven writes to Ferdinand Ries,—"He certainly possesses many admirable qualities, but he thinks himself quite faultless, whereas the very defects that he discovers in others are those which he possesses himself to the highest degree." One of the most natural and truthfully, as well as forcibly, drawn characters in Mrs. Inchbald's "Simple Story,"—Sandford,—a man of understanding, of learning, and a complete casuist, yet all whose faults were committed for the want of knowing better, is described as constantly reproving faults in others, and most assuredly too good a man not to have corrected and amended his own, had they been known to him; but known to him they were not. He had been, we are told, for so long a time the spiritual superior or preceptor of all with whom he lived, and so busied with instructing others, that he had not once recollected that he needed instruction himself; and in such awe did his habitual severity keep all about him, that although he had numerous friends, not one of them told him of his failing. "Was there not then some reason for him to suppose he *had* no faults?

His enemies, indeed, hinted that he had; but enemies he never hearkened to; and thus, with all his good sense, he wanted the sense to follow the rule, 'Believe what your enemies say of you rather than what is said by your friends.'" He had yet to learn, and to learn by heart, the wide and practical import of the prayer—

"Teach me to love and to forgive,
Exact my own defects to scan,
What others are to feel, and know myself a Man."

Well may the demoniac guide of Don Cleofas, in Le Sage's symbolical fiction, say, and well does he say, "J'admire messieurs les hommes; leurs propres défauts leur paraissent des minuties, au lieu qu'ils regardent ceux d'autrui avec un microscope." To their own faults more than a little blind, to those of others they are not a little unkind.

Gay begins his fable of the Turkey and the Ant with the smoothly-turned truism, that

"In other men we faults can spy,
And blame the mote that dims their eye;
Each little speck and error find;
To our own stronger errors blind."

One of the most classical masters of modern English, whether in verse or prose, was employing the same metre—of fatal facility, as it is called—when he closed his address to a brother bard in a strain that must also close this chapter of instances:

"We, who surround a common table,
And imitate the fashionable,
Wear each two eye-glasses: *this* lens
Shows us our faults, *that* other men's.
We do not care how dim may be
This by whose aid our own we see;
But, ever anxiously alert
That all may have their whole desert,
We would melt down the stars and sun
In our heart's furnace, to make one
Through which th' enlightened world might spy
A mote upon a brother's eye."

——o——

STRANGERS AND PILGRIMS.

1 PETER ii. 11.

PETER, an apostle of Jesus Christ, to the strangers scattered throughout Asia Minor, addressed the urgent appeal that *as* strangers—strangers and pilgrims—they should abstain from fleshly lusts, which war against the soul.

Consider what you are, he seems to say, as his words are paraphrased by the greatest of all commentators on his first epistle: "If you were citizens of this world, then you might drive the same trade" with the men of this world, "and follow the same lusts; but seeing you are chosen and called out of this world, and invested into a new society, made free of another city, and are therefore here but travellers passing through to your own country, it is very reasonable that there be this difference betwixt you and the world, that while they live at home your carriage be such as fits strangers, not glutting yourselves with their pleasures, nor surfeiting upon their delicious fruits, as some unwary travellers do abroad; but as wise strangers living warily and soberly, and still minding most of all your journey homewards, suspecting dangers and snares in your way, and so walking with a holy fear, as the Hebrew word for a stranger imports."

The topic is one upon which Archbishop Leighton ever writes feelingly. As again in his comment on the psalmist's profession of being a stranger with God, and a sojourner as all his fathers were, the same devout expositor observes that he who looks on himself as a stranger, and is sensible of the darkness round about him in this wilderness, will often put up that request with David, "I am a stranger in the earth: hide not Thy commandments from me." What, Leighton asks, is the joy of our life, but the thoughts of that other life, our home before us? "And certainly he that lives much in these thoughts, set him where you will here, he is not much pleased nor displeased; but if His Father call him home, that word gives him his heart's desire."

Once again, in the sixth of his lectures on the immortality

of the soul, Leighton expatiates on the fact that this is not our rest, that we have no place of residence here below: "it is the region of fleas and gnats; and while we search for happiness among these mean and perishing things, we are not only sure to be disappointed, but also not to escape those miseries which, in great numbers, continually beset us; so that we may apply to ourselves the saying of the famous artist confined in the island of Crete, and truly say,—

"'Nec tellus nostræ, nec patet unda fugæ,
Restat iter cœli, cœlo tentabimus ire.'"

("The earth and the sea are shut up against us, and neither of them can favour our escape; the way to heaven is alone open, and this way we will strive to go.")

Incidentally, it adds to the interest of every such passage in Leighton's writings to remember a noteworthy circumstance respecting his death. He had been used to say that if he were to choose a place to die in it should be an inn—for that would look so like a pilgrim's going home, to whom this world was all as an inn. It was his opinion, also, as we read in the memoir of him by Aikman, that "the officious tenderness and care of friends was an entanglement to a dying man, and that the unconcerned attendance of those who could be procured in such a place would give less disturbance." He had his wish. At the Bell Inn, Warwick Lane, Robert Leighton, in his seventy-fourth year, stranger and pilgrim, drew his last breath.

"An inn receives me, where, unknown,
I solitary sit me down;
Many I hear, and some I see—
I nought to them, they nought to me.

Thus, in those regions of the dead,
A pilgrim's wandering life I lead;
And still at every step declare
I 've no abiding city here.

*   *   *   *   *

The world is like an inn; for there
Men call and storm and drink and swear;
While undisturbed the Christian waits,
And reads and writes and meditates.

Though in the dark ofttimes I stray,
The Lord shall light me on my way;
And to the city of the sun
Conduct me, when my journey 's done.

There by these eyes shall He be seen,
Who sojourned for me at an inn;
On Sion's hill I those shall hail
From whom I parted in the vale."

Of him who walks by faith and not by sight, who places eternity by the side of time, and so regards the one as a mere path or stepping-stone to the other, it is well said by Dr. Chalmers that he actually moves through life in the spirit of a traveller, feels his home to be heaven, and all his dearest hopes and interests to be laid up there; "walking therefore over the world with a more light and unencumbered step than other men, just because all its adversities to him are but the crosses of a rapid journey, and all its joys but the shifting scenery of the land through which he is travelling, and visions of passing loveliness."

As in the pilgrim's song of a contemporary clerical poet:

"My rest is in heaven; my rest is not here:
Then why should I murmur when trials are near?
Be hushed, my dark spirit! the worst that can come
But shortens thy journey, and hastens thee home.

* * * * * *

A scrip on my back, and a staff in my hand,
I march on in haste through an enemy's land:
The road may be rough, but it cannot be long;
And I 'll smooth it with hope, and I 'll cheer it with song."

The second of Bishop Beveridge's Resolutions comprises this utterance,—after the expression of a longing that he could be ever on the mount, taking a view of the land of Canaan, for then what dreams and shadows would all things here below appear to be,—"Well! by the grace of God, I am resolved no longer to tie myself to sense and sight, the sordid and trifling affairs of this life, but always to walk as one of the other world; to behave myself in all places, and at all times, as one already possessed of my inheritance and an inhabitant of the

New Jerusalem;—by faith assuring myself I have but a few more days to live below, a little more work to do, and be admitted to a nearer vision and fruition of God, and see Him face to face." And thus, although at present here in the flesh, the believer's resolve is to look upon himself as more really an inhabitant of heaven than abiding (for here we have no continuing city) upon earth.

In the words of *l'exilé* of Lamennais, "La patrie n'est point ici-bas; l'homme vainement l'y cherche; ce qu'il prend pour elle n'est qu'un gite d'une nuit." Happy they, exclaims Pascal in his *Pensées,* whose tears are shed, not at the evanescence of all things earthly and perishable, but when they remember Sion—*dans le souvenir de leur chère patrie*—the heavenly Jerusalem, after which they sigh continually in the weariness of their exile. But as Schiller's Thekla replies to Neubrunn's comment on "the journey's weary length,"—

> "The pilgrim, travelling to a distant shrine
> Of hope and healing, does not count the leagues."

John Foster describes the Israelite indeed, who is a pilgrim indeed, as resembling a person whose eye, while he is conversing with you about an object or a succession of objects, should glance every moment towards some great obstacle appearing on the distant horizon. "He seems to talk to his friends in somewhat of the manner of expression with which you can imagine that Elijah spoke, if he remarked to his companion any circumstance in the journey from Bethel to Jericho, and from Jericho to the Jordan; a manner betraying the sublime anticipation which was pressing on his thoughts." To other pilgrims the vision of the land that is very far off may be, as Professor Maurice puts it, not so clear as they wish; but it is more clear than their vision of anything which lies about them; and without it all would be shadow and darkness. "There, in that state, must lie all that they dream of and hope for." "There only they must live, or have no life." "When they pray 'Thy kingdom come,' they ask that the Great Shepherd will lead them and their brethren out of a land of pits, a thirsty wilderness, a valley of the shadow of death, to a peaceable habitation and a sure dwelling-place." There is a bleak desert, in the words of one who wrote sacred songs, though himself no sacred poet,—

. . . "where daylight grows weary
Of wasting its smiles on a desert so dreary—
What may that desert be?
'Tis life, cheerless life, where the few joys that come
Are lost like that daylight, for 'tis not their home.

There is a lone pilgrim, before whose faint eyes
The water he pants for but sparkles and flies—
Who may that pilgrim be?
'Tis man, hapless man, through this life tempted on
By fair shining hopes, that in shining are gone."

In that essay of John Foster's, from which a citation has already been made, the essayist protests against the care so many popular writers seem to take to guard against the inroad of ideas pertaining to another life—as much care as the inhabitants of Holland take against the irruption of the sea; and their writings, he adds, do really form a kind of moral dyke against the invasion from the other world. "They do not instruct a man to act, to enjoy, and to suffer, as a being that may by to-morrow have finally abandoned this orb; everything is done to beguile the feeling of his being 'a stranger and a pilgrim on the earth.'" They fail to recognise the *c'est vrai* of the Christian lyrist's avowal, the—

"'*Tis true*, we are but strangers
And sojourners below;
And countless snares and dangers
Surround the path we go:

Though painful and distressing,
Yet there 's a rest above;
And onward still we 're pressing,
To reach that land of love."

The object of such a pilgrim is progress—or, rather, progress is the means to an end; and the end is not yet, is not here, but will surely come, and come quickly, and will not tarry.

There is a wicket gate towards which they are making progress, and it is the portal of a city that hath foundations, whose builder and maker is God. They who professedly sojourn here as in a strange country, who obey the call to go out into a place which they shall after receive for an inheritance; who confess, and act on the confession, that they are strangers and pilgrims on the earth; they that say and do such things declare plainly that they seek a country, a better country—that is, a heavenly.

Chaucer's "old style" conveys a meaning the world can never be too old to learn:

> "Here is no home, here is but wyldyrnesse.
> Forth, pilgrime! forth, best out of thy stalle!
> Look up on hye, and thonke God of alle;
> Weyve thy lust, and let thy goste thee lede,[1]
> And trouthe shall thee delyver, it is no drede."

We are strangers and sojourners before God, as were all our fathers. By faith it was that Abraham sojourned in the land of promise, as in a strange country, dwelling in tabernacles with Isaac and Jacob, the heirs with him of the same promise; in tabernacles, that bespeak the stranger and pilgrim upon earth; not in houses built to endure. For he confessed, and denied not, but confessed that here he had no continuing city. True, a citizen he was of no mean city. But it was not of the earth, earthy. For he looked for a city which hath foundations, more everlasting than the hills. Meanwhile, God's statutes were his songs in the house of his pilgrimage.

The Bird of God is Wordsworth's epithet for that "resplendent wanderer" called by Eastern islanders the Bird of Heaven, and by us of the West, Bird of Paradise; and, as usual with the serenely meditative bard of Rydal, there is moral, nay, religious teaching in the symbolism of his strain:—

> "The Bird of God! whose blessed will
> She seems performing as she flies

[1] That is, "Let thy spirit (goste), not thy appetite, lead thee." In St. Peter's words, "Abstain from fleshly lusts."

Over the earth and through the skies,
In never-wearied search of Paradise—
Region that crowns her beauty with the name
She bears for us—for us how blest,
How happy at all seasons, could like aim
Uphold our spirits urged to kindred flight
On wings that fear no glance of God's pure sight,
No tempest from His breath, their promised rest
Seeking with indefatigable quest
Above a world that deems itself most wise
When most enslaved by gross realities!"

An appalling pestilence raged in Carthage, and so gave deadly emphasis to the exhortations of St. Cyprian, when he, a good shepherd, sought to lead the sheep of his flock to green pastures and still waters of comfort; reminding them, as he stood between the living and the dead, while as yet the plague was stayed not, that they had renounced the world, and were abiding here as strangers and pilgrims only. "Let us," he besought them, "embrace that time which gives to each one his home, which, delivering us from this world, and loosing us from worldly snares, restores us to paradise and the kingdom." Who, he asks, that is placed in a foreign land, would not hasten to return to his own country? Who that saileth towards his own, would not eagerly desire a prosperous wind to bring him swiftly to the embrace of those he loves? "Our country we believe to be paradise: the patriarchs we esteem our parents. Why, then, do we not speed and run, that we may behold our country and salute our parents?"

Salutary though the sentiment be, however, it admits of one-sided exaggeration. There are good people who, for instance, exalt and expatiate upon the death of godly infants, as though to quit this earth of ours at the very earliest date were the most blessed of privileges. The idea of man being sent into the world for any definite purpose never seems, it has been justly said, to enter the minds of these good people. "With them life is but an irksome omnibus-journey—the shorter the better—and to be got over by each without any regard to the comfort or requirements of his fellow-travellers." Only in part are these strictures on "the shorter the better" applicable, if at all, to the theme and expression of Mrs. Browning's sonnet:—

"I think we are too ready with complaint
In this fair world of God's. Had we no hope
Indeed beyond the zenith and the slope
Of yon grey blank of sky, we might grow faint
To muse upon eternity's constraint
Round our aspirant souls. But since the scope
Must widen early, is it well to droop
For a few days consumed in loss and taint?
O pusillanimous heart! be comforted,
And, like a cheerful traveller, take the road,
Singing beside the hedge. What if the bread
Be bitter in thine inn, and thou unshod
To meet the flints?—At least it may be said,
'Because the way is *short*, I thank thee, God!'"

Addison devotes a paragraph in one of his *Spectators* to the fact of men being in Scripture called strangers and sojourners upon earth, and life a pilgrimage. And he refers to several heathen as well as Christian authors, who under the same kind of metaphor have represented the world as an inn, which was only designed to furnish us with accommodation in this our passage. It is therefore very absurd, urges our moral essayist, to think of setting up our rest before we come to our journey's end; and not rather to take care of the reception we shall there meet with, than to fix our thoughts on the little conveniences and advantages which we enjoy one above another in the way to it.

"The Illusiveness of Life" is the title of a sermon on the patriarchs as sojourners in a strange country, by the late F. W. Robertson, of Brighton; who with characteristic force and insight explains the deception of life's promise, and the meaning of that deception. He shows how our natural anticipations deceive us—every human life being a fresh one, bright with hopes that will never be realized. With our affections, he goes on to say, it is still worse, because they promise more. "Men's affections are but the tabernacles of Canaan—the tents of a night—not permanent habitations, even for this life."

Where, he asks, are the charms of character, the perfection and the purity and the truthfulness which seemed so resplendent in our friend? They were only the shape of our own conceptions —our creative shaping intellect projected its own fantasies on him; and hence we outgrow our early friendships—outgrow the intensity of all: we dwell in tents; we never find a home, even in the land of promise, any more than Abraham did. "Life is an unenjoyable Canaan, with nothing real or substantial in it." But there is another beside the sentimental way, trite enough, of considering this aspect of life—as a bubble, a dream, a delusion, a phantasm, and that other is the way of faith. "The ancient saints felt as keenly as any moralist could feel the brokenness of life's promises: they confessed that they were strangers and pilgrims here; they said that they had here no continuing city; but they did not mournfully moralize on this; they said it cheerfully, and rejoiced that it was so." Strangers —the very term implies a distant home. Pilgrims—the law of whose pilgrimage is to make progress. Forgetting the things behind; rating at their true worth the things around; earnestly pressing forward to the things before. Keble's devout lyric on the escape to Zoar is pitched in this key:—

> "Sweet is the smile of home; the mutual look
> When hearts are of each other sure;
> Sweet all the joys that crowd the household nook,
> The haunt of all affections pure;
> Yet in the world even these abide, and we
> Above the world our calling boast:
> Once gain the mountain-top, and thou art free:
> Till then, who rest, presume; who turn to look, are lost."

——o——

THE FALSITY OF THE FAMILIAR FRIEND.

PSALM xli. 9.

THE psalmist's enemies were speaking evil of him: when should he die, and his name perish? All that hated him were whispering together against him, and devising hurt.

But this he could bear, on the part of declared foes. What he could not bear was that his own familiar friend, in whom he trusted, and who ate of his bread, should have lifted up his heel against him.

Hengstenberg remarks that in Judas the expression, "Which did eat of my bread," receives its full, its frightful verification, in the fact of his participating in the Last Supper—to say nothing of habitually sharing in previous and everyday meals.

Even a comparatively slight wound may be severe when dealt by a friend. Dr. Colani thinks that never could the Son of man have felt so acutely the pain caused by opposition and non-recognition as when He received the message from John the Baptist, inquiring into the credentials of His Divine mission. That the rulers of the people, that one of the twelve, that those of His own kin, should doubt or dispute His mission, was hard enough to bear, but perhaps easy to foresee. But when he who had baptized Him, who had, so to speak, revealed Him to Himself,—when His "spiritual father" took his stand among the doubters, "Jesus must have felt a heartrending surprise, a veritable consternation:" for the Baptist was not a reed shaken with the wind, and yet, if the Divine hand rested on that support, what but a reed was it, to pierce, even while it gave way?

The *Et tu, Brute!* of dying Cæsar is a large utterance, hardly more deep in reproachful pathos than wide of application. The bitterness of its import, varying in intensity, has sufficed to choke bad men and good and indifferent,—as a pang more sharp than all. What stung Jugurtha to the heart was the treachery of his confidential agent, Bomilcar, who intrigued to betray him to the Romans. What Cicero professes to have felt most keenly, during the Clodian troubles, was the perfidious conduct to him of that Serranus to whom, when consul, he had been so kind; nor was it the least bitter drop in the cup he had to drain at the last, that the leader of the band who took his life was one whose life Cicero had once saved, as counsel for the defence. Antony in the tragedy is naturally made to brood most resentfully on the being betrayed by one on whose bosom he had "slept secure of injured faith." He can forgive a foe, but not a friend :

> "Treason is there in its most horrid shape,
> Where trust is greatest."

Herod the Great felt the pang when that dark and horrible secret, as Milman calls it, came to light, that Antipater, the beloved son, for whom he had imbrued his hands in the blood of his own children—Antipater, the heir of his kingdom—was "clearly proved to have conspired with Pheroras (B.C. 5) to poison his old and doting father, and thus to secure and accelerate his own succession." Michelet's narrative of the decline and death of the Emperor Frederick II. comprises this record : "Finally his chancellor, his dearest friend, Peter de Vineâ, attempted to poison him. After this last blow it only remained for him to veil his face, like Cæsar on the ides of March." And familiar to us all is the story of our Henry II., sick and bedridden, inquiring the names of the supporters of his rebellious son Richard. He was for declaring John, the youngest of his sons, and as he thought the most attached to him, heir to all his continental dominions. But on hearing the name of his beloved John, highest on the list of Richard's adherents, Henry was seized with a sort of convulsive agitation, sat up in bed, and gazing around with searching and haggard look, exclaimed, "Can it be true that John, my heart, the son of my choice, on whom I doted more than on all the rest, and my love for whom has brought on me all my woes, has fallen from me?" Assured that so it was, "Well then," sighed Henry, falling back on his bed, and turning his face to the wall, "henceforward let all go on as it may; I no longer care for myself nor for the world." And in this connection may be mentioned the dying exclamation of Henry's murdered chancellor. "What is this, Reginald?" cried Becket to Fitzurse, when the latter made up to him, bared sword in hand : "I have loaded you with favours, and *you* come to me armed, and in the church?" The last stroke that broke down the aged Pope Boniface VIII., bowed with the weight of eighty-six years, was the defection of his favourite and favoured nephew. One may apply to such defections the upbraidal in a latter-day poem on Old Pictures in Florence:

> "Giotto, how, with that soul of yours,
> Could you play me false who loved you so?
> Some slight if a certain heart endures,
> It feels, I would have your fellows know.
> Well—I perceive not why I should care
> To break a silence that suits them best;
> But the thing grows somewhat hard to bear
> When I find a Giotto join the rest."

Most painful to Luther, in his last moments, was the controversy forced upon him by the defection of so dear a friend as Agricola, the leader of the Antinomians. He had long before that expressed his "astoundment" at the secession of Œcolampadius and Regius, and other intimate associates. "Why should I fret and fume against the papists?" he wrote in 1531: "all they have done against me has been in fair, open war; we are declared enemies, and act as such. They who hurt me are my own dear children. My brothers, *fraterculi mei, aurei amiculi mei.* . . . . I thought I had gone through, had exhausted all the adversities the evil one could inflict; but it was not so. My Absalom, the child of my heart, had not deserted his father, had not poured out ignominy upon David; my Judas, the traitor who delivered up his master, had not sold me: he has done so now."

If Mary Stuart had any quarter to which, in her disastrous condition, she might look for love and favour, it was, says the most popular of historians of Scotland, her brother Murray. *His* kindness and compassion she deserved, after loading him with favours, as well as pardoning him considerable offences. But his acceptance of the regency broke all remaining ties of tenderness betwixt him and his sister. Scott is not romancing when, in an historical romance, he describes her reception of the news. "The queen gave a sort of shriek, and clapping her hands together, exclaimed, 'Comes the arrow out of his quiver? —out of my brother's bow?'" When Elizabeth appointed commissioners to inquire into Mary's case, the Regent Murray appeared before them, "in the odious character of the accuser of his sister, benefactress, and sovereign." To adopt the sentiment of the most sententious of stage moralists, When ingratitude barbs the dart of injury, the wound has double danger in it.

What touched Cortez most nearly, at the time of the expulsion from Mexico, was to find the name of his trusted friend, his *intimado*, his *privado*, the secretary Duero, at the head of the paper of remonstrance presented by his disaffected soldiers. We find Louis XVI., on the eve of his execution, inquiring with calm curiosity, and as though not personally affected, how certain members of the convention whom he knew had voted at his trial. Told that his cousin of Orleans had voted for his death, "Ah!" he exclaimed to Malesherbes, "that affects me more than all the rest." It was, remarks Lamartine, the comment of Cæsar when he recognised the face of Brutus amongst his murderers; he alone roused him to speak.

So spake the captain of Plymouth, but with more of anger in his sorrow, in the New England hexameters devoted by Longfellow to Miles Standish, when he charged John Alder with having supplanted, defrauded, betrayèd him:—

"Yours is the greater treason, for yours is a treason to friendship!
You, who lived under my roof, whom I cherished and loved as a brother;
You, who have fed at my board and drunk of my cup, to whose keeping
I have entrusted my honour, my thoughts the most sacred and secret,—
You too, Brutus! ah, woe to the name of friendship hereafter!"

It was the revolt of his beloved son Conrad which crushed to the earth the emperor Henry IV. What Dean Milman calls "the almost fatal effect" of his conduct on his father, can only be ascribed to profound affection, deeply, cruelly, wantonly wounded. "The revolt of Conrad seemed to crush the aged Emperor to the earth. He had borne all the vicissitudes of his earlier life with unbroken courage, he had risen from his humiliation at Canosa with refreshed energy; he now abandoned himself to despair, threw off the robes and insignia of royalty, and was hardly prevented by his friends from falling on his own sword."—There is a spice of the *et tu Brute* bitterness in Becket's exclamation to John of Poitiers, when even that most ardent of his admirers followed him to Etampes, and implored him to yield. "And you too," cried the primate, in a pang of wrath, "will you strangle us"—*ut quid nos et vos strangulatis?*—The great Emperor Frederick II. reproached Pope Gregory IX., in the height of their contest, as having been, while in the lower orders of the Church, his familiar friend; but that no sooner had he reached the height of his ambition than he threw off all gratitude, and became his determined foe.—When Queen Elizabeth broke out on a party of the peers for urging her whither she would not, Norfolk she as good as called traitor and conspirator, and Pembroke she said talked like a foolish soldier; but to Leicester it was that she exclaimed, "You, my lord, you! If all the world forsook me I thought that you would be true!"—Charles I.'s celebrated letter to Prince Rupert after the loss of Bristol, depriving him of his command, begins with assuring him that the surrender, in such a manner, and by his trusted, no longer trusty nephew, of that most important city, was the greatest trial of his constancy that had yet befallen him: "For what is to be done, after one that is so near me as you are, both in blood and friendship, submits himself to so mean an action (I give it the easiest term)? such——I have so much to say, that I will say no more of it." The tone is that of the duke in Mr. Browning's *Colombe's Birthday*:

> "Ah, the first bitterness is over now!
> Bitter I may have felt it to confront
> The truth, and ascertain those natures' value
> I had so counted on—that was a pang."

Corneille, in his historical tragedy of *Cinna*, treats in a like strain the effect upon Augustus of the discovered conspiracy:

> "Quoi! mes plus chers amis! quoi! Cinna! quoi! Maxime!
> Les deux que j'honorais d'une si haute estime,
> A qui j'ouvrais mon cœur, et dont j'avais fait choix
> Pours les plus importants et plus nobles emplois!
> Après qu'entre leurs mains j'ai remis mon empire,
> Pour m'arracher le jour l'un et l'autre conspire!"

But a later scene proves that Augustus is not even yet aware of all the accomplices; and the conviction of Æmilie as one of them, wrings from him, as Brutus from the elder Cæsar, the upbraiding cry, *Et toi, ma fille, aussi!*

One touching incident marks the horror of the murder of the Czar Paul in 1801. The dress of Ouvaroff, one of the conspirators, is said to have caused him to be mistaken by the Emperor for his son Constantine; and, according to Bignon, the last words which the unhappy monarch uttered were, "And you too, my Constantine!"

Very worthless objects have sometimes been very undeservedly Et-tu-Brutefied. The first Lord Holland, when forsaken by the selfish friends, as they have justly been described, with whom he had jobbed and made merry and laughed at principle, had yet retained enough belief in the social virtues to be made seriously unhappy by the conduct of his worthless companions, particularly by that of Rigby, the most worthless of them all;

"White-liver'd Grenville and self-loving Gower
Shall never cause one peevish moment more; . . .
Slight was the pain they gave, and short its date;
I found I could not both despise and hate;
But, Rigby, what did I for thee endure?"

A man as pious as Henry Fox was otherwise, has declared that he knew few things which so darken one's views of the moral government of God, as the experience of baseness and treachery in persons who have won our confidence; that it tempts one to question the reality of human virtue, to suspect the hollowness of all appearance of truth and piety, whence there is but a step to calling in question the moral purpose for which we are placed on earth. Hawthorne somewhere intimates that the young and pure are not apt to find out how actually sin is in the world, until that miserable truth is brought home to them by the guiltiness of some trusted friend. "Trust ye not in a friend,"—but ah, the pity of it, for him who has to take up with these words of the Morasthite,—"A man's enemies are the men of his own house."—How many variations on this general theme might be played from Shakespeare's plays! Sir Valentine, for instance, denouncing the falsity of that other, so-called, but so far mis-called, Gentleman of Verona:

> . . . "Now I dare not say
> I have one friend alive; thou wouldst disprove me.
> Who should be trusted now, when one's right hand
> Is perjured to the bosom? Proteus,
> I am sorry I must never trust thee more,
> But count the world a stranger for thy sake.
> The private wound is deepest: O time most curst!
> 'Mongst all foes that a friend should be the worst!"

Polixenes, again, argues touching the breach of amity between him and Leontes, that revenge is like to be all the more bitter for the cordiality of past confidence. Then, too, the implication of Lord Scroop, of Masham, in the conspiracy with Grey and Cambridge against Henry V.,—

> "Nay, but the man that was his bedfellow,
> Whom he hath cloy'd and graced with princely favours,—
> That he should, for a foreign purse, so sell
> His sovereign's life to death and treachery!"

Henry reminds Scroop that he bore the key of all his counsels, and knew the very bottom of his soul; and he wept for *him*,—"for this revolt of thine, methinks, is like another fall of man."—A later king of England, Edward IV., is made to despair when he sees his brother Clarence among the supporters of the foe: "Yea, brother of Clarence, art thou here too? Nay, then, I see that Edward needs must down."—And once again, there is the *Et tu Brute* cue from which we started, thus set forth in all its suggestive force by Shakespeare's Antony:

> "For Brutus, as you know, was Cæsar's angel:
> Judge, O you gods, how dearly Cæsar loved him!
> This was the most unkindest cut of all:
> For when the noble Cæsar saw *him* stab,
> Ingratitude, more strong than traitor's arms,
> Quite vanquish'd him: then burst his mighty heart."

But as we recur to this, as the first among these secular annotations on a Scripture text, so we recur to Scripture, in conclusion, for a pathetic parallel, also from the Book of

Psalms: "For it was not an enemy that reproached me; then I could have borne it; neither was it he that hated me that did magnify himself against me: then I would have hid myself from him. But it was thou, a man mine equal, my guide, and mine acquaintance. We took sweet counsel together, and walked unto the house of God in company." The companionship past intensifies the cruelty present. Without so recent and vivid a remembrance of sweet counsel together, and companionship hallowed by the sanctuary itself, the present cruelty could have been borne; but with them it hardly can.

—o—

"*JUDGE NOT.*"

ST. MATTHEW vii. 1.

A STRINGENT motive is adduced to enforce the strenuous monition, "Judge not,"—and it is, "that ye be not judged. For with what judgment ye judge, ye shall be judged; and with what measure ye mete, it shall be measured to you again." There is one Lawgiver, who is able to save and to destroy; even He who hath committed all judgment unto the Son: who art thou that judgest another?

Appalled were all who gazed on the last struggles of Cardinal Beaufort, rendered hideous by the tortures of agonizing remorse. Hope had he none. Despair was impersonated in the frenzied contortions of that dying man. King and peers stood beside the death-bed, awe-stricken and shocked. The king prayed for the cardinal, that the Eternal mover of the heavens might "look with a gentle eye upon this wretch:

> O beat away the busy meddling fiend
> That lays strong siege upon this wretch's soul,
> And from his bosom purge this black despair."

See, says a less gentle observer, Warwick, how the pangs of death do make him grin. Royal Henry, on devouter thoughts intent, bids "peace to his soul," in parting, "if God's pleasure be." And then the monarch solemnly, urgently, importunes the moribund cardinal to give some token, ere he quite depart, that Despair has not made him all her own: "Lord cardinal, if thou think'st on heaven's bliss, hold up thy hand, make signal of thy hope." But the cardinal—dies, and makes no sign. The appeal is fruitless: no hand is held up; no signal of hope displayed. The baffled prince, cut to the heart, can but exclaim, "He dies, and makes no sign: O God, forgive him!" Warwick again interposes a harsher voice, "So bad a death argues a monstrous life," he is sure. But his sovereign hushes his damning criticism with a right royal veto:—

> "FORBEAR TO JUDGE, *for we are sinners all.*
> * * * * *
> Close up his eyes, and draw the curtain close;
> And let us all to meditation."

Forbear to judge. And the Shakspearean Henry practises in person the monition thus enforced. It is his rule to check in himself every tendency to uncharitable judgment. As when proof all but positive distresses him of his uncle Gloster's death being due to violence, he yet restrains the bent of his convictions by the prayer,—

> "O Thou that judgest all things, stay my thoughts:
> My thoughts, that labour to persuade my soul
> Some violent hands were laid on Humphrey's life!
> If my suspèct be false, forgive me, God;
> For judgment only doth belong to Thee!"

It is by the deathbed of the man self-convicted of Duke Humphrey's death, that Henry can yet say, even of him, when from so bad a death is argued a monstrous life, Forbear to judge, for we are sinners all.

Are we to infer that Shakspeare was himself for backing to the full this royal veto? That, perhaps, were going too far. The veto is dramatically true to character, and designedly characteristic of the royal speaker. But if Shakspeare himself (we are assuming him to *be* the author of this disputed play) would or could scarcely in this particular instance have enforced such a lesson of charity, we may at least be assured, from the large tolerance and subtle apprehension so patent in his own kingly nature, that he would in spirit have echoed the king's *forbear*. Perhaps his own feeling might be as nearly as possible expressed in other words of his, put into the mouth of quite another character, and referring to quite another occasion :—

> "And how his audit stands, who knows, save heaven?
> But, in our circumstance and course of thought,
> 'Tis heavy with him."

Forbear to judge, is, nevertheless, the moral of this strain, as of the other. Human ignorance in the one case, human frailty in the other, ousts human nature from the judgment-seat.

No man, avers Sir Thomas Browne, can justly censure or condemn another; because, in fact, no man truly knows another. "This I perceive in myself; for I am in the dark to all the world, and my nearest friends behold me but in a cloud. . . . Further, no man can judge another, because no man knows himself." In a former section of this his profession of faith, this good physician warns those who, upon a rigid application of the law, sentence Solomon unto damnation,* that they condemn not only him, but themselves, and the whole world; "for, by the letter and written word of God, we are without exception in the state of death: but there is a prerogative of God, and an arbitrary pleasure above the letter of His own law, by which alone we can pretend unto salvation, and through which Solomon might be as easily saved as those who condemn him."

The Vicar of Gravenhurst, in his position of parish priest, owns himself compelled to confess that the best people are not the best in every relation of life, and the worst not bad in every relation of life; so that, with experience, he finds himself growing lenient in his blame, if also reticent in his praise. "Again and again I say to myself that only the Omniscient can be the equitable judge of human beings—so complicated are our

* St. Augustine, Lyra, Bellarmine, and others, are chargeable with this judgment and sentence.

virtues with our failings, and so many are the hidden virtues, as well as hidden vices, of our fellow-men." If judge at all we dare, and do, be it in the spirit and to the letter of Wordsworth's counsel:—

> "From all rash censure be the mind kept free;
> He only judges right who weighs, compares,
> And, in the sternest sentence which his voice
> Pronounces, ne'er abandons Charity."

Well and wisely said La Bruyère, that "La règle de Descartes, qui ne veut pas que l'on décide sur les moindres vérités avant qu'elles soient connues clairement et distinctement, est assez belle et assez juste pour devoir s'étendu au jugement que l'on fait des personnes." Real character, as William Hazlitt says, is not one thing, but a thousand things: actual qualities do not conform to any factitious standard in the mind, but rest upon their own truth and nature. "The dull stupor under which we labour in respect of those whom we have the greatest opportunities of inspecting nearly, we should do well to imitate, before we give extreme and uncharitable verdicts againsts those whom we only see in passing, or at a distance."

> "Well—after all—
> "What know we of the secret of a man?
> His nerves were wrong. What ails us, who are sound,
> That we should mimic this raw fool, the world,
> Which charts us all in its coarse blacks or whites,
> As ruthless as a baby with a worm,
> As cruel as a schoolboy ere he grows
> To pity—more from ignorance than will."

Who can say, asks Samuel Rogers, "In such circumstances I should have done otherwise?" Who, did he but reflect by what slow gradations, often by how many strange occurrences, we are led astray; with how much reluctance, how much agony, how many efforts to escape, how many sighs, how many tears—who, did he but reflect for a moment, would have the heart to cast a stone? *

* "Fortunately these things are known to Him, from whom no secrets are hidden; and let us rest in the assurance that His judgments are not as ours."—*Rogers's Italy.*

The autobiographer of one of Mr. Wilkie Collins's earlier fictions proposes in an opening chapter to give a sketch of his character. But he sensibly refrains from the execution of a too ambitious plan. For, "what man can say: I will sound the depth of my own vices and measure the height of my own virtues; and be as good as his word? We can neither know nor judge ourselves—others may judge, but cannot know us—God alone judges and knows too."

"Who made the heart, 'tis He alone
  Decidedly can try us;
He knows each chord—its various tone,
  Each spring, its various bias:
Then at the balance let's be mute,
  We never can adjust it."

Dunsford the essayist's objection to all hasty judgment of our fellow-creatures is based on the ground of its being "such an unscientific proceeding." You comment, he says, upon another man's conduct, and attribute motives to him. Now an ingenious and imaginative person—a lawyer making a speech for him—might show many different motives of equal probability. You fix upon one, perhaps because it is consonant to your own mind and nature, or because it is the uppermost or easiest one to conjecture; but really you often ignore the doctrine of chances, and perhaps you will find upon strict calculation that the chances are fairly four to one against your having named the right motive. As the winning horse is often "a dark one," at any rate not the favourite, so after all some obscure and improbable motive is often the true cause of a man's actions. In short, Dunsford maintains that our condemnation of others is often as unscientific as it is unchristian.

When the Doge of Venice, Foscari, in Byron's tragedy, agitated by the summons to judge his son, speculates somewhat wildly on the burden of the mystery of all this unintelligible world, Marina submissively suggests that

"These are things we cannot judge
On earth."

And how then, demands the old man,—

> "And how then shall we judge each other,
> Who are all earth?"

Mr. Lockhart, in the closing chapter of his admirable Life of Scott, quoting Keble's lines,—

> "Not even the tenderest heart, and next our own,
> Knows half the reasons why we smile or sigh,"

declares considerations of this kind to have always induced him to regard with small respect any attempt to delineate fully and exactly any human being's character. He avows his distrust of our capacity for, even in very humble cases, judging our neighbour fairly; and cannot but pity the presumption that must swell in the heart and brain of any ordinary brother of the race, when daring to pronounce, *ex cathedrâ,* on the whole structure and complexion of a great mind, from the comparatively narrow and scanty materials which can by possibility have been placed before him.

Men who see *into* their neighbours, observes Dr. Oliver Wendell Holmes, are very apt to be contemptuous; but men who see *through* them find something lying behind every human soul which it is not for them to sit in judgment on, or to attempt to sneer out of the order of God's manifold universe.

The same wise-hearted writer—wise of heart as well as head—has a dialogue between doctor and minister concerning a quasi-reprobate, to whom the former has been kind, and about whose destiny the other is hardly more severe than certain. "Bad enough, no doubt," Doctor Kittredge owns this scampish half-breed to be; "but might be worse. Has some humanity left in him yet. Let him go. God can judge him—I can't." "You are too charitable, doctor," objects the minister. "He has saved his neck—but his soul is a lost one, I am afraid, beyond question." "I can't judge men's souls," the doctor replies. "I can judge their acts, and hold them responsible for those; but I don't know much about their souls. If you or I had found our soul in a half-breed body, and then been turned loose to run among the Indians, we might have been playing just such tricks as this fellow has been trying." What said a greater doctor when Boswell asked him whether, in the case of an aggressor forcing on a duel by ill usage, and getting killed in it, there is not almost no "ground to hope that he is gone to a state of happiness"? "Sir," said Johnson, "we are not to judge determinately of the state in which a man leaves this life. He may in a moment have repented effectually." And then Johnson quoted, apparently with approval, at any rate with hopeful interest, an epitaph, from Camden's Remains, upon a very wicked man, who was killed by a fall from his horse, in which epitaph he is supposed to say, "Between the stirrup and the ground, I mercy asked, I mercy found." On another occasion Johnson appealed to Richard Baxter's avowed belief that a suicide—if hurried by sudden passion to self-slaughter—may be saved. And "if," says Baxter, "it should be objected that what I maintain may encourage suicide, I answer, I am not to tell a lie to prevent it." Who, as Campbell asks, after surmising that the hand which smote its kindred heart, might yet be prone to deeds of mercy,—

> . . . "Who may understand
> Thy many woes, poor suicide, unknown?
> He who thy being gave shall judge of thee alone."

Qualis vita, finis ita, is a rhyming proverb not quite worthy of all acceptation. That Country Parson whose Recreations made him a name (such name, at least, as four initials may comprise) declares himself to have no look but one of sorrow and pity to cast on the poor suicide's grave, and thinks the common English verdict is right as well as charitable, which supposes that in every such case reason has become unhinged, and responsibility is gone. "No doubt it is the saddest of all sad ends; but I do not forget that a certain Authority, the highest of all authorities, said to all human beings, 'Judge not, that ye be not judged.' The writer has, in the course of his duty, looked upon more than one suicide's dead face; and the lines of Hood appeared to sketch the fit feeling with which to do so:—

> "'Owning her weakness,
> Her evil behaviour;

And leaving, with meekness,
Her soul to her Saviour.'"

A different spirit informs the Kirk from the day when Wishart complained that, in their arrogance, her ministers, "as if they had been privy to the councils of God, or the dispensers of His vengeance to the world," presumed to pronounce upon the future state of their adversaries, and "doomed them, both body and soul, to eternal torments." Pity but the poet had been better man and Christian who wrote these strong lines on damnatory sentences *de mortuis*, even when there remains nought to show—

. . . "save a life misspent,—
And soul—but who shall answer where it went?
'Tis ours to bear, not judge the dead; and they
Who doom to hell, themselves are on the way,
Unless those bullies of eternal pains
Are pardoned their bad hearts for their worse brains."

More in a reverent spirit, and in a farther-seeing one, is the mystic finale of the Laureate's memorable Vision of Sin, and its open verdict on the obscure crime of a great criminal:—

"At last I heard a voice upon the slope
Cry to the summit, 'Is there any hope?'
To which an answer pealed from that high land,
But in a tongue no man could understand;
And on the glimmering limit far withdrawn,
God made Himself an awful rose of dawn."

Never let it be forgotten, insists a Quarterly Reviewer, that there is scarcely a single moral action of a single human being of which other men have such a knowledge—its ultimate grounds, its surrounding incidents, and the real determining causes of its merits,—as to warrant their pronouncing a conclusive judgment.

The writings of Mr. Arthur Helps are honourably distinguished by an oft-recurring plea for mutual tolerance, on the ground of the little we really know one of another. In "Companions of my Solitude," for instance, the author remarks that were it only considered how utterly incompetent men are to talk of the conduct of others as they do, the talkers would often be silenced at once, and the sufferers as readily consoled. Take the one question merely of difference of temperament—which, amongst men, is probably as great as that amongst the different species of animals—as between that, for example, of the lively squirrel and the solemn crane. "Now, if only from this difference between them, the squirrel would be a bad judge of the felicity, or generosity, or the domestic conduct, of the crane.

"Probably when we are thinking or talking of a person, we recall some visual image of that person. I have thought what an instructive thing it would be, if under some magic influence—like that, for example, which would construct a 'palace of truth'—it were arranged that as we gave out our comments on the character or conduct of any person, this image on the retina of memory should change according to the truth, or rather the want of it, in our remarks. Gradually, feature after feature would steal away till we gazed at nonentity, or we should find another image glide into the field of view,—somebody we had never seen, perhaps, but to whom the comments we were uttering really did apply."

Accordingly, our author would have the sufferers from injurious and unjust comment treat the whole thing as one which lacked reality. No thoughtful man, he urges, ought to be long vexed at such stuff, immaterial in every sense: such stuff as dreams are made of.

In one of his Dialogues, again, he makes Dunsford declare the most curious thing, as regards people living together, to be the intense ignorance they sometimes are in of each other. And Milverton follows up the remark by adding, that people fulfil a relation towards each other, and only know each other in that relation: they perform orbits round each other, each gyrating, too, upon his own axis, so that there are parts of the character of each which are never brought into view of the other. In another Dialogue, Milverton refers to the habit divines have of reminding us, that, in forming our ideas of the government of Providence, we should recollect that we see only a fragment. The same observation, in its degree, he holds to be true as regards human conduct. "We see a little bit here and there, and assume the nature of the whole. Even a very silly man's actions are often more to the purpose than his friends' comments on them."

In yet another of his works, this popular essay-writer devotes an entire essay to the subject of our judgments of other men. Who does not feel, he asks, that to describe with fidelity the least portion of the entangled nature that is within him would be no easy matter? And yet the same man who feels this, and who, perhaps, would be ashamed of talking at hazard about the properties of a flower, of a weed, of some figure in geometry, will put forth his guesses about the character of his brother-man, as if he had the fullest authority for all that he was saying. It is shown in detail how an opinion of some man's character and conduct gets abroad which is formed after a wrong method, by prejudiced persons, upon a false statement of facts, respecting a matter which they cannot possibly understand; and how this is then left to be inflated by Folly, and blown about by Idleness.

There is among Wordsworth's Poems on the Naming of Places, one which is memorable if only as containing one of the most admired lines he ever wrote, descriptive of Lady of the Mere—

> "Sole-sitting by the shores of old romance,"

—but which is also pertinent to the present occasion, as pointing a moral, after the poet's wont to moralise his song. A man had been seen in the distance by the poet and his friends, angling. No great harm in that, my masters? Nay; but the angler was in peasant's garb, and the season was mid-harvest, and therefore, and on the spot, they voted him improvident and reckless. But when they came up to him, these over-hasty judges found in the man they had summarily condemned, a poor mortal wasted by sickness, and all too weak to labour in the harvest-field, but using his best skill to gain a pittance from the dead unfeeling lake that knew not of his wants :—

> "I will not say
> What thoughts immediately were ours, nor how

The happy idleness of that sweet morn
With all its lovely images, was changed
To serious musing and to self-reproach.
Nor did we fail to see within ourselves
What need there is to be reserved in speech,
And temper all our thoughts with charity.
—Therefore, unwilling to forget that day,
My friend, myself, and she who then received
The same admonishment, have called the place
By a memorial name, uncouth indeed
As e'er by mariner was given to bay
Or foreland on a new-discovered coast;
And POINT RASH-JUDGMENT is the name it bears." *

Forbear to judge: for how pitifully little is the all we really know one of another! Mr. Froude has forcibly remarked—even admitting the remark to be a truism—that whoever has attended but slightly to the phenomena of human nature has discovered how inadequate is the clearest insight which he can hope to attain into character and disposition. "Every one is a perplexity to himself and a perplexity to his neighbours; and men who are born in the same generation, who are exposed to the same influences, trained by the same teachers, and live from childhood to age in constant and familiar intercourse, are often little more than shadows to each other, intelligible in superficial form and outline, but divided inwardly by impalpable and mysterious barriers." And yet how ready each "weak unknowing hand" to hurl the bolts of Heaven against whomsoever it deems to be Heaven's foe.

Sir James Stephen bids all hail to Rhadamanthus on his posthumous judgment-seat in the nether regions. But when Rhadamanthus comes above ground, holds in his hand the historical pen, and resolves all the enigmas of hearts which ceased to beat long centuries ago, more confidently than most of us would dare to interpret the mysteries of own, Sir James for one wishes him back again at the confluence of Styx, Phlegethon, and Cocytus. For, "it is, after all, nothing more than

* The friends spoken of were Coleridge and Miss Wordsworth. The scene was the eastern shore of Grasmere. The date of the poem is 1800.

the surface of human character which the retrospective scrutiny of the keenest human eye is able to detect." It is in a subsequent portion of the same instructive treatise, that the writer pronounces human justice to be severe, not merely because man is censorious, but because he reasonably distrusts himself, and fears lest his weakness should confound the distinctions of good and evil; and Divine justice to be lenient, because there alone love can flow in all its unfathomable depths and boundless expansion, impeded by no dread of error, and diverted by no misplaced sympathies.*

In the course of some remarks on the harshness with which man is disposed to regard the fellow-man whose doctrine, in matters of religious faith, differs from his own, the author of the "Caxton Essays" is impressive on the fact that He who hath reserved to Himself the right of judging, has imperatively said to man, whose faculty of judging must be, like man himself, erring and human, "Judge not, that ye be not judged." Now, argues the essayist, of all our offences, it is clear that that offence of which man can be the least competent judge is an offence of defective faith. "For faith belongs to our innermost hearts, and not to our overt actions. And religious faith is therefore that express tribute to the only Reader of all hearts, on the value of which man can never, without arrogant presumption, set himself up as judge."

If even-handed justice, says Mr. Anthony Trollope, were done throughout the world, some apology would be found for most offences. Not that the offences would thus be wiped

* On the "false humility" which shrinks from all censure or reprobation of what is evil, under cover of the text "judge not, that ye be not judged,"—as if it were the intent of that text, not to warn us against rash, presumptuous, and uncharitable judgments, but absolutely to forbid our taking account of the distinction between right and wrong,—see Sir Henry Taylor's essay on Humility and Independence in his valuable "Notes from Life." The man of true humility, we are there taught, will come to the task of judgment, on serious occasions, not lightly or unawed, but praying to have "a right judgment in all things;" and whilst exercising that judgment in no spirit of compromise or evasion, he will feel that to judge his brother is a duty and not a privilege; and he will judge him in sorrow, humbled by the contemplation of that fallen nature of which he is himself part and parcel. (See "Notes from Life" (1847), pp. 46, *sqq.*)

away, and black become white; but much that is now very black would, he submits, be reduced to that sombre, uninviting shade of ordinary brown which is so customary to humanity." * It is much the same humane thought which underlies Pelayo's apology for Roderick, when we read how closely that generous prince would and did

> . . . "cherish in his heart the constant thought
> Something was yet untold, which, being known,
> Would palliate his offence, and make the fall
> Of one till then so excellently good,
> Less monstrous, less revolting to belief,
> More to be pitied, more to be forgiven."

As one of George Eliot's good parsons has it, God sees us as we are altogether, not in separate feelings or actions, as our fellow-men see us. We are always doing each other injustice, and thinking better or worse of each other than we deserve, he says, because we only hear and see separate words and actions —not each other's whole nature. Do not philosophic doctors tell us, again, the reflective author in person elsewhere muses, that we are unable to discern so much as a tree, except by an unconscious cunning which combines many past and separate sensations; that no one sense is independent of another, so that in the dark we can hardly taste a fricassee, or tell whether our pipe is alight or not, and the most intelligent boy, if accommodated with claws or hoofs instead of fingers, would be likely to remain on the lowest form? If so, it is easy to understand that our discernment of men's motives must depend on the completeness of the elements we can bring from our own susceptibility and our own experience. "See to it, friend, before you pronounce a too hasty judgment, that your own moral sensibilities are not of a hoofed or clawed character." For, as this penetrating writer insists, in continuation of the metaphor, the keenest eye will not serve, unless you have the delicate fingers, with their subtile nerve filaments, which elude scientific

* Were we all turned inside out, however, Mr. Trollope elsewhere surmises, some of us might find "our shade of brown to be very dark."—*The Bertrams*, chap. xix.

lenses, and lose themselves in the invisible world of human sensations.

Deeds which, to quote another popular though less powerful penwoman, our acquaintance designate our follies, may at another tribunal be our virtues—our single redeeming points; who judges rightly, who can rightly judge, where so many of our efforts are bent to seem other than we are, and the universal conjuring trick of this world is to throw dust expertly in our neighbours' eyes?

Centuries ago, well-nigh two score, it was written by the most philosophic, and perhaps the best, of Roman emperors, that men's actions look worse than they are; and, says he, "one must be thoroughly informed of a great many things before one can be rightly qualified to give judgment in the case." The sceptic Bayle was a better Christian than Scaliger, when he protested against the assertion of that peremptory scholar that Bellarmin did not believe a word of what he wrote, and was at heart an atheist: besides the testimony of Bellarmin's life and deathbed to the contrary, such judgments are, said Bayle (and no friend to the Jesuits he), a usurpation of the rights of One who alone is the Judge of hearts, and before whom there is no dissembling.

An apostle's reason given for the counsel, Speak not evil one of another, brethren,—is this: that whoso speaketh evil of his brother, and judgeth his brother, speaketh evil of the law, and judgeth the law. Now, there is one Lawgiver, who is able to save and to destroy; who art thou that judgest another?

> "Oh what are we,
> Frail creatures as we are, that we should sit
> In judgment man on man! and what were we,
> If the All-merciful should mete to us
> With the same rigorous measure wherewithal
> Sinner to sinner metes!"

No observant reader of Mr. Carlyle but will have noticed, if not (which were better) laid to heart, his habitual abstention from that dogmatism of the judgment-seat in which smaller spirits delight. For instance, in his moral estimate of so erring a genius as Hoffmann, if, in judging him, Mr. Carlyle is forced to condemn him, it is with mildness, with a desire to do justice. Let us not forget, urges the critic, that for a mind like Hoffmann's, the path of propriety was difficult to find—still more difficult to keep. "Moody, sensitive, and fantastic, he wandered through the world like a foreign presence, subject to influences of which common natures have happily no glimpse." A good or a wise man we must not call him; but among the ordinary population of this world, "to note him with the mark of reprobation were ungrateful and unjust." So, again, in the same author's review of the life and writings of Werner—who, always in some degree an enigma to himself, may well be obscure to us. For "there are mysteries and unsounded abysses in every human heart; and that is but a questionable philosophy which undertakes so readily to explain them." Religious belief especially, Mr. Carlyle urges, at least when it seems heartfelt and well-intentioned, is no subject for harsh or even irreverent investigation. "He is a wise man that, having such a belief, knows and sees clearly the grounds of it in himself; and those, we imagine, who have explored with strictest scrutiny the secret of their own bosoms, will be least apt to rush with intolerant violence into that of other men's." Still more elaborate and emphatic is the exposition of this doctrine as applied to the case of Robert Burns. The world, it is alleged, is habitually unjust in its judgments of such men, since it decides, like a court of law, by dead statutes, and not positively but negatively,—less on what is done right, than on what is or is not done wrong. Whereas, by Mr. Carlyle's doctrine, not the few inches of deflection from the mathematical orbit, which are so easily measured, but the *ratio* of these to the whole diameter, constitutes the real aberration. "This orbit may be a planet's, its diameter the breadth of the solar system; or it may be a city hippodrome; nay, the circle of a ginhorse, its diameter a score of feet or paces. But the inches of deflection only are measured; and it is assumed that the diameter of the ginhorse, and that of the planet, will yield the same ratio when compared to them!" Here, according to our author, lies the root of many a blind, cruel condemnation of Burnses, Swifts, Rousseaus, which one never listens to with approval. "Granted, the ship comes into harbour with shrouds and tackle damaged; the pilot is blameworthy; he has not been all-wise and all-powerful: but to know *how* blameworthy, tell us first whether his voyage has been round the globe, or only to Ramsgate and the Isle of Dogs."

To a very different style of sinners the same judgment—rather the same refusal to judge—is accorded, when the doom of Chaumette, Gobel, and other reddest of red-republican reprobates, is rehearsed, in the history of France's reign of terror, while the revolution was devouring so greedily her own children. "For Anaxagoras Chaumette, the sleek head now [April 1794] stript of its *bonnet rouge* [and a traveller by tumbril to Sainte Guillotine], what hope is there? Unless Death *were* 'an eternal sleep'? Wretched Anaxagoras! God shall judge thee, not I."

Once more: "Unhappy soul! who shall judge him?" is the historian's deprecating query in the instance of August of Poland, the physically strong,—who dies, confessedly a *very* great sinner, early in 1733. Who shall judge him?

"Hereafter?—And do you think to look
On the terrible pages of that Book
To find his failings, faults, and errors?
Ah, you will then have other cares,
In your own shortcomings and despairs,
In your own secret sins and terrors!"

Corporal Trim was once moved to avow his belief—rather hotly, for his *esprit de corps* was piqued—that when a soldier "gets time to pray, he prays as heartily as a parson—though not with all his fuss and hypocrisy. Thou shouldst not have said that, Trim, said my uncle Toby—for God only knows who is a hypocrite, and who is not. At the great and general review of us all, Corporal, at the day of judgment (and not till then)—it will be seen who have done their duties in this world, and who have not."

In a like spirit, another clerical novelist, of a more recent type, and whose distinctive evangel is Muscular Christianity, introduces a "double-first" candidate for orders who reminds him of Mr. Bye-Ends in Bunyan: "And yet," comes the charitable clause conditional, "I believe the man was really in earnest. He was really desirous to do what was right, as far as he knew it; and all the more desirous, because he saw, in the present state of society, what was right would pay him. God shall judge him, not I. Who can unravel the confusion of mingled selfishness and devotion that exist even in his own heart, much less in that of another?"

In Mr. Thackeray's instance, exception has been taken, on ethical grounds, by no vulgar critic, to his habit of shrinking from moral estimate as well as moral judgment, in dealing with his characters. Into that distinction not without a difference, this is not the place (nor this the pen) to enter. But the critic in question—for some years a main support of the *National Review*—recognises this avoidance of moral judgment as springing from kindly feeling, from the just and humble sense we all should have that our own demerits make it unseemly for us to ascend the judgment-chair, and from a wide appreciation of the variety and obscurity of men's real motives of action.*

——o——

PART KNOWLEDGE.

1 CORINTHIANS xiii. 9.

"WE know in part," said the apostle; who, therefore, prophesied in part; always with the assurance that when that which is perfect is come, then shall that which is in part be done away. Meanwhile, we see through a glass darkly, through a medium obscurely—"now I know in part."

* The avoidance of moral *estimate*, on the other hand, is imputed to an insufficient sense of the duty incumbent on all of us to form determinate estimates of men and actions, if only as bearing on our own conduct in life. (See "W. C. Roscoe's Essays," vol. ii., p. 308.)

If so it was with him that once was caught up into the third heavens, much more with his readers. For we are but of yesterday, and know nothing. "Behold, God is great, and we know Him not." At the height of our knowledge we can but fall back upon the old saying, "Lo, these are parts of His ways; but how little a portion is heard of Him!" And when we consider the heavens, the work of His hands; the moon and the stars, which He hath ordained; the earth beneath, the ocean round about, the waters under the earth, the pent-up fires within it,—verily He is a God that hideth Himself still, and that revealeth but a portion of His work, clouds and darkness covering the rest. His thoughts are very deep; and what is man that he should know them, or the son of man that he should find them out unto perfection? From the topmost pinnacles attained by science he can see but the utmost part of them, and cannot see them all.

Locke argues the intellectual and sensible world to be in this perfectly alike: that the part which we see of them holds no proportion with what we see not; and that whatsoever we can reach with our eyes, or our thoughts, of either of them, is but a point, almost nothing, in comparison with the rest. Shall he whose birth, maturity, and age, as Beattie has it, scarce fill the circle of one summer day—shall the poor gnat conclude nature in collapse because of a passing cloud, not transparent to the insect's vision?

"One part, one little part, we dimly scan
  Through the dark medium of life's feverish dream;
Yet dare arraign the whole stupendous plan,
  If but that little part incongruous seem.
  Nor is that part perhaps what mortals deem;
Oft from apparent ill our blessings rise.
  Oh then renounce that impious self-esteem,
That aims to trace the secrets of the skies;
For thou art but of dust: be humble and be wise."

Freethinking Lord Shaftesbury begins a section of his "Characteristics" with the remark, that when we reflect on any ordinary frame or constitution, either of art or nature, and consider how hard it is to give the least account of a particular *part* without a competent knowledge of the *whole*, we need not wonder to find ourselves at a loss in many things relating to the constitution and frame of the universe. Elsewhere he suggestively observes, that in an infinity of things mutually relative, a mind which sees not infinitely, can see nothing fully; "and since each particular has relation to all in general, it can know no perfect or true relation of anything in a world not perfectly and fully known." And supposing the case of an ignorant landsman presuming to question the details of a ship's rigging, his lordship breaks out into the apostrophe, "O my friend, let us not thus betray our ignorance, but consider where we are, and in what a universe. Think of the many parts of the vast machine in which we have so little insight, and of which it is impossible we should know the ends and uses; when instead of seeing to the highest pennons, we see only some lower deck, and are in this dark case of flesh, confined even to the hold and meanest station of the vessel." There is Mrs. Browning's usual energy of diction in the exclamation,

> "Ay, we are forced, so pent,
> To judge the whole too partially, confound
> Conclusions. Is there any common phrase
> Significant, when the adverb's heard alone,
> The verb being absent, and the pronoun out?
> But we, distracted in the roar of life,
> Still insolently at God's adverb snatch,
> And bruit against Him that His thought is void,
> His meaning hopeless."

The same good Providence, as Madame de Sévigné writes, that governs all, shall one day unravel all; we poor mortals being, in the meanwhile, so many all but stone-blind and utterly ignorant lookers-on. We suffer, as the author of "Thorndale" says—there is no doubt about that—and we naturally speak and think under the sharp pang of our present agony; but the ultimate and overruling judgment which we form of human life, should be taken from some calm, impersonal point of view. "We should command the widest horizon possible. Of the great whole of humanity we see but a little at a time. We pause sometimes on the lights only of the picture, sometimes only on the shadows. How very dark those shadows seem! Yet if we could embrace in our view the whole of the picture, perhaps the very darkest shadows might be recognised as effective or inevitable portions of a grand harmonious whole." How closes Thomson his poem of "The Seasons," drear Winter then his cue?—with the memorable lines:—

"Ye good distress'd!
Ye noble few! who here unbending stand
Beneath life's pressure, yet bear up awhile;
And what your bounded view, which only saw
A little part, deemed evil, is no more:
The storms of wintry time will quickly pass,
And one unbounded spring encircle all."

The theme of our part knowledge, so strictly cabin'd, cribb'd, confined, is one to which Thomson repeatedly recurs. For instance, in an earlier book:—

"But here the cloud,
So wills Eternal Providence, sits deep.
Enough for us to know that this dark state,
In wayward passions lost, and vain pursuits,
This infancy of being, cannot prove
The final issue of the works of God,
By boundless love and perfect wisdom form'd
And ever rising with the rising mind."

Again, with emphasis and discretion (as Polonius says), he puts the query—

"Shall little haughty ignorance pronounce
His works unwise, of which the smallest part
Exceeds the narrow vision of her mind?
As if upon a full proportioned dome,
On swelling columns heaved, the pride of art,
A critic-fly, whose feeble ray scarce spreads
An inch around, with blind presumption bold,
Should dare to tax the structure of the whole."

Horace Walpole makes use of a similar figure in one of his three or four thousand published letters: "We are poor silly animals: we live for an instant upon a particle of a boundless universe, and are much like a butterfly that should argue

Q 2

about the nature of the seasons, and what creates their vicissitudes, and does not exist itself to see one annual revolution of them."

> "Earth's number-scale is near us set;
> The total God alone can see;
> But each some fraction." *

Addison, in one of his essays, comments on the body of an animal as an object comparatively adequate to our senses, it being a particular part of Providence that lies within a narrow compass, so that the eye is able to command it, and by successive inquiries to search into all its parts. Could the body of the whole earth, he goes on to say, or indeed the whole universe, be thus subjected to the examination of our senses, were it not too big and disproportioned for our inquiries, too unwieldy for the management of the eye and hand, "there is no question but it would appear to us as curious and well-contrived a frame as that of a human body. We should see the same concatenation and subserviency, the same necessity and usefulness, the same beauty and harmony, in all and every of its parts, as what we discover in the body of every single animal." To adopt an illustration of Fénélon's to the same purpose: imagine the letters of a sentence to be so enormous in size, that a man could only make out one of them at a time; in that case he could not read, that is, collect the letters together and discover the sense of them in combination. So it is, argues the benign prelate, with the *grands traits* of Providence in the conduct of the world at large during the lapse of centuries. It is only the whole that is intelligible, and the whole is too vast to be scrutinised near at hand. Each event in the process of ages is like a separate letter or sign, which is too large for our petty organs, and which is without a meaning when taken apart from the rest. A more vigorous philosopher than the gentle Fénélon compares the universe to a picture, the beauty of which is then alone perceptible when the true stand-point of perspective is taken. There are certain inventions in perspective, or certain

* Owen Meredith: "The Artist."

beautiful designs, he says, which look all confusion until you either inspect them from the right point of view, or make use of some kind of glass or mirror as the medium of observation. In the same manner the apparent deformities of our fractional side-views, resolve themselves into harmonious unity when the eye is directed aright.

Dr. Johnson was in an unwontedly placid and benignant frame of mind, by Boswell's account, when the two stood together, one serene autumn night, in Dr. Taylor's garden, and the sage delivered himself, in meditative mood, of this noteworthy surmise: "Sir," said he, "I do not imagine that all things will be made clear to us immediately after death, but that the ways of Providence will be explained to us very gradually." Be that as it may, few could have been found more ready than the melancholic Johnson to agree that meanwhile, until the day star arise and the shadows flee away,

> "The ways of Heaven are dark and intricate,
> Puzzled in mazes, and perplexed with errors :
> Our understanding traces them in vain,
> Lost and bewildered in the fruitless search ;
> Nor sees with how much art the windings run,
> Nor where the regular confusion ends."

It was at a time of national and household tribulation, when darkness that might be felt seemed to encompass altar and hearth, that Joseph de Maistre wrote to a friend in trouble: "Be it enough for us to know, that for everything there is a reason with which we shall one day become acquainted; let us not weary ourselves with seeking out the why and the wherefore, even when possibly they might be discerned." He would have his correspondent bear in mind that the epithet "very good" is a necessary adjunct to "very great;" and that is sufficient. The inference is self-evident, that under the sway of the Being who combines in himself those two qualities—the *très-bon* and the *très-grand*—all the evils we either suffer or witness must needs be acts of justice or means of reformation equally indispensable. In the declared love of God to man, M. de Maistre found a general solution of all the enigmas that can offend (*scandaliser*, in the New Testament sense of putting a stumbling-block in the way of) our ignorance. "Fixed to one little point of time and space, we are insane enough to refer all to this point; and in so doing we are at once blameworthy and absurd." If De Maistre's collation of the *très-bon* with the *très-grand* resembles the lines of Drummond's hymn beginning,

"O King, whose greatness none can comprehend,
Whose boundless goodness doth to all extend,"

so is the scope of his argument at one with what follows:

"Here, where, as in a mirror, we but see
Shadows of shadows, atoms of Thy might,
Still owly-eyed when staring on Thy light."

What we call this life of men on earth, as Mr. Browning's island-poet has it, is, as he finds much reason to conceive,

"Intended to be viewed eventually
As a great whole, not analysed to parts,
But each part having reference to all." *

Pope's well-worked line is of perpetual application,

"'Tis but a part we see, and not the whole."

So is the avowal of the present laureate:

"I see in part
That all, as in some work of art,
Is toil co-operant to an end."

To us, as Sir Benjamin Brodie remarks, in one of his psychological discussions, the universe presents itself as an assemblage of heterogeneous phenomena, some of which we can reduce to laws of limited operation, while others stand by themselves, bearing no evident relation to anything besides. We may well, he thinks, suppose that there are in the universe beings of a superior intelligence, and possessed of a greater range of observation, who are sufficiently "behind the scenes" to be able to contemplate all the immense variety of material phenomena as the result of one great general law. Their standpoint may

* "Cleon," by Robert Browning.

enable them to see a Cosmos, a world of order, where to lower intelligences Chaos alone is discernible, a world comparatively without form and void, with darkness upon the face of its deep. And as with the physical, so with the metaphysical. As with the material, so with the moral.

"Experience, like a pale musician, holds
A dulcimer of patience in his hand;
Whence harmonies we cannot understand
Of God's will in the worlds, the strain unfolds
In sad perplexèd minors. . . .

"We murmur—'Where is any certain tune
Of measured music, in such notes as these?'—
But angels leaning from their golden seat,
Are not so minded! their fine ear hath won
The issue of completed* cadences,—
And, smiling down the stars, they whisper—Sweet."†

——o——

RULING THE WAVES.

PSALM cxiv. 1–5; ST. MARK iv. 39.

WHEN Israel went out of Egypt, it was under the guidance of One whose hand being mighty to save, the sea saw it, and fled; Jordan was driven back. "What ailed thee, O thou sea, that thou fleddest? thou Jordan, that thou wast driven back?" The trembling was at the presence of Him who hath placed the sand for the bound of the sea, by a perpetual decree, that it cannot pass it; and though the waves thereof toss themselves, yet can they not prevail; though they roar, yet can they not pass over it. The commotion, the fleeing, the driving back, was at the bidding of Him

* Completed. *Finis coronat opus.* Children and fools, it has been observed, should not see a work that is half done, they not having the sense to make out what the artist is designing. "The whole of this world that we see, is a work half done; and thence fools are apt to find fault with Providence."—ARCHBISHOP WHATELY.

† Sonnets, by Elizabeth Barrett Browning: "Perplexed Music."

who, and who alone, can say to the sea, Thus far shalt thou come, and no farther; and here shall thy proud waves be stayed.

The men of Galilee marvelled when, at the storm that once arose on their sea, and the ship was in jeopardy, there arose One who rebuked the winds and the sea; and there was a great calm. What manner of man was this, that even the winds and the sea obeyed Him?

What manner of man? Be it legend or history, the story of royal Cnut on the seashore, forbidding, at his flatterers' instigation, or by his own desire to rebuke their folly—forbidding the farther approach of the incoming tide, is pregnant with instruction on this head. The royal Dane might be a man of men, but the surging waves were not obedient unto his voice. King though he was, the tide was responseless as deaf adder to any charming of his, charmed he never so wisely, enjoined he never so straitly. What manner of man, then, but the Son of man? What manner of king but the King of kings?

The Dane might have enforced the lesson on his parasites by such a strain as that of a defeated monarch in Shakspeare:—

> "Farewell king!
> Cover your heads, and mock not flesh and blood
> With solemn reverence; throw away respect,
> Tradition, form, and ceremonious duty,
> For you have but mistook me all this while:
> I live with bread, like you, feel want, taste grief,
> Need friends:—subjected thus,
> How can you say to me I am a king?"

A king, that is, in *their* sense of right Divine, and Divine extent. So with poor, mad, discrowned Lear, drenched in that terrible storm on the heath, and remembering soft speeches of cozening courtiership, only of yesterday too. "When the rain came to wet me, and the wind to make me chatter; when the thunder would not peace at my bidding; there I found them, there I smelt them out. Go to, they are not men of their words: they told me I was everything; 'tis a lie, I am not ague-proof." Mark, again, from the opening scene of the

"Tempest," the rough, blunt, uncivil words with which the boatswain cuts short the addresses of his royal passengers :—

> "Hence! What care these roarers [the waves] for the name of king? To cabin: silence: trouble us not.
>
> "*Gonzalo.* Good; yet remember whom thou hast aboard.
>
> "*Boatswain.* None that I love more than myself. You are a counsellor; if you can command these elements to a silence, and work the peace of the present [instant], we will not hand a rope more: use your authority. If you cannot, give thanks you have lived so long, and make yourself ready in your cabin for the mischance of the hour, if so it hap. Cheerily, good hearts.—Out of our way, I say!"

Of Antiochus Epiphanes, and his pride that had a fall, it is written in the book of Maccabees: "And thus he that a little afore thought he *might command the waves of the sea* (so proud was he beyond the condition of man), and weigh the high mountains in a balance, was now cast on the ground."

An elder king than Cnut, and not a wiser, not only lashed the winds that blew contrary to his will, but bound the sea with fetters, after a sort:

> "Ipsum compedibus qui vinxerat Ennosigæum."

Much good it did him: witness his return from his great expedition, in a poor skiff, wind-tossed across waves red with the blood of his slaughtered host, *cruentis fluctibus.* The stars in their courses once fought against Sisera, and the fettered waves were little more propitious to speed the fortunes of Xerxes. He might have spared his chains. At any rate he lost his army. Archdeacon Hare practically applied the extravagance of the Great King, as they of Persia were styled, in designating the present (or, rather, what was to him the present) as an age when men will scoff at the madness of Xerxes, yet themselves try to fling their chains over the ever-rolling, irrepressible ocean of thought; nay, they will scoop out a mimic sea in their pleasure-ground, he goes on to say, and make it ripple and bubble, and spout up prettily into the air, and then fancy that they are taming the Atlantic; which, however, keeps advancing upon them, until it sweeps them away with their toys.

It is edifying to read in the Diary of Mr. Pepys how, one July afternoon, soon after the king had come back to enjoy his own again, that gentleman went upon the river, but had to put ashore and shelter himself from the rain that rained so hard; during which time came by the king in his barge, going down towards the Downs to meet the queen: "But methought it lessened my esteem of a king, that he should not be able to command the rain."

Instructive, too, is the tenor of the legend of King Robert of Sicily, which has been so attractively treated in prose by Leigh Hunt, in his Jar of Honey from Mount Hybla, and in verse by Professor Longfellow, in his Tales of a Wayside Inn. There we read how the king with his nobles proudly sat at vespers, on St. John's Eve, and heard the priests chant the Magnificat:—

"And, as he listened, o'er and o'er again
Repeated, like a burden or refrain,
He caught the words, '*Deposuit potentes*
De sede, et exaltavit humiles;'
And slowly lifting up his kingly head,
He to a learned clerk beside him said,
'What mean these words?' The clerk made answer meet,
'He hath put down the mighty from their seat,
And hath exalted them of low degree.'
Thereat King Robert muttered scornfully,
''Tis well that such seditious words are sung
Only by priests, and in the Latin tongue;
For unto priests and people be it known
There is no power can push me from my throne!'"

The sequel teaches him a different lesson, which he learns by (and lays to) heart.

In those days, however, if any order of men might, or did, claim authority over such turbulent subject-matter as the sea, it was not kings, but priests. Ecclesiastical history relates the calamitous visitation of earthquake and inundations by which Epidaurus must once, and for ever, have been overwhelmed, had not the prudent citizens placed St. Hilarion, an Egyptian monk, on the beach. "He made the sign of the cross; the mountain-wave stopped, bowed, and returned." One's respect for the great qualities of the fearless Akbah, traversing the wilds of Africa, and at length penetrating to the verge of the Atlantic, is not lessened by what Gibbon relates of him:—that his career, though not his zeal, being checked by the prospect of a boundless ocean, Akbah spurred his horse into the waves, and raising his eyes to heaven, exclaimed with the tone of a fanatic, "Great God, if my course were not stopped by this sea, I would still go on, to the unknown kingdoms of the West, preaching the unity of Thy holy name." And the picture reminds us of another, some eight centuries later, when Constantinople was besieged and taken by Mahomet II., who, while his ships were engaged against those of the Genoese, sat on horseback on the beach, to encourage by voice and presence the valour of the faithful: "The passions of his soul, and even the gestures of his body, seemed to imitate the action of the combatants; and, as if he had been the lord of nature, he spurred his horse with a fearless and impotent effort into the sea." Sir Archibald Alison moralises on the spectacle of Napoleon, in 1804, reviewing, or intending to review, the naval force by which he designed to crush the British power: the flotilla being tempest-tost when it hove in sight, and several vessels stranded—an event "destined to teach the French Emperor, like Canute the Dane, that there were bounds to his power, and that his might was limited to the element on which his army stood." The sea—*c'est autre chose.*

It is of Tiberius, absolute master of the vastest, richest empire ever seen under the sun, that an eminent French preacher is treating when he says that an adulatory senator kept repeating to him in every tone and accent that his authority was without bounds. Tiberius would fain have believed the assurance, if the illusion had been possible,—if he had not felt himself at every instant *heurté contre une barrière infranchissable.* The emperor's flatterers had forgotten, for one thing, to secure a peremptory decree against the inconvenient limitation called time. His days were numbered. And in vain Tiberius essayed to trick and elude death, and dissembled with himself as to the stubborn fact of its resistless advance.

Kings, great nobles, and the like, as a popular essayist observes, have been known, even to the close of life, to violently curse and swear, if things went against them; going the length of stamping and blaspheming even at wind and rain, and branches of trees and plashes of mud, for insubordination and disrespect of persons. A popular novelist, again, having to describe a fashionable wedding in the country on a portentously wet and stormy day, makes the Lisford beadle, "who was a sound Tory of the old school," almost wonder that the heavens themselves should be audacious enough to wet the uncovered head of the lord of Jocelyn's Rock. "But it went on raining nevertheless." It was in no such spirit that John Bunyan once was all but resolved on putting to the test the reality of his faith, by commanding some water puddles to be dry.

Mr. Carlyle made a picturesque application of the royal Dane's injunction to the waves, in his survey of the advancing tide of the French Revolution—grim host marching on, the black-browed Marseillese in the van, with hum and murmur, far-heard; like the ocean-tide, "drawn up, as if by Luna and Influences, from the great deep of waters, they roll gleaming on; no king, Canute or Louis, can bid them roll back." To quite another effect is Judge Haliburton's application of the incident, in his panegyric on the capabilities of the Southampton docks. It was here, he says, that Cnut sat in his arm-chair, to show his courtiers (after he gave up drinking and murder) that though he was a mighty prince, he could not control the sea. "Well, what Canute could not do, your dock company has accomplished. It has actually said to the sea, 'Thus far shalt thou go, and no farther:' and the waves have obeyed the mandate."

By poetical licence a Cornish poet of the present day ascribes to his rock-bound coast a *ne plus ultra* control over an ever-aggressive sea: he pictures the embattled advance of the waves, and their discomfiture and retreat:

"They come—they mount—they charge in vain.
Thus far, incalculable main;

No more ! Thine hosts have not o'erthrown
The lichen on the barrier stone.
Have the rocks faith that thus they stand,
Unmoved, a grim and stately band,
And look, like warriors tried and brave,
Stern, silent, reckless, o'er the wave ? "

One, and one alone, is veritably the ruler of the waves. When the floods are risen, when the floods have lift up their voice, and lift up their waves, to Him only it pertaineth to still their tumultuous clamour, and to level their aspiring crests. The waves of the sea are mighty, and rage horribly; yet the Lord, who dwelleth on high, is mightier. "O Lord God of hosts, who is like unto Thee ? . . . Thou rulest the raging of the sea : Thou stillest the waves thereof when they arise."

With a moral application we conclude, borrowed from one whose was ever the pen of a ready writer to point a moral. Some dream, says Cowper, that

. . . "they can silence when they will
The storm of passion, and say, 'Peace, be still :'
But 'Thus far and no farther,' when addressed
To the wild wave, or wilder human breast,
Implies authority that never can,
That never ought to be the lot of man."

——o——

IN DEADLY PERIL UNAWARES.

1 SAMUEL xxvi. 8–25.

SOUNDLY the stalwart king of Israel slept within the trench, while David and Abishai gazed on him by stealth in the night-watches—his spear stuck in the ground at his bolster, and Abner and the people lying round about him. Abishai was for smiting him with the spear at once, promising that once should be quite enough. Could David hesitate? Was it not a special Providence? Had not God delivered his enemy into his hand? Let but David give the word, the look, the nod, and Abishai would at one fell swoop send Saul to his account, with all his imperfections on his head. "Now, therefore, let me smite him, I pray thee, with the spear, even to the earth at once, and I will not smite him the second time." But David was inflexible in repudiating the regicide. Not for him was it to stretch forth a hand against the Lord's anointed. So Saul slept on, and the shadow of death passed away. Unaware of the peril that had approached him, his awaking was an ordinary awaking. But, to convict the watchers of unwatchfulness, if not to convince the king of a narrow escape and a generous foe, David took the spear and the cruse of water from Saul's bolster; and he and his companion gat them away unperceived—for no man saw it, nor knew it, neither awaked; for they were all asleep; because a deep sleep from the Lord was fallen upon them. Anon David roused the host with the story of that narrow escape, charging Abner with criminal neglect worthy of death. And as he recited the story, Saul was touched; and there was emotion in his voice and in his words when he felt what the peril had been, and knew whom he had to thank for its harmless issue.

Had we eyes sharp enough, observes Cowper in a letter to Hayley, we should see the arrows of death flying in all directions, and account it a wonder that we and our friends escape them but a single day. Many years previously the poet had written to the same effect to Unwin,—that could we see at a glance of the eye what is passing every day upon all the roads in the kingdom, we should indeed find reason to be thankful for journeys performed in safety, and for deliverance from dangers we are not perhaps even permitted to see. "When in some of the high southern latitudes, and in a dark tempestuous night, a flash of lightning discovered to Captain Cook a vessel which glanced along close by his side, and which but for the lightning he must have run foul of, both the danger and the transient light that showed it were undoubtedly designed," as Cowper is devoutly convinced, "to convey to him this wholesome instruction, that a particular Providence attended him, and that he was not only preserved from evils of which he had notice, but from many more of which he had no information or even the least suspicion." It is noticeable, as Mr. de Quincey points out, that a danger which approaches, but wheels away—which threatens, but finally forbears to strike—is more interesting by much on a distant retrospect than the danger which accomplishes its mission. "The Alpine precipice, down which many pilgrims have fallen, is passed without much attention; but that precipice, within one inch of which a traveller has passed unconsciously in the dark, first tracing his peril along the snowy margin on the next morning, becomes invested with an attraction of horror for all who hear the story." In another of his books, and the most celebrated of them all, the same impassioned master of English prose, recites the thoughts that arose within him, at a crisis in his youthful life, on the suggestive opening of that beautiful collect, "Lighten our darkness, we beseech thee, O Lord!" in which the great shadows of night are made symbolically significant—those great powers, night and darkness, that belong to aboriginal chaos, being made representative of the perils that, unseen, continually menace poor afflicted human nature. "With deepest sympathy I accompanied the prayer against the perils of darkness,—perils that I seemed to see, in the ambush of mid night solitude, brooding around the beds of sleeping nations; perils from even worse forms of darkness shrouded within the recesses of blind human hearts; perils from temptations weaving unseen snares for our footing." As Marcello has it, in Beddoes' tragedy,

> "Each minute of man's safety he does walk
> A bridge, no thicker than his frozen breath,
> O'er a precipitous and craggy danger
> Yawning to death!"

With admirable subtlety and suggestiveness, Mr. Hawthorne illustrates this subject in that *fantasiestück* of his, called "David Swan." A young man of that name falls asleep on the roadside, of a summer's day, and *we* see, what he sees not, nor dreams of happening to him, a series of incidents that go near to alter the current of his being, and very near, in one instance, to stop altogether its earthly course. When he awakes from that sound sleep, and hies him cheerily homeward, he knows not, nor ever will know, in this world at least, that while he slumbered, all in one brief hour, wealth was all but made over to him by one heirless passer-by, and death all but dealt him by two reckless ruffians. They were interrupted, and left him, and he never was to know of the narrow escape. The moral of the fantasy is, that sleeping or waking, we hear not the airy footsteps of the strange things that almost happen. And the moralist's query ensues, Does it not argue a superintending Providence, that while viewless and unexpected events thrust themselves continually athwart our path, there should still be regularity enough in mortal life to render foresight even partially available?

The moral of "David Swan" is implicitly conveyed in that passage in "Waverley" which relates Colonel Gardiner's unconscious escape from the raised and pointed weapon of the Highlander, Callum Beg. An incident that appeals to his superstition makes the intending slayer drop his piece; and "Colonel Gardiner," we read, "unconscious of the danger he had escaped, turned his horse round, and rode slowly back to the front of his regiment."

So with Mrs. Hilyard, in "Salem Chapel," on the evening of the secret interview upon the chapel steps. A hidden witness there is of that interview, who, however, sees not the gesture of her companion which bodes, and almost involves, a fatal, a murderous issue. "But even Mrs. Hilyard herself never knew how near, how very near, she was at that moment to the unseen world."

Or glance, again, at the Azteca, in Southey's "Madoc," gliding like a snake to where Caradoc lay sleeping—all unconscious of peril, as happy, and happily unconscious, David Swan:—

> "Sweetly slept he, and pleasant were his dreams
> Of Britain, and the blue-eyed maid he loved.
> The Azteca stood over him; he knew
> His victim, and the power of vengeance gave
> Malignant joy. Once hast thou 'scaped my arm;
> But what shall save thee now? the Tiger thought,
> Exulting, and he raised his spear to strike.

That instant, o'er the Briton's unseen harp
The gale of morning passed, and swept its strings
Into so sweet a harmony, that sure
It seemed no earthly tune. The savage man
Suspends his stroke ; he looks astonished round ;
No human hand is near :—and hark ! again
The aërial music swells and dies away.
Then first the heart of Tialala felt fear :
He thought that some protecting spirit watched
Beside the stranger, and, abashed, withdrew."

To Cremona went together, in seeming amity, the Emperor Sigismund and Pope John XXIII., and there an incident had nearly taken place, which, as the historian of Latin Christianity says, might, by preventing the Council of Constance, have changed the fortunes of the world. Gabrino Fondoli, who from podestâ had become tyrant of Cremona, "entertained his distinguished guests with sumptuous hospitality. He led them up the lofty tower to survey the rich and spacious plains of Lombardy. On his deathbed Fondoli confessed the sin, of which he deeply repented, that he resisted the temptation, and had not hurled pope and emperor down, and so secured himself an immortal name." Pope and emperor on the tower-top were as little inclined to suspect how closely the shadow of death was then and there overshadowing them, as they would have been able to comprehend the ultimate repentance of the intending murderer, not for having intended murder, but for having not carried his intention out.

It is one of Young's night thoughts that "the farthest from the fear, are often nearest to the stroke of fate." Often the stroke menaces them unawares, but after all is not dealt; and to the last they are unaware that on such a day, and at such a minute, there was but a step between them and death.

Quid quisque vitet, says Horace, *nunquam homini satis cautum est, in horas.* The ignorance of what is impending is bliss, in a certain sense. Just as

"The kid from the pen, and the lamb from the fold,
Unmoved may the blade of the butcher behold ;
They dream not—ah, happier they !—that the knife,
Though uplifted, can menace their innocent life.

It falls ;—the frail thread of their being is riven ;
They dread not, suspect not, the blow till 'tis given."

Mais qu'il me soit permis de ne le savoir pas, is the wish of some in regard even of escaped peril.

Scott vividly illustrates in "Rokeby" the position of unconscious and therefore unconcerned borderers on the grave; it is where Bertram creeps on hands and knees through the spreading birch and hazels, and takes aim at Redmond, and twice Matilda comes between the carabine and Redmond's breast, "just ere the spring his finger pressed;" and the interruption of Guy Denzil's approach makes the ruffian retire, *rê infectâ:*

"They whom dark Bertram, in his wrath,
Doomed to captivity or death,
Their thoughts to one sad subject lent,
Saw not nor heard the ambushment.
Heedless and unconcerned they sate,
While on the very verge of fate;
Heedless and unconcerned remained,
When Heaven the murderer's arm restrained;
As ships drift darkling down the tide,
Nor see the shelves o'er which they glide."

——o——

NO LEISURE.

ST. MARK vi. 31.

THAT must have been a busy time with the apostles, careful and troubled about many things, cumbered with much serving, worn with many anxieties, and kept in unrest by continual demands on their services, when the Divine Master—knowing their frame and remembering that they were dust—bade them come by themselves "apart into a desert place, and rest a while; for there were many coming and going, and they had *no leisure* so much as to eat."

Our own age has been rightly described as one of stimulus and high pressure: we live as it were our lives out fast; effect is everything; results produced at once; something to show, and something that may *tell.* "The folio of patient years is replaced by the pamphlet that stirs men's curiosity to-day, and to-morrow is forgotten." Or as an eminent reviewer puts it—writing to the same effect as the eminent divine just quoted—without grudging to contemporary productions the applause which they receive, or the interest which they excite, thoughtful minds cannot see them with complacency obscuring by their brilliance, or perhaps their "glare," the more temperate and wholesome light of the elder classics of our land. "At no moment in the intellectual progress of England has repose ever been more needful, if the literature of the present century be to take its place among its great antecessors." For want of repose our prose is declared on the same authority to be growing turgid, our verse empty or inflated; and as a good cooling regimen is required to correct these exorbitances, nothing would rejoice our censor more than to be assured, on the credit of sound publishers' statistics, that the number of new books was diminishing, while that of re-editions of old books was on the increase. Dr. Arnold, we are told, once preached a sermon to the boys at Rugby against taking in the monthly numbers of "Nicholas Nickleby," by way of protest against systematic and uninterrupted excitement. "Society keeps up as much excitement as it can. It wants its new number of something to appear incessantly. There is no rest or repose, and one subject of thought succeeds another faster than wave succeeds wave." A rather ironical apology for dull sermons sets up at least this plea in their behalf: that so easy is it for a man who lives in such a society never to be alone with himself, that a compulsory half-hour of quietude at a wakeful time of the day, in a place which recalls to him the most solemn thoughts, is no slight advantage.

La Bruyère, two centuries ago, complained of French society in his day, that there was no getting any one to abide quietly at home, and there in patience possess his soul, and make sure to himself that he had one. All was hurry and flurry. Not to be excitedly busy was to be idle. But that the philosopher denied. A wise man turns his leisure to account. He is not idle who devotes his leisure to tranquil meditation, and converse and reading. Rather is this a species of work—at any rate a means for working with fresh energy and better effect when the working hour comes round again. There is such a thing as what Wordsworth wisely calls a wise passiveness.

Chateaubriand, again, more than a century afterwards, complained—not indeed of Frenchmen alone, but of all men—that all was done helter-skelter and in haste, post-haste; that amid this din and distraction of coming and going there was no leisure so much as to eat; or that if men did set about a meal, there was no such thing as sitting down to it, but it was eaten by them with their loins girded, their shoes on their feet, and their staff in their hand—eaten in haste, as was the Jewish passover.

The most eminent political economist of our day owns himself to be "not charmed" with the ideal of life held out by those who think that the normal state of human beings is that of struggling to get on; that the trampling, crushing, elbowing, and treading on one another's heels, which form the existing type of social life, are the most desirable lot of human kind, or anything but the disagreeable symptoms of one of the phases of industrial progress. The town, complains one of the most thoughtful and influential of latter-day divines,—the town, with its fever and its excitements, and its collision of mind with mind, has spread over the country, and there is no country, scarcely home. "To men who traverse England in a few hours, and spend only a portion of the year in one place, home is becoming a vocable of past ages." He echoes Wordsworth's lament that

> "Plain living and high thinking are no more;"

and in another place he declares our want to be the vision of a calmer and simpler beauty, to tranquillise us in the midst of artificial tastes, and the draught of a purer spring to cool the flame of our excited life. It is many years ago since the most genial of essayists avowed his preference for "coaching it," and could have been well content to live upon the road, in those roomy antiques, instead of getting on at the present rate, and being impatient to arrive at some town, only perhaps to be equally restless when arrived there. Not that he was insensible to the pleasure of driving fast—stirring the blood as it does, and giving a sense of power; but he complained that everything was getting a little too hasty and business-like, "as though we were to be eternally getting on, and never realizing anything but fidget and money—the means instead of the end." A distinction is duly recognised between haste and hurry—hurry adding to rapidity the element of painful confusion; but in the case of ordinary people, as Dr. Boyd observes, haste generally implies hurry, and very strenuously he dilates on "what a horrible thing" it must be to go through life in a hurry. The self-styled country parson made a name ("letters four do make that name") by his "Recreations." And he has since then maintained its popularity by a series of "Leisure Hours." In his essay concerning Hurry and Leisure he avows his utter contempt for the idler—the loafer, as Yankees term him—who never does anything, whose idle hands are always in his idle pockets, and who is always sauntering to and fro. Leisure, we are reminded, is the intermission of labour—the blink of idleness in the life of a hard-working man; and it is only in the case of such a man that leisure is allowed to be dignified, commendable, or enjoyable. "But to him it is all these, and more. Let us not be ever driving on. The machinery, physical and mental, will not stand it." Only in leisure, it is further contended, will the human mind yield many of its best products. Calm views, sound thoughts, healthful feelings, do not originate in a hurry or a fever.

It was in wistful remembrance of the silence in heaven for the space of half an hour, as recorded by the Seer of Patmos, that Mrs. Browning penned a sonnet which expressed a prayer, suggestive in its earnestness and of wide application,

> "Vouchsafe us such a half-hour's hush alone,
> In compensation for our stormy years!"

Never to be forgotten amid the tranquillising sweets of leisure hours, with healing on their wings, is the serene solemnity of that silent half-hour.

Professor Longfellow, in one of his earliest works, proclaimed to his countrymen as the great want of the national character, that of the "dignity of repose." "We seem," he said, "to live in the midst of a battle—there is such a din, such a hurrying to and fro. In the streets of a crowded city it is difficult to walk slowly. You feel the rushing of the crowd, and rush with it onward. In the press of our life, it is difficult to be calm. In this stress of wind and tide, all professions seem to drag their anchors, and are swept out into the main." The following stanza is so thoroughly conceived in the spirit and expressed in the style of the same author—the author of the "Psalm of Life"—that few readers might have hesitated to attribute it to him, were it not known to be from one of the "Palm Leaves" of Lord Houghton, who, a quarter of a century ago, as Richard Monckton Milnes, after contrasting the din, and stir, and turmoil of the West with the reposeful air of the East, counselled the poet of the West to wander eastward now and then:

> "There the calm of life comparing
> With his Europe's busy fate,
> Let him gladly homeward faring,
> Learn to labour and to wait."

It is perhaps the most gifted of American writers of fiction to whom we owe the avowal, that were he to adopt a pet idea, as so many people do, and fondle it in his embraces to the exclusion of all others, it would be that the great want which mankind labours under at this present period is—sleep. The world, he urges, should recline its vast head on the first convenient pillow, and take a prolonged nap. It has gone distracted, on his showing, through a morbid activity, and while preternaturally wide awake, is nevertheless tormented by visions that seem real to it now, but would assume their true aspect and character were all things once set right by an interval of sound repose. This he declares to be the only method of getting rid of old delusions and of avoiding new ones—of restoring to us the simple perception of what is right, and the single-hearted desire to achieve it, both of which have long been lost in consequence of this weary activity of brain and torpor or passion of the heart that now afflict the universe. "Stimulants, the only mode of treatment hitherto attempted, cannot quell the disease; they do but heighten the delirium." Sleep, therefore, is the panacea he prescribes for the physical and metaphysical regeneration of our race, so that it may in due time awake, as an infant out of dewy slumber.

To the like effect protests an able essayist of our day against tendencies to overrate the endless facilities of speedy locomotion now enjoyed, as if they were a boon without a drawback; and he professes not to regard as particularly attractive or elevating the sight of mankind scouring and bustling endlessly hither and thither over the face of the earth, like eager, energetic ants, with little bits of straw or other rubbish packed on their heads. Ought we not rather, it is asked, to look on tranquillity, and equilibrium, and regularity, as the normal condition of things? and in the thousand encomiums which are poured forth upon steam and speed, do we often take into account the waste and havoc which they make in "plain living"—how they practically shorten the days of a man?

The haste and hurry of modern English civilization, it has been elsewhere observed, ever increasing and carrying us more impetuously forward, tend to deaden all capacity for simpler enjoyments, and all sense of the worth of a tranquil life on which the eyes of all the world are not fixed. And whenever, as a reflective discourser remarks, people set their heads to constant work, we may be perfectly certain that they are losing more than they gain, and are sinking in the scale at once of meditative and social beings. The accomplished author of an essay on Leisure—the cultivation of which as an art is thought to be in danger of dying out amongst us—says of that activity which never relaxes sufficiently to allow time for a calm and more or less passive contemplation of life as a whole, that it is "apt to degenerate into mere hand-to-mouth fussiness or drudgery, and can be justified only by necessity." The very repose of leisure is accordingly pronounced a by no means purely selfish enjoyment—it being one of the most communicable, nay, contagious, of pleasures; for there are people, we are reminded, whose company is as restful as sleep, in whose presence hurry seems like a bad dream when it is past, and whom one leaves with a sense of refreshment and renewed energy such as is produced by a good night's rest. And this writer contends that to afford such refreshment to others may often be turning time to better account than to crowd it with self-chosen business. Not that the fact is not duly insisted upon that too little work is as fatal as too much to that lightness and alacrity of spirit which are needed for the conversion of spare time into hours of leisure worthy to be so called. Some natures, indeed, and they are of a high order, sometimes of the highest, find one leisure hour at a time as much as they can away with, and anon

"The hour of rest is gone,
And urgent voices round them cry,
'Ho, lingerer, hasten on!'

"And has the soul, then, only gained,
From this brief time of ease,
A moment's rest, when overstrained,
One hurried glimpse of peace?"

Nay something better and more abiding than that.

But to conclude. The notion, as expounded by an essayist on "Short Cuts," that if a thing is to be done at all, "then 'twere well it were done quickly," admirable as it may be on the Exchange, is justly said to rub the delicacy and bloom off life when it is made the ruling maxim in all other relations and positions: a life with leisure hours in it for watching and examining all that we pass being a much more enviable and rational lot than a swift rushing from one goal to another, from one sort of fame or power or opulence to another and more remote. When the ambitious hero in Sir Henry Taylor's dramatic poem declares in the storm and stress of his career,

"We have not time to mourn,"

"The worse for us!" is his good counsellor's rejoinder:

"*He that lacks time to mourn lacks time to mend.*
Eternity mourns that. 'Tis an ill cure

For life's worst ills, to have no time to feel them.
Where sorrow's held intrusive and turn'd out,
There wisdom will not enter, nor true power,
Nor aught that dignifies humanity.
Yet such the barrenness of busy life!
From shelf to shelf Ambition clambers up
To reach the naked'st pinnacle of all,
While Magnanimity, absolved from toil,
Reposes self-included at the base."

——o——

A PROPHYLACTIC KNIFE TO THE THROAT.

PROVERBS xxiii. 2.

KING Solomon's discreet counsel to him that feasts with royalty, to put a knife to his throat, if he be a man given to appetite, may be advantageously enlarged in its application to diners-out, or for the matter of that, to diners at home, all and sundry. Sitting to eat with a ruler, the guest is admonished to consider diligently what is before him; and at the same time to be not desirous of the great man's dainties, for they are deceitful meat. Any and every man given to appetite will do well to chew the cud of this bitter fancy; and the prophylactic application of a knife to the throat, forbidding rash ingress and intemperate speed of swallow, is wholesome for all estates and degrees of men among us, and might beneficially be a standing order for all times.

Adam Smith, in his "Theory of the Moral Sentiments," calls it "indecent" to express any strong degree of those passions which arise from a certain situation or disposition of the body; because the company, not being in the same disposition, cannot be expected to sympathize with them; and he mentions violent hunger as being, though upon many occasions not only natural, but unavoidable, yet "always indecent; and to eat voraciously is universally regarded as a piece of ill manners." There is, however, he allows, some degree of sympathy, even with hunger, and we may add, even on the part of a ruler at whose table sits the man given to appetite. Lewis the Fourteenth, himself a gourmand, and, which is different, an enormous eater, liked to see a dinner guest disposing wholesale of the royal cates, if only by way of keeping himself in countenance, while achieving the like result. Royalty has, indeed, again and again been addicted to surfeiting, and sometimes of a memorably fatal sort. Alexander Jannæus died of gluttony, during the siege of Ragaba. Soliman, the seventh khalif of the race of the Ommiyades, died of a surfeit at Chalcis, in Syria, while preparing to lead an army to Constantinople.* Of the emperor Jovian, we read in Gibbon, that one night, at the obscure town Dadastana, after indulging himself with a redundant supper, he retired to rest, and was next morning found dead in his bed—an event ascribed by some, though not by all, to the quality of the mushrooms, *plus* the quantity of wine, which he had swallowed in the evening. The same historian rather more than suspects that the mortal disease of Athanaric the Goth "was contracted amidst the pleasures of the imperial banquets," by Theodosius provided. Pope Benedict XI. is said to have died of a surfeit of fruit—some beautiful fresh figs, of which he was very fond, being offered to him in a silver basin by a veiled novice, as if from the abbess of the convent of St. Petronilla, in Perugia: "The pope, not suspecting a gift from such a hand, ate them eagerly, and without having them previously tasted." That he died of poison, few in that age, as Milman says, would venture to doubt, but the poisoning power of arrears of undigested food has never been quite rated at its full value. The same hesitation between fruit surfeit and poison, obtains in the case of King John, whose death, by one account due to the fatal drug administered by a Cistercian monk, by another is attributed to an intemperate indulgence at supper in fruit and new cider. The Emperor Frederick III. contracted his last

* He is said to have emptied two baskets of figs and of eggs, which he swallowed alternately, and the repast was concluded with marrow and sugar. In one of his pilgrimages to Mecca, Soliman is asserted to have eaten, at a single meal, seventy pomegranates, a kid, six fowls, and a huge quantity of the grapes of Tayaf. "If," says, Gibbon, "the bill of fare be correct, we must admire the appetite rather than the luxury of the sovereign of Asia."—*Hist. Rom. Empire*, ch. lii.

illness, some say, by a surfeit of melons. And is there not, in the case of our Henry I., what has been called that tale of royal excess so concisely and pathetically told in nursery history? "He never smiled again, and died of a surfeit of lampreys." The *regicide* lampreys, Moore calls them in one place; and in another, after citing Hume's remark on them, as "a food which always agreed better with his [Henry's] palate than his constitution," a dish so indigestible, that a late novelist, at the end of his book, could imagine no more summary mode of getting rid of all his heroes and heroines than by a hearty supper of stewed lampreys. In yet another the same squib-writer has a cruel simile, "just as honest King Stephen his beaver might doff to the fishes that carried his kind uncle off." To a surfeit of red herrings is ascribed the death of Robert Greene, the dramatist. The trap for the life of the Emperor Antoninus Pius was baited, as De Quincey expresses it, with toasted cheese. Kaiser Karl VI. was the victim of a voracious repast on mushrooms stewed in oil.

When Hadrian found his illness on the increase, and his end approaching, he removed to Baiæ, where, "in spite of the prescriptions [or proscriptions?] of his physicians, he began to eat and drink according to his pleasure." The excesses of Charles V. in the same way are exceptionally notorious. Of that "little, spare, aguish, peevish, supper-eating" sovereign, Frederick the Great, who loved his dishes the more they tormented him, it is on record, that on the approach of death, "this warrior full of courage and sage speculation," could not resist the customary pepper and sauce piquante, though he knew it would inevitably result in a nightmare, "turning his bed into a nest of monsters." So with the Duke Augustus commemorated by Perthes: "All medical skill was in vain, for this half crazy prince could not deny himself the stimulus of the hottest spices." Mr. Tennyson's dying Northern Farmer is only too true a type of his kind:—

> "What atta stannin' theer for, an' doesn bring ma the yaäle?
> Doctor's a'tottler, lass, an a's hallus i' the owd taäle;
> I weänt breäk rules for doctor, a knaws naw more nor a floy;
> Git ma my yaäle I tell tha, an' gin I mun doy I mun doy."

Swift is giving Pope a significant and not uncalled-for hint, when he writes to express his uneasiness at ever hearing of the poet's being out to dinner: "For the least transgression of yours, if it be only two bits and one sup more than your stint, is a great debauch; for which you certainly pay more than those sots who are carried dead drunk to bed." An entry in Mrs. Trench's diary begins, "Dined at the Duke of Queensberry's. He is very ill—has a violent cough, but *will* eat an immense dinner, and then complains of a *digestion pénible.*" Another of his quality has been described as taking all sorts of pains to get a little enjoyment which must produce for him a world of misery. "One of his passions which he *will* not resist, is for a particular dish, pungent, savoury, and multifarious, which sends him almost every night into Tartarus." Mr. Thackeray's moribund old Madame Bernstein *will* have her supper luxurious, "nor could any injunction of ours or the doctor's teach her abstinence." The Sir Miles St. John of another popular fiction does himself to death after the same manner: "He would have his own way; and he contrived to coax or to force his doctor into an authority on his side." For doctors are not all of the kind that Sancho Panza had to deal with when governor of Barataria. *The Doctor* cites the case of an eminent member of "the faculty," who could never refrain from eating toasted cheese, though he was subject to an alarming pulmonary complaint which was uniformly aggravated by it, and which terminated fatally at an age by no means advanced. Another he relates, of a physician who, at an autumnal dessert never ceased eating all the filberts he could lay his hands upon, while candidly acknowledging what indigestible and hurtful things they were.

Not a doctor apparently of medicine, but (*proh pudor!*) of divinity, was that Cambridge don of whose end Gray makes memorable mention, as having gone to his grave with five fine mackarel (large and full of roe) in his inside. "He ate them all off at one dinner; but his fate was a turbot on Trinity Sunday, of which he left little for the company besides bones. He had not been hearty all the week; but after this sixth fish he never held up his head more." Like Milton's Eve, in one sense at least :—

> "Greedily he ingorged without restraint,
> And knew not eating death."

Dr. Johnson's friend, Thrale, is a noteworthy example, or warning, of the man of appetite, who *will not* restrain it; will not put a knife to his throat, but prefers sending a full laden fork in that direction. His wife describes his natural disposition to conviviality as degenerating into a preternatural desire for food. "No one could control his appetite." "Burney and I and Queeney tease him every meal he eats, and Mrs. Montagu is quite serious with him; but what *can* one do? He will eat, I think; and if he does eat, I know he will not live." The lampreys that were one too many for Henry the king, were one too many for Thrale the brewer. He begged some of an old friend, and the old friend complied, despite the frowns and negative signals of the ladies of the house—whom following out of the room, the too compliant visitor thus made his apology to Mrs. Thrale, "I understand you ,Madam, but *must* disobey. A friend I have known thirty-six years shall not ask a favour of me in his last stage of life and be refused. What difference can it make?" Tears stood in *his* eyes, and Mrs. Thrale's own —*les larmes dans la voix*—prevented all reply. What difference did it make? That day was Mr. Thrale's last. The tone of the apology reminds us of General Paoli's answer to Boswell, when whispering his fear lest Johnson, very aged and very ailing, might be hurt by the amount and variety of what he was despatching at the general's table, "where he loved to dine." Boswell begged Paoli not to press him. Why urge a too willing horse? "Alas!" said the host, "see how very ill he looks: he can live but a very short time. Would you refuse a slight gratification to a man under sentence of death?" And the general cited approvingly the "humane custom" in Italy, by which those in Johnson's position were indulged with having whatever they liked best to eat and drink, even with expensive delicacies. A parallel case we have in Sir Walter Scott, during his melancholy sojourn in Italy, as Sir W. Gell describes his dining at a Roman palace, and his own fears lest, from the hospitality of the Torlonia family, and "with servants on all sides pressing him to eat and drink, as is their custom at Rome," Sir Walter might be induced to eat more than was safe for his malady. "Colonel Blair, who sat next him, was requested to take care that this should not happen. Whenever I observed him, however, Sir Walter appeared always to be eating; while the duchess, who had discovered the nature of the office imposed on the colonel, was by no means satisfied, and after dinner observed that it was an odd sort of friendship which consisted in starving one's neighbour to death, when he had a good appetite, and there was dinner enough."

The selfish club-man *par excellence* has been depicted as earthing himself from pursuit in the sanctuary of his club, there to eat his fill unmolested, with no remonstrant at hand to remind him of the gout when enjoying his turtle, or to talk of cupping when the glass of champagne is at his lips. "There he may eat his asparagus *tout à l'huile*—there he may pepper his cream-tart," and none to say him nay. Drawn with pitiless realism from the life is Acton Bell (Anne Bronte)'s picture of the dying master of Wildfell Hall, whose extreme dread of death, when and while it seems imminent, renders easy his wife's task of curbing his unruly greed, but who becomes intractable as the danger to dear life seems receding. "I watch and restrain him," she writes, "as well as I can, and often get bitterly abused for my rigid severity; and sometimes he contrives to elude my vigilance, and sometimes acts in opposition to my will." William Collins, the painter, notes in his diary a certain "dinner at C——'s," where he "sat next to H——, who took some highly seasoned omelet. I asked him how he could venture on such stuff; he said he could not resist it, though he knew how much he should suffer from it. He took a great deal of wine, to overcome the effects of the omelet, and assured me he should be ill for four days after such a dinner, and that he always suffered in the same way after dining with C——! How absurd such weakness appears, and yet how common it is!" George Herbert's counsel is never out of date, any more than King Solomon's, in the matter of putting a knife to one's throat, if edacious and a diner-out:—

> "Look to thy mouth: diseases enter there. . . .
> . . . Carve, or discourse; do not a famine fear.
> Who carves is kind to two, who talks to all.
> Look on meat, think it dirt, then eat a bit;
> Then say withal, Earth to earth I commit."

——o——

HAZAEL'S ABHORRENT REPUDIATION OF HIS FUTURE SELF.

2 KINGS viii. 13.

WHY wept Elisha in the presence of Hazael, when that envoy from the sick king of Syria courted the man of God, in his sovereign's behalf, with a consignment of every good thing of Damascus, forty camels' burden? Courteous and gentle was Benhadad's messenger who came to inquire of the Lord of Elisha, if the royal Syrian should recover of the disease which had brought him so low. Why wept the prophet, when his prophecy had been uttered, ominously vague? "Go, say unto him [Benhadad], Thou mayest certainly recover. Howbeit the Lord hath showed me that he shall certainly die." And he settled his countenance stedfastly, until he was ashamed.

"And Hazael said, Why weepeth my lord? And he answered, Because I know the evil that thou wilt do unto the children of Israel; their strongholds wilt thou set on fire, and their young men wilt thou slay with the sword, and wilt dash their children," etc. And Hazael said, "But what! is thy servant a dog, that he should do this great thing?"

Yet Hazael went home, and on the very morrow commenced his justification of the seer's previsionary tears, by spreading a thick wet cloth on the face of his master, so that Benhadad, who else would have recovered, died, and Hazael reigned in his stead.

Well might the man of God weep, nor could anything be

more natural, or at least naturally assumed, than the shuddering repudiation, the deprecating protest, of the envoy that now was, the king—and dog—that to-morrow should be.

> "Lui-même, à son portrait forcé de rendre hommage,
> Il frémira d'horreur devant sa propre image."

The man who is weak, observes Miss Lee in the "Canterbury Tales," is always in danger of becoming a villain; and she exemplifies this liability in the instance of Villars, who, by indulging a passion calculated to enfeeble his understanding and corrupt his heart, is soon to be found touching that point which his high tone of romantic refinement had once induced him to believe it impossible he should even approach. But he protests too much who strenuously protests, with protestation heaped on protestation, against any such possible lapse and collapse on his part; and there are cases of this kind, of which one may say with Molière—

> "Que c'est être à demi ce que l'on vient de dire,
> Que de vouloir jurer qu'on ne le sera pas."

Martial is in the right in answering the inquiry of Priscus, how would he live if he became rich and great all at once, with another query, Who can say beforehand what his future conduct will be? *Quemquam posse putas mores narrare futuros?* If Priscus were to become a lion, what sort of one would he turn out to be? Perhaps like Hazael, a dog.

In sight of a corpse suspended to a tree, the "miserable remnant of a wretch that was hanged there for murder," Robert, in one of Tobin's dramas, protests to his mother that, robber though he be, *he* is no murderer; she replies:—

> "You are a robber;
> And he who robs, by sharp resistance pressed,
> Will end the deed in blood: 'twas so with him;
> He once possessed a soul quick as your own
> To mercy, and would quake, as you do now,
> At the bare apprehension of the act
> That has consigned him to yon blasted tree."

Dr. Hamilton somewhere adverts to a sort of gambling in

our large cities which does not look particularly repulsive—not being carried on in "hells," and pleading the sanction of some titled names; the results, however, of which are hanging like a millstone round the neck of many a once promising young man; while, to say nothing of those whom it has reduced to beggary or blackguardism, numbers of its victims must be sought in the Portland hulks or Dartmoor prison. "They went to the race-course, or, without going there, they laid wagers on horses, and sooner or later they lost more than they could pay, and in dread of dishonour they took means to get the money at the very suggestion of which, once upon a time, they would indignantly have exclaimed, 'Is thy servant a dog?' and after a few miserable makeshifts, only adding sin to sin, there came detection and ruin and disgrace." It is of the riotous living of prodigal sons that the same preacher is treating, when he shows, in his graphic way, how speedily riot, whether coarse or refined, wastes the reveller's substance—not only sapping the constitution, and softening the brain, and shattering the nerves, and enfeebling the mind, but exhausting the estate, and soon bringing the spendthrift to poverty. And, as the discourser goes on to say, if the passion still urges, and the fear of God has departed, wild methods will be used to meet the demand and assuage the frantic craving. "Keepsakes will be sold or pledged, to part with which would, once upon a time, have looked like sacrilege." Perhaps money will be taken from the till, and so on and on, or rather downwards and downwards, deeper and deeper, till the lowest deep is sounded, and darkness is the burier of the dead.

It has been remarked by one of the most reflective of our popular authors, that there is a terrible coercion in our deeds which may first turn the honest man into a deceiver, and then reconcile him to the change, for this reason—that the second wrong presents itself to him in the guise of the only practicable right. "The action which before commission has been seen with that blended common-sense and fresh untarnished feeling which is the healthy eye of the soul, is looked at afterwards with the lens of apologetic ingenuity, through which all things that men call beautiful and ugly are seen to be made up of textures very much alike." Europe, it is suggestively added, adjusts itself to a *fait accompli;* and so does an individual character—until the placid adjustment is disturbed by a convulsive retribution.

Recording the appointment of Bonaparte to succeed Scherer in command of the French forces on Genoese territory, Southey observes that although the former had given indications of his military talents at Toulon, and of his remorseless nature at Paris, "the extent either of his ability or his wickedness was at this time known to none, and perhaps not even suspected by himself." Of all the lessons derived from the history of human passion, says Lavalette, the most important is the utter impossibility which even the best men will always experience of stopping, if they are once led into the path of error. If, a few years before they were perpetrated, the crimes of the first French Revolution, he goes on to surmise, could have been portrayed to those who committed them, "even Robespierre himself would have recoiled with horror." Men, in the case suggested, are seduced at first by plausible theories, which their heated imaginations represent as beneficial and easy of execution: "they advance unconsciously from errors to faults, and from faults to crimes, till sensibility is destroyed by the habitual spectacle of guilt, and the most savage atrocities come to be dignified by the name of state policy."

The world, and the spirit of the world, observes Sir Fowell Buxton in one of his letters, are very insidious; "and more than once I have seen a person who, as a youth, was single-eyed and single-hearted, and who, to any one who supposed he might glide into laxity of zeal, would have said, 'Am I a dog?' in maturer age become, if not a lover of the vices of the world, at least a tolerator of its vanities." But as M. de Sainte-Beuve sententiously puts it, in one of his maxims after the manner of La Rochefoucauld, "La plupart des défauts qui éclatent dans la seconde moitié de la vie existaient en nous tout formés bien auparavant; mais ils étaient masqués, en quelque sorte, par la pudeur de la jeunesse." The faults of after-life were there, and only the modest reserve and self-restraint of youth kept them under cover. With riper years comes less regard for others, and the cover is taken off.

A clerical essayist on "Future Years," "can well believe," he tells us, "that many a man, could he have a glimpse in innocent youth of what he will be twenty or thirty years after, would pray in anguish to be taken before coming to *that!*" "Mansie Wauch's glimpse of destitution was bad enough; but a million times worse is a glimpse of hardened and unabashed sin and shame." And it would be no comfort, we are reminded—it would be an aggravation in that view—to think that by the time you have reached that miserable point, you will have grown pretty well reconciled to it—*that* being the worst of all.

Hazael stands out in large type, black letter type, or red letter, if you will—the hue of blood—a degraded instance of the degrading power of guilt—a warning of the stealthy yet swift aggression of criminal impulse, or criminal policy, seducing, subduing, and transforming its subjects,—

"Till creatures born,
For good (whose hearts kind Pity nursed)
Will act the direst crimes they cursed
But yester-morn."

——o——

THE OPEN RIGHT HAND'S SECRET FROM THE LEFT.

St. Matthew vi. 3.

TO some of us, to very many, it may seem that the Sermon might well be on a Mount, that set forth such a text as this: "But when thou doest alms, let not thy left hand know what thy right hand doeth." The atmosphere is of other altitudes than here below. We may not sound a trumpet before us, as the hypocrites did in the synagogue and in the streets, to have glory of men; and verily, every man his own trumpeter, they had their reward. But as to keeping our open-handed doles and donations a secret, as it were, from our other self; as to concealing from the left hand the furtive bounties and stealthy almsgiving of the right, that is a practical transcendentalism mostly undreamt of in our philosophy.

Yet are there, and ever will be, those—else had this earth of ours lost the salt of the earth, and wherewith then should it be salted?—who—

> "Do good by stealth, and blush to find it fame."

The larger number of benefactors, who, as the caustic French wit, Chamfort, puts it, pretend to conceal themselves after effecting a deed of kindness, betake themselves to flight and a hiding-place only as Virgil's Galatea did, with a decided wish to be seen first: *Et se cupit ante videri.* Another of Chamfort's cynical *maximes et pensées* runs thus: "Il y a peu de bienfaiteurs qui ne disent comme Satan, *Si cadens adoraveris me.*" Whom the vulgar succour, they oppress, says Crabbe. They have as little sympathy with, or interest in, the rule of keeping the right hand's largesse a secret from the left, as with Peter of Aragon's famous refusal to let Pope Martin IV. know what were his designs against the infidel. Peter implored the blessing of the Holy Father on his scheme of action; "but if he thought his right hand knew his secret, he would cut it off, lest it should betray it to his left." And the vulgar mean the commonalty, the many, the *polloi.* The doer of good, therefore, who does it by stealth, is the exception to a rule; and as an exception he is treated in literature and life as what is called a "character." Goldsmith makes a highly pronounced character of his man in black, whose hand is open as day to melting charity, while he professes to keep it closed tight as wax and hard as steel. He bullies in words a petitioner for aid, while he is but studying what method he shall take to relieve him unobserved. "He had, however," writes the Chinese citizen of the world, "no easy part to act, as he was obliged to preserve the appearance of ill-nature before me, and yet relieve himself by relieving the sailor." And by contrivance he gains his end. The mandarin's curiosity to know "what could be his motives for thus concealing virtues which others take such pains to display," is natural, and finds natural expression; and thereby hangs the tale of the "reluctantly good" Man in Black. Smollett, again, makes one of his heroes, though young and pleasure-loving, retrench his expenses in order to help the needy: "Numberless were the objects to which he extended his charity in private. Indeed, he exerted this virtue in secret, not only on account of avoiding the charge of ostentation, but also because he was ashamed of being detected in such an awkward, unfashionable practice by the censorious observers of this humane generation. In this particular he seemed to confound the ideas of virtue and vice; for he did good as other people do evil, by stealth; and was [like the man in black] so capricious in point of behaviour, that frequently, in public, he wagged his tongue in satirical animadversions upon that poverty which his hand had, in private, relieved." It cannot be affirmed of him that he exemplified, in detail, all the attributes of a portrait from life, but after death, by Cowper; but some of them he did:

> "Yet was thy liberality discreet,
> Nice in its choice, and of a tempered heat;
> And though in act unwearied, *secret still*,
> As in some solitude the summer rill
> Refreshes, where it winds, the faded green,
> And cheers the drooping flowers, *unheard, unseen.*"

When a biographer can accredit the subject of his narrative with a disposition to hide his bounty, he is usually apt enough to catch at so catching a quality. Wellington, we are told, though his name so rarely figured on subscription lists, was very liberal in his charities, and was not unfrequently victimized by impostors. During the Irish famine he is said to have distributed at least £10,000 among the relief committees; but "he never said a word about it at Exeter Hall." Free gifts by stealth are often characteristic of such natures as Byron's; of whom, for instance, we read that, soon after Lord Falkland's death, the poet reminded the unfortunate widow that he was to be godfather to her infant [Byron a sponsor!—but let that pass]; and that after the "christening" he inserted a five-hundred pound note in a breakfast cup; but in so cautious a manner that it was not discovered until he had left the house. Montesquieu was even hard and harsh in his repudiation of thanks from those he helped; his kindness was accordingly (to speak by quibble) less than kind; insomuch that one critic recognises in him "un de ces dieux bienfaiteurs de l'humanité, mais qui n'en partagent point la tendresse." Grimm is another example of a satirical tongue with an open hand, only the hand was opened behind his own back: *il sut être bienveillant en secret.* Amid James Watt's donations in aid of sound and useful learning, testifies one biographer, were not wanting others prescribed by true religion, for the consolation of the poor, and relief of the afflicted; but these works were done in secret, and with injunctions that his name should not be made known. Goethe seems to have preserved profound secrecy with respect to some signal exercises of his beneficence. Cowper tells Unwin, in one of his letters, that a recent endeavour of that good pastor to relieve the indigent of his flock would probably have succeeded better "had it been an affair of more notoriety than merely to furnish a few poor fellows with a little fuel to preserve their extremities from the frost." "Men really pious delight in doing good by stealth;* but nothing less than an ostentatious display of bounty will satisfy mankind in general." The Olney bard, in after years, had pleasant dealings with a signal exemplar of the benefactor by stealth. He was made the almoner of a charitable stranger, to whom he thus refers in a letter to John Newton: "Like the subterraneous flue that warms my myrtles, he does good and is unseen. His injunctions of secrecy are still as rigorous as ever, and must therefore be observed with the same attention." A year later: "I shall probably never see him," writes Cowper, in relating a fresh tide of benefactions; but "he will always have a niche in the museum of my reverential remembrance." Even without *that,* the Unknown had his reward.

"Charity ever
Finds in the act reward, and needs no trumpet
In the receiver."

* A broken-down old schoolmaster bore witness to Dr. Chalmers' *modus operandi.* "Many a pound-note has the doctor given me, and he always did the thing as if he were afraid that any person should see him. May God reward him!"—Hanna's "Life of Chalmers," chap. i.

TO-MORROW.

ST. JAMES iv. 13, 14.

THE rich man in the parable was self-complacently far-sighted in his foresight, when he took stock of his much goods laid up for many years; but that very night his soul was to be required of him. Take thine ease; eat, drink, and be merry, was his easy-going style of self-communing: many are the years in store for thee, and all of these well stored with whatever makes this life worth the living. And just in the same easy-going style is pitched the prospective self-assurance of the worldlings censured by St. James. "Go to now, ye that say, to-day or to-morrow we will go into such a city, and continue there a year, and buy, and sell, and get gain: whereas ye know not what shall be on the morrow. For what is your life? it is even a vapour that appeareth for a little time, and then vanisheth away." Boast not thyself of to-morrow, for thou knowest not what a day may bring forth. To-day, while it is called to-day,—hardly this can be called thine. But to-morrow, whose is that? Even the uttermost sensualist owns it to be none of his, when he sets up for his motto, at once a reminder to live fast and a *memento mori*,—Let us eat and drink to-day, for to-morrow we die. So far he is at least verbally wiser than his brethren of the cup and the platter, whose style is, "Come ye, I will fetch wine, and we will fill ourselves with strong drink; and to-morrow shall be as this day, and much more abundant." Little reck they of the platitude that all flesh is grass, which to-day is, and to-morrow is cast into the oven.

Macbeth's threefold To-morrow is a triplet that by no means goes trippingly off the tongue:—

> "TO-MORROW, AND TO-MORROW, AND TO-MORROW,
> Creeps in this petty pace from day to day,
> To the last syllable of recorded time;
> And all our yesterdays have lighted fools
> The way to dusty death."

So muses the usurper, besieged in his last fastness, while the cry is still, *They come*—even the enemy and the avenger; a cry varied by one of women bewailing their mistress dead. He has supped full of horrors; and the cry of "The queen, my lord, is dead," but elicits for response, "She should have died hereafter; there would have been a time for such a word.—*To-morrow, and to-morrow, and to-morrow.*" . . .

In some such mood was usurping Gloster, on the eve of destruction, pitching his tent on Bosworth Field, and meditating,—

> . . . "Here will I lie to-night;
> [*Soldiers begin to set up the King's tent.*
> But where to-morrow?—Well, all's one for that."

To the meanest private in rank and file the to-morrow that shall bring on a battle cannot but be a momentous thought. As his grace of York says, on the eve of Hotspur's encounter with the king's forces at Shrewsbury,—

> "To-morrow, good Sir Michael, is a day
> Wherein the fortune of ten thousand men
> Must 'bide the touch."

While there's life there's hope, and hope is, by the nature of it, intent on to-morrow. As with hopes, so with fears. And hopes and fears together make up the sum of what has interest in life. No wonder, then, if to-morrow is a frequent word with the poet-philosopher of human life; and that in comedy and in tragedy alike, it serves his turn. Be it a wedding for to-morrow or an execution for to-morrow, Shakspeare iterates and re-iterates the phrase, with all the dramatic realism that informs and vivifies his creations. Is it the wedding of Hero with Claudio, for instance? "When are you married, madam?" asks Ursula of the bride; who, with affected levity, replies,—

> "Why, every day; to-morrow. Come, go in;
> I'll show thee some attires; and have thy counsel,
> Which is the best to furnish me to-morrow."

Little she recks of what is to betide her ere to-morrow dawn. Or is it an execution? Hear Angelo's decree against another (quite another) Claudio:

> "Were he my kinsman, brother, or my son,
> It would be thus with him;—he must die to-morrow.

Isab. To-morrow! O, that's sudden! Spare him, spare him;
He's not prepared for death."

Many scenes later we have the Provost imparting his fate to the doomed man: —

"Look, here's the warrant, Claudio, for thy death:
'Tis now dead-midnight, and by eight to-morrow
Thou must be made immortal."

Presently the disguised duke comes in, and asks of the Provost,—

"Have you no countermand for Claudio yet,
But he must die to-morrow?
Prov. None, sir; none.

One may wonder whether Macbeth, brooding on the vague and vasty gloom of that word, bethought him of the fatal first use of it in his incipient designs against his sovran. The gracious Duncan, he tells his wife, on reaching home, is to become his guest to-night:

Lady M. And when goes hence?
Macb. To-morrow,—as he purposes.
Lady M. O, never
Shall sun that morrow see!"

Reason good, or rather, in a bad sense, reason of the worst, had Macbeth to brood in after-days, when the morrow that never came to Duncan, had come blood-stained to *him*,—on the far-reaching capacities of so memorable a phrase. But from Shakspeare turn to other sources of illustration.

Truth as well as pathos has been justly ascribed to the following expansion of a very natural sentiment—"the fear of personal oblivion in one's own home"—artistically rendered by one of a gifted family of artists:

"I listened to their honest chat;
Said one: 'To-morrow we shall be
Plod, plod along the featureless sands
And coasting miles and miles of sea.'
Said one: 'Before the turn of tide
We will achieve the eyrie-seat.'
Said one: 'To-morrow shall be like
To-day, but much more sweet.'

'To-morrow,' said they, strong with hope,
  And dwelt upon the pleasant way;
'To-morrow,' cried they, one and all,
  While no one spoke of yesterday.
Then life stood still at blessed noon,
  I, only I, had passed away:
'To-morrow and to-day,' they cried:
  I was of yesterday."

It is a critical point in Mr. Charles Reade's story of what he calls very hard cash, when Noah Skinner, the fraudulent banker's clerk, old and dying, proposes to himself, and resolves to deliver up, to-morrow, the receipt for fourteen thousand pounds, his criminal possession and crafty retention of which has caused such profound and wide-spread misery. "A sleepy languor now came over him; . . . but his resolution remained unshaken; by-and-by waking up from a sort of heavy dose, he took, as it were a last look at the receipt, and murmured, 'My head, how heavy it feels.' But presently he roused himself, full of his penitent resolution, and murmured again brokenly, 'I'll—take it to—Pembroke-street to—morrow: to—mor—row." Fool—like other us fools of nature—that night his soul was required of him. The to-morrow found him, and so did the detectives, dead.

Among other visitors and applicants at the mystical Intelligence Office thrown open to our gaze by Nathaniel Hawthorne, there totters hastily in a grandfatherly personage, so earnest in his uniform alacrity that his white hair floats backwards as he hurries up to the desk, while his dim eyes catch a momentary lustre from his vehemence of purpose. This venerable figure explains that he is in search of To-morrow.

"I have spent all my life in pursuit of it," adds the sage old gentleman, "being assured that To-morrow has some vast benefit or other in store for me. But I am now getting a little in years, and must make haste, for unless I overtake To-morrow soon, I begin to be afraid it will finally escape me."

"This fugitive To-morrow, my venerable friend," said the Man of Intelligence, "is a stray child of Time, and is flying from his father into the region of the infinite. Continue your pursuit, and you will doubtless come up with him; but as to the earthly gifts which you expect, he has scattered them all among a throng of Yesterdays."

The grandsire is obliged to content himself with this enigmatical response, and hastens forth with a quick clatter of his staff upon the floor; and as he disappears, a little boy scampers through the door in chase of a butterfly, which has got astray amid the barren sunshine of the city. Had the old gentleman, suggests our ever-suggestive moralist, been shrewder, he might have detected To-morrow under the semblance of that gaudy insect.

J'ai vécu—I managed to keep alive—was the Abbé Siéyès' answer to those who, in after days, asked him how he spent his time in the Reign of Terror. And it is in allusion to his position at that season of peril, when no one could reckon on a morrow—*nul ne pouvait se promettre un lendemain*—that he quotes the *vers charmants* made in 1708 by Maucroix, then fourscore and upwards:—

> "Chaque jour est un bien que du Ciel je reçoi!
> Jouissons aujourd'hui de celui qu'il nous donne:
> Il n'appartient pas plus aux jeunes gens qu'à moi,
> Et celui de demain n'appartient à personne."

"What shall we be doing to-morrow at this time?" said Ducos, as the Girondins were whiling away their last evening here on earth. And each of them replied as the humour took him, or the subject impressed him. The favourite answer seems to have been, We shall sleep after the fatigues of the day. To some the feeling may have been, too literally and very bitterly, what Wordsworth versified as he gazed from Rydal Mount on a slowly-sinking star:

> "We struggle with our fate,
> While health, power, glory, from their height decline,
> Depressed; and then extinguished; and our state,
> In this, how different, lost Star, from thine,
> That no to-morrow shall our beams restore!"

To-morrow, and to-morrow, and to-morrow. For some time had the Emperor Francis—Maria Theresa's consort—been threatened with an apoplexy, when, on the morning of the 18th of August, 1764, being pressed by his sister to be blooded, he answered, "I am engaged this evening to sup with Joseph, and will not disappoint him; but I promise you I will be blooded to-morrow." At the opera in the evening he was taken ill. Retiring, he was struck with apoplexy, and died at Joseph's feet, for he had fallen from Joseph's arms. At his feet—like one of old time—he bowed, he fell, he lay down: at his feet he bowed, he fell: where he bowed, there he fell down dead.

Boast not thyself of to-morrow. Hardly less hackneyed in the ear of scholar and schoolboy, yet hardly less impressive as truisms with ever-living truth in them, are Horace's

> Quis scit an adjiciant hodiernæ crastina summæ
> Tempora Di superi?

(who knows whether the powers above will add a morrow to the day that now is?), and Seneca's Never was man so in favour with the gods as to be able to promise himself a morrow:

> Nemo tam divos habuit faventes,
> Crastinum ut possit sibi polliceri.

When Archias, the polemarch at Thebes, dissolved in wine and pleasure, received from his pontifical namesake at Athens a full and particular account by letter of the conspiracy of Pelopidas and the exiles, who were even then counting the minutes ere they struck the blow,—although the messenger expressly urged his excellency to read the missive forthwith, as the contents were of instant import, Archias only smiled a tipsy smile, and said, "Business to-morrow." Then he put the unopened letter under the bolster of his couch, and resumed his colloquy with his host, Philidias, who was in the plot, and who was taking good care to ply the polemarch with wine. Business to-morrow. To-morrow as he purposed! Oh, never should sun that morrow see.

Si hodie non es paratus, quo modo cras eris? CRAS *est dies incertus: et qui scis si crastinum habebis?* To-morrow, in this its prospective, procrastinating sense, is denounced by Mr. Sala, with all due asperity, as a wretched, cowardly, idiotic subterfuge and apology—a "suicidal delusion and pitfall." Yes, to-morrow I will begin to learn Syro-Chaldaic (we overhear him saying): I will read the novel of the day to-day. To-morrow I will dine on a mutton-chop and a glass of water. To-day I will ask the *chef* at the club to send me up a pretty little dinner, not forgetting that irresistible *choufleur au gratin*, and bid the butler bring me that curious pommard with the iron-grey seal. To-morrow I will finish my *magnum opus*, my "Treatise on the Books of Job and Ecclesiastes in their relation to Human Wisdom and Knowledge." To-day flippant rubbish or frothy egotism shall flow from my pen. To-morrow I will pay my tailor. To-day I will order a new coat. In fine: "To-morrow I will atone for the wrong, and pray for strength to continue in the right. To-day I will follow my devices, and listen to the promptings of the world, the flesh, and the devil. To-morrow, and to-morrow, and to-morrow."

For many years, the late Alfred de Vigny continued slowly amassing poetical materials, though publishing nothing, and murmuring always, like André Chenier,—

> "Rien n'est fait aujourd'hui, tout sera fait *demain*."

The morrow has come, wrote the *Journal des Débats*, in recording his death, and his artist hands are cold in the grave.

Says the Cordelier to the condemned Thief in Mat Prior's derry-down ballad,—

> "Courage, friend; to-day is your period of sorrow;
> And things will go better, believe me, to-morrow."

But what says the Thief in reply?

> "To-morrow? our hero replied in a fright:
> He that's hanged before noon, ought to think of to-night."

But Prior will supply us with more than one study of the subject. Here is a variation, for instance, in matter, manner, and metre:—

> "The hoary fool, who many days
> Has struggled with continued sorrow,
> Renews his hope, and blindly lays
> The desperate bet upon to-morrow.

"To-morrow comes ; 'tis noon, 'tis night ;
This day like all the former flies :
Yet on he runs, to seek delight
To-morrow, till to-night he dies."

The gaming allusion of the first stanza reminds us of the picture of a certain devotee at the *roulette* table at Hombourg, who kept his seat—tranquil, immovable, vigilant,—the Napoleon of *roulette;* in whose victorious progress Marengos and Austerlitzes succeeded each other, as if Moscow and the Beresina were phantoms—as if to-morrow would never come. "To-morrow; ay, that dread to-morrow that comes to all: the fateful *Demain* of Victor:

"Demain est la sapin du trône,
Aujourd'hui c'en est le velours."

Yes, to-morrow is the coarse deal, with its ten sacks, that forms the framework of the throne, as to-day is its velvet and gilding.

"Demain c'est le coursier qui s'abat plein d'écume ;
Demain, O conquérant, c'est Moscou qui s'allume
La nuit comme un flambeau :
C'est not' vieille garde qui jonche au lointain la plaine,
Demain c'est Waterloo ! Demain c'est Ste. Helène !
Demain c'est le tombeau !"

And yet to-morrow was, for good or bad, for better for worse, a favourite phrase with Napoleon. His last words to Murat at nightfall, in the hope of battle with the Russians on the Dwina next day, were, "To-morrow, at five, the sun of Austerlitz!" After the combat of Reichenbach, which lost him Duroc, he sat alone, in moody meditation, neither speaking nor to be spoken with; appealed to in vain for orders by Caulaincourt and Maret: "To-morrow—everything," was the only answer their most urgent demands could wring from him, in his hour of dejection and theirs of need. In another mood was the emperor when, after Leipsic, he pressed the Austrian cabinet to side with him, and at once. If they were wise, he said, they would do so forthwith. They could do so, he told their representative, that evening. To-morrow it might perhaps be too late; for who could foretell the events of to-morrow?

So thought Sunderland, in that "agony of terror," almost over-wrought or over-coloured, perhaps, by Macaulay, which impelled him to resign office, in a sort of frenzied haste. He had asked some of his friends to come to his house that he might consult them; they came at the appointed time, but found that he had gone to Kensington, and had left word that he should soon be back. When he joined them, they observed that he had not the gold key which is the badge of the Lord Chamberlain, and asked where it was. "At Kensington," answered Sunderland. They found that he had tendered his resignation, and that it had been, after a long struggle, accepted. They blamed his haste, and told him that since he had summoned them to advise him on that day, he might at least have waited till the morrow. "To-morrow," he exclaimed "would have ruined me. To-night has saved me."

A signal contrast the despairing minister presents to the poet's picture of credulous hope which ever promises a morrow better than to-day (like the voluptuaries branded by the Hebrew prophet, who hug themselves in the assurance that To-morrow shall be as this day, and much more abundant):

> . . . "Credula vitam
> Spes fovet, ac melius cras fore semper ait."

They say that To-morrow never comes. The great Greek father with the golden mouth seems to have based an ethical warning on this thought, when he bids us defer not till to-morrow, for to-morrow is a vanishing quantity. Μὴ εἰς τὴν αὔριον ἀναβάλλου· ἡ γὰρ αὔριον οὐδέ ποτε λαμβάνει τέγος. The moral is one with that of the Latin satirist—though *he* makes to-morrow come fast enough, one *per diem*,—and go quite as fast as it came:

> . . . "Cum lux altera venit,
> Jam cras hesternum consumpsimus; ecce aliud cras
> Egerit hys annos."

Matter-of-fact people will tell you that To-morrow does come, and fix by their stop-watch the instant of its arrival. Nay, they can appeal to the *primus inter poetas* for poetical verification of their view. Says the Messenger to the Provost, while it is yet dark, on the morning whichis appointed to be Claudio's last, "Good morrow; for, as I take it, it is almost day." And so with the peers who enter sleepless King Henry's chamber, at the hour they name:

> "*Warwick.* Many good morrows to your majesty.
> *K. Hen.* Is it good morrow, lords?
> *War.* 'Tis one o'clock, and past.
> *K. Hen.* Why then, good morrow to you all, my lords."

But, in its own sense, the saying holds good, and is good sense too, that To-morrow never comes. One might take for emblem of its import the touching story told by Southey, of a lady on the point of marriage, whose affianced husband usually travelled by the stage-coach to visit her, and who, going one day to meet him, found instead of her betrothed an old friend, despatched to announce to her his sudden death. She uttered a scream, and piteously exclaimed, "He is dead!" But then all consciousness of the affliction that had befallen her ceased. From that fatal moment she had daily, for fifty years, at the time Dr. Uwins wrote, and "in all seasons, traversed the distance of a few miles, where she expected her future husband to alight from the coach; and every day [adds the doctor, writing in the then present tense] she utters in a plaintive tone, "He is not come yet! I will return to-morrow." *To-morrow, and to-morrow, and to-morrow*—that to her never was, but always was to be.

Why, and how, To-morrow never comes, might be discussed in a strain of transcendental metaphysics. Mr. Carlyle, in a memorable chapter headed Natural Supernaturalism, expounds in his mystic suggestive way the philosophic thesis, that Time and Space are but creations of God,—with whom as it is a universal HERE, so it is an everlasting NOW. And as regards Man: is the Past annihilated, or only past? is the Future non-extant, or only future? "The curtains of Yesterday drop down, and the curtains of To-morrow roll up; but Yesterday and To-morrow both *are.* Pierce through the Time-element, glance into the Eternal."

It is but a glance the strongest eye can take, in that direction. But even a glance may secure a glimpse of things which filmy, unpurged, downlooking eye hath not seen, nor ear heard—for they seem to involve unspeakable words, which it is not lawful for a man to utter. To-morrow thou hast never seen; to thee it has never come. But it shall come. And it that shall come, will come; and will not tarry. Wait the great teacher, Death. CRAS *iterabimus æquor:* to-morrow we shall be sounding our dim and perilous way across the dark waters of that fathomless sea. If the prospect appals, happy he that can adapt to his own hopes, in serenest confidence, yet eager anticipation,—as he speculates on what a day, and the Better Land, may bring forth: To-morrow, to fresh woods and pastures new.

——o——

THE DIVINE AUTHORSHIP OF ORDER.

I CORINTHIANS xiv. 33, 40.

PRACTICALLY, the amount of confusion prevalent in the church of Corinth, arising from irregularities incident to the exercise of "tongues," and to the undisciplined energies of a mixed congregation, appears to have almost rivalled the disorder in the theatre of Ephesus, when the whole city was filled with confusion, and some cried one thing, and some another; for the assembly was confused, and the most part knew not wherefore they were come together. So, when the whole church of Corinth were come together into one place, and all spoke with tongues, to outsiders that for the nonce stepped inside they must appear mad. All things were done indecorously and in most admired disorder. Now, St. Paul was for having all things done decently and in order. "For God is not the author of confusion, but of peace." Order is Heaven's first law. The same apostle is prompt to remind the Thessalonians that he behaved himself not disorderly among them; and this he did because he heard that there were some among them which walked disorderly—ἀτάκτως. The apostolic canon for both

Corinth and Thessalonica, and all other churches, is, Πάντα δὲ κατὰ τάξιν γινέσθω. Let them all walk by this same rule, and all mind this same thing.

As with the sect of Pythagoreans, virtue was defined to be a harmony, unity, and an endeavour to resemble the Deity,—so the whole life of man, they taught, should be an attempt to represent on earth the beauty and harmony displayed in the order of the universe. It was the doctrine of Pythagoras himself, that by action as well as by thought the individual as well as the state should represent in themselves "an image of the order and harmony by which the world was sustained and regulated." But as Prior puts it, when he considers the heavens, the starry worlds of God's ordaining, or ordering,—

> "How mean the order and perfection sought
> In the best product of the human thought,
> Compared to the great harmony that reigns
> In what the Spirit of the world ordains!"

Lord Lytton suggestively pictures to us one of his characters alone in the streets by night, striding noiselessly on, under the gaslights, under the stars; gaslights primly marshalled at equidistance; stars that seem to the naked eye dotted over space without symmetry or method—"Man's order, near and finite, is so distinct; the Maker's order, remote, infinite, is so beyond man's comprehension of what *is* order." Chauncy Hare Townshend expresses the same idea in an address to the stars:—

> "Distance deceives the sight. Ye move and sway
> With life; yet are your hoverings on the brink
> Of ruin but the freedom and the play
> That binds your dance of beauty, link to link,
> In woven joy that shall not fail nor shrink.
> . . . Thrones arise and sink,
> Earth is transformed beneath you: ye remain,
> Clasping distracted man with Order's sacred chain."

So Wordsworth, addressing as it were a deified idea of Duty, pays this homage:—

> . . . "Thou dost preserve the stars from wrong,
> And the most ancient heavens through Thee are fresh and strong."

Well may Hooker speculate on what would become of man, were Nature to intermit her course, and leave altogether, though but for a while, the observation of her own laws; if the frame of that heavenly arch erected over our heads should loosen and dissolve itself; if celestial spheres should forget their wonted motions, and by irregular volubility turn themselves any way as it might happen; if the prince of the lights of heaven, which now as a giant doth run his unwearied course, should, as it were through a languishing faintness, begin to stand and rest himself; if the moon should wander from her beaten way, the times and seasons of the year blend themselves by disordered and confused mixture—"See we not plainly that obedience of creatures unto the law of Nature is the stay of the whole world?" Again to quote from "The Mystery of Evil," the same star-gazer speaking:—

"Do I not climb in you, O blessèd host,
  The way of symbols, shining steps to God?
When most man knows you, he is certain most
  One law unswerving reigns from star to clod."

"Of law," says Hooker, at the close of his first book of Ecclesiastical Polity, with an eloquence which has ever been most admired by the most admirable masters of English prose,—"Of law there can be no less acknowledged, than that her seat is the bosom of God, her voice the harmony of the world; all things in heaven and earth do her homage, the very least as feeling her care, and the greatest as not exempted from her power: both angels and men, and creatures of what condition soever, though each in different sort and manner, yet all with uniform consent, admiring her as the mother of their peace and joy." Considering when he wrote, what he wrote, and to what purpose and in what spirit he wrote, there seems to us a beautiful consistency in Richard Hooker's deathbed meditations, as related in the familiar memoir by Izaak Walton. Found by his trustiest visitor, "deep in contemplation, and not inclinable to discourse," and asked what was the subject of his present thoughts, he replied, "That he was meditating the number and nature of angels, and their blessed obedience and order, without which, peace could not be in heaven; and oh, that it might be so on earth!"

There is not, affirms a modern divine, a corner of the world, nor a process of nature, nor a piece of God's handiwork of any kind whatever, on which His love of order is not written with a plainness not to be mistaken. "System and method, law and order, symmetry and punctuality, are conspicuous everywhere; indicating at once the value attached to these things in the mind of God, and his dislike for their opposites—confusion, fitfulness, irregularity." Nor is the Divine love of order a quality that ever leads to stiffness, formality, or monotony; for it is shown to be constantly associated with beauty, variety, and freedom.

M. Jules Simon interpolates into his argument for the vast preponderance of good over evil in the world, a casually expressed identification of good with order: "le bien, c'est-à-dire, l'ordre, car dans le monde le bien et l'ordre ne font qu'un."

"Some think Disorder means God's moral plan;
But Evil oscillates in certain bounds.
Ten thousand causes check the rage of man:
His utmost crimes a wall of brass surrounds;
Mere weariness exhausts War's yelling hounds;
And, if all fail, Death comes with his great wave,
That levels all the hollows and the mounds
Of human life. Who then shall be so brave
As of Confusion found in God's large thoughts to rave?"

Readers familiar with the writings first and last of Mr. Carlyle, will readily call to mind many a terse utterance in vindication of the Divine authorship and Divine authority of order. *Dis*order he pronounces to be a thing which "veracious created Nature, even because it is not Chaos and a waste-whirling baseless Phantasm," rejects and disowns. "*Dis*order, insane by the nature of it, is the hatefullest of things to man, who lives by sanity and by order." "All Anarchy, all evil, all injustice, is, by the nature of it, . . . suicidal, and cannot endure." "Arrangement is indispensable to man; Arrangement, were it grounded only on that old primary evangel of Force, with Sceptre in the shape of Hammer!" Such sentences admit of almost infinite multiplication. "Anarchy, hateful as Death, is abhorrent to the whole nature of man; and so must itself soon die." Hence this philosopher's partiality for "heroes," even of the least estimable type, provided they have will and force to replace confusion by order. Cortes is not among the specified Heroes of his special Hero-worship; but he deserves a place by reason of the preamble to that code of ordinances, as the conqueror of Mexico himself terms them, which he set forth in restraint of his army: the essential purport of this preamble being, that in all institutions, whether Divine or human (if the latter have any worth), order is the great law.

It was in support of the cause of social order that Luther took to exposing the dangers due to ignorant innovators, and strenuously declared that "God Himself constituted certain authorities to direct the world; for it is a great feature in His magnificent system, that there shall be order here below." Doctor Martin may, in this respect, be called a man after our Hero-worshipper's own heart; such another as the one of whom he wrote,—"Wheresoever Disorder may stand or lie, let it have a care; here is the man that has declared war with it, that will never make peace with it. Man is the Missionary of Order; he is the servant, not of the Devil and of Chaos, but of God and the universe." And Christian doctrine teaches that the order and beauty of the outward world are symbols of that inward order and symmetry, that peace and purity of heart, that universal harmony between God's will and man's will, which it is one great object of Christianity to establish.

> "Then quick I ran my glance about the globe,
> To find Religion link'd with Order's aim,
> Ruling by love and light,"

says the Christian poet, who has, however, to deplore the disappointments of his quest. Of all orderly things that are beautiful in God's eyes, it has been said, there can be none so beautiful as an orderly or holy soul. "Once in this world the sight presented itself in spotless beauty and brilliancy." Everything there seen was in its place: reason, conscience, will, feeling, instinct, appetite, "all most beautifully arranged; each was in perfect health, and all were in thorough harmony with the will of God." But that was God manifest in the flesh. Order incarnate. Without Him, in the material world, was not anything made that was made. Apart from Him, the moral world is without form and void, and darkness covers the face of its deep. Order, in fine, is the indispensable postulate of every given cosmos. In the words of Schiller—

> "It is the keystone of the world's wide arch;
> The one sustaining and sustained by all,
> Which, if it fall, brings all in ruin down."

Of the Church as a family, George Herbert, ever quaint in his devotion, sings or says—after a depreciation of his own unruly thoughts :

> "But, Lord, the house and family are Thine,
> Though some of them repine.
> Turn out these wranglers, which defile Thy seat :
> For where Thou dwellest all is neat.
>
> "First Peace and Silence all disputes control,
> Then *Order* plays the soul;
> And giving all things their set forms and hours,
> Makes of wild woods sweet walks and bowers."

So Dryden traces to harmony this universal frame—a cosmos evolved from chaos, from a heap of jarring atoms that, at the Divine summons,—

> "*In order* to their stations leap."

Shaftesbury contends that the admiration and love of order, in whatever kind, is "naturally improving to the temper, advantageous to social affection, and highly assistant to virtue—which is itself no other than the love of order and beauty in society." In the meanest subjects of the world, he goes on to say, the appearance of order gains upon the mind, and draws the affections towards it. "For 'tis impossible that such a Divine order should be contemplated without ecstasy and rapture; since in the common subjects of science, and the liberal arts, whatever is according to just harmony and proportion is so transporting to those who have any knowledge or practice in the kind." In another place he elaborates the thesis, that whatever things have order, have unity of design, and concur in one, and are parts constituent of one whole—just as a symphony is a certain system of proportioned sounds. It is noteworthy that Pythagoras deduced his celebrated theory of the music of the spheres from his assumption that everything in the great arrangement (κόσμος) which he called the world must be harmoniously arranged (and that, accordingly, the planets were at the same relative distance as the divisions of the monochord, etc.) Divine as the philosophy of Plato is commonly esteemed, there are, on the other hand, occasional glimpses in it of what one of his commentators calls the "appalling doctrine" that God alternately governs and forsakes the world—the world when he forsakes it, suddenly changing its orbit, so that all things are in disorder, and mundane existence is totally disarranged: "only after some time do things settle down to a sort of order, though of a very imperfect kind." Spinoza takes order to be a thing of the imagination, as also he does right and wrong, useful and hurtful—these being merely such, he argues, in relation to us. But this would not prevent him, from his stand-point, assenting to the ethical import of order—as expounded for instance by the Shakspearian Ulysses:

> "The heavens themselves, the planets, and this centre,
> Observe degree, priority, and place, . . .
> Office, and custom, in all line of order. . . .
> Take but degree away, untune that string,
> And hark, what discord follows! each thing meets
> In mere oppugnancy."

Order, writes Southey, is the sanity of the mind, the health of the body, the peace of the city, the security of the State. Diogenes held with the Dorian lawgivers, that order (κόσμος) is the basis of civil government. As the beams to a house, it has been said, as the bones to the microcosm of man, so is order to all things. Balzac is treating of *harmonie politique* when he says that harmony is the poetry of order, and that "the peoples" have a keen need of order. The racy author of the "Biglow Papers" discourses in his shrewd, homely style, on the indispensableness (not that he uses such a word) of orderly established law :—

> " Onsettle *that*, an' all the world goes whiz,
> A screw is loose in everything there is."

Mr. Carlyle, in his apology for Knox in the act of pulling down cathedrals—as if he were a seditious rioting demagogue—urges that he was precisely the reverse of that. Knox, he maintains, wanted no pulling down of stone edifices, but wanted leprosy and darkness to be thrown out of the lives of men. "Tumult was not his element; it was the tragic feature of his life that he was forced to dwell so much on that." Every such man, on Mr. Carlyle's showing, is the born enemy of disorder—hates to be in it; but what then? "Smooth falsehood is not order; it is the general sum total of disorder. Order is truth—each thing standing on the basis that belongs to it. Order and falsehood cannot subsist together." And it is in treating of another of his heroes elect, that the same philosopher contends on behalf of such others of them as seem to have worked as revolutionary men, that nevertheless every great man, every genuine man, is by the nature of him a son of order, not of disorder—a seeming anarchist, yet to his whole soul anarchy is hostile, hateful. "His mission is Order; every man's is. He is here to make what was disorderly, chaotic, into a thing ruled, regular. He is the missionary of Order." Is not all work of man in this world, we are emphatically asked, a making of Order?

The Abbé Duval, writing to Mme. Récamier, as her spiritual counsellor, bids her engrave this elementary truth on her heart of hearts: "Gravez au-dedans de vous-même cette première vérité que la religion veut *l'ordre* avant tout." Whatsoever doth make manifest is light, and it is light that reveals a cosmos where before, in the words of Thomson, a formless grey confusion covered all :—

> " As when of old (so sung the Hebrew bard)
> Light, uncollected, through the chaos urged
> Its infant way; nor Order yet had drawn
> His lovely train from out the dubious gloom."

That a scrupulous regard for order, in some sort, is nevertheless compatible with a very low standard of moral worth, is recognised and illustrated by poet Crabbe—prose-poet the good parson was, not quite in the accepted sense—in a series of pithy, if not pungent rhymes :—

"The love of order—I the thing receive
From reverend men, and I in part believe—
Shows a clear mind and clean, and whoso needs
This love, but seldom in the world succeeds ;
And yet with this some other love must be,
Ere I can fully to the fact agree ;
Valour and study may by order gain,
By order sovereigns hold more steady reign ;
Through all the tribes of nature order runs,
And rules around in systems and in suns :
Still has the love of order found a place
With all that's low, degrading, mean, and base,
With all that merits scorn, and all that meets disgrace :
In the cold miser, of all change afraid,
In pompous men in public seats obeyed ;
In humble placemen, heralds, solemn drones ;

. . . . . .

Order to these is armour and defence,
And love of method serves in lack of sense."

Exceptions allowed for, as in every rule, yet is the rule sufficiently approved, that order is heaven's first law. The poet of "The Angel in the House" in style, and spirit, and sentiment, how salient a contrast to Crabbe, utters the conceit (*poeticè*) in one of his tender preludes, that—

"Sweet Order has its draught of bliss
Graced with the pearl of God's consent,"—

a conceit that allows of wide application, as do many of those of so suggestive a writer.

But to conclude. When the judicious Hooker—to call him by his conventional epithet—lay a-dying, he expressed his joy at the near prospect of entering a World of Order. The author of "The Book of the Church" emphasises the import of holy Richard's "placid and profound contentment," by reminding us that because he had been employed in ecclesiastical polemics, and because his life had been passed under the perpetual discomfort of domestic discord, the happiness of heaven must have seemed in Hooker's estimation, to consist primarily in Order, as, indeed, in all human societies this is the first thing needful.

——o——

SWEET SLEEP, AND ITS FORFEITURE.

PROVERBS iii. 24.

TO him that keepeth sound wisdom and instruction is the promise given, not only that he shall walk in his way safely, and his foot shall not stumble,—this for daytime and its activities,—but further, as regards night-time and its contingencies, that when he lies down he shall not be afraid; yea, he shall lie down, and his sleep shall be sweet. So He giveth His beloved sleep, of whom the Psalmist said, "I laid me down and slept; I awaked; for the Lord sustained me." Surely, in order that one may pray with full purpose of heart the prayer, Let me die the death of the righteous, and let my last end be like his! one should live the life that may warrant the nightly petition, Let me sleep the sleep of the just, and let mine eyes close quietly in slumber even as his.

Macbeth, within this minute a murderer, *ipso facto* realizes the appalling truth, that between him and placid sleep there is, from henceforth and for evermore, a great gulf fixed, as impassable as abysmal.

> " Methought I heard a voice cry, 'Sleep no more!
> Macbeth does murder sleep, the innocent sleep;
> Sleep, that knits up the ravell'd sleave of care,
> The death of each day's life, sore labour's bath,
> Balm of hurt minds, great nature's second course,
> Chief nourisher in life's feast,——'
> *Lady M.* What do you mean?
> *Macb.* Still it cried, 'Sleep no more!' to all the house:
> 'Glamis hath murder'd sleep; and therefore Cawdor
> Shall sleep no more. Macbeth shall sleep no more!' "

How sleeps Lady Macbeth after that night? Ask her physician

and waiting-woman, and watch with them the sleep-walking scene. "To bed, to bed, to bed." But what avails *that* to the somnambulist, ever in semblance washing her hands, and complaining of the smell of blood upon them still, and that all the perfumes of Arabia will not sweeten them? Now and then one meets with a sceptic as to lost sleep being the inevitable sequent upon crime; and no doubt there are exceptions. Mr. G. Wingrove Cooke, in his letters from Chinese waters, thus describes the captive Mandarin, Yeh, whose fellow-passenger to Calcutta he was: "He goes to bed at eight o'clock, and while we are reading or writing or playing chess, he sleeps the sleep of infancy—an unbroken slumber, apparently undisturbed by visions of widowed women and wailing orphans. This man-killer, after slaying his hundred thousand human beings, enjoys sweeter sleep than an innocent London alderman after a turtle dinner." Perhaps that is not saying much,—considering what a turtle dinner comprehends and superinduces. But the next sentence says a good deal; it is to be hoped, a great deal too much: "So false are traditions; so false are the remorseful scenes of Greek and English tragedies." One would be sorry, for the dignity of human nature, to believe that all is fiction the poets tell us of cases in which *non avium citharæque cantus*, or any other aids and appliances, *somnum reducent*. "Wherefore to me," asks Clytemnestra,—

. . . "is solacing sleep denied?
And honourable rest, the right of all?
So that no medicine of the slumbrous shell,
Brimmed with divinest draughts of melody,
Nor silence under dreamful canopies,
Nor purple cushions of the lofty couch,
May lull this fever for a little while."

Impressive in history, not romance, as Plutarch tells it, is the story of Pausanius as a haunted man, from the hour that Cleonice fell dead at his feet, pierced by his sword. "From that hour he could rest no more." Her spectre perturbed him every night. Henceforth, nor poppy, nor mandragora, nor all the drowsy syrups of the world, could ever medicine him to that sweet sleep which he owed yesterday. As a guilty spirit says of guilt, in one of Landor's fragments,—

> "It wakes me many mornings, many nights,
> And fields of poppies could not quiet it."

Modern fiction abounds with examples to the purpose. There is Colonel Whyte Melville's remorseful woman of the world bidding her young friend good night, and meaning it all the more because her own good nights are dead and gone: "What would I give to yawn as honestly as you do, and to sleep sound once again, as I used to sleep when I was a girl!" There is Mr. Trollope's Lady Mason, so wistfully, so vainly longing for rest—to be able to lay aside the terrible fatigue of being ever on the watch. From the burden of that necessity she has never been free since her crime was first committed. "She had never known true rest. She had not once trusted herself to sleep without the feeling that her first waking thought would be one of horror, as the remembrance of her position came upon her." As with the royal lady pictured by the laureate,—

> "Many a time for hours
> In the dead night, grim faces came and went
> Before her, or a vague spiritual fear—
> Like to some doubtful noise of creaking doors,
> Heard by the watcher in a haunted house,
> That keeps the rust of murder on the walls—
> Held her awake. Or if she slept, she dream'd
> An awful dream . . .
> . . . and with a cry she woke.
> And all this trouble did not pass, but grew."

There is Donatello, in Hawthorne's "Transformation," succumbing to a stupor, which he mistakes for such drowsiness as he has known in his innocent past life. There is Albert Maurice, in "Mary of Burgundy," gazing on the Vert Gallant of Hannut as he lay in a deep, sweet sleep—so calm and tranquil, though within the walls of a prison, suffering from injuries, and exposed to constant danger; gazing with a sense of envy and regret, "which few, perhaps, can appreciate fully, who have not felt the sharp tooth of remorse begin its sleepless gnawings on the heart. He would not have disturbed such slumbers for the world; and, withdrawing again with a noiseless step, he retired to his own chamber, and cast himself down upon his bed, to snatch, at least, that heated and disturbed sleep, which was all the repose that he was ever more to know on earth." To such as him can nothing bring back, in the hour and power of darkness, more than an embittered memory of times

> "When that placid sleep came o'er him
> Which he ne'er can know again."

An innocent comforter in a modern tragedy offers a disquieted spirit the assurance, as regards the object of his disquiet, that "'twill away in sleep." But his answer is,—

> "No, no! I dare not sleep—for well I know
> That then the knife will gleam, the blood will gush,
> The form will stiffen!"

From the night of the massacre of Glencoe, Glenlyon, as Macaulay tells us, was never again the man that he had been before that night. The form of his countenance was changed; and "in all places, at all hours, whether he waked or slept, Glencoe was for ever before him." As with a distinguished foreigner of a later generation, *Depuis ce moment, point de sommeil, point de repos; il croyait toujours voir un glaive arrêté sur sa tête.* In such cases, the sleepers start from broken slumbers, as if starting back from the edge of a precipice; for,—

> "Their whole tranquillity of heart is gone;
> The peace wherewith till now they have been blest
> Hath taken its departure. In the breast
> Fast following thoughts and busy fancies throng;
> Their sleep itself is feverish, and possest
> With dreams that to the wakeful mind belong."

"Something like a stupid sleep oppresses me," writes one of Henry Mackenzie's characters; "last night I could not sleep. Where are now those luxurious slumbers, those wandering dreams of future happiness? Never shall I know them again." Falkland avows to Caleb Williams, the involuntary master of his master's fatal secret, that "from the hour the crime was committed" he has not had an hour's peace: "I became changed from the happiest into the most miserable being that lives; sleep has fled from my eyes." And Caleb Williams himself testifies in an after chapter, "The ease and light-heartedness of my youth were for ever gone. The voice of an irresistible necessity had commanded me to 'sleep no more.'" They that do murder, says Roscoe's Violenzia,—

"Never sleep more, never more taste of peace,
Quaff poison in their drink, see knives in the dark,
And ever at their elbow horror walks,
Shaking them like a palsy."

The bitter contrast—ah, for the change 'twixt now and then! —is forcibly worded by Bosola in the "Duchess of Malfi":—

"O sacred innocence, that sweetly sleeps
On turtle's feathers! whilst a guilty conscience
Is a perspective that foreshows us hell."

——o——

ONCE DENIED, THRICE DENIED.

St. Matthew xxvi, 69, *sq.*

LIE engenders lie. Once committed, the liar has to go on in his course of lying. It is the penalty of his transgression, or one of the penalties. To the habitual liar, bronzed and hardened in the custom, till custom becomes second nature, the penalty may seem no very terrible price to pay. To him, on the other hand, who, without deliberate intent, and against his innermost will, is overtaken with such a fault, the generative power of a first lie to beget others, the necessity of supporting the first by a second and a third, is a retribution keenly to be felt, while penitently owned to be most just.

Though it was afar off that Peter followed his Master to the high-priest's house, yet he did follow; and, we may be sure, with little thought, and still less intention, of denying Him even once. But as he sat by the fire and warmed himself, the identification of him by a certain maid as certainly a disciple of Christ was boldly met by the affirmation, or negation, "Woman, I know Him not." The lie was uttered; the winged word of falsehood was on its way. And there an end, he perhaps hoped. But after a little while, another bystander recognised him, and asserted the damaging recognition, "Thou art also of them." Another denial was the consequence: "Man, I am not." An hour passed away, and Peter, in sullen misery and bewilderment, self-consciously an abject coward and confirmed liar, had to deny for the third time Him he had denied once and again. "Of a truth," affirmed another of the mixed company, "this fellow also was with Him; for he is a Galilean." And Peter said, "Man, I know not what thou sayest." And then the cock crew. And then the Lord turned and looked upon Peter. And at that look—so upbraidingly expressive, so pathetically recalling recent protestations of unfaltering allegiance, and the concurrent prediction of lapse and abandonment—what could Peter do, but with shame and confusion of face, and with a heart full to bursting, go out, and weep bitterly.

When he thought thereon, he wept: thought of the Master's look, that recalled to him the vehement assurance of loyalty met by the foretelling of his fall. Thought, too, of the gradua-tion of his denials; a first involving a second, and the second exacting yet a third. The third was the cost of the first. He had not counted the cost then. He had to pay it now.

It was part of the prophet's burden of woes against the doomed city, that she had "wearied herself with lies." Easily uttered, they may multiply at a rate to trouble the teller of them, and weary him, if only with the necessity of inventing new ones to back the old. He must ever be devising fresh vouchers for his impaired and imperilled credit. He must continually be endorsing his forged notes, and forging fresh ones that will stand inspection. *Fallacia alia aliam trudit.* And this is weary work.

> "En quel gouffre de soins et de perplexité
> Nous jette une action faite sans equité."

And as with actions, so with words. The same speaker of the foregoing couplet utters elsewhere the lament,—

> "Ma fourbe est découverte. Oh ! que la vérité
> Se peut cacher longtemps avec difficulté !"

So we read in Molière. And Corneille has a play (not original) entirely devoted to the illustration of this subject, showing *qu'il faut bonne mémoire après qu'on a menti;* the Menteur κατ' ἐξοχὴν, being one who *entasse fourbe sur fourbe,* and is constrained by the law of his nature, at least of habit, which is second nature, to be ever adding to the heap of lies to which he has committed himself. A Spanish proverb—and *Le Menteur* is from the Spanish—declares that "for an honest man half his wits is enough, while the whole are too little for a knave;" the ways, that is, as Archbishop Trench expounds the adage, of truth and uprightness are so simple and plain, that a little wit is abundantly sufficient for those who walk in them; whereas the ways of falsehood and fraud are so perplexed and tangled, that sooner or later all the wit of the cleverest rogue will not preserve him from being entangled therein—a truth often and wonderfully confirmed in the lives of evil men.

Among the aphorisms of Dean Swift we read: "He who tells a lie is not sensible how great a task he undertakes; for he must be forced to invent twenty more to maintain that one."

It has been called the severe, but appropriate, punishment of historians who desert the paths of truth for those of paradox, to be compelled to defend the falsehood to which they have committed themselves against the ever-accumulating evidences of the truth. Mr. Robertson, of Brighton, feelingly sketches the case of one who, being unprepared and accosted suddenly, says hastily that which is irreconcileable with strict truth; then to substantiate and make it look probable, misrepresents or invents something else; and so has woven round himself a mesh which will entangle his conscience through many a weary day and many a sleepless night.* One burden laid on fault,

* The case of St. Peter was expressly within the preacher's view. "It is shocking, doubtless, to allow ourselves even to admit that this is

he goes on to show, is that chain of entanglement which seems to drag down to fresh sins. "One step necessitates many others. One fault leads to another, and crime to crime. The soul gravitates downward beneath its burden. It was profound knowledge which prophetically refused to limit Peter's sin to once. 'Verily I say unto thee . . . thou shalt deny me thrice.'"

Mr. Froude shows us Queen Elizabeth stooping to "a deliberate lie." At times, he says, writing of her embarrassed policy in 1565, she "seemed to struggle with her ignominy, but it was only to flounder deeper into distraction and dishonour." In October of that year she publicly denied that she had encouraged the rebellion in Scotland. In November, we read, "Never had Elizabeth been in greater danger; and the worst features of the peril were the creations of her own untruths." Again, in May, 1566: "Meanwhile Elizabeth was reaping a harvest of inconveniences for her exaggerated demonstrations of friendliness" to the Queen of Scots. Mary taking her at her word, "Vainly Elizabeth struggled to extricate herself from her dilemma; resentment was still pursuing her for her treachery in the past autumn. . . . She could but shuffle and equivocate in a manner which had become too characteristic."* She was but paying the price of lies—the being constrained to go on lying still. It is certain, affirms a popular essayist, that nobody yet ever did anything wrong in this world without having to tell one or more falsehoods to begin with: the embryo murderer has to tell a lie about the pistol or dagger, the would-be suicide about the poison he purchases; and in fine, "the ways down which the bad ship

---

possible; yet no one knowing human nature from men and not from books, will deny that this might befall even a brave and true man. St. Peter was both; yet this was his history. In a crowd, suddenly, the question was put directly, 'This man also was with Jesus of Nazareth?' Then a prevarication—a lie: and yet another."—*Sermon on the Restoration of the Erring.*

* Froude, "History of Reign of Elizabeth," vol. ii., pp. 126, 215, 226, 277, 278.

Wickedness slides to a shoreless ocean must be greased with lies."*

English reviewers not long since were prompt to recognise in Balzac's "La Marâtre," as revived to Parisian popularity, what they rightly accounted wonderful, a moral immaculate and beyond reproach. And what is that moral? "The necessity of a life of lying as a punishment for the one great lie of a mercenary marriage." One great lie is put out to interest, and the interest is compound. One great lie involves a ramification of others, great or small, if there be comparatives of magnitude in such matters; and memory, if not conscience, is for ever on the stretch. The sad expedient of renewed issues is a necessity. As with the involved victim in one of Crabbe's Tales:—

"Such is his pain, who, by his debt oppress'd,
Seeks by new bonds a temporary rest."

To another section, and with another starting-point from Holy Writ, may be referred some remaining illustrations of the subject.

——o——

LINKED LIES.

GENESIS xxvii. 19–24.

JACOB in Esau's goodly raiment, and his smooth skin overlaid with goatskins, was duly prepared for a consistent course of deception. But the lie upon lie he had to tell

* Mr. Thackeray incidentally opposes the quasi-apologists for smuggling on the ground that it is a complicated tissue of lying. In his very last and unfinished work, he makes a good old rector allow that to run an anker of brandy may seem no monstrous crime; but when men engage in these lawless ventures, who knows how far the evil will go? "I buy ten kegs of brandy from a French fishing-boat, I land it under a lie on the coast, I send it inland ever so far, and all my consignees lie and swindle. I land it, and lie to the revenue officer. Under a lie (that is, a mutual secrecy), I sell it to the landlord of the Bell at Maidstone, say. . . . My landlord sells it to a customer under a lie. We are all engaged in crime, conspiracy, and falsehood; nay, if the revenue looks too closely after us, we out with our pistols, and to crime and conspiracy add murder. Do you suppose men engaged in lying every day will scruple about a false oath in a witness-box? Crime engenders crime, sir."—*Denis Duval*, chap. vii.

before his end was gained, must have sorely tried what of conscience he then had. The primary falsehood,—distinctly enounced in answer to his blind sire's "Who art thou?" "I am Esau, thy firstborn," come back from the chase with the venison Isaac had desired of his firstborn,—this initial lie had immediately to be backed by another. How had he found it so quickly? There is something revolting in the style of the unfaltering fabrication at once ready to hand, "Because the Lord thy God brought it to me." Then ensued that solution of the old man's misgivings by a manual examination of the disguised pretender; it was Esau's hirsute skin, sure enough, though the voice was Jacob's. But the blessing was given. And even after that eventful benediction, the patriarch, with a yet lingering apprehension, renewed the pointed question, in its directest form, "Art thou my very son Esau?" And Jacob said, "I am." Lie linked to lie, in a concatenation accordingly.

Solent mendaces luere pœnas malefici, says Phædrus: liars usually pay the penalty of their guilt. And Mrs. Browning vigorously states one distinctive penalty, where she speaks of those who--

> . . . "Pay the price
> Of lies, by being constrained to lie on still."

The author of "Romola" powerfully illustrates in that remarkable book the embarrassments involved in one cowardly departure from truth. In the chapter headed "Tito's Dilemma," the occasion arises for Tito to fabricate an ingenious lie; an occasion "which circumstance never fails to beget on tacit falsity." Many chapters farther on we find him experiencing the inexorable law of human souls, that we prepare ourselves for sudden deeds by the reiterated choice of good or evil that gradually determines character; and it becomes a question whether all the resources of lying will save him from being crushed by the consequences of his habitual choice. At another juncture we read: "Tito felt more and more confidence as he went on; the lie was not so difficult when it was once begun; and as the words fell easily from his lips, they gave him a sense of power such as men feel when they have begun a muscular feat successfully." The penalty is enforced a few pages later. "But he had borrowed from the terrible usurer Falsehood, and the loan had mounted and mounted with the years, till he belonged to the usurer, body and soul." Again: "To-night he had paid a heavier price than ever to make himself safe." *

---

* From Sir Walter Scott we might gather numerous examples and aphorisms to the purpose. "It's a sair judgment on a man," says Ratcliffe, in the "Heart of Mid-Lothian," "when he has once gane sae far wrang as I hae dune"—the present thief-taker being in fact an ex-thief—that never a bit "he can be honest, try't whilk way he will." The career of Effie Deans, anon Lady Staunton, in the same story, is a practical sermon on the same text. "I drag on," she owns, "the life of a miserable impostor, indebted for the marks of regard I receive to a tissue of deceit and lies, which the slightest accident may unravel." Her sister, on perusing the letter which contains these confessions, is impressed with such an instance of the staggering condition of those who have risen to distinction by undue arts, and the "outworks and bulwarks of fiction and falsehood, by which they are under the necessity of surrounding and defending their precarious advantages."

Then again there is old Caleb Balderstone, querulous at being what he calls "forced" to imperil his soul "wi' telling ae lee after another faster than I can count them,"—and elsewhere at the "cost" of "telling twenty daily lees to a wheen idle chaps and queans, and, what's waur, without gaining credence."

And for another instance we have the titular Earl of Etherington, in "St. Ronan's Well," in the position as of a spider when he perceives that his deceitful web is threatened with danger, and sits balanced in the centre, watching every point, and uncertain which he may be called upon first to defend. "Such is one part, and not the slightest part, of the penance which never fails to wait on those, who, abandoning the 'fair play of the world,' endeavour to work out their purposes by a process of deception and intrigue."

In one of Mr. Disraeli's earlier fictions, there is a young man whose frankness is proverbial, but who finds himself involved in a course of prevarication—due effect being given to its preliminary process, though "only the commencement of the system of degrading deception which awaited him."

But perhaps the most direct and forcible illustration of the subject in modern fiction, is to be found in the "White Lies" of Mr. Charles Reade, a work the title of which declares its didactic scope. Rose Beaurépaire in an unguarded moment equivocates, or tells a white lie, and thereby hangs the tale. Soon we have her bitterly bewailing the imbroglio in which she has involved herself and others, and the necessity of fresh fibs to maintain the meaning and credit of the first. "There is no end to it," she sobs despairingly. "It is like a spider's web: every struggle to be free but multiplies the fine yet irresistible thread that seems to bind me." In the next chapter a significant paragraph intimates, "This was the last lie the poor entangled wretch had to tell that morning." And the penultimate chapter opens with a notice anew of the "fatal entanglement" into which

In the American story of "The Gayworthys," the like moral attaches to the course of one unhappy woman who lets herself slide, half involuntarily, into deeper wrong: she holds her peace; she makes herself passive. "Her very soul lied to itself in its false, bewildered reasonings; that is the inherent retribution of false souls." There are some acts of folly, remarks the most popular, probably, of contemporary English penwomen, which carry falsehood and dissimulation at their heels as certainly as the shadows which follow us when we walk towards the evening sun; and we very rarely swerve from the severe boundary-line of right without being dragged ever so much farther than we calculated upon across the border.

Corneille's celebrated play, "Le Menteur,"—but for reading which Moliére asserts his belief that he would never have written a comedy himself,—is "conveyed" from a Spanish original, and has itself been Englished by Fielding; the ingenuity of the piece consisting in the manner in which one lie is made to call for another, until their wholesale employer is inextricably caught in the toils.

> "This is the curse of every evil deed,—
> That, propagating still, it brings forth evil,"

laments the elder Piccolomini, in Schiller's trilogy. The commission of one wrong, says Owen Feltham, puts a man upon a thousand wrongs, perhaps, to maintain that one: injury, with injury is defended; and we commit a greater, to maintain a less. "A lie begets a lie, till generations succeed." Mr. Carlyle sternly moralises on the growth of accumulated falsities, —"sad opulence descending by inheritance, always at compound interest, and always largely increased by fresh acquirement on

two high-minded sisters had been led, through yielding to a natural foible: the desire, namely, to hide everything painful from those they loved, even at the expense of truth. The author lays stress on the inextricable complications due to their "amiable dishonesty," and he importunes the reader to take notice that after the first White Lie or two, circumstances overpowered them, and drove them on against their will. It was no small part, he insists, of all their misery, that they longed to get back to truth and could not.

such immensity of standing capital." One lie, says Owen, must be thatched with another, or it will soon rain through.

Benvenuto Cellini records in his autobiography, the bitter experiences he endured in being tempted to lie to the duke, his patron, lest he should forfeit the favour of the duchess—he who "was always a lover of truth and an enemy to falsehood, being then under a necessity of telling lies." "As I had begun to tell lies, I plunged deeper and deeper into the mire,"—till a very Slough of Despond it became to him.

Fool that he was, exclaims Mr. Trollope, of one of his characters in "Framley Parsonage:" "A man can always do right, even though he has done wrong before. But the previous wrong adds so much difficulty to the path—a difficulty which increases in tremendous ratio, till a man at last is choked in his struggling, and is drowned beneath the waters." Mr. Thackeray sermonises to the same effect: "And so, my dear sir, seeing that after committing any infraction of the moral laws, you must tell lies in order to back yourself out of your scrape, let me ask you whether you had not better forego the crime, so as to avoid the unavoidable, and unpleasant, and daily-recurring necessity of the subsequent perjury?" And the cleverest character this master of social satire ever drew, confesses how it jarred on her to begin telling lies to a confiding, simple friend: "But that is the misfortune of beginning with this kind of forgery. When one fib becomes due as it were, you must forge another to take up the old acceptance; and so the stock of your lies in circulation inevitably multiplies, and the danger of detection increases every day."

Jeremy Taylor quaintly says of the devil in the ancient oracles, "When he was put to it at his oracles, and durst not tell a downright lie, and yet knew not what was truth, many times he was put to the most pitiful shifts, and trifling equivocations, and acts of knavery, which, when they were discovered, ... it made him much more contemptible and ridiculous than if he had said nothing or confessed his ignorance."

A lie has been called a two-edged sword without a hilt, which is sure to slip and cut the hand that holds it. "After telling one lie, we are sure to tell another; and usually, after spinning a silly, very complicated, and disgusting web, which entangles and chokes us, we find out that if we had told the truth, it would have been much the easier and better plan." Lying is likened, again, to borrowing of money-lenders; for the credit which we get by it we have always to pay heavily for; and at last we find that the interest by far exceeds the principal, and we get so inextricably involved that we never fully recover. "He who tells a lie," says Pope, "is not sensible how great a task he undertakes; for he must be forced to invent twenty more to maintain that one." Johnson observes that nobody can live long without knowing that falsehoods of convenience or vanity are very lightly uttered, and when once uttered are sullenly supported. He reminds us that Boileau, who desired to be thought a rigorous and steady moralist, having told a petty lie to Lewis the Fourteenth, continued it afterwards by false dates, thinking himself obliged in honour to maintain what, when he said it, was so well received. Pope himself is taxed with similar mendacity by Mr. de Quincey, who charges him, on a certain literary question, with knowingly "preparing for himself a dire necessity of falsehood. . . . Once launched upon such a course, he became pledged and committed to all the difficulties which it might impose. Desperate necessities would arise, from which nothing but desperate lying and hard swearing could extricate him." And at a subsequent stage in the *facilis descensus* he is described, rather imaginatively, as feeling, and groaning as he felt, that fresh falsehoods were in peremptory demand. "This comes of telling lies," is supposed to be his bitter reflection: "one lie makes a necessity for another."

The Leucippus of Beaumont and Fletcher thus admonishes an intimate :—

> "My sin, Ismenus, has wrought all this ill:
> And I beseech thee to be warned by me,
> And do not lie, if any man should ask thee
> But how thou dost, or what o'clock 'tis now;
> Be sure thou do not lie, make no excuse

For him that is most near thee; never let
The most officious falsehood 'scape thy tongue,
For they above (that are entirely Truth)
Will make the seed which thou hast sown of lies,
Yield miseries a thousand-fold
Upon thine head, as they have done on mine."

——o——

A TIME TO WEEP, AND A TIME TO LAUGH.

ECCLESIASTES. iii. 4.

AS to everything there is a season, and a time to every purpose under the sun,—for as Shakspeare words it, "How many things by season seasoned are to their right praise and true perfection!"—be sure that the Wise King includes laughter and weeping in the list. "A time to weep, and a time to laugh." Acquainted with grief, he had also been familiar with merriment. He had said in his heart, Go to, now, I will prove thee with mirth; but the result was that he said of laughter, It is mad; and of mirth, What doeth it?—For all this, he freely recognises a time to laugh, so that one keep to the time. So much depends, here, on the due observance of times and seasons. It is with the frivolous habit of laughing out of season, and at all seasons, that the following notes are concerned.

The laureate's is a good keynote to begin with:—

"Prythee weep, May Lilian!
Gaiety without eclipse
Wearieth me, May Lilian."

So with Barry Cornwall and his Hermione:—

"Something thou dost want, O queen!
(As the gold doth ask alloy,)
Tears,—amidst thy laughter seen,
Pity,—mingling with the joy."

Such a conjunction as the courtier records of Cordelia in "King Lear"—sunshine and rain at once: "her smiles and tears were like a better day: those happy smiles that played on her ripe lip, seemed not to know what guests were in her eyes:" "in brief, sorrow would a be rarity most beloved, if all could so become it." Nothing, we often hear it said, is so tedious as uniformity; and under the bright sky of Italy one sometimes sighs for a cloud. "A gay writer, who," says Horace Walpole, "should only express satisfaction without variety, would soon be nauseous." Johnson's Papilius winds up his confession, in the "Rambler," with a whine on the melancholy necessity of supporting that character by study, which he gained by levity; having learned too late that gaiety must be recommended by higher qualities, and that mirth can never please long but as the efflorescence of a mind loved for its luxuriance, but esteemed for its usefulness. There must be fruitage as well as blossomy "efflorescence;" as Cowper is fain to enforce, when in the closing lines of the "Task," he records how he once, when called to dress a sofa with the flowers of verse, played awhile with that light task, obedient to the fair:—

> . . . "but soon, to please her more,
> Whom flowers alone I knew would little please,
> Let fall the unfinished wreath, and roved for fruit."

Mark Mrs. Browning's picture of the Lady Geraldine:—

> "In her utmost lightness there is truth—and often she speaks lightly—
> Has a grace in being gay, which even mournful souls approve,
> For the root of some grave earnest thought is understruck so rightly
> As to justify the foliage and the waving flowers above."

So with Lord Lytton's Helen Mainwaring, the sunny gladness of whose nature must have vent like a bird's, though he forbids us to fancy that that gladness speaks the levity which comes from the absence of thought: "it is rather from the depth of thought that it springs, as from the depth of a sea comes its music.' Well and wisely Molière's Cléonte exclaims, "Veux-tu de ces enjouements épanouis, de ces joies toujours ouvertes? et vois tu rien de plus impertinent que des femmes qui rient à tout propos?" Such a *femme* as the same author's Zerbinette, a self-convicted giggler in and out of season, yet whose confession may be twisted into an example the other way, when she says, "J'ai l'humeur enjouée, et sans cesse je ris: mais, tout en riant, je suis sérieuse sur de certains chapitres."

Among the writings of M. de St. Evremond there is an essay on the Idea of a Woman that never was, nor ever will be found. Emilia he calls this all too perfect, impossible she. And amongst the foremost of Emilia's fine qualities he reckons the co-existence of seriousness *au fond* with vivacity of mien. "For we find that the gayest humour doth, at length, become tiresome; . . . the most effervescent liveliness either disgusts or wearies you." In the case of the celebrated Duchesse de Longueville, De Retz notices the exquisite effect of the sudden bursts of gaiety which would at times dispel her habitual but not inexpressive languor. Mdlle. de Scudéry, in her "Clélie," was painting a well-known, perhaps too well-known, contemporary in the person of Clarice, when, "parmi toute cette disposition qu'elle a pour la joie," she ascribes to this charmer, *qui rit si aisément*, a facile faculty of tear-shedding: *elle sait pleurer*, whenever occasion justifies weeping. As Lady Eastlake says, in her little treatise on Music, a change of key is the most powerful engine in the hands of a musician: we cannot bear the monotony of one key long, even the most joyful: "Gaiety without eclipse wearieth me, May Lilian." We long for "a mournful muse, soft pity to infuse." The Hon. Miss Byron takes the liberty of telling the sister of Sir Charles Grandison that "Your brother has hinted, Charlotte, that he loves you for your vivacity, and should still more, if you consulted time and occasion." The affections are justly said to be more readily called into play by a mixture of mirth and melancholy; ours being a twofold life, the union of mortal with immortal, we covet happiness, yet turn back anon to the more majestic form of sorrow. There is a form of cheerfulness which, we are assured, nobody can stand:—

> "Send me hence a thousand miles
> From a face that always smiles;"

people ostentatiously and pretentiously cheerful being not unfrequently foolish people: their spirits of a brisk but thin quality

—nothing about them in good working order. "For, in truth, the most fortunate existence has cares enough to make gravity our normal condition." Roland Graeme, in the "Abbot," earnestly assures his vivacious companion, "Ay, but, fair Catherine, there are moments of deep and true feeling, which are worth ten thousand years of liveliest mirth." Melancholy Minna is a fine relief by contrast to laughter-loving Brenda; and it is suggestively told us of the old Udaller, their sire, that he liked his graver damsel better in the walk without doors, and his merry maiden better by the fireside; and that if he preferred Brenda after the glass circulated in the evening, he gave the preference to Minna before noon. So with Molly and Cynthia in "Wives and Daughters:" Molly always gentle, but very grave and silent; Cynthia merry, full of pretty mockeries, and hardly ever silent—only this constant brilliancy became a little tiresome in everyday life, being not the sunshiny rest of a placid lake, so much as the "glitter of the pieces of a broken mirror, which confuses and bewilders." The union of what can be harmonized of the two distinctive characters, is sure to be engaging in no ordinary degree. As in the Beryl of "George Geith." "You imagine," says Beryl, on one occasion, "because it is necessary to my existence to laugh at people's oddities, that I never feel for their woes. You think, because I have a quick sense of the ludicrous, that I have no eyes for grief. And there you do me an injustice." Such as Beryl will be found to take exception to predominant levity in the masculine gender, after the manner of the fair tenant of Wildfell Hall: "I do wish he would be sometimes serious," she writes of her endeared Arthur: "I cannot get him to write or speak in real, solid earnest. I don't mind it now, but if it be always so, what shall I do with the serious part of myself?" Tired out with such çompanionship, a complainant in one of Lovell Beddoes' tragedies exclaims,—

> "I'm weary of their laughter's empty din.
> Methinks, these fellows, with their ready jests,
> Are like to tedious bells, that ring alike
> Marriage or death."

Rather than have her uniformly saccharine and smiling, Ben Jonson's Curius avowedly would have his mistress "angry sometimes, to sweeten off the rest of her behaviour."

Sir Walter Scott, in one page of his Diary, noting the break-up of a hilarious group of guests at Abbotsford, adds the avowal, "I am not sorry, being one of those whom too much mirth always inclines to sadness." Even the bright extremes of joy, as Thomas Hood the elder words it, bring on conclusions of disgust:—

"There is no music in the life
That sounds with idiot laughter solely;
There's not a string attuned to mirth
But has its chord in melancholy."

Leigh Hunt tenderly tells one of his grandchildren how, when *he* was a child, and in excessive spirits, his dear mother would sometimes say to him, "Leigh, come and sit down here by me, and let us try to think a little." Better that than *riant sans cesse,* even for a child. When I was a child, says the apostle, I thought as a child. Thinking was not out of the question even then, though it might, and by comparison with the man's it must, be childish thinking. For children as for men, a time to laugh and a time to weep. True, there are differences of gifts and temperaments:—

"To some men God hath given laughter; but tears to some men He hath given:
He bade us sow in tears, hereafter to harvest holier smiles in Heaven;
And tears and smiles, they are His gift: both good, to smite or to uplift.
He knows His sheep: the wind and showers beat not too sharply the shorn lamb:
His wisdom is more wise than ours: He knew my nature—what I am:
He tempers smiles with tears: both good, to bear in time the Christian mood."

——o——

DISALLOWED DESIGNS.

PROVERBS xix. 21.

"THERE are many devices in a man's heart; nevertheless, the counsel of the Lord, that shall stand." Even the counsels of the prudent He bringeth to nought. "There is no wisdom, nor understanding, nor counsel, against the Lord," nor any that prospers without Him. Without Him, where is the wise? where is the scribe? What, after all, is the wisdom of the children of this world, wiser in their generation than the children of light? Hath not God made foolish the wisdom of this world? For it is written, "I will destroy the wisdom of the wise." Nay; unworldly wisdom, in its forming of plans, and elaboration of schemes, and devising of devices, enjoys no privileged immunity from failure, at the veto of Him who chargeth His angels with folly. "L'homme propose, Dieu dispose." The Divine disposal of human proposals is ofttimes very summary and entire.

The proverb, "Man proposes, God disposes," is believed by one learned in such lore to be naturalised in every nation of Europe:—thus the Spanish, "La gente pone, y Dios dispone;" the German, with its corresponding jingle, "Der Mensch denkt's, Gott lenkt's," etc., so deeply upon all men is impressed the sense of Hamlet's assertion of a Divinity that shapes our ends, rough-hew them how we will. Molière's shrewd-spoken Dorine enounces a truism when reminding Damis that,—

> "On n'exécute pas tout ce qui se propose;
> Et le chemin est long du projet à la chose."

A wise man endeavours, it has been said, by considering all circumstances, to make conjectures and form conclusions: but the smallest accident intervening (and in the course of affairs it is impossible to foresee all) often produces such turns and changes, that at last he is just as much in doubt of events as the most ignorant and inexperienced person. What Shakspeare in his sonnets calls "millioned accidents" creep in between design and result, between plan and performance, between scheme and issue, and "blunt the sharpest intents." As the old moralising poet, modernised by Dryden, puts it—

> "But see how Fortune can confound the wise,
> And when they least expect it, turn the dice."

Fortune, or fate, is the popularly recognised agent in these reversals and collapses; and subtile philosophers speculate curiously on the plenipotent character of this agency. One such, for example, predisposed to paradox may-be, yet no heedless or hasty penman, affirms, that if you look closely into the matter, it will be seen that whatever appears most vagrant, and utterly purposeless, turns out, in the end, to have been impelled the most surely on a preordained and unswerving track. Chance and change, he goes on to remark, love to deal with men's unsettled plans, not with their idle vagaries. So that, as he argues the matter, if we desire unexpected and unimaginable events, we should contrive an iron framework, such as we fancy may compel the future to take one inevitable shape; for then comes in the unexpected, and shatters our design in fragments.

The biographer of Columbus, narrating the story of his shipwreck in 1492, describes him as passing, with his usual excitability, from a state of doubt and anxiety to one of sanguine anticipation, and thus coming to consider his present misfortune as a providential event mysteriously ordained by Heaven to work out the success of his enterprise. At once, therefore, he began to look forward to glorious fruits to be reaped from this seeming evil, and laid his plans accordingly. "Such was the visionary yet generous enthusiasm of Columbus, the moment that prospects of vast wealth broke upon his mind. What in some spirits would have awakened a grasping and sordid avidity to accumulate, immediately filled his imagination with plans of magnificent expenditure. But how vain are our attempts to interpret the inscrutable decrees of Providence! The shipwreck, which Columbus considered the act of Divine favour, to reveal to him the secrets of the land, shackled and limited all his after-discoveries." For it is shown to have linked his fortunes, for the remainder of his life, to this island, which was doomed to be to him a source of cares and troubles, to involve him in a thousand perplexities, and to becloud his declining years with humiliation and disappointment.

> "Le ciel agit sans nous en ces événements,
> Et ne les régle point dessus nos sentiments."

It is instructive to note in the memoirs of Gabriel Naudé, that great scholar's exultant anticipation of the public opening of the library he had mainly helped to form. He must have reckoned on that day as a *beau jour* for him, the happiest day of his life; and he arranged a fête accordingly, to be celebrated with his most intimate friends. But that very day broke out the public troubles of the Fronde; and barricades in the streets of Paris ill accorded with Gabriel Naudé's cherished hopes. "Ainsi vont les projets humains sous l'œil d'en haut qui les déjoue." The Scotch ploughman-poet, eyeing the mouse and its "wee bit housie, too, in ruin," as turned up by his plough, gave racy utterance to but a trite reflection, when, apostrophising the "wee sleekit, cow'rin, tim'rous beastie," he thus moralised his song:—

> "But, mousie, thou art no thy lane,
> In proving foresight may be vain:
> The best-laid schemes o' mice an' men
> Gang aft a-gley,
> And leave us nought but grief an' pain,
> For promised joy."

As the good friar in Shakspeare has it,—

> "A greater power than we can contradict
> Hath thwarted our intents,"

well laid and discreetly devised as they seemed to be.

And as with the seemingly laudable plans of the prudent, so with the arrogant designs of the self-confident. The enemy said, "I will pursue, I will overtake, I will divide the spoil; my lust shall be satisfied upon them; I will draw my sword; my hand shall destroy them." Thus said the enemy, even

Pharaoh's host, on the shores of the Red Sea. But then sang Moses and the children of Israel this song unto the Lord: "Thou didst blow with Thy wind, the sea covered them; they sank as lead in the mighty waters." It is but an emphasised reading of the standard text, that the Lord bringeth the counsel of the heathen to nought, and maketh the devices of the people of none effect, and casteth out the counsel of princes. Whereas, turning from man proposing to God disposing, "The counsel of the Lord shall endure for ever, and the thoughts of His heart from generation to generation." The same is He of whom it is written that He turneth wise men backwards, and maketh their knowledge foolish.

Wordsworth, ever a moralist, moralised his song when, at a critical juncture in the legend of the "White Doe of Rylstone," he interposed this reflection:—

> "But quick the turns of chance and change,
> And knowledge has a narrow range;
> Whence idle fears, and needless pain,
> And wishes blind, and efforts vain."

For a closing variation on the present theme, a worse might be found than this from the play within the play of "Hamlet:"—

> "But, orderly to end where I begun,—
> Our wills, our fates, do so contrary run,
> That our devices still are overthrown;
> Our thoughts are ours, their ends none of our own."

But, with a slight change of title and text, the same theme is pursued, in the section next ensuing, through another fugue-course of variations.

———o———

MAN DEVISING, GOD DIRECTING.

PROVERBS xvi. 9.

"A MAN'S heart deviseth his way; but the Lord directeth his steps." Man devises, God directs; man proposes, God disposes. There is a way that seemeth right unto a man, and practicable, plausible, easy of accomplishment, and sure of success. But the counsel of the Lord puts a veto on the scheme; and the counsel of the Lord, that shall stand.

Luther charges it against princes and potentates in his day, that when they take in hand an enterprise, they do not pray before they begin, but set to work calculating: three times three make nine, twice seven are fourteen—so-and-so will do so-and-so—in this manner will the business come to a prosperous issue: "but our Lord God says unto them, For whom then do ye hold me? for a cypher? Do I sit here above in vain, and to no purpose? Ye shall know, that I will twist your accounts about finely, and make them all false reckonings."

Says old Alice, in "Mary Barton," "I sometimes think the Lord is against planning. Whene'er I plan over much, He is sure to send and mar all my plans, as if He would ha' me put the future into His hands. Afore Christmas-time I was as full as full could be of going home for good and all; yo has heard how I've wished it this terrible long time. . . . Many a winter's night did I lie awake and think that, please God, come summer, I'd go home at last. Little did I think how God Almighty would baulk me for not leaving my days in His hands, who had led me through the wilderness hitherto." It is very like Rousseau to say, in reference to a fully determined project of his, for the fulfilment of which nothing was wanting but "ce qui ne dépend pas des hommes dans les projets les mieux concertés,"—that "on dirait qu'il n'y a que les noirs complots des méchants qui réussissent; les projets innocents des bons n'ont presque jamais d'accomplissement." But who can hope for anything like contentment, as Mr. Helps somewhere asks, so long as he continues to attach that ridiculous degree of importance to the events of this life which so many

X

people are inclined to do? Observe, he bids us, the effect which it has upon them: they are most uncomfortable if their little projects do not turn out according to their fancy—nothing is to be angular to them—they regard external things as the only realities; and as they have fixed their abode here, they must have it arranged to their mind. Lady Mary Wortley Montagu assures one of her correspondents that never had she been so little mistress of her own time and actions as since she lived alone; and going on to account for this, she observes, "Mankind is placed in a state of dependency, not only on one another (which all are in some degree), but so many inevitable accidents thwart our designs and limit our best-laid projects." The poor efforts of our utmost prudence, and political schemes, she fancies must appear in the eyes of some superior beings, like the pecking of a young linnet to break a wire cage, or the climbing of a squirrel in a hoop. If to this bit of morality from the greatest of lady letter-writers in England, a parallel passage may readily be cited from the greatest of lady letter-writers in France, there is a characteristic difference, in the tone of religious feeling, conspicuous generally by its absence in Lady Mary's case, but a pervading, though underlying, force in that of Madame de Sévigné. The latter describes on one occasion the "cruel derangement" of her family plans, so nicely arranged, and so ripe for completion; then adds, if with a sigh, with a sigh of gentle resignation, "La Providence le veut ainsi. Elle est tellement maitresse de toutes nos actions, que nous n'exécutons rien que sous son bon plaisir, et je tache de ne faire de projets que le moins qu'il m'est possible, afin de n'être pas si souvent trompée; car qui compte sans elle compte deux fois." How vain, exclaims the author of "Destiny," are all our schemes for futurity! Human wisdom exhausts itself in devising what a higher Power shows to be vanity. We decide for to-day, and a passing moment scatters our decisions as chaff before the wind. We resolve for to-morrow, to-morrow comes but to root up our resolutions. We scheme for our works to remain monuments of our power and wisdom, and the most minute, the most trivial event is sufficient to overturn all our purposes, and cast down to the dust the thoughts and the labours of a life. Truly, "it is not in man that walketh to direct his steps."

Were the affairs of this world to be guided implicitly by human wisdom, suggests one of Scott's sententious doctors of divinity, or were they uniformly to fall out according to the conjectures of human foresight, events would no longer be under the domination of that time and chance which happen unto all men; since we should, in the one case, work out our own purposes to a certainty, by our own skill; and, in the other, regulate our conduct according to the views of unerring prescience. "But man is, while in this vale of tears, like an uninstructed bowler, so to speak, who thinks to attain the jack by delivering the bowl straightforward upon it, being ignorant that there is a concealed bias within the spheroid, which will make it, in all probability, swerve away, and lose the cast." The future, in the words of a later fiction, is not a blank sheet of paper, for us to write any story we please upon, but a wonderful chart, mapped out by a Divine and unerring hand.

> *Ούδέ τις ἀνθρώπων ἐργάζεται, ἐν φρεσὶν εἰδὼς*
> *'Es τέλος, εἴτ' ἀγαθὸν γίγνεται εἴτε κακόν.*
> *Πολλάκι γαρ δοκέων θήσειν κακόν, ἐσθλὸν ἔθηκε,*
> *Καί τε δοκῶν θήσειν ἐσθλόν, ἔθηκε κακόν.*
> *'Ουδέ τῳ ἀνθρώπων παραγίγνεται ὅσσ' ἐθέλησεν.*

When Mr. Thackeray propounds the query, Who can foresee everything, and always? and returns his own answer (a sufficiently safe one), Not the wisest amongst us,—he does so in reference to the counsels of the worldly woman who governed and directed the Newcome family; which counsels bore results so different from what that elderly lady desired, and foresaw. And he proceeds to point his moral by the tale of a French king's fall. "When his majesty, Louis XIV., jockied his grandson on to the throne of Spain (founding thereby the present revered dynasty of that country), did he expect to peril his own, and bring all Europe about his royal ears? Could a late King of France, eager for the advantageous establishment of one of his darling sons, and anxious to procure a beautiful Spanish princess, with a crown and kingdom in reversion, for the simple and obedient youth, ever suppose that the welfare of his whole august race and reign would be upset by that smart speculation?" The master of irony professes to take only the most noble examples to illustrate the conduct of such a noble old personage as her ladyship of Kew, who brought a prodigious deal of trouble upon some of the innocent members of her family, whom no doubt she thought to better in life by her experienced guidance, and undoubted worldly wisdom. We may be as deep as Jesuits, he continues,—may know the world ever so well, lay the best ordered plans, and the profoundest combinations,—and by a certain not unnatural turn of fate, we, and our plans and combinations, are sent flying before the wind. "We may be as wise as Louis Philippe, that many-counselled Ulysses whom the respectable world admired so; and after years of patient scheming, and prodigies of skill; after coaxing, wheedling, doubling, bullying wisdom, behold, yet stronger powers interpose: and schemes and skill and violence are nought." As Schiller's Wallenstein puts it, in his rather heathenish way—

> "For jealous are the powers of destiny.
> Joy premature, and shouts ere victory,
> Encroach upon their rights and privileges.
> We sow the seed, and they the growth determine."

"Il y a," in the words of a masterly French moralist, "je ne sais quelle *force cachée*, a dit Lucrèce (ce que d'autres avec Bossuet nommeront Providence), qui semble se plaire à briser les choses humaines, à faire manquer d'un coup l'appereil établi de la puissance, et à déjouer la pièce, juste au moment ou elle promettait de mieux aller." O fate of fools! exclaims Zara, in the "Mourning Bride,"—"officious in contriving; in executing, puzzled, lame, and lost;" a rebuke which Selim deprecates in his reply :—

> "Prescience is Heaven's alone, not given to man.
> If I have failed in what, as being man,
> I needs must fail, impute not as a crime
> My nature's want."

So with the resolute undertaking of Argantes, in Tasso, to slay Tancred, the slayer of his betrothed; all the people applauding his resolve, and rejoicing in the assurance that this—

> ". . . boaster stout
> Would kill the prince who late had slain his love.
> O promise vain! it otherwise fell out.
> Men purpose, but high gods dispose above;
> For underneath his sword this boaster died,
> Whom there he scorned and threatened in his pride."

In Homer, again, how grieves Achilles, and, impetuous, vents to all his myrmidons his loud laments?

> "By what vain promise, gods! did I engage,
> When, to console Menætius' feeble age,
> I vowed his much-loved offspring to restore;
> Charged with rich spoils to fair Opuntia's shore.
> But mighty Jove cuts short, with just disdain,
> The long, long views of poor designing man!"

—o—

A PURSEBEARER'S PROTEST AGAINST PURPOSELESS WASTE.

St. John xii. 5.

IT was very costly ointment of spikenard that Mary took and anointed therewith the feet of Jesus, so that the house was filled with the odour of the ointment. So costly, that it set one of His apostles to work, counting the cost. Judas Iscariot was this ready reckoner. He was conversant with figures. He was the pursebearer of the apostolic circle, and knew, it seems, how and when and why to keep a tight finger on the purse-strings. The wasted contents—waste he accounted it—of that alabaster box might have been sold for three hundred denarii, and the proceeds given to the poor. As pursebearer he protested. And nominally his protest was in behalf of the poor.

Referring to that text in Exodus which tells how the people brought much more than enough for the service of the work which the Lord commanded to make, the question was put by a divine who, being dead, yet speaketh: When will the earth again hear that glad announcement? Yet, until we bring more than enough, he said, at least until there is kindled in us a spirit which will make us desire to do so, we shall never bring enough. "And ought we not? Your economists will say *No.* They who would think the sun a useful creature, if he would come down from the sky and light their fires, will gravely reprehend such wasteful extravagance." This last figure of speech has its parallel in Mr. Carlyle's estimate of "the uses of this Dante:" he declines to say much about his "uses;" he holds that an influence working, like Dante's, into the depths of our existence, and feeding through long times the life-roots of all excellent things whatsoever, is not to be very satisfactorily computed by "utilities." Dante shall therefore be invaluable, or of no value: "We will not estimate the sun by the quantity of gas-light it saves us."

Judas the pursebearer was, as a French divine characterizes him, *exact, positif, calculateur;* one who habituated himself to compute everything by a ready-money standard, and to appraise every action by the rule of immediate utility. He might be accurate to a fraction in his reckoning of what that "wasted" ointment would have fetched in the market; but, had not his heart been already in some sort ossified, he would have comprehended that "au dessus de l'utile il y a le beau, et au dessus du calcul le dévouement, et qu' à une âme qui déborde d'une joie extraordinaire il faut des moyens extraordinaires aussi pour exprimer ce qu'elle éprouve. Judas a perdu le sens des réalités purement spirituelles, qui lui paraissent vagues, parce que, comme l'infini, elles résistent aux chiffres."

When Dr. Justus Jonas told Dr. Martin Luther of a certain potent landholder, who said to Duke John Frederic, when commending to him the gospel of Christ, "Sir, the gospel pays no interest,"—"Have you no grains?" was Luther's interrogative comment,—citing the words of the swine at the lion's feast, when invited to feast on recondite dainties. Even so, said Dr. Martin, there are inveterate worldlings who, when invited to the spiritual feast of fat things well refined, "turn up their snouts, and ask for guilders. Offer a cow nutmeg, and she will reject it for old hay."

It is a too true bill of indictment against the mass of men, that, knowing that two and two make four, and that four is of a higher value than three, they practically conclude, carrying out into practice the conclusion, that to amass is to become wealthy, and that to bestow is to become the poorer. With this arithmetic the children of this world are wise in their generation, and add field to field, house to house, to some purpose. But by what right, asks a voice from the sanctuary, do they take upon themselves to pronounce on such qualities and realities as devotion and charity, as detachment from the "good things of this life" and renunciation of indulgence to the senses? If they witness a deed of noble self-sacrifice, they can but wag their heads, in shocked surprise and bewilderment at such a blunder in arithmetic, *une telle faute de calcul.* "Ils ne comprennent pas qu'on puisse soupirer après d'autres biens que ceux de la matière, après d'autres vérités que celles de l'arithmétique." There are many, very many more things than are dreamt of in their philosophy; dreaming, indeed, is rather out of their way; and perhaps philosophy too, for the matter of that.

Coleridge, denouncing the "moral" consequences of Napoleon's tyranny, as far more to be dreaded than the worst of those outward and calculable evils, which chiefly shock the imaginations of men, is out of all patience with such objections as, "What *good* will the Tyrolese do themselves by their heroic resistance?" "What are the Spaniards fighting for?" etc.,—as if man were made only to eat above ground, and be eaten; as if we had no dignity to preserve, no conscience to obey, no immortality to expect.

What good can it do him? demands the vulgar fine lady in "Cecil," who hears that a certain well-to-do man of genius has written a book. A man, she argues, writes for money or distinction: what can be this man's object? he don't want to be made a baronet, nor does he want to increase his income. Where can be the *use* of writing? And where, she is (by cross-questioning) answered, can be the use to the aloe of its flower, to the mine of its gold? Oldbuck of Monkbarns might have done worse than parody, as he did, the "brutal ignorance" of your *cui bono* querists of the baser sort, in the strain of Gray's Bard,—

" Weave the warp and weave the woof,
The winding-sheet of wit and sense;
Dull garment of defensive proof
'Gainst all that does not gather pence."

That a new machine, a new experiment, the discovery of a salt, or of a bone, should, in England, receive a wider homage, than the most profound speculation from which no obvious results are apprehended,—this way of contemplating affairs Mr. Buckle was prompt to own as certainly productive of great good. But he also took care to declare it to be, with equal certainty, a one-sided way, satisfying a part only of the human mind—many of the noblest intellects craving for something which it cannot supply. There are mortals who, as a clerical essayist has said, cannot understand or sympathise with the gratification arising from a study of graceful and beautiful objects; who think that the supply of animal necessities is all that any man (but themselves, perhaps) can need. What more can he want? they exclaim, if the man be well-fed, and well-dressed, and well-lodged. Why, if he had been a horse or a pig, is the answer, he would have wanted nothing more; but the possession of a rational soul brings with it pressing wants which are not of a material nature, not to be supplied by material things, and not felt by pigs and horses. And the craving for surrounding objects of grace and beauty is held to be one of these. Mr. Emerson, in his far-going way, goes so far as to say, as regards the "base rate at which the highest mental and moral gifts are held" in his country,—that let a man attain the highest and broadest culture that any American has possessed, then let him die by sea-storm, railroad collision, or other accident, "and all America will acquiesce that the best thing has happened to him; that, after the education has gone far, such is the expensiveness of America, that the best use to put a fine person to, is, to drown him to save his board." M. de Tocqueville somewhere observes, that to cross almost impenetrable forests, to swim deep rivers, to encounter pestilential marshes, to sleep exposed to the damp air of the woods,—these are efforts which an American easily conceives, if a dollar is to be gained by them—that is the point; but that a man should take such journeys from curiosity, he cannot understand. The German poet is often cited for his remark, that the Cow of Isis is to some the divine symbol of knowledge, to others but the milch cow, only regarded for the pounds of butter she will yield. An English sympathiser exclaims, "O tendency of our age, to look on Isis as the milch cow! Gaze on the goddess," he bids a sordid aspirant, "and get ready the churn and thy scales, and let us see what butter will fetch in the market." When Judge Haliburton's typical Yankee is asked by the old minister what he thinks of Niagara, and forthwith expatiates on the "grand spec" it offers for factory purposes—for carding mills, fulling mills, cotton mills, grain mills, saw mills, plaster mills, and never a want of water for any or all of them, his pastor upbraids him with almost sacrilege in that style of talk; exclaiming, "How that dreadful thirst of gain has absorbed all other feelings in our people, when such an idea could be entertained for a moment! It [Niagara] is a grand spectacle, it is the voice of nature in the wilderness, proclaiming to the untutored tribes there of the power and majesty and glory of God. . . . Talk not to me of mills, factories, and machinery, sir, nor of introducing the money-changers into the temple of the Lord."

——o——

LIGHT AT EVENING-TIME.

ZECHARIAH xiv. 7.

THE promise, or prediction, to be found in the words of the son of Berechiah, that "at evening-time it shall be light," is gratefully accepted by devout souls in perhaps a strained and wrested sense; but a sense so comforting, so full of tenderness and beauty, that one is fain to believe the words may favour, if they cannot be said to warrant, this "accommodation of Scripture." Divines are fain to give technical divinity the go-by for the nonce, while, as they confess, the deepening twilight seldom fails to suggest to them this cheering promise, a promise which "tells how the Christian's day shall end, how the day of life may be somewhat overcast and dreary, but light shall come on the darkened way at last." In the same spirit are welcome the words of Amos, the herdsman of Tekoa, concerning One who turneth the shadow of death into the morning. To Him the darkness and the light are both alike; and at His bidding, when despondent sufferers are in a horror of great darkness, and say surely the darkness shall cover them,—even the night shall be light about them; and in some sort to them, even as to Him, the night shineth as the day; or at least, in the language of Zechariah, there is light, which if not clear, is yet not dark; neither wholly day nor night, but twilight—soft, soothing, tranquillizing—instead of the dreaded darkness which may be felt. Even thus He brings the blind by a way that they knew not, making darkness light before them.

Even thus, at the last, He delivers them who through fear of death were all their lifetime subject to bondage. Bunyan exemplifies such in Mr. Fearing, the pilgrim, who at the entrance of the Valley of the Shadow of Death was "ready to die for fear." But the valley was quiet from troublers. "I suppose those enemies here had now a special check from our Lord, and a command not to meddle until Mr. Fearing had passed over it." "And here also I took notice of what was very remarkable—the water of that river was lower at this time than ever I saw it in all my life; so he went over at last, not much above wetshod.

"*Honesty:* Then it seems he was well at last?"

"*Greatheart*: Yes, yes; I never had a doubt about it."

Often, observes Schleiermacher in one of his letters, the last radiant moment is called rapidly into being, even in souls wherein the eternal Light has not always shone with bright effulgence.

Biographers of Dr. Johnson tell us how, when at length the moment, dreaded through so many years, came close, the dark cloud passed away from his mind; how his temper became unusually patient and gentle, and he ceased to think with terror of death, and of that which lieth beyond death, and spoke much of the mercy of God and of the propitiation of Christ. One might apply to him in effect the lines of the poet of the Seasons.

> "Joy seized his withered veins, and one bright gleam
> Of setting life shone on her evening hours."

Meditating on various senses in which the words of the promise of light at evening-time speak truly, in which its great principle holds good, the signal blessing shall come when it is needed most and expected least, Dr. Boyd, thinks mainly how sometimes, at the close of the chequered and sober day, the Better Sun has broken through the clouds and made the flaming west all purple and gold. He pictures the chamber of death, while hushed and mournful gazers see also the summer sun in glory going down. "But it is only to us who remain that the evening darkness is growing, only for us that the sun is going down." As the evening falls on us, but not on the departing believer; as the shadows deepen on us, but not on him; as the darkness gathers on us, but not on him; the "glorious promise has found its perfect fulfilment, that 'at the evening-time there shall be light.'"

Secular literature has its analogous instances. Dr. Holmes describes Elsie Venner's storm-tossed, vagrant spirit as composed and serene at the last; the cold glitter died out of the diamond eyes, and the stormy scowl disappeared from the dark brows. "It seemed to her father as if the malign influence—evil spirit it might almost be called—which had pervaded her being had at last been driven forth or exorcised," and that the tears she now shed were "at once the sign and the pledge of her redeemed nature. But now she was to be soothed and not excited. After her tears she slept again, and the look her face wore was peaceful as never before." And the devoted father, to whom her life-long career had been until now a perturbing trial, now thanked God for the brief interval of peace which had been granted her, and for the sweet communion they had enjoyed in these last days. There are those of whom it may be said that it comes to pass, when midday is over, and they cast wistful glances, and perhaps even reproachful petitions heavenwards, until evening-time, that there is from above neither voice, nor any to answer, nor seemingly any that regardeth; but with evening-time comes an answer and comes light. Applicable to the subject, in this sense, are the lines in "Paracelsus," on one who lived without God in the world :—

> "Then died, grown old; and just an hour before—
> Having lain long with blank and soulless eyes—
> He sate up suddenly, and with natural voice
> Said, that in spite of thick air and closed doors
> God told him it was June."

Of Margaret Arundel, in "The Gordian Knot," we read, in her hour of household desolation and distress, that could we have seen her fair face, now pale with pain, now flushed with emotion, we should have pitied her; but "it may be that some superior intelligence witnessed her suffering, and pitied her not; knowing that all she was to undergo was but the fiery trial destined for those for whom in the evening there is light." Stephen Blackpool, in "Hard Times," who has found life "aw a muddle," and meets with his death in the pit, is tranquillized with light at the last—light which he identifies with the star that shone upon him while he lay mangled in the old shaft. "Often as I coom to myseln, and found it shinin' on me down there in my trouble, I thowt it were the very star as guided to our Saviour's home. I awmost think it be the very star." His rescuers lift him up, and he is overjoyed to find they are about to take him in the direction whither the star seems to him to lead. Very gently they carry him along the fields and down the lanes; but it is soon a funeral procession. "The star had shown him where to find the God of the poor; and through humility and sorrow and forgiveness, he had gone to his Saviour's rest." It is not every life the early prime of which has been blissful enough to warrant the exclamation,—

"Ne'er tell me of glories serenely adorning
The close of our day, the calm eve of our night:
Give me back, give me back, the wild freshness of morning,
Its smiles and its tears are worth evening's best light."

For sometimes the light comes at evening-time that has never come before.

Cellini opens his autobiography with a placid record of the enjoyment of his present lot, in life's decline, in contrast with the storms and turmoil of his previous course. We read of James Watt, that not until he had reached what is termed the grand climacteric of man's life did he know real freedom from bodily infirmities; and that his spirits became more equable as the principal causes of his anxiety and occasional depression were removed; so that although he was destined to be one of those "who are so strong that they come to fourscore years," his strength even then, while it could scarcely be termed "labour," was certainly very far from "sorrow." The cloud which had so long hung over him was gently lifted up, and the curtain parted, to disclose a happier scene. "It is curious that even physical ease and enjoyment should come so late; but so it was. The term which commenced with his release from the evils of active business was a serene and golden time, in which he found repose"—with the softening retrospect of a struggle past and a victory won. John Galt, in "The Entail," exemplifies a kindred experience in the widow Walkinshaw, whose deliverance from an all but lifelong thraldom, late in the day as it came, yet came in time enough to "allow the original brightness of her mind to shine out in the evening with a serene and pleasing lustre."

Dr. Boyd quotes the dying speech of a poor English day labourer, than which, he affirms, few sentences ever touched him more with their hopeless pathos: "Wut wi' faeth, and wut wi' the earth goin' round the sun, and wut wi' the railways all a-whuzzing and a-buzzing, I 'm clean muddled, confoozled, and bet!" It is Stephen Blackpool again in spirit, and to the letter. With that sentence the dying man is said to have feebly turned to the wall, and spoken no more. "Well, let us hope that light came at the evening-time upon that blind, benighted way."

Among the dying words of Mrs. Schimmelpenninck, honourably known by her "Memoirs of Port Royal," and other works, the remark is preserved that she had often in her life been inclined to occupy herself with the prospect close at hand, from finding the bleak, hard outline of the eternal hills cold and barren to her sight; but that, as she drew nearer, God's mercy made His light to shine full upon them, so that she could now perceive they were covered with magnificent trees of the forest, and were rich in fruit and flowers far more pleasant than those close at hand, and yet a continuation of them.

A commentator on the text of "promised light at evening-time," explains that by evening is understood the gradual withdrawal of the light; it is the lessening light that makes the evening-time: because of *that* the daisies close, and the birds fly to their nests, and a hush comes over nature. And it is just because evening is the time when, in the ordinary course of things, the light is going and the darkness is coming, that there is found to be anything remarkable in the text of *um den Abend wird es licht seyn*, as Luther's version runs. The promise, or prophecy, is that "light shall come at a time when it is not natural, when in the common course of things it is not looked for." It would be no surprise, as this divine proceeds to remark, that light should come at noonday: we expect it then, it is just what we are accustomed to see. "But if, when the twilight shadows were falling deeper and deeper, . . . with a sudden burst the noonday light were to spread around,—that would be a surprise." One of his personal illustrations of its import is the instance of the Christian poet who passed away almost in despair,—the gloom that overshadowed his spirit enduring almost to the end: "but even in the last moment there came a wonderful change"—and they tell us how even on his dead face there remained, till it was hidden for ever, a look of bright and beautiful and sudden surprise; the reflection of that light at evening that had been long in coming, but had come at last. At eventide light may break forth as the morning; light rising in obscurity, and darkness becoming as the noonday.

Light in darkness—light springing up out of darkness—the blessedness of this is emphatically recognised both by signal example and in special promise, in Holy Writ. When the hand of Moses was stretched out toward heaven, and darkness fell over the land of Egypt, even darkness which might be felt—a thick darkness in all the land of Egypt for three days—the Egyptians saw not one another, neither rose any from his place for three days. But all the children of Israel had light in their dwellings. "When I sit in darkness, the Lord shall be a light unto me." "For thou wilt light my candle; the Lord my God will enlighten my darkness." In the same Psalm that tells how clouds and darkness are round about Him, the Father of lights, is contained the exulting assurance, that "light is sown for the righteous." The light of the righteous rejoiceth, when the lamp of the wicked hath been put out. Well may spiritual aspirations be fervent for light to be sent forth, to lead and to guide to His holy hill and tabernacle, lest the feet of the wayfarer slip in a way that he knows not; and, above all, when they stumble on the dark mountains, or lose their footing in the swelling of Jordan.

Lux è tenebris—who will not prize it? who does not need it? For—

> "What am I?
> An infant crying in the night,
> An infant *crying for the light*,
> And with no language but a cry."

An exceeding bitter cry this crying for the light sometimes is, in such as those, for instance, whom Robertson of Brighton describes as "turning from side to side," feeling with horror the old, and all they hold dear, crumbling away—the ancient light going out—more than half suspecting the falsehood of the rest, and with an earnestness amounting to agony, leaving their home, like the Magians, and inquiring for fresh light.

Turning from side to side, with the wailing note of interrogation, "Who will show us any good?" And then, more earnestly than ever, "Lord, lift Thou up the LIGHT of Thy countenance upon us." In vain we turn from side to side. To whom should we go but unto Thee? Turn us again, O Lord God of hosts; show the LIGHT of Thy countenance, and we shall be saved.

Observable for special application is what Locke makes observable as a general fact, that new-born children always turn their eyes to that part whence the light comes, lay them how you please.

When the blind are operated on for the restoration of sight, it is suggestively remarked by an eminent author, that the same succouring hand which has opened to them the visible world, immediately shuts out the bright prospect again for a time, a bandage being passed over the eyes, lest in the first tenderness of their recovered sense, they should be fatally affected by the sudden transition from darkness to light. But, as he goes on to say, between the awful blank of total privation of vision, and the temporary blank of vision merely veiled, there lies the widest difference. "In the moment of their restoration the blind have but one glimpse of light, flashing on them in an overpowering gleam of brightness, which the thickest, closest veiling cannot extinguish. The new darkness is not like the void darkness of old: it is filled with rapid, changing visions of brilliant colours and ever-varying forms, rising, falling, whirling hither and thither with every second." And thus is it made evident that even when the handkerchief is passed over them, the once sightless eyes, though bandaged fast, are yet not blinded as they were before. All the more, however, they now dread the blankness of that total eclipse, now that, as it were, to them that walked in the shadow of death, light is sprung up. Light, how much the more precious for that background of blackness of darkness, darkness that still may be felt!

Light that may be felt, is the theme of blind old Œdipus, in Sophocles, at the hour of his mysterious departure—the hour and the power of darkness. Farewell he bids to—

> "Light, sweet Light!
> Rayless to me—mine once, and even now
> I feel thee palpable, round this worn form
> Clinging in last embrace."

Immortal as Homer is the prayer of his Ajax to die, if die he must, in the light. Contrast with this the *modus moriendi* of Pompey the Great, as pictured in Corneille:—

> "D'un des pans de sa robe il couvre son visage,
> A son mauvais destin en aveugle obéit,
> Et dédaigne de voir le ciel qui le trahit."

So with the Greek wife in Landor's Hellenics, who resists the bidding to fall not on her knees, but to look up:—

> "The hand
> That is to slay me, best may slay me thus.
> I dare no longer see the light of heaven." *

But to die in the light is the almost universal craving. "As a matter of fact, nothing," it has been remarked, "is more common than the craving and demand for light a little before death;" a remark confirmed by the sad experience of many who have tended and watched the last moments of a friend. "What more frequent than a prayer to open the shutters, and let in the sun? What complaint more repeated, and more touching than that 'it is growing dark'?" We are told of a sufferer who did not seem in immediate danger, suddenly ordering the sick room to be lit up as for a gala. When this was mentioned to the physician, he said, gravely, "No worse sign." We all

* In apposition, or opposition, to which, note the bidding and the demur in Talfourd's tragedy of "Ion":—

> "*Adrastus.* No; strike at once; my hour is come: in thee
> I recognise the minister of Jove,
> And, kneeling thus, submit me to his power.
> *Ion.* Avert thy face.
> *Adras.* No; let me meet thy gaze," etc.

remember the tenor of the last words of Dr. Adam, of the High School, Edinburgh, as recorded (however variously) by Scott and Lord Cockburn and others. It was in his bed-chamber, and in the forenoon, that he died; and finding that he could not see, the old schoolmaster, believing himself in the familiar school-room, exclaimed, "It is getting dark, boys; we must put off the rest till to-morrow." It was the darkness of death. And to the living, to-morrow, above all, *that* to-morrow, never comes.

M. de Lescure, dying of the wounds he had received at the battle of Chollet, awaited with his usual serenity the advent of his last hour. "Open the windows," said he to his wife, who was watching by his bedside, "is it clear?" "Yes," she said, "the sun is shining." "I have, then," replied the dying general, "a veil before my eyes." A veil that no man could raise. Chateaubriand, in describing the last hours of his sister, Madame de Beaumont—the Lucile of his "Memoires d'outre-tombe"—incidentally relates that "she begged of me to open the window. . . . A ray of sunshine rested upon her bed, and seemed to rejoice her spirit." The same circumstance is related of the dying Emperor Alexander. So it is of Dr. Channing. Karl Ludwig Sand, on the scaffold, begged that the bandage over his eyes might be so placed that he could, until his last moment, see the light. And it was so. Turner's biographer tells us that almost at the very hour of the old painter's death, his landlady wheeled his chair to the window, that he might see the sunshine he had loved so much, mantling the river, and glowing on the sails of the passing boats. "The old painter died with the winter-morning sun shining upon his face, as he was lying in his bed. The attendant drew up the window-blind, and the morning sun shone on the dying artist—the sun he had so often beheld with such love and such veneration," and painted, at sundry times and in divers manners, with such force.

Rousseau's wish, when in a dying state, to be carried into the open air, that he might have "a parting look at the glorious orb of day," is referred to by one of the many biographers of

Robert Burns, in recording that poet's remark one beautiful evening, when the sun was shining brightly through the casement. The hand of death was then upon him, and a young friend rose to let down the window-blinds, fearing the light might be too much for him. Burns thanked her, with a look of great benignity, but prayed her to let the sun shine on: "he will not shine long for me."

Tender and true is the pathos in one of Mrs. Richard Trench's letters, touching the death of her endeared child, Bessy, where we read: "The last phrase she uttered, except those expressive of her latest wants and pain, was a desire the window-curtain might be withdrawn, that she might look at the stars." Sunlight or starlight, it is light we cherish, and that cherishes us. Light from the first, light to the last. Happy, if the light we cherish is the shining light, that shineth more and more unto the perfect day.

Another set of variations on the same theme will form the section next ensuing.

——o——

WISHED-FOR DAY.

ACTS xxvii. 29.

IT was in a ship of Alexandria, sailing into Italy, when sailing was now dangerous, because of the advanced season; it was during a voyage which Paul, a passenger, foresaw and foretold would be with hurt and much damage, not only of the lading and ship, but also of lives two hundred threescore and sixteen; it was after there had arisen against the ship a tempestuous wind called Euroclydon, before which the vessel became a helpless drift; then it was that the crew and passengers, exceedingly tossed with the tempest, and not comforted—except the apostle, gave up, with the same exception, all hope of escape, and gloomily awaited the bitter end. On the third day they cast out the tackling of the ship. And when neither sun nor stars in many days appeared, and no small tempest lay on them, all hope that they should be saved was then taken away. The fourteenth night was come, and they were driven up and down in Adria, and about midnight the shipmen deemed that they drew near to some country, and sounded once and again, and found reason to fear lest they should have fallen upon rocks. So they cast four anchors out of the stern, and *wished for the day*—ηὔχοντο ἡμέραν γενέσθαι. If 'tis double death to die in sight of shore, as Shakspeare says, it is also, or nearly, double death to die in the dark. Some would almost say, Surely the bitterness of death is past, if light be vouchsafed to the dying, and so the shadows flee away. Well can they understand a pregnant symbolism in that incident of patriarchal days, when a deep sleep fell upon Abram as the sun was going down; and, lo, a horror of a great darkness fell upon him. With something of a shuddering sympathy can they connect the fact that, on the day whence all Good Fridays take their name, there was darkness over all the land unto the ninth hour, with that other fact that about the ninth hour there was heard a wailing cry, whose echo reverberates through all space and time, *Eli, Eli, lama sabachthani?*

Ever memorable in classical lore is the supplication of the Greek warrior in Homer, not to die in the dark. Let him see his foe, and see his end, however imminent, however inevitable. King Edward II., in Christopher Marlowe's historical tragedy, left alone in the Berkeley Castle dungeon with Lightborn, a murderer, exclaims:—

> "I see my tragedy written in thy brows;
> Yet stay awhile, forbear thy bloody hand,
> And let me see the stroke before it comes,
> That even then, when I shall lose my life,
> My mind may be more steadfast on my God."

Frequent in historical narrative are instances like that of Labedoyère, who when brought out to be shot, refused to have his eyes bandaged, and looking straight at the levelled muskets, exclaimed in a loud voice, "Fire, my friends!" Marshal Ney, a week or two later, also refused to have his eyes bandaged. "For five-and-twenty years," he said, "I have been accustomed to face the balls of the enemy." Then taking off his hat with his left hand, and placing his right upon his heart, he too said in a loud voice, fronting the soldiers, "My comrades, fire on me." Murat fell in a like manner, after a like request,—but gazing to the last on a medallion which contained portraits of his wife and four children.

What mainly tends to pile up the agony of Goisvintha, in the historical romance of "Antonina," when alone in the vaults with the madman Ulpius, is the distracting absence of light. "Bewildered and daunted by the darkness and mystery around her, she vainly strained her eyes to look through the obscurity, as Ulpius drew her on into the recess. . . . Suddenly he heard her pause, as if panic-stricken in the darkness, and her voice ascended to him, groaning, 'Light! light! oh, where is the light?'" She is held forth at this crisis, as a terrible evidence of the debasing power of crime, as she now stands, enfeebled by the weight of her own avenging guilt, and "by the agency of darkness, whose perils the innocent and the weak have been known to brave." It is only your melodramatic villain that flings forth his flourish in the style of Velasquez in "Braganza,"—addressing the duke, his judge:—

> "Yes, in your gloomiest dungeons plunge me down.
> Welcome, congenial darkness! horrors, hail!
> No more these loathing eyes shall see that sun
> Whose irksome beams light up thy pageant triumph."

And thus Sir Walter Scott has full warranty for proving the exceptional courage of his captive Englishman, when subjected to a midnight trial in the vaults of the *Vehmgericht*, by showing him unappalled by even the utter darkness of that terrible court. "Even in these agitating circumstances, the mind of the undaunted Englishman remained unshaken, and his eyelid did not quiver nor his heart beat quicker, though he seemed, according to the expression of Scripture, to be a pilgrim in the valley of the shadow of death, beset by numerous snares, and encompassed by total darkness, where light was most necessary for safety." It is only in an oblique sense that what Euripides says is true, of the coward being very valiant in the dark—ἐν ὄρφνῃ δραπέτης μέγα σθένει.

Dr. Croly applies the Homeric prayer of Ajax to an incident in the long war with France, when twenty-seven thousand British were eager, under Abercrombie and the Duke of York, to attack the French lines, and at the first tap of the drum a general cheer was given from all the columns. But the day, we read, had scarcely broke when a dense fog fell suddenly upon the whole horizon, and rendered movement almost impossible. "Nothing could exceed the vexation of the army at this impediment, and if our soldiers had ever heard of Homer there would have been many a repetition of his warrior's prayer, that 'live or die, it might be in the light of day.'" One is reminded of the lines in Racine:—

> "Enfin toute l'horreur d'un combat ténébreux ;
> Que pouvait la valeur dans ce trouble funeste?"

It has been observed of a certain railway catastrophe, where the crash and collision occurred in a tunnel—in that very place which nobody, even on ordinary occasions, passes through without a slight shudder and an undefined dread of some such disaster as the one in question—that "Ajax's prayer has been muttered by many who never heard of Ajax; and if we are to die, it is at least a mitigation of the hour of fate when it overtakes us in daylight."

In tracing, psychologically, the development within us of the sense of awe, Professor Newman attributes to the gloom of night (*deadly night*, as Homer terms it), more universally perhaps than to any other phenomenon, the first awakening of an uneasy sense of vastness. A young child, as he says, accustomed to survey the narrow limits of a lighted room, wakes in the night, and is frightened at the dim vacancy. "No nurse's tales about spectres are needed to make the darkness awful." Nor, he adds, is it from fear of any human or material enemy: it is the negation, the unknown, the unlimited, which excites and alarms; and sometimes the more if mingled with glimpses of light.

The last words audible of Goethe were, "*More light!*" The final darkness grew apace, in the words of his ablest biographer; and he whose eternal longings had been for more light, gave a parting cry for it as he was passing under the shadow of death.

"Light! give me more light," is the cry of the dying woman in "The Dead Secret,"—whereby hangs that tale. How often Lord Lytton remarks, is "light!" the last word of those round whom the shades are gathering. And he says it in reference to the last hours of one of the characters he has described with most success as well as elaboration, John Burley, who discourses of what is precious in light, as the darkness closes about him. When he lies down, and the attendant would withdraw the light, he moves uneasily. "Not that," he murmurs, "light to the last!" And putting forth a wan hand, he draws aside the curtain, so that the light may fall full on his face. When his only friend returns, and steals back to Burley's room on tiptoe, it is to see light stream through the cottage lattice—not the miserable ray lit by a human hand—but the still and holy effulgence of a moonlit heaven. Burley has died in sleep—calmly, and the half open eyes have the look of inexpressible softness which death sometimes leaves; "and still they were turned towards the light; and the light burned clear." Which things are an allegory.

Mr. Dickens intensifies the wretchedness of his prisoner at Marseilles by the deprivation of light in a prison that, like a well, like a vault, like a tomb, had no knowledge of the brightness outside, and would have kept its polluted atmosphere intact, in one of the spice islands of the Indian Ocean. What light he does get comes languishing down a square funnel that blinds a window in the staircase wall, through which the sky is never seen—nor anything else. What he does see of the "light of day" he calls the light of yesterday week, the light of six months ago, the light of six years ago: so slack and dead. Bitter indeed is the import of the curse, "Let it look for light and have none." Piteous indeed is the import of the pathetic remonstrance, "Wherefore is light given to him in misery?" Graphic indeed is the description of a place "where the light is as darkness." Darkness and light are both alike to One only.

The record of the last day in the life of Patrick Fraser Tytler opens as follows:—"On Sunday, the 23rd, he grew confused in memory, experienced difficulty in swallowing, and complained of darkness. The curtain was drawn, and the light of the winter morning was suffered to stream on his bed; but in vain. He folded his hands, and exclaimed, 'I see how it is.'"

John Foxe relates this incident in his narrative of the martyrdom of William Hunter, apprentice to a silk weaver in London, but discharged from his master's employment for refusing to attend mass, and finally condemned to the stake as an incorrigible heretic. "Then said William, 'Son of God, shine upon me!' and immediately the sun in the element shone out of a dark cloud so full in his face that he was constrained to look another way, whereat the people mused, because it was dark a little time before."

—o—

THE MORE THAN BROTHERHOOD OF A BOSOM FRIEND.

PROVERBS xviii. 24.

IN the last book of the Pentateuch we meet with a verse which, incidentally, seems to recognise how much more vitally close and intimate may be the affinity between a man and his bosom friend, than between the same man and his own brother. The brother is spoken of without descriptive epithet or adjunct of any kind; while of the friend it is added, "which is as thine own soul."* An ever memorable verse in

* Deut. xiii. 6. Observe too the seeming climax,—ascending from "thy brother, the son of thy mother," through the successive stages of "thy son, thy daughter," and "the wife of thy bosom," to "thy friend, which is as thine own soul." As though

"The force of Nature could no further go."

the book of Proverbs has immortalized the truth, that "there is a friend that sticketh closer than a brother."

None too many are the testimonies on record of brotherly attachment such as Columbus signalizes in his correspondence. To his elder son, Diego, the affectionate father writes concerning the younger, Fernando, then a stripling midway in his teens, "To thy brother conduct thyself as the elder brother should unto the younger. Thou hast no other, and I praise God that this is such a one as thou dost need. Ten brothers would not be too many for thee. Never have I found a better friend to right or left than my brothers." General testimony points the other way. Cicero, who, himself a good brother, in one place moots the question whether it is just to prefer our friends to our relations—*quæritur sitne æquum amicos cognatis anteferre,*—in another decides that friendship is better than relationship: *præstat amicitia propinquitati.* It has been remarked by Samuel Bailey, of Sheffield, that parents and children, husbands and wives, brothers and sisters, reciprocally complain of each other's deficiency of affection, and think it hard that the tie of relationship should not secure invariable kindness and indestructible love: expecting some secret influence of blood, some physical sympathy, some natural attraction, to retain the affection of their relatives, without any solicitude on their part to cherish or confirm it; and forgetting that man is so constituted as to love only what in some way or other, directly or indirectly, immediately or remotely, gives him pleasure,—that even natural affection is the result of pleasurable associations in his mind, or at least may be overcome by associations of an opposite character, and that the sure way to make themselves beloved is to display amiable qualities to those whose regard they wish to obtain.* Crabbe has a terse couplet on—

* "If our friends appear to look upon us with little interest, if our arrival is seen without pleasure, and our departure without regret, instead of charging them with a deficiency of feeling, we should turn our scrutiny upon ourselves."—*Essays on the Formation and Publication of Opinions,* v. i.

. . . "those
Who are called friends because they are not foes;"

meaning by friends, kinsfolk; but such as, though not more than kin, are less than kind. Dr. Croly's hero, Marston, soldier and statesman, on receiving, in his isolation, three letters from three proved friends, yet comparative strangers, describes himself as feeling, "while holding their letters in my hand, and almost pressing them to my heart, how much more strongly friendship may bind us than the ties of cold and negligent relationship." So Mr. Thackeray is bitter on what it is to have sham friends and no sympathy; ties of kindred which bind one, as it were, to the corpse of friendship, and oblige one to bear through life the weight and the embraces of this lifeless, cold connection.

Noteworthy among the avowals of Sir Thomas Browne, in his "Religio Medici," is this: "I confess I do not observe that order that the schools ordain our affections,—to love our parents, wives, children, and then our friends; for, excepting the injunctions of religion, I do not find in myself such a necessary and indissoluble sympathy to all those of my blood. I hope I do not break the fifth commandment, if I conceive I may love my friend before the nearest of my blood, even those to whom I owe the principles of life." The father and the son may, as Montaigne says, be of quite contrary humours, and brothers be without any sympathy with brothers. So Feltham asserts it to be likeness which makes the true love-knot of friendship. When we find another of our own disposition, what is it, he asks, but the same soul in a divided body? "We are then intermutually transposed into each other; and nature, which makes us love ourselves, makes us for the same reason love those who are like us; hence a friend is a more sacred name than a brother." What avails it, he further asks, to have bodies of the same original, when the souls within them differ?

The autobiographer in a modern work of fiction, having occasion to acknowledge, after being thrust amongst strangers to sicken, and all but die, that among strangers he received as much sympathy and kindness as he should have done among his own people, and in his father's house,—characterizes this sort of confession as one which people are apt to make as a reflection upon their relations, "whereas it disgraces only themselves." It is a case of rare misfortune, he contends, when we are not loved by our nearest of kin, in proportion as we desire and deserve to excite affection. Nevertheless, there is a too ample *consensus* of authorities whose testimony affirms, and confirms, the often slight and slender tenure of mere family ties, as such. "None of your family parties for me," quoth one of Justice Haliburton's shrewd spokesmen; "connections at best are poor friends, and commonly bitter enemies. If you want nothing, go to them, and you are sure to get it; if you are in want of any assistance, go to a stranger friend you have *made for yourself*, and that's the boy that has a heart and a hand for you." The Earl of Dudley, Bishop Copleston's correspondent, in one of his always interesting letters to that prelate, adverting to the death of an uncle who had never taken the smallest interest in him, or showed him the smallest kindness, makes the avowal: "And, though I flatter myself that there is no person more capable of returning affection than myself, yet I fairly own that I am wholly unable to bestow it quite gratuitously even upon a near relation." Richardson harps on this note again and again in his history of Clarissa. How much more binding and tender, that young lady writes—and the writing comes of bitter experience—are the ties of pure friendship and the union of like minds, than the ties of nature! And her chief correspondent, in commenting on the terms of a kinsman's assurance, that he will not see Clarissa "imposed on either by friend or foe,"—interposes the verbal amendment: "By *relation* or foe, should he not have said? For a friend will not impose upon a friend." Elsewhere the same writer has to put the home-question: "Would you side with a false brother against a true friend? A brother may not be a friend; but a friend will be always a brother."

It was one of the aphorisms—or call them paradoxes—of M. de Stendhal (Henri Beyle) that our next of kin are our natural enemies when we enter the world; the simple matter of fact being, as an Edinburgh reviewer alleges, that his own character, tendencies, and aspirations had been invariably opposed to the plans, wishes, and modes of thinking of his family. Mr. Froude has depicted in Edward Fowler a young man who in his dealings with every one except with his own family, was frank, generous, and unselfish; and whose affections, naturally very strong, finding themselves forced out of their proper channel, poured themselves out on any one that happened to attract him. A few kind words from his father, now and then, implying real sympathy and inviting confidence, might, we are given to understand, have averted in this case, as in so many others, a bitter result of estrangement and desolation. Perhaps, as Mr. Disraeli somewhere intimates, with all their anxiety and opportunities for observation, the parent and tutor are rarely skilful in discovering the character of their child or charge. "Custom blunts the fineness of psychological study: those with whom we have lived long and early, are apt to blend our essential and our accidental qualities in one bewildering association." Strange, exclaims Hamilton Aïde, how little we often know of those who are next us in the battle-ranks through this long march of life! Our daily familiar life, as George Eliot has remarked, is but a hiding of ourselves from each other behind a screen of trivial words and deeds; and those who sit with us at the same hearth are often the farthest off from the deep human soul within us, full of unspoken evil and unacted good. "Strangers yet," as Lord Houghton has it:—

> "After childhood's winning ways,
> After care, and blame, and praise,
> Counsel asked, and wisdom given,
> After mutual prayers to heaven,
> Child and parent scarce regret
> When they part—are strangers yet."

Or as Chauncy Hare Townshend expresses the same relative truth, too absolutely true:—

> "Kindred are oft but kin by name,
> Our thoughts they never knew."

MANY YEARS TO ENJOY LIFE: THIS NIGHT TO DIE.

St. Luke xii. 19, 20.

THE rich man was getting richer to his heart's content. So plentiful was the produce of his land, that he must needs enlarge his premises. There was not room enough in his barns for those golden harvests; the barns must be pulled down, and greater ones built, wherein to bestow all his fruits and his goods. Happy man he accounted himself that day; happy in a prosperous present, happier still in a promising future. A future of happiness not less prolonged than assured. So he would say to his soul that day, "Soul, thou hast much goods laid up for many years; take thine ease, eat, drink, and be merry." That day he said it. Fool! that night his soul was required of him.

Woe was denounced by one of old on another of the Dives family, who said, "I will build me a wide house, and large chambers," and who cut him out windows, and ceiled his house with cedar, and painted it with vermilion. "Shalt thou reign because thou closest thyself in cedar?" Man's sanguine and sure "I will"—how little of the future tense there sometimes is about it after all!

> "Tu secanda marmora
> Locas sub ipsum funus; et sepulchri
> Immemor, struis domos."

In Homer we see from his tall ship the king of men descend, there fondly thinking the gods conclude his toil, where, in fact, awaits him murder most foul and most unnatural. In Homeric figure—

> "So, whilst he feeds luxurious in the stall,
> The sovereign of the herd is doomed to fall."

Bitterly the shade of Atrides repeats his tragic story to Odysseus, telling how, "Alas! he hoped, the toils of war o'ercome, to meet soft quiet and repose at home. Delusive hope!" for at home the hand was already upraised to smite him.

The Turkish prince, Alp Arslan, dying of Joseph's dagger-stroke, bequeathed an admonition to the pride of kings, which

Gibbon has preserved. "Yesterday, as from an eminence I beheld the numbers, the discipline, and the spirit of my armies; the earth seemed to tremble under my feet; and I said in my heart, 'Surely thou art the king of the world, the greatest and most invincible of warriors.' These armies are no longer mine; and in the confidence of my personal strength, I now fall by the hand of an assassin." The inscription on his tomb invited those who had seen the glory of Alp Arslan exalted to the heavens, to meditate on its present burial in the dust.

Michelet moralises with trenchant irony on the fate which overtook our Henry V. on French soil. It is to the "Dance of Death" he refers in the exclamation, "What sport for death, what a malicious pastime to have brought the victorious Harry within a month's reach of the crown of France! After a life of unremitting toil for that end, he wanted but one little month added to his existence to be the survivor of Charles VI. . . . No! not a month, not a day more was to be his."

Splendid was that festival at Cæsarea at which Herod Agrippa, in the pomp and pride of power, entered the theatre in a robe of silver, which glittered, says the historian, with the morning rays of the sun, so as to dazzle the eyes of the assembly, and excite general admiration. Some of his flatterers set up the shout, "A present god!" Agrippa did not repress the impious adulation which spread through the theatre. At that moment he looked up, and saw an owl perched over his head on a rope, and Agrippa had been forewarned that when next he saw that bird, "at the height of his fortune," he would die within five days. The fatal omen, according to Josephus, pierced the heart of the king, who, with deep melancholy, exclaimed, "Your god will soon suffer the common lot of mortality." He was immediately struck, in the language of the sacred volume, by an angel. Seized with violent pains, he was carried to his palace, lingered five days in extreme agony, being "eaten of worms," and so died.

Fielding forcibly presents a certain sanguine projector, lusty and strong, in the heyday of middle age, who reckons confidently on becoming heir to the estate of a senior of immense wealth, and has all his plans elaborately prepared for his disposal of the same. Nothing is wanting to enable him to enter upon the immediate execution of these plans, but the death of the elder man, in calculating which he has studied every book extant that treats of the value of lives, reversions, etc.; from all which he has satisfied himself, that as he has every day a chance of this happening, so has he more an even chance of its happening before long. "But while the captain was one day busied in deep contemplations of this kind, one of the most unlucky, as well as most unseasonable, accidents happened to him. The utmost malice of fortune could, indeed, have contrived nothing so cruel, so *mal-à-propos*, so absolutely destructive to all his schemes." It was, that just at the very instant when his heart was exulting in meditations on the happiness which would accrue to him by the other's death, he himself was cut off by an apoplexy. As Léontine complains in "Heraclius,"—

> "Et lorsque le hasard me flatte avec excès,
> Tout mon dessein avorte au milieu du succès."

It was just when Kleber was beginning to reap the fruits of his intrepidity and discretion, that he was cut off by the obscure assassin, Souliman. One is reminded of Thomson on the massacre of the bees,—

> "At evening snatched,
> Beneath the cloud of guilt-concealing night,
> And fixed o'er sulphur; while not dreaming ill,
> The happy people in their waxen cells,
> Sat tending public cares, and planning schemes
> Of temperance, for winter poor," etc.

A tory historian, recording the close of the parliamentary session in July 1827, takes occasion to observe that Mr. Canning now saw every wish of his heart gratified, having raised himself to the highest position in the State, and being looked up to in every part of the world as the protector of the oppressed and the advocate of freedom. In the prime of life, "his sway in Parliament was unbounded, and he might hope for a long career of fame, fortune, and usefulness." *Vanitas vanitatum!* The hand of fate was already upon him, and he was to be suddenly snatched from the scene of his glory, at the very moment when he seemed to have attained the summit of earthly felicity. Even, however, when death is not concerned, as in his memorable case, in the sudden and final collapse of a great career, and the abrupt extinction of exuberant promise, how often is Cowper's picture realized, where—

> "Runs the mountainous and craggy ridge
> That tempts ambition. On the summit, see,
> The seals of office glitter in his eyes;
> He climbs, he pants, he grasps them. At his heels,
> Close at his heels, a demagogue ascends,
> And with a dexterous jerk soon twists him down,
> And wins them, but to lose them in his turn."

The picture is, in some sort, and for moral uses, a pendent to that by another poet, of those who are pushing hard up hill the cumbrous load of life; just as they trust to gain the farthest steep, and put an end to strife,—

> "Down thunders back the stone with mighty sweep,
> And hurls their labours to the valley deep,
> For ever vain."

But this is diverging farther and farther from the direct import of our theme. More to the purpose is the same poet's description of Celadon assuring his betrothed of perfect safety, and triumphantly asserting her absolute immunity from the perils of the storm, and as exultingly inferring his own, from his relationship to her; when,—

> "From his void embrace,
> Mysterious heaven! that moment to the ground,
> A blackened corse, was struck the beauteous maid."

Some innocents, as Cleopatra has it, escape not the thunderbolt. Innocence, as well as iniquity, may know something of that breach ready to fall, swelling out in a high wall, whose breaking cometh suddenly at an instant.

The loving friends of Charlotte Brontë, after her marriage, are described by one among them as catching occasional glimpses of brightness, and pleasant peaceful murmurs of sound, telling to them who stood outside, of the gladness within; and they said among themselves, "After a long and a hard struggle—after many cares and bitter sorrows—she is tasting happiness now." Remembering her trials, they were glad in the idea that God had seen fit to wipe away the tears from her eyes. "But God's ways are not as our ways," Mrs. Gaskell adds. Just as Currer Bell's happiness seemed beginning, and her goodness ripening, came fever, delirium, death. Mrs. Gaskell's own career was similarly cut short, just when she was finishing, but ere yet she had finished, the completest and ablest of her works; just when public recognition of her merits was growing earnest as well as general. It is the old, old story. For what, as the old ballad says,—

"is this worldys bliss,
That changeth as the moon!
My summer's day in lusty May
Is darked before the noon."

——o——

GREAT BABYLON BUILT: A BUILDER'S BOAST.

DANIEL iv. 29–33.

WALKING in the palace of his kingdom of Babylon—that Babylon of which the foundations, indeed, had been laid ages ago, but which he had so enlarged and adorned as to make it one of the world's wonders—Nebuchadnezzar the king, elate with pride at the pomp of architectural results, flushed with the triumph of enterprises so costly, and achievements so manifest to the eye, gave utterance, in complacent soliloquy perhaps, to the exultant sense of being a master builder indeed, and of seeing his power reflected in so gorgeous a form. The king spake and said, "Is not this great Babylon, that I have built for the house of the kingdom, by the might of my power, and for the honour of my majesty?"

While the word was in the king's mouth, there fell a voice

from heaven, saying, "O king Nebuchadnezzar, to thee it is spoken: The kingdom is departed from thee." And the sequel we know. How that same hour was the thing fulfilled upon Nebuchadnezzar, and he was driven from men, and did eat grass as oxen, and his body was wet with the dew of heaven, till his hairs were grown like eagles' feathers, and his nails like birds' claws,—is it not written in the book of the prophecies of Daniel, whose name was Belteshazzar, and whom the king made ruler over the whole province of that same Babylon the Great?

The royal builder's boast was on the instant reproved by a degradation literally brutal in its extremity. While the word of complacent self-glorification was in the king's mouth, the sentence of bestial doom went forth against him. Just when he was resting on his laurels, a taint overtook them. Just when he rejoiced in asserting himself a king of kings, commenced the working of a curse which levelled him with grazing flocks and herds.

The lesson is for all time, and for all sorts and conditions of men. Verifications of it—varying, of course, in kind, and still more in degree—are rife in records historical and biographical, and in the unrecorded experiences, the moving accidents, of everyday life. Just when a man is apt to set up his rest, the fiat goes forth against him which shatters to its base the structure he has reared. The house he has just finished building tumbles to pieces like a house of cards. The castle in whose defences, at last completed, he felt so secure, dislimns like a castle in the air.

". . . The engineer
Who lays the last stone of his sea-built tower,
It cost him years and years of toil to raise,—
And, smiling at it, tells the wind and waves
To roar and whistle now—but, in a night,
Beholds the tempest sporting in its place—
May look aghast."

Belshazzar the king made a great feast to a thousand of his lords, and drank wine before the thousand, and displayed the golden vessels which his father Nebuchadnezzar had taken out of the temple at Jerusalem, and was jubilant with the excitement of revelry, and joyously confident in the stability of his realm; when, in the same hour, there came forth fingers of a man's hand, and wrote over against the plaster of the wall of the king's palace; and what they wrote was, that God had numbered his kingdom, and finished it. And in that night was Belshazzar the king of the Chaldeans slain.

A noble chamber had Pope John XXI. built for himself in the palace of Viterbo; and by the falling in of the roof he so admired, he was crushed to death. "John XXI.," writes Dean Milman, "was contemplating with too great pride the work of his own hands, and burst out into laughter; at that instant the avenging roof came down on his head." The catastrophe was held at the time to be a special judgment on a reprobate pontiff. Nebuchadnezzar's boast, and worse than Nebuchadnezzar's doom. The mention of Babylon the Great will serve, with some, to eke out a parallel.

The historian of Mexico tells us of Montezuma, while exacting from his people the homage of an adulation worthy of an oriental despot, and the profuse expenditure of whose court was a standing marvel, that "while the empire seemed towering in its most palmy and prosperous state, the canker had eaten deepest into its heart." Ruin was at hand. The hour was come, and the man; and that man was Hernando Cortès.

Significantly opens a fifth act—for a fifth act is the last—of Ben Jonson's "Sejanus," with the joyous exultations of that prosperous upstart, in the confidence of power: "Swell, swell, my joys," he exclaims,—

"I did not live till now; this my first hour;
Wherein I see my thoughts reached by my power.
* * * * *
My roof receives me not; 'tis air I tread;
And, at each step, I feel my advanced head
Knock out a star in heaven!"

and so forth, with other hyperboles of frantic arrogance. His soliloquy is interrupted by messengers of ill news. Destruction dogs his path; and very soon the magniloquent braggart has to subdue his tone, and his cue is then to upbraid the higher powers whom alone he recognises :—

> "If you will, Destinies, that after all,
> I faint now ere I touch my period,
> You are but cruel."

Of constant recurrence among the commonplaces of biography are such "buts," inopportune and inevitable, as Cicero's biographer prefixes to a critical paragraph : "But while all things were proceeding very prosperously in his favour, and nothing seemed wanting to crown his success, . . . all his hopes and fortunes were blasted at once, by an unhappy rencounter with his old enemy Clodius."

There is a popular historical fiction in which we see the Cardinal Alberoni musing on the greatness he has achieved for Spain and for himself, only to find himself overtaken by ruin and disgrace. The rope which he has twisted so carefully, proves to be of sand. In another we see a successful adventurer at the culminating point of his success. There seems nothing wanting to him in "that supreme moment," as the phrase goes. He is in "a tumult of gratified ambition and selfish joy." "This glory and grandeur" repay a thousand-fold his patient endeavours and strenuous schemings. But at this very moment a dark shadow overlays the sunshine on his pathway; and we look on a changed countenance—"no longer full of triumph and pleasure, but ghastly pale" at a sudden but very present and very pressing sense of impending disaster. *Fortuna vitrea est, tum cum splendet frangitur.*

At the opening of the twelfth century all was prosperity with the Emperor Henry IV. ; his turbulent and agitated life seemed, in the words of Dean Milman, "as if it would close in an august and peaceful end." But, as an after page in the history of Latin Christianity is prompt to prove, this most secure and splendid period in the life of Henry was one calm and brilliant hour of evening before a night of utter gloom.

Columbus had just welcomed tranquillity in exchange for the troubles and dangers of his island, when intelligence arrived of the discovery of a large tract of country rich in mines. He now anticipated the prosperous prosecution of his favourite enterprise, and was exultant at the turn of the tide. "How illusive were his hopes!" exclaims his biographer. "At this moment events were maturing which were to overwhelm him with distress, strip him of his honour, and render him comparatively a wreck for the remainder of his days." Who, the chronicler of the conquest of Granada may well ask, who can tell when to rejoice in this fluctuating world? "Every wave of prosperity has its reacting surge, and we are often overwhelmed by the very billow on which we thought to be wafted into the haven of our hopes." *Et subito casu, quæ valuere, ruunt.*

Olivarez was requested by his royal master to resign, just at the moment when the death of Richelieu (1643) opened to him an almost royal road, it might seem, to success.

> "O momentary grace of mortal men,
> Which we more hunt for than the grace of God!
> Who builds his hope in air of your fair looks,
> Lives like a drunken sailor on a mast,
> Ready, with every nod, to tumble down
> Into the fatal bowels of the deep."

Such is the state of man, as Shakspeare's Hastings feels it. And this is the state of man, as Shakspeare's Wolsey finds it: to-day he puts forth the tender leaves of hope, to-morrow blossoms, and next day comes a frost, a killing frost, and,—when he thinks, good easy man, full surely his goodness is a ripening,—nips his root, and then he falls. Shakspeare's Belarius again, will furnish us with another text, of practical application:—

> ". . . Then was I as a tree,
> Whose boughs did bend with fruit: but in one night,
> A storm, or robbery, call it what you will,
> Shook down my yellow hangings, nay, my leaves,
> And left me bare to weather."

And as with the pride and pomp and circumstance of life, so with life itself. Typical for all time is the fate of Lycidas:—

> "Fame is the spur that the clear spirit doth raise
> (That last infirmity of noble mind)

To scorn delights, and live laborious days ;
But the fair guerdon when we hope to find,
And think to burst out into sudden blaze,
Comes the blind fury with the abhorrèd shears,
And slits the thin-spun life."

——o——

INVOCATION AND INACTION.

EXODUS xiv. 15.

WITH the Red Sea close before them, and with Pharaoh and his host close behind them, what were the children of Israel to do? Was it for this that Moses had brought them out of the house of bondage, which yet had its fleshpots and creature comforts after all? What were they to do? They lifted up their eyes, and saw the sea in front, and the enemy in the rear; and then they lifted up their voice in querulous fear and expostulation. Should they go back? Then Moses lifted up his voice, and bade them stand still, and they should see a great deliverance. But the will of God was not that they should either go back, or stand still and merely look on. For "the Lord said unto Moses, Wherefore criest thou unto me? speak unto the children of Israel that they go forward." Invocation may be excellent in itself, but, as a concomitant, inaction mars it. A hallowed thing is prayer; but to pray and sit still, when the need is to go forward and push on, is the sign or stigma of feeble folk.

When Nelson told the King of Naples, in plain terms, that he had his choice—either to advance, trusting to God for His blessing on a just cause, and prepared to die sword in hand; or to remain quiet, and be kicked out of his kingdom; the king made answer that he would go on, and trust in God and Nelson. Of the same stuff as Nelson, but his superiors in moral character and in practical recognition of Him that is Holy, Holy, Holy, as well as Lord God Almighty, were those early English navigators, characterized by a modern pen as "indomitable God-fearing men, whose life was one great liturgy."

"The ice was strong, but God was stronger," says one of Frobisher's men, after grinding a night and a day among the icebergs; not waiting for God to come down and split them, but toiling through the long hours, himself and the rest fending off the vessel with poles and planks, with death glaring at them out of the rocks, and so saving themselves and it. We read in Turell's Life of Dr. Benjamin Colman, "that reverend father in our New England Israel," as Mr. Lowell calls him, that when the vessel in which he had taken passage for England was attacked by a French privateer, he "fought like a philosopher and a Christian, . . . and prayed all the while he charged and fired." His the practice was, if not on his lips the maxim, to pray to God and keep his powder dry. It is expressly noted of the Maid of Orleans, in the *Procès* on record, that while she rather evaded the question of resorting to miraculous aids and appliances, and of affecting supernatural power, she "used the Gallic proverb, *Ayde-toi, Dieu te aydera.*"

> "In daily toil, in deadly fight,
> God's chosen found their time to pray;
> And still He loves the brave and strong,
> Who scorn to starve, and strive with wrong,
> To mend it, if they may."

Forcible is the portrait drawn in a recent work of fiction, of a man now steeped in moral degradation, who had once tried to be honest, and prayed to God to prosper his honesty; but then he only tried to do right in a spasmodic, fitful kind of way, and expected his prayers to be granted as soon as uttered, and was indignant with a Providence that seemed regardless of his entreaties.

Bentley is held to have happily ridiculed the helpless Chorus of Greek tragedy, who, when a deed of violence was to be acted, instead of interfering to prevent the atrocity to which the perpetrator had made them privy, could only, by the rules of the theatre, exhaust their sorrow and surprise in dithyrambics. He burlesqued this characteristic by introducing into "The Wishes" a Chorus after the manner of the ancient Greeks, who are informed by one of the *dramatis personæ*, that a madman with a firebrand has just entered the vaults beneath the place which they occupy, and which contain a magazine of gunpowder. The Chorus, instead of stirring from the dangerous vicinity, immediately commence a long complaint of the hardship of their fate, exclaiming pathetically, "O unhappy madman—or rather unhappy we, the victims of this madman's fury—or thrice, thrice unhappy the friends of the madman, who did not secure him, and restrain him from the perpetration of such deeds of frenzy—or three and four times hapless the keeper of the magazine, who forgot the keys in the door," etc., etc.

The cry of Charles and his Paladins at Arles, "Help us, oh blessed martyr St. Trophimus!" is thus disposed of by Torfrid, Hereward's forefather, in the story of the Wake, "What use in crying to St. Trophimus? A tough arm is worth a score of martyrs here," in the thick of the fight for dear life.

When Lord Rea, in 1630, as recorded in a well-known passage from Rushworth, uttered the pious conventionalism or devout platitude, "Well, God mend all!" his companion, Sir David Ramsay, impatiently exclaimed, "Nay," with an undevout expletive, "Nay, Donald, we must help him to mend it!" One is reminded of what Mr. Froude says of the Protestant leaders in Scotland, during the autumn of 1559, when the Queen Regent returned to Holyrood, once more absolutely victorious: "Notwithstanding all their talk about God, it had come to this. God had as much interest in them as they had themselves courage, energy, capacity, understanding, and perseverance—so much precisely, and not more." Or again of that homely thrust in the "Biglow Papers," where one of the interlocutors, on a critical occasion, avowing a wish to know where and when to strike, is thus answered by his plain-spoken mate :—

"'Strike soon,' sez he, 'or you'll be deadly ailin',—
Folks thet's afear'd to fail are sure o' failin';
God hates your sneakin' creturs thet believe
He'll settle things they run away an' leave.'"

There is something to be said—indeed in our present sense

there is more to be said, for the farmer than for the clergyman in the story of the latter congratulating the former on the state of his crops, and finding him not free from apprehensions, in regard of former bad years—"My friend," urged the rector, "trust in Providence." "Providence! Yes, yes," replied the other; "that's all very well: but give me the doong cart." Dr. John Brown relates with zest how one of his faculty was attending a poor woman in labour—a desperate case, that required a cool head and a firm will, while the good man, "for he *was* good," had neither of these,—and losing his presence of mind, gave up the poor woman as lost, and retired into the next room to pray for her. "Another doctor, who perhaps wanted what the first one had, and certainly had what he wanted, brains and courage, meanwhile arrived, and called out, 'Where is Dr. ——?' 'Oh, he has gone into the next room to pray.' 'Pray! Tell him to come here this instant, and help me; he can work and pray too;'" and by the new-comer's, the *snell* working doctor's, assistance the woman's life was saved.

Sir Robert Peel, in his reply to certain suggestions offered by Lord Kenyon in reference to the potato-disease, coupled with the recommendation of a "special public acknowledgment of our dependence on God's mercy in our present distressed state," was mildly sarcastic on the seeming inconsistency of making such an acknowledgment, while at the same time leaving "in full operation the restraints which man has imposed on the import of provisions."

Not likely to be soon forgotten, on either side the Tweed, is Lord Palmerston's reply as Home Secretary, to the Presbytery of Edinburgh, touching the national attitude pending a visitation of Asiatic cholera. He advised them that it was better to cleanse than to fast. Let them see to purifying the foul wynds and overcrowded flats tenanted by the poor, and so get rid of "those causes and sources of contagion which, if allowed to remain, will infallibly breed pestilence, and be fruitful in death, in spite of all the prayers and fastings of a united, but inactive nation." To apply what a north country bishop says in Shakspeare :—

> "The means that Heaven yields must be embraced,
> And not neglected; else, if Heaven would,
> And we will not, Heaven's offer we refuse;
> The proffered means of succour and redress."

A recent apologist for the captain of a lost steamship submitted that the destruction of that fine vessel was what is called in the old-fashioned language of a charter-party, "the act of God." Less partial critics, on the other hand, affirmed it to be the act of the folly and madness of man,—the term quoted belonging to an age when they who go down to the sea in ships had not learned the irreverent practice of imputing to the Deity the direct consequences of human rashness. "Let us, if we can, amend this folly; or, if we will persist in it, let us at least take the blame upon ourselves." They that go down to the sea in ships have, however, in all ages, though not so much one people as another (English for instance as Italians), been prone to waste in wailing outcries to patron saints the energy that, in peril of wreck, they might have expended to better purpose. The "Colloquies" of Erasmus give a lively sample of this run-to-waste invocation. The last of the heroes of La Vendée, Charette, while still a youth, sailed from Brest in a cutter which lost its mast, and was in imminent jeopardy of going down; the sailors, on their knees, were praying to the Virgin, and had entirely given up all notion of exertion, "till Charette, by killing one, succeeded in bringing the others to a sense of their duty, and thereby saved the vessel." Lord Broughton describes a scene of the kind, in a Turkish ship of war: the Greeks on board called on all the saints, the Mussulmans on Allah; the captain burst into tears and ran below deck, telling his passengers to call on God: he rung his hands, and wept aloud, and being asked what he could do, said he could do nothing. "Could he get back to the main land?" "If God chooses," was his answer. "Could he make Corfu?" "If God chooses." One thinks of the testy old patrician's rejoinder in "Coriolanus" to the tribune's exclaimer, "The gods be good unto us!" "No; in such a case the gods will not be good unto us." In Scott's tale of the Crusaders, "I will vow a golden candlestick to the Holy Sepulchre—a shrine of silver to our Lady of Engaddi—a pall, worth one hundred bezants to Saint Thomas of Orthez," cries the Queen in extremity.—" Up, up, madam," says Edith; "call on the saints an you list, but be your own best saint." In "Ivanhoe," again, when the Grand Master forbodes the contingent extinction of his order (the Templars), " Now may God avert such a calamity!" says the Preceptor. " Amen!" rejoins the Grand Master, with solemnity, "but we must deserve His aid."

It is all in keeping with the practical character of the man, the prayer which on one critical occasion Benvenuto Cellini records his offering: "Almighty God, favour my cause, for Thou knowest it is a just one, and that I am not on my part wanting in my utmost efforts to make it succeed." On another he tells us how he " told Lionardo, who was incessantly crying out, 'Jesus, Jesus!' that Jesus would assist him, if he strove to help himself." Elsewhere again Cellini emphatically asserts his systematic habit of " always exerting his utmost efforts to extricate" himself from difficulty, as well as of devoutly recommending himself to God, by whom alone those efforts could achieve success, and who so often had delivered him when the best of these had clearly and entirely failed.

Saintly as well as Saint Francis of Sales bids his brethren, " En toutes vos affaires, appuyez-vous totalement sur la providence de Dieu, par laquelle seule tous vos desseins doivent réussir; travaillez néanmoins de votre côté tout doucement pour co-opérer avec icelle." The counsel is at one, *au fond*, with that of the heathen stoic in the old play :—

> "I am plain, fathers. Here you look about
> One at another, doubting what to do,
> With faces, as you trusted to the gods,
> That still have saved you; and they can do it: but
> They are not wishings, or base womanish prayers,
> Can draw their aids; but vigilance, counsel, action;
> Which they will be ashamèd to forsake.
> 'Tis sloth they hate, and cowardice."

——o——

CO-OPERANT UNITS.

EPHESIANS iv. 16.

THE universal Church is designated by the apostle a body, which whole body is fitly joined together and compacted by that which every joint supplieth, according to the effectual working in the measure of every part. And every part in its measure, and according to its imparted power. Very little are some of the joints and fibres; but every little helps. Who shall despise the whole of small things? But for the accumulated atoms, the aggregated littles, where were the body?

"Let me not deem that I was made in vain,
Or that my Being was an accident,
Which Fate, in working its sublime intent,
Not wished to be, to hinder would not deign.
Each drop uncounted in a storm of rain
Hath its own mission, and is duly sent
To its own leaf or blade, not idly spent
'Mid myriad dimples on the shipless main.
The very shadow of an insect's wing,
For which the violet cared not while it stayed,
Yet felt the lighter for its vanishing,
Proved that the sun was shining by its shade:
Then can a drop of the eternal spring,
Shadow of living lights, in vain be made?"*

As the author of "Felix Holt" says, we see human heroism broken into units, and are apt to imagine, this unit did little—might as well not have been. But in this way we might break up a great army into units; in this way we might break the sunlight into fragments, and think that this and the other might be cheaply parted with. "Let us rather raise a monument to the soldiers whose brave hearts only kept the ranks unbroken, and met death—a monument to the faithful who were not famous, and who are precious as the continuity of the sunbeams is precious, though some of them fall unseen and on

* Hartley Coleridge, Sonnets.

barrenness." Suppose but a solution of that continuity; the sequel is, darkness that may be felt.

There is a latter-day apologue of a gimlet that grew exceedingly discontented with its vocation, envying all the other tools in the carpenter's basket, and thinking scorn of its own mean duty of perpetually boring and picking holes everywhere. "The saw and the axe had grand work to do; and the plane got praise always; so did the chisel for its carving; and the happy hammer was always ringing merrily upon the clenching nail." But for *it*, a wretched, poking, paltry, gimlet, its work was hidden away, and very little seemed its recognised use. But the gimlet is assured, on the best authority, that nothing could compensate for its absence, and is therefore bidden be content, nay happy; for though its work seems mean and secret, it is indispensable. To its good offices, the workman is said to look chiefly for coherence without splitting; and to its quiet influences, the neatness, the solidity, the comfort of his structure may greatly be ascribed. The apologue has, of course, its practical application. "Are there not many pining gimlets in society, ambitious of the honour given to the greater-seeming tools of our Architect, but unconscious that in His hands they are quite as useful? The loving little child, the gentle woman, the patience of many a moral martyr, the diligence of many a duteous drudge, though their works may be unseen and their virtues operate in obscurity, yet are these main helpers to the very joints and bands of our body corporate, the quiet home influences whereby the great edifice, Society, is so nicely wainscoted and floored without split-boards."

To recognise one's being entrusted with but one talent, after all, and not with five or with ten, as one's vanity had previously taken for granted, has even bee n hailed as, in some sort, a soothing sensation. When one of us who has been led by native vanity or senseless flattery, says Dr. Holmes, to think himself or herself possessed of talent, arrives at the full and final conclusion that he or she is really dull, it is one of the most tranquillizing and blessed convictions that can enter a mortal's mind: "All our failures, our short-comings, our strange disappointments in the effect of our efforts, are lifted from our bruised shoulders, and fall, like Christian's pack, at the feet of that Omnipotence which has seen fit to deny us the pleasant gifts of high intelligence,—with which one look may overflow us in some wider sphere of being." That the one talent be employed, is the one thing needful. So feels the girl in one of Charlotte Brontë's tales, whose exclamation is, "Mother, the Lord who gave each of us our talents will come home some day, and will demand from all an account. The tea-pot, the old stocking-foot, the linen rag, the willow-pattern tureen, will yield up their barren deposit in many a house: suffer your daughters, at least, to put their money to the exchangers, that they may be enabled at the Master's coming to pay His own with usury." A man is accepted according to that he hath, not condemned in respect of what he never had. Whatsoever his hand findeth to do, that is what a man is to do with his might, to do with a will,—be it to govern a nation, or to dust a warehouse. To apply a passage in Ben Jonson's "Catiline,"

> "They are no less part of the commonwealth
> That do obey, than those that do command."

John Newton said that if two angels came down from heaven to execute a Divine command, and one was appointed to conduct an empire, and the other to sweep a street in it, they would feel no inclination to change employments. So again, the same robust divine affirmed that a Christian should never plead spirituality for being a sloven; "if he be but a shoe-cleaner, he should be the best in the parish." As the old servant tells Ruth, in Mrs. Gaskell's story, "There 's a right and a wrong way of setting about everything—and to my thinking, the right way is to take a thing up heartily, if it is only making a bed. Why, dear ah me! making a bed may be done after a Christian fashion, I take it, or else what 's to come of such as me in heaven, who 've had little enough time on earth for clapping ourselves down on our knees for set prayers?" This quaint speaker had laid to heart the lesson once for all enforced upon her, to do her duty in that state of life to which it had pleased God to call her; her station was that of a servant, and, looked at aright, as honourable as a king's: she was to help and serve others in one way, just as a king is in another. Her parting counsel to Ruth runs thus: "Just try for a day to think of all the odd jobs as to be done well and truly in God's sight, not just slurred over any how, and you 'll go through them twice as cheerfully," besides doing them more efficiently. John Brown, of Haddington, being waited on by a lad of excitable temperament, who informed him of his desire to become a preacher, and whom the shrewd pastor saw to be as weak in intellect as he was strong in conceit, advised him to continue in his present vocation. The young man said, "But I wish to preach and glorify God." The old commentator replied, "My young friend, a man may glorify God making broom besoms; stick to your trade, and glorify God by your life and conversation." As it was said of Bossuet, in the seventeeth century, that he could not walk, or sit down, or even pluck a currant, without your recognising in him the great bishop (so asserts a modern French divine, not of Bossuet's church), just so the workman and the domestic servant who are animated by their Master's spirit, distinguish themselves among their fellows by a certain air of nobility; under their blouse or their livery may be seen to shine the signal light of their *aristocratie spirituelle*, the image of the Most High Himself. However mean their employment, they go about it with neither disgust nor indifference; but with an intelligent interest, because, in the sight of God, and indeed in their own eyes, their occupation is on a level with that of king or emperor. What constitutes the difference between man and man, is not, urges M. Colani, the wielding a sceptre or plying a needle, but the being loyal to the trust, be it great or small, committed to us. This, he contends, is the only true point of view from which men and women should regard their occupations,—they should consider themselves as *collaborateurs du Tout-Puissant.* If their work seem the reverse of noble, let them ennoble it by this thought, in Wordsworth's phrase,—

> "And with the lofty sanctify the low."

A Christian nursemaid is pictured, forgetting the thousand *désagréments* of her humble functions, and reminding herself that in reality she is in charge of souls, as much as pastor or preacher is, and this *grande conviction* suffices to save her from servile dejection. So, again, the artisan and day labourer may be sustained by the Spirit from on high, and taught to magnify their calling, in a deep and a wide sense, because it is what they are called to, and because they respond to the call, in the spirit of it. They are toilers co-operant to an end; and the end, the result, is with God. "They also serve who only stand and wait." But the whole sonnet of Milton's which closes with that grand line, is too germane to the matter, and too largely suggestive in its main issue, to be omitted here; the sonnet which the blind poet wrote touching his blindness:—

> "When I consider how my light is spent,
> Ere half my days, in this dark world and wide,
> And that one talent which is death to hide,
> Lodged with me useless, though my soul more bent
> To serve therewith my Maker, and present
> My true account, lest He, returning, chide;
> 'Doth God exact day-labour, light denied?'
> I fondly ask: but Patience, to prevent
> That murmur, soon replies, 'God doth not need
> Either man's work, or His own gifts; who best
> Bear his mild yoke, they serve Him best; His state
> Is kingly; thousands at His bidding speed,
> And post o'er land and ocean without rest;
> They also serve who only stand and wait."

——o——

SUBORDINATE, NOT SUPERFLUOUS; OR, DEPRECIATED MEMBERSHIP.

I CORINTHIANS xii. 22.

STRENUOUSLY St. Paul insists on the importance of not overlooking the feebler members of the body—be it physical, politic, or ecclesiastical,—and of upholding their rights to due consideration, on the mere score of membership. Subordinate they may be, but superfluous they are not. The body would not be a body without them. "Nay, much more, those members of the body, which seem to be more feeble, are necessary." "Now ye are the body of Christ, and members in particular." If all were one member, where were the body? But now are they many members, but one body. And one member differeth from another in honour; yet, without the seeming minor and meaner ones, for all the abundant honour of the greater ones, where were the body?

Human society, it has been said, is a vast and intricate machine, composed of innumerable wheels and pulleys:—every one has his special handle to grind at; some with great and obvious effects, others with little or no assignable result; but if the object ultimately produced by the combined efforts of all is in itself a good one, it is not to be denied that whatever is essential to its production is good also. Human society is thus regarded as a body corporate, made up of different members, each of which has its own special function: one class tilling the ground, another combining and distributing its produce, a third making, and a fourth executing laws, and so on, through every class of society. "If all these functions are properly discharged, the whole body corporate is in a healthy condition; and thence it follows that whoever contributes to the full and proper discharge of any one of these functions, is contributing to the general good of the whole body; so that a person occupied in them is doing good in the strictest sense of the words." An able discourser on social subjects, arguing against a current crotchet, utterly denies that a girl in a respectable family does not earn the honourable title of a worker, though she be only employed in assisting in housekeeping and at the family work-table, just as fairly and as completely as if she walked to a solicitor's office for an eight hours' daily task of copying briefs and making out bills of costs.

"They work in spirit who for service wait."

Frederick Robertson glowingly expatiates on the glory of womanhood, as surely one which, if woman rightly comprehended her place on earth, might enable her to accept its apparent humiliation unrepiningly; the glory, as he defines it, of unsensualizing coarse and common things, sensual things, the objects of mere sense, meat and drink and household cares, elevating them by the spirit in which she ministers them, into something transfigured and sublime. "The humblest mother of a poor family, who is cumbered with much serving, or watching over a hospitality which she is too poor to delegate to others, or toiling for love's sake in household work, needs no emancipation in God's sight. It is the prerogative and the glory of her womanhood to consecrate the meanest things by a ministry which is not for self." What hundreds and thousands of female invalids have felt, and almost in the same words said, with Lucy Aikin, when enfeebled with age and other ailments, "The thought which sits heavy on my mind is that of my own inutility. Alas! what important end of existence do I fulfil? To whom is it of any real consequence whether or not I continue to fill a place in the world? I hope that involuntary uselessness will not be imputed, and that we may say, 'They also serve who only stand and wait.'" A fellow-worker of the same sex, but made of sterner stuff, in the dedication of a book written in illness, tells her friend, "You know, as well as I, how withering would be the sense of our own nothingness, if we tried to take comfort from our own dignity and usefulness." And she goes on to say how ridiculous, if it were not shocking, would be any complacency on the ground of having followed the instincts of her nature to work, while work was possible,—the issues of such divinely appointed instrumentality being wholly brought out and directed by Him who framed and actuated her. To apply the words of Aurora Leigh :—

. . . "Though we fail indeed,—
You, I, a score of such weak-workers,—He
Fails never. If He cannot work by us,
He will work over us. Does He want a man,
Much less a woman, think you? Every time
The star winks there, so many souls are born,
Who all shall work too. Let our own be calm:
We should be ashamed to sit beneath those stars,
Impatient that we're nothing."

So Mrs. Browning. And pitched in the self-same key is this stanza of her husband's:—

"All service ranks the same with God:
If now, as formerly He trod
Paradise, His presence fills
Our earth, each only as God wills
Can work—God's puppets, best and worst,
Are we; there is no last nor first."

Wordsworth is eloquently suggestive in those prefatory lines of his, which weave a moral and infer a solace, from the fact, that the stars pre-eminent in magnitude, and they that from the zenith dart their beams, are yet of no diviner origin, no purer essence, than the one he watched from Rydal Mount, burning like an untended watch-fire on the ridge of some dark hill-top; or than those which seem

"Humbly to hang, like twinkling winter lamps,
Among the branches of the leafless trees;
All are the undying offspring of one Sire.
Then, to the measure of the light vouchsafed,
Shine, poet, in thy place, and be content."

If we weave a yard of tape in all humility, says Emerson, and as well as we can, long hereafter we shall see that it was "no cotton tape at all, but some galaxy which we braided, and that the threads were Time and Nature." Without number, as Archdeacon Hare puts it, are the sutlers and pioneers, the engineers and artisans, who attend the march of intellect; many of them busied in building and fitting up and painting and emblazoning the chariot; others in lessening the friction of the wheels; while others move forward in detachments, and level the way it is to pass over, and cut down the obstacles which would impede its progress. And these too, he proceeds to say, "have their reward. If so be they labour diligently in their calling, not only will they enjoy that calm contentment which diligence in the lowliest task never fails to win; not only will the sweat of their brows be sweet, and the sweetener of the rest that follows; but, when the victory is at last achieved, they come in for a share of the glory; even as the meanest soldier who fought at Marathon or at Leipsic became a sharer in the glory of those saving days." Remember, with Owen Meredith,—

"Remember, every man God made
Is different: has some deed to do,
Some work to work. Be undismay'd
Though thine be humble: do it too.

An elder teacher would qualify the Remember by a Do not forget, that "it matters infinitely less what we *do* than what we *are.*" If we cannot pursue a trade or a science—says a memorable voice from a sick-room,—if we cannot keep house, or help the state, or write books, or earn our own bread or that of others, we can do the work to which all this is only subsidiary; "we can cherish a sweet and holy temper; we can vindicate the supremacy of mind over body; we can, in defiance of our liabilities, minister pleasure and hope to the gayest who come prepared to receive pain from the spectacle of our pain; we can, here as well as in heaven's courts hereafter, reveal the angel growing into its immortal aspect, which is the highest achievement we could propose to ourselves, or that grace from above could propose to us, if we had a free choice of all possible conditions of human life."

To all those possible conditions, so manifold in their potentialities, the doctrine applies. The membership is a constant quantity. *Nil me officit unquam*, says Horace, *Ditior hic, aut est quia doctior; est locus uni Cuique suus.* And we have Shakspeare's word for it, that nought so vile upon the earth doth live, but to the earth some special good doth give; and though he is speaking of stones and the like, are there not sermons in stones, as well as good in everything?

Holy George Herbert shall furnish us with a versicle to the purpose. As ever, he is looking upwards when he says,—

> "Indeed the world's Thy book
> Where all things have their leaf assign'd:
> Yet a meek look
> Hath interlined.
> Thy board is full, yet humble guests
> Find nests."

But more pertinent, and less quaintly obscure, is that stanza from another little lyric of his, in which the Country Parson exalts the exalting power of a simple trust in God and devotion to His service:

> "A servant with this clause
> Makes drudgery divine:
> Who sweeps a room, as for Thy laws,
> Makes that and the action fine."

—o—

THE WRATH-DISPELLING POWER OF A SOFT ANSWER.

PROVERBS XV. I.

WHILE it is the effect, if not the end and aim, of grievous words to stir up anger,—"a soft answer turneth away wrath." Though "the wrath of a king is as messengers of death, a wise man will pacify it." "By long forbearing is a prince persuaded, and a soft tongue breaketh the bone."

When the men of Ephraim, enraged at Gideon's failing to invoke their aid when he went to fight with the Midianites, chided with him sharply, his soft answer was of instant avail to turn away their wrath. What had he done now in comparison of them? the champion deferentially exclaimed; and what was he able to do in comparison of them? Was not the mere gleaning of the grapes of Ephraim better than the entire vintage of Abi-ezer? "Then their anger was abated toward him, when he had said that." What threatened to be a very bone of contention,—well, so soft a tongue as that of Jerubbaal, who is Gideon, breaketh the bone.

Discussing Lord Aberdeen's settlement of the vexed question of the right of search, in 1843, the historian of Europe observes that never was there a truer maxim than that it requires the consent of two persons to make a quarrel; a soft word, a seasonable explanation, often turns aside wrath, and sometimes prevents the most serious wars that threaten to devastate the world. Æsop Smith says he never knew a downright quarrel yet, where two people were not in the wrong; "drop your battledore, and the shuttlecock will fall. 'A soft answer turneth away wrath.' No doubt it does, in nine cases out of ten," —but not quite always, this authority affirms; there being some unreasonable quarrellers, who will batter the peacemaker when he drops his battledore. But as a rule, and on the authority of an older and still more widely recognised maker of proverbs, the mere fact of yielding pacifieth great offences.

The historian of the conquest of Peru tells us how Gasca was assailed by reproaches and invectives which, however, had no power to disturb his equanimity; he patiently listened, and replied to all in the mild tone of expostulation best calculated to turn away wrath. "By this victory over himself," says Garcilasso, "he acquired more real glory, than by all his victories over his foes." As Spenser has it,—

"Words well-disposed
Have secret power t' appease inflamèd rage."

Sir Matthew Hale's celebrated letter of advice includes this counsel,—if a person be passionate, and give you ill language, rather to pity him than be moved to anger. We shall find, the pious judge asserts, that silence, or very gentle words, are the most exquisite revenge for reproaches; they will either cure the distemper in the angry man, and make him sorry for his passion, or they will be a severe reproof and punishment to him. "But at any rate," adds Sir Matthew, "they will preserve your innocence, give you the deserved reputation of wisdom and moderation, and keep up the serenity and composure of your mind. Passion and anger make a man unfit for everything that becomes him as a man or as a Christian."

The fact is, maintains the author of "The Gentle Life," all hard words are a mistake: most of our quarrels arise from a total misunderstanding of each other; and at any rate, hard words will not mend the matter. One might as well, he says, try to mend glass windows by pelting them with stones. Soft words, on the other hand, fall like a healing balm on the hearts of all. "Such power," in the words of one who loved to be written, if not to write himself, Leontius, "such power has the least shadow of a pleasant speech, to do away an ill-feeling of the moment, in the complacency it produces, both in the giver and receiver." To apply, again, a passage from Spenser, descriptive of a damsel's success in deterring two doughty knights from mortal encounter, so effective was her speech to

> . . . "calm the sea of their tempestuous spite :
> Such power have pleasing words ! Such is the might
> Of courteous clemency in gentle heart !"

We are all of us fond of gentle words, once more to quote an *ex titulo* authority on all that concerns gentle living; and he denies the truth of the common rough proverb, "Soft words butter no parsnips," which is shown to be, after all, an apologetic proverb, meaning that the hearer is tickled with the politeness, albeit real satisfaction is not yet made. "Soft words do butter parsnips; and many an oily fellow, whose talent, industry, and conscientiousness are small, owes his position and advancement in life to the soft words which drop continually from his mouth." The soft answer that avails to dispel wrath, comes of practised patience; and when patience has its perfect work, it works miracles, as detailed by that fine old forgotten poet, Decker :—

> "It is the greatest enemy to law
> That can be, for it doth embrace all wrongs,
> And so chains up lawyers and women's tongues ;
>
> . . . .
>
> And last of all, to end a household strife,
> It is the honey 'gainst a waspish wife."

This reminds us of a passage in "The Gordian Knot," where the gentle laying of a husband's hand in an irritated wife's, or *vice versâ*, is recommended (by example) as a good plan to adopt in conjugal discussions when differences arise. The tongue, says our author, is very proud, abominably proud and sulky, and often refuses to say what the heart desires should be said; but the fingers know their duty, and are ready to convey an apologetic or forgiving pressure, which, he makes bold to assert, "will stop ninety-nine quarrels out of a hundred, if the parties love one another."

The greatest, widest, deepest of all observers of human nature puts into the mouth of one of the sagest of kings this counsel to a younger son, in respect to his bearing towards the elder:—

. . . "Blunt not his love; . . .
For he is gracious, if he be observed; *
Yet notwithstanding, being incensed, he's flint:
As humorous as winter, and as sudden
As flaws† congealed in the spring of day.
His temper, therefore, must be well observed:
Chide him for faults, and do it reverently,
When you perceive his blood inclined to mirth:
But being moody, give him line and scope;
Till that his passions, like a whale on ground,
Confound themselves with working."

In a later one, again, of his noble series of English history plays—indeed the latest—Shakspeare makes a ducal politician, astute in practical psychology as well as in politics, utter this apophthegm, of his own coinage:—

"Anger is like
A full-hot horse, who being allowed his way,
Self-mettle tires him."

* That is, if attention be shown him.
† Gusts of wind.

A TWICE-TOLD TALE OF YEARS.

ECCLESIASTES vi. 6.

THE preacher, whose text was Vanity of vanities, all is vanity, pictures in one section of his homily a man who has lived many years, "so that the days of his years be many," but whose soul is not filled with good, but aches rather with a gnawing sense of emptiness, so that his many years, gloomy as they have been, are all too few. "Yea, though he live a thousand years twice told, yet hath he seen no good: do not all go to one place?" What more tedious than such a twice-told tale of years? Yet, to look back upon, how fleet their transit, how imperceptible their lapse, how petty the sum of them! That tale is soon told, even if told twice.

The days of our life are threescore years and ten, and though men be so strong that they come to fourscore years, yet is their strength then but labour and sorrow; nor do the fourscore seem longer to the retrospective reviewer than do to the sexagenarian his sixty years, or to the septuagenarian his threescore and ten. The most popular of contemporary authors describes a man of seventy-eight, of whom a loveless, sad-hearted questioner asks whether his seventy-eight years would not be seventy-eight heavy curses, if he could say to himself, as the questioner can, "I have secured to myself the love and attachment, the gratitude or respect, of no human creature; I have won myself a tender place in no regard; I have done nothing good or serviceable to be remembered by." The Royal Preacher would apply context as well as text to such a retrospect, with an "I say, that an untimely birth is better than he. For he cometh in with vanity, and departeth in darkness, and his name shall be covered with darkness. Moreover he hath not seen the sun, nor known anything: this hath more rest than the other. Yea, though he live a thousand years twice told, yet hath he seen no good."

The same questioner, already cited, asks the same old man if his childhood seems far off,—if the days when he sat at his mother's knee seem days of very long ago? To which the experience of threescore and eighteen years gives this reply: "Twenty years back, yes: at this time of my life, no. For, as I draw closer and closer to the end, I travel in the circle, nearer and nearer to the beginning." But he is not one to feel and say with the French cynic, "Mais enfin la vie se passe, et mourir après s'être amusé ou s'être ennuyé dix ou vingt ans, c'est la même chose." He has not so learned life, and the meaning of life, and its purpose, and its end.

Infinite is the swiftness of time, says Seneca, as seen by those who are looking back at time past. *Infinita est velocitas temporis, quæ magis apparet respicientibus.* Looked forward to, it is another matter altogether. As Cowper has it, when retracing the windings of his way through many years,—

> "Short as in retrospect the journey seems,
> It seemed not always short; the rugged path,
> And prospect oft so dreary and forlorn,
> Moved many a sigh at its disheartening length."

But as Cowper elsewhere draws the contrast, in the Latin motto he wrote for the king's clock,—

> "Quæ lenta accedit, quam velox præterit hora!"

(Slow comes the hour; its passing speed how great!—so Hayley Englished the line.) "Since this new epoch in my life," writes Schleiermacher on a certain occasion, "time seems to fly twice as quickly as before, and I can quite fancy that when Jatte and I are grown old and grey, we shall still feel as if only a few days had gone by." Moore was in his sixtieth year when Lord John Russell talked with him of the speed with which time seems to fly; and Moore records in his Diary the question he put, "If you find it so now, what will you say of it when you are as old as I am?" The "peculiar melancholy" of the answer given is emphasised in the same journal.

Another retrospective reviewer pictures our race as struggling ever onward, toiling up towards some air-built goal never to be attained—while the past crumbles instantly away behind our steps, like the staircase of the Epicurean, as we advance in our progress; and every step, which was of such magnitude when we passed it, is forgotten in the "collectiveness of retrospection," insomuch that at times a passing thought would compass the events of years.

Few and evil the patriarch declares the days of the years of his pilgrimage to have been, when, in answer to Pharaoh's "How old art thou?" the answer is, A hundred and thirty years. Man that is born of a woman is of few days, said another patriarch, and full of trouble. His days are swifter than a post, they flee away, they see no good. They are passed away as the swift ships; they are swifter than a weaver's shuttle. *Festinat enim decurrere velox Flosculus angustæ miseræque brevissima vitæ Portio.* And thus in Juvenal's pregnant phrase, *obrepit non intellecta senectus.* Or, as with the ageing subject of the Three Warnings,—

> "Old Time whose haste no mortal spares,
> Uncalled, unheeded, unawares,
> Brought him on his eightieth year."

We bring our years to an end, as it were a tale that is told.

In one of his letters to his old friend Mrs. Hughes, Southey commences a paragraph with the truism, "The last twenty years, to you and me, are but as yesterday;" and he adds, that if we could but bring ourselves to feel, as truly as we know, that the next twenty years are but as to-morrow, that feeling, with a trust in God's mercy, would be sufficient consolation under all sorrows. Half a year later we find him writing to her in the same strain: "It seems but as yesterday when I look back twenty, thirty, forty, and even more years; the end, therefore, of my mortal term would seem but as to-morrow if it were rightly looked on to. A little while, and we shall be young again, beyond all power of time and change, with those whom we love, and to continue with them for ever and ever." Madame de Sévigné utters her pure French hélas! over the like retrospect of twenty years: "Hélas! est-il possible qu'il y ait vingt-un ans? il me esembleque ce fut l'année passée; mais je juge, par le peu que m'a duré ce temps, ce que me paraîtront les années qui viendront encore." Home, straight home to every heart comes the homely moral of the bard addressing the busy, curious, thirsty fly he freely welcomed to his cup, and whose little life he compared with his longer yet little own :—

> "Both alike are mine and thine,
> Hastening quick to their decline :
> Thine's a summer, mine no more,
> Though repeated to threescore ;
> Threescore summers, when they're gone,
> Will appear as short as one."

If for threescore we read fourscore, it would not mar the metre, or the rhyme or reason.

Man is never so deluded as when he dreams of his own duration, says Cowper; and he goes on to cite Jacob's retrospective reviewal of years elapsed : "The answer of the old patriarch to Pharaoh may be adapted by every man at the close of the longest life. 'Few and evil have been the days of the years of my pilgrimage.' Whether we look back from fifty or from twice fifty, the past equally appears a dream; and we can only be said truly to have lived while we have been profitably employed." And as the sovereign lady of French letter-writers has her Hélas ! so one of the princes among English letter-writers has his Alas ! to utter on this trite topic, "Alas, then, making the necessary deductions, how short is life !" Though the life be made up of a thousand years twice told, the tale is told so soon, and the teller seems to himself but as a dreamer, and his little life is rounded with a sleep; like as a dream when one awaketh.

The good emperor Marcus Antoninus, one of those whom a broad churchmanship is free and fain to recognise as Seekers after God, is taken to intimate that the difference between a so-called long and a short life is insignificant, in regard of Eternity, when he indites this aphorism, among his Meditations : "When frankincense is thrown upon the altar, one grain usually falls before another; but then the distance of time is of no moment." The moments, so to speak, of difference, are not momentous. Do not all go to one place ?

But in the issue, all depends on the using. Happy the few

and evil years of a patriarch, if a patriarch indeed, of a pilgrim going home. Be they few and evil in one sense, or in another very many,—

> "They will appear like moments when he soars
> Beyond those sunbreaks."

——o——

DAYBREAK NO SOLACE: NIGHTFALL NO RELIEF.

DEUTERONOMY xxviii. 36, 37.

NOT the least impressive of the afflictions denounced against a disloyal people, in the book Deuteronomy, is that which should make day and night a fear and a trouble to them; so that in the morning they should say, "Would God it were even!" and at even, "Would God it were morning!" There is at once terrible realism and suggestiveness in words but too familiar to most who have themselves suffered, or watched by the couch of sleepless suffering. Job utters a complaint of wearisome nights as appointed to him; so that when he lay down, he said, "When shall I arise, and the night be gone?" and thus was he full of tossings to and fro unto the dawning of the day. Like the Psalmist, he cried in the daytime, but it seemed that God heard not; and in the night season he was not silent, but it seemed as though from above there was neither voice, nor any to answer, nor any that regarded. In such cases, one day telleth another of seeming desolation; and one night certifieth another almost of despair. And the eventide is longed for in broad daylight, if haply, with mere change, it may bring relief. But when it has set in, and eve has saddened into night, there is wearying for daybreak, as possibly the bringer of a boon that, however, it fails to bring.

A stanza in one of Shakspeare's poems contains an example to the purpose:—

> "Thus ebbs and flows the current of her sorrow,
> And time doth weary time with her complaining:
> She looks for night, and then she longs for morrow;
> And both she thinks too long with her remaining:
> Short time seems long in sorrow's sharp sustaining.

Though woe be heavy, yet it seldom sleeps;
And they that watch, see time how slow it creeps."

And thus runs one of Landor's imitations from the Greek, of an address to Hesperus:—

"I have beheld thee in the morning hour,
A solitary star, with thankless eyes,
Ungrateful as I am! who bade thee rise
When sleep all night had wandered from my bower."

One of, and not the least fearful of, the curses denounced against Byron's Manfred is, that to him shall Night deny all the quiet of her sky; and the day shall have a sun which shall make him wish it done. Crabbe's Tale of Edward Shore has to tell how, at one stage of that sombre career,—

"Struck by new terrors, from his friends he fled,
And wept his woes upon a restless bed;
Retiring late, at early hour to rise,
With shrunken features, and with bloodshot eyes;
If sleep one moment closed the dismal view,
Fancy her terrors built upon the true;
And night and day had their alternate woes,
That baffled pleasure, and that mocked repose."

The hero of one popular prose fiction describes himself as lying awake night after night, quivering with his great sorrow—wishing that the first dull grey of morning would appear at the window; and when it came, longing for night and darkness once more. Of the heroine in another we read that "the terrible 'demon of the bed,' that invests our lightest sorrows with such hopeless and crushing anxiety, reigned triumphant over its gentle victim; and yet, when the daylight crept through her uncurtained windows, she shrunk from it, as though in her broken spirit she preferred to hide her distress in the gloom of night, fearful and unrelieved as was its dark dominion." How sickening, how dark, exclaims Keats, in the fantastic diction of "Endymion," "the dreadful leisure of weary days, made deeper exquisite by a foreknowledge of unslumbrous night!" Mr. Tennyson pictures to us the simple maid Elaine, who went half the night repeating, Must she die?

"And now to right she turned, and now to left,
And found no ease in turning or in rest"—

like one of those depicted by Keble—

". . . who darkling and alone,
Would wish the weary night were gone,
Though dawning morn should only show
The secret of their unknown woe."

Shelley sings of the desire "of the night for the morrow" when expressing the devotion to something afar from the sphere of our sorrow. Gray vividly depicts the state of mind of one who—

". . . starts from short slumbers, and wishes for morning—
To close his dull eyes when he sees it returning."

Of Mrs. Gaskell's Jemima we read, that "the night, the sleepless night, was so crowded and haunted by miserable images, that she longed for day; and when day came, with its stinging realities, she wearied and grew sick for the solitude of night." So with Shenstone's Jessie:—

"Amid the dreary gloom of night I cry,
When will the morn's once pleasing scenes return?
Yet what can morn's returning ray supply,
But foes that triumph, or but friends that mourn?"

BUYER'S BARGAIN AND BOAST.

PROVERBS XX. 14.

CONSIDERING what goes to make up a proverb, it would be strange if, in the book of Proverbs, part though it be of holy writ, there should be no touches of the humorous, however restrained and dignified its manifestation. Shrewd insight into character, finding expression in phrases of homely vigour, or tranquil irony, or two-edged sarcasm,—without much of this, what were a book of proverbs? Assuredly the collected proverbs of Solomon, the son of David, king of Israel, are not careful to eschew a touch of humour when the subject invites, or allows of, not to say requires it. Such a subject we have, and such a touch of the jocose, in a verse which sets forth so tersely the tactics of traffickers and bargain-makers; how the bidder depreciates the wares he is bidding for, until they are his; and how he alters his tone then, and brags at once of their superior worth, and of his own superior skill in effecting a purchase. He haggles, and beats them down, and pooh-poohs them, as all but unsaleable, while yet they are on sale; but so soon as the bargain is struck, he goes on his way rejoicing, and perhaps calls his kinsfolk and acquaintance together, to rejoice with him, for he has bought dirt cheap what was worth its weight in gold. "It is naught, it is naught, saith the buyer; but when he is gone his way, then he boasteth."

The Paris of "Troilus and Cressida" compliments, or, as may be, upbraids a subtle Greek with his dexterity in this line of policy:—

> "Fair Diomede, you do as chapmen do,
> Dispraise the thing that you desire to buy."

In measure with the intending buyer's dispraise, is kept up by the would-be seller a song of praise. As Horace has it, *Laudat venales qui vult extrudere merces;* and the laudation is apt to be in inverse proportion to the intrinsic worth of his wares. Good wine may need no bush; but bad wine, on that showing, may need one as big as a tree; and the wine merchant is equal to the occasion.

A. K. H. B. has said of men in towns, aware of the value of time, that by long experience they are assured of the uselessness of trying to overreach a neighbour in a bargain, because he is so sharp that they will not succeed. But in agricultural districts such practical essayists in the art of overreaching are declared to be common enough and to spare; and it is one of the Recreations of the Country Parson aforenamed (initially at least) to mark out in detail the course which these bargain-makers are alleged invariably to follow. "If they wish to buy a cow or rent a field, they begin by declaring with frequency and vehemence that they don't want the thing,—that in fact they would rather not have it,—that it would be inconvenient for them to become possessors of it. They then go on to say that still, if they can get it at a fair price, they may be induced to think of it. They next declare that the cow is the very worst that ever was seen, and that very few men would have such a creature in their possession." And so on,—till the strenuous haggler, after wasting two hours, telling sixty-five lies, and stamping himself as a cheat, ends the negotiation, without taking anything at all by his petty trickery, so complicated and so clumsy withal in its convolutions.

It is in his estimate of the real merits of English horses, that Fuller discreetly observes, in meting out temperate but cordial praise of their good points, "And whilst the seller praiseth them too much, the buyer too little, the indifferent stander-by will give them their due commendation." What was true of horseflesh and its breeders and purchasers, in old Fuller's day holds good still. Type of a large class is that manœuvring major in a popular fiction, of whom, and of his "bargains" in the stable—mostly sedate, elderly animals—we read, that certainly, if the animals could have spoken, they would have expressed their surprise at the difference in the language used by the major when a buyer and when a seller; for while, as a buyer, he made them out to be, like Gil Blas' mule, all faults, as a seller he suddenly came round to believe in them as paragons of perfection.

Leigh Hunt records as his experience of the Italians at home, that to cheat you through thick and thin was the universal endeavour—so that a perpetual warfare was inevitable, in which you were obliged to fight in self-defence. "If you paid anybody what he asked you, it never entered into his imagination that you did it from anything but folly. You were pronounced a *minchione* (a ninny), one of their greatest terms of reproach. On the other hand, if you battled well through the bargain, a perversion of the natural principle of self-defence led to a feeling of respect for you." Dispute might increase, it is added; the man might grin, stare, threaten; might pour out torrents of argument and of "injured innocence," as they always do; but be firm, and he went away equally angry and admiring. "Did anybody condescend to take them in, the admiration as well as the anger was still in proportion, like that of the gallant knights of old when they were beaten in single combat." Such chaffering, or "prigging," as Burns calls it (in his satiric touch at town councillors waddling down the street, in all the pomp of ignorant conceit,—

"Men wha grew wise prigging owre hops and raisins),"

such haggling, and stickling, and demurring, and deferring, are too truly said to distinguish the British system of arranging settlements—in which, embodying completely the Oriental theory of marriage, a woman is dealt with "as a valuable security, to be exchanged for due consideration." A marriage conducted according to the approved principles is therefore "a matter of sharp, close bargaining. No sooner is the romantic part of it over, than it is surrendered to the lawyers, who proceed to chaffer over it and cheapen their adversary's claim, as they might do if they were purchasing a cow." A self-styled Oriental student of the modern Syrians, in a book bearing that title, graphically sketches a representative bargaining scene in a café at Damascus, between a Christian indigo-dealer, in Beyrout costume, and a Jewish dyer; the former pretending to feel insulted at being offered so low a price, and the latter pretending to get into a passion at having his time taken up with a fruitless negotiation. Captain Marryat's Travels in North America supply a plurality of parallel passages; now of two misses "swopping" bonnets, with an assumed indifference and a suppressed ardour almost ridiculous enough to verge on the sublime; and now of a couple of Down-Easters, whittling all the while they are bargaining, and doing both with all their might and main. Fiction-writers who make a study of character and manners are fond of introducing scenes of this kind. Scott's Antiquary chuckles over his feats in cheapening old curiosities, and delights to tell how often he has stood haggling on a halfpenny, lest, by a too ready acquiescence in the dealer's first price, he should be led to suspect the value Mr. Oldbuck sets upon the article: "And then, Mr. Lovel, the sly satisfaction with which one pays the consideration, and pockets the article, affecting a cold indifference, while the hand is trembling with pleasure!" The bargaining match with Maggie, the Fairport fishwife, is one of the gems of the story. Mr. Charles Reade offers a racy pendant in his trafficking encounter between Christie Johnstone, the pride of Newhaven, and the four Irish merchants who have agreed to work together, and to make a show of competition, the better to keep the price down within bounds, but who are no match for woman's wit and woman's tongue, as exercised by Christie. The author of "Doctor Jacob" depicts in Herr Schmidt a rosy, round man, with eyes that were never in tune with his mouth; the former being sharp, Jewish, and speculative; the latter, supine, commercial, and conservative: "He made use of his eyes when he bought, and of his mouth when he sold, giving his customers to understand that he was the easiest going man in the world, only desirous of small profits, and by no means miserable if a gold watch or any other article went for half its value." Canon Kingsley enlivens the adventures of "Hereward" with a certain Dick Hammerhand, the richest man in Walcheren, who tries to overreach the hero, and fails to his cost; one stage of the transaction taking this turn: "The less anxious the stranger seemed to buy, the more anxious grew Dick to sell; but he concealed his anxiety, and let the stranger turn away, thanking him for his drink," but anon renewing the treaty with as much semblance of disregard as he could put on. The author of "The Gayworthys" works up a clever bit of homely chaffering between Mrs. Vorse and Widow Horke the strawberry-dealer. And we find ourselves between a couple of horse-dealers again in "Silas Marner:" "Bryce of course divined that Dunstan wanted to sell the horse, and Dunstan knew that he divined it (horse-dealing is only one of many human transactions carried on in this ingenious manner); and they both considered that the bargain was in its first stage, when Bryce replied ironically, [to the other's boast of a recent high bid,] 'I wonder at that now, I wonder you mean to keep him; for I never heard of a man who didn't want to sell his horse, getting a bid of half as much again as the horse was worth,'" etc. Trust Bryce to boast of that horse, and of that bargain, so soon as he is gone his way, the horse his, and the bargain made. It must be a distorted type of human nature that resembles the discontented man of Theophrastus, who, after taking a great deal of pains to beat down the price of a slave, and after he has paid his money for him,—instead of boasting, breaks out into the grumble, "I am sure thou art good for nothing, or I should not have had thee so cheap." A companion picture, in its way, but with the difference between an inveterate grumbler and an impenetrable oaf, is that by Plautus of a fool with an old grange to sell, of which property he advertises the singular attractions to draw buyers to bid and buy. Nothing ever thrived on it, he says; no owner of it ever died in his bed; the trees were all blasted; the swine died of the measles, the cattle of the murrain, the sheep of the rot; nothing was ever reared there, not a duckling, or goose. *Hospitium fuit calamitatis.* It is naught, it is naught, saith the buyer? No, the seller, in this case.

——o——

GRAY-HAIRED UNAWARES.

HOSEA vii. 9.

AMONG the reminders and remonstrances which it was the mission of the prophet, the son of Beeri, in the days of Ahaz and Hezekiah, to deliver to Ephraim, there was this significant passage, expressive of a reckless people's unconscious decline, whose lapses were taken account of on high, and Ephraim knew it not—"Yea, gray hairs are here and there upon him, yet he knoweth not."

Who, asks Hartley Coleridge, ever saw their first gray hairs, or marked the crow feet at the angle of their eyes, without a sigh or a tear, a momentaneous self-abasement, a sudden sinking of the soul, a thought that youth is fled for ever? "None but the blessed few that, having dedicated their spring of life to Heaven, behold in the shedding of their vernal blossoms a promise that the season of immortal fruit is near." Gray hairs, in an advancing stage of the plural number, may be here and there upon us before we know of it. But the actual discovery of the first is a bit of an epoch in one's life; and if one exclaims Eureka! it is hardly in the most jubilant of tones or the most exultant of tempers.

Falstaff was surprised into a full purpose of amendment of life when he lighted on the first white hair on his chin; but only to keep on renewing the purpose weekly, long after chin and head, too, must have been covered with silver or snow.

With some the humour is to pass off the discovery in seeming glee; and perhaps it is the saturnine, melancholy temperament that is likeliest to do this. For instance, Gerbier relates of Charles the First, that one morning "as the King was combing his head, he found a white hair, which he sent to the Queen in merriment. Henrietta Maria immediately wrote back that Don Carlos would cause many more to come up before the Emperor gave up the Palatinate." Had the King not been himself combing his head on this not too auspicious occasion, the probability is, as courts and courtiers go, that his first white hair would not thus have been allowed to attract and invite attention. A courtly dresser would have been shocked to reveal what he saw, and would have kept the secret with *ex officio* conscientiousness. Many and many are the uncrowned heads upon which gray hairs are gathering here and there—a familiar sight enough to overseeing (and not overlooking) attendants or friends, but by the owners themselves unsuspected as yet. Mrs. Browning lets Aurora Leigh espy one such straggler, which even the neat-handed maid-in-waiting overlooks, at Lady Waldemar's toilet:—

"Her maid must use both hands to twist that coil
Of tresses, then be careful lest the rich
Bronze rounds should slip:—she missed, though, a gray hair,
A single one,—I saw it; otherwise
The woman looked immortal."

It is among the graver of his Recreations that a clerical essayist pictures to himself man or woman, thoughtful, earnest, and pious, sitting down and musing, at the sight of the first gray hairs. Here is the slight shadow, he puts it, of "a certain great event which is to come;" the earliest touch of a chill hand which must prevail at length. "Here is manifest decay: we have begun to die. And no worthy human being will pretend that this is other than a very solemn thought. And we look backward as well as forward: how short a time since we were little children, and kind hands smoothed down the locks now grown scanty and gray." So in Mrs. Southey's (Caroline Bowles') tender, simple verses on the same trite theme:—

"Some there were took fond delight,
Sporting with these tresses bright,
To enring with living gold
Fingers now beneath the mould
(Woe is me!) grown icy cold.
* * * * *
Now again a shining streak
'Gins the dusky cloud to break;—
Here and there a glittering thread
Lights the ringlets, dark and dead—
Glittering light!—but pale and cold—
Glittering thread!—but *not* of *gold*.

Silent warning! silvery streak!
Not unheeded dost thou speak.
Not with feelings light and vain,
Not with fond, regretful pain,
Look I on the token sent
To declare the day far spent."

Mr. Thackeray makes his youngish widow, Amelia Osborne, take tranquilly enough this sort of revelation. "In these quiet labours and harmless cares the gentle widow's life was passing away, a silver hair or two marking the progress of time on her head, and a line deepening ever so little on her fair forehead. She used to smile at these marks of time." Which accords with her placid temperament. Quite otherwise constituted is Currer Bell's Madame Beck. "A loud bell rang for morning school. She got up. As she passed a dressing-table with a glass upon it, she looked at her reflected image. One single white hair streaked her nut-brown tresses; she plucked it out with a shudder." That is an early phase of the decadence of which Mr. Robert Browning graphically depicts a later stage :—

> "One day, as the lady saw her youth
> Depart, and the silver thread that streaked
> Her hair, and, worn by the serpent's tooth,
> The brow so puckered, the chin so peaked—
> She wondered who the woman was,
> So hollow-eyed and haggard-cheeked."

Mr. Trollope's Captain Cutwater is the representative of a large constituency in at least this one salient particular, that he "had no idea that he was an old man. He had lived for so many years among men of his own stamp, who had grown gray and bald and rickety and weak alongside of him," that when he moved into a younger circle, and settled there, he ignored the disparity of ages. In Juvenal's emphatic phrase, old age steals upon us unawares,—unperceived, unrecognised : *obrepit non intellecta senectus.* This stealthy in-coming, or on-coming, of old age is an iterated topic in the classics. Cicero, indeed, had been beforehand with Juvenal, almost word for word : *non intelligitur quando obrepit senectus.* There is Ovid, again, with his "stealthy lapse" of age, beguiling as it wears away : *labitur occulte, fallitque volubilis ætas ;* and with his elsewhere reminder, that time glides on, and with noiseless years we grow older till we grow old : *Tempora labuntur, tacitisque senescimus annis.* Without, as Hazlitt says, our in the least suspecting it, the mists are at our feet, and the shadows of age encompass us. Leigh Hunt somewhere comments feelingly on the difficulty of learning how narrow and dim a boundary separates mature from old age ; and quoting his own personal experience, says, that a single illness made the line of demarcation clear to him. So M. de Ste.-Beuve : *Rien n'est penible à démêler comme les confins des ages : il faut souvent que quelque chose vienne du dehors et coupe court.*

There is all the more force in the kindly wish of Mr. Tennyson's Will Waterproof, that the plump object of it may live long, ere from his topmost head the thickset hazel dies ; long, ere the hateful crow shall tread the corners of his eyes; all the more force as coming from one who has to own of himself—

"For I had hope, by something rare,
To prove myself a poet;
But, while I plan, and plan, my hair
Is gray before I know it."

—o—

RESTRAINED ANGER.

PROVERBS xvi. 32.

"HE that is slow to anger is better than the mighty; and he that ruleth his spirit than he that taketh a city." To be ruled by one's angry spirit is cruel bondage indeed, for that taskmaster never spares the lash. To rule or to be ruled,—that is the question.

"Ira furor brevis est: animum rege; qui, nisi paret,
Imperat: hunc frenis, hunc tu compesce catenâ."

Marcus Antoninus, in his Meditations, calls rage and resentment marks of an unmanly disposition; mildness and temper being not only more humane, but, he contends, more masculine too. And the philosophic emperor wrote and spoke as one of, what Mr. Matthew Arnold calls, those

". . . milder natures, and more free,
Whom an unblamed serenity
Hath freed from passions, and the state
Of struggle these necessitate."

From that state of struggle many a victor emerges with honourable scars, but deep. Famous and significant is the story of the physiognomist who detected in the features ot Socrates the traces of that fiery temper which for the most part he kept in severe control, but which, when it did break loose, is described by those who witnessed it as absolutely terrible, overleaping both in act and language every barrier of the ordinary decorum of Grecian manners. Le Clerc's *éloge* ot John Locke includes the remark that if he had any defect, it was the being somewhat passionate; "but he had got the better of it by reason, and it was very seldom that it did him or any one else any harm." Of Rudolf of Hapsburg we are told that he was by nature warm and choleric, but that as he advanced in years he corrected this defect. To some of his friends, expressing their wonder that since his elevation to the imperial dignity he had restrained the vehemence of his temper, the founder of the House of Austria replied, "I have often repented of being passionate, never of being mild and humane." One of Cromwell's biographers reports his "temper exceeding fiery; but the flame of it kept down for the most part, or soon allayed with those moral endowments he had." The admirable Frederick Borromeo was admired for a placability, a sweetness of manner nearly imperturbable, which, however, as Manzoni reminds us, was not natural to the devout prelate, but was the effect of continual combat against a quick and hasty disposition. Lord Clarendon more than once in his autobiography, plumes himself on having mastered and "suppressed that heat and passion he was naturally inclined to be transported with." "They who knew the great infirmity of his whole family, which abounded in passion, used to say he had much extinguished the unruliness of that fire." Lord Macaulay turns to the advantage of his favourite chancellor the assertion of his detractors, that the disposition of the great Somers was very far from being so gentle as the world believed, that he was really prone to the angry passions, and that sometimes, while his voice was soft, and his words kind and courteous, his delicate frame was almost convulsed by suppressed emotion. His brilliant advocate is fain to accept this reproach as the highest of all eulogies. Again: Sir Archibald Alison assures us of Sir Robert Peel, that he was by nature afflicted with a most violent temper, and that so extreme were his paroxysms of anger, when a young man, that he used, while they were coming on, to shut himself up alone till the dark fit was over. "By degrees, however, he obtained the mastery of this infirmity, and this at length so effectually that he passed with the world, at a distance, as a man of a singularly cold and phlegmatic temperament."

Lady Holland reports her distinguished father to have been naturally choleric,—prefacing the statement by a reflection, that, although it is not the part of a daughter to reveal faults, yet a fault nobly repaired, or repented of, adds to the respect and interest which a character inspires. By her showing, then, Mr. Sydney Smith was by nature quick and hasty, but always struggled against the failing, and made many regulations to avoid exciting any such emotions; and when he did give way, it often excited his biographer's admiration to see him gradually subduing his chafed spirit, and to observe his dissatisfaction with himself till he had humbled himself and made his peace, it mattered not with whom, groom or child. "He could not bear the reproaches of his own heart." So Mr. Henry Rogers observes of Locke, and his success, by dint of "immense pains" taken, in subjugating his choleric propensity, that his anxiety for its complete subjugation appears in his never being so angry with another as he always was with himself—for being angry. Those who are conversant with the journal and letters of Dr. Chalmers, may remember how often that good man takes himself to task for infirmities of temper, and how strenuously he resolves to strive to keep down every tendency to irritation when in company, to "try to maintain a vigorous contest with this unfortunate peculiarity of my temper," to "school down every irritable feeling;" and how remorsefully he records such instances as getting "into a violent passion with Sandy," and getting "ruffled with Jane," in a manner and to a degree "quite unchristian." Passages abound such as, "Now is the time for reflecting on the evils of intemperate passion;" "erred egregiously this evening in venting my indignation;" "I may at least ward off the assaults of anger;" "erred in betraying my anger to my servant and wife;" "constant visitations of indignancy; this exceedingly wrong: there is not a greater foe to spirituality than wrath." "O my God, deliver me from all rancour and much irritableness," * etc., etc. "Here," to apply the lines of Wordsworth's son-in-law,—

* See Hanna's Life of Chalmers, Journal of 1810 and of 1825-6, *passim*.

> "Here was a temper less by nature tuned
> Than harmonized by discipline to rule,
> And by religion sanctified to peace."

The pen is too truly said to be a fruitful source of regrets to some of us, in regard of the outbreaks of temper we allow it to put on paper; and never is the sting sharper, says one essayist, than when we realize that our imprudence is in black and white, beyond our reach, irrevocable. "We send off our letter, to repent sometimes how bitterly!" *Litera scripta manet.* Hence the advice of another, never to write in anger, or, at any rate, to keep your letter till you are cool. We are recommended, when indignant at any one's conduct, to write a letter couched in the strongest terms possible, as satirical and cutting as we can make it, and having done this, to direct, seal, and put it in our desk for a few hours, then read it for our own satisfaction, and tear it up. Another popular authority, earnestly deprecating angry letters, lays down as a rule to be observed throughout the letter-writing world, that no angry letter be posted till four and twenty hours shall have elapsed since it was written. "We all know how absurd is that other rule, of saying the alphabet when you are angry. Trash! Sit down and write your letter; write it with all the venom in your power; spit out your spleen at the fullest; it will do you good: you think you have been injured; say all that you can say with all your poisoned eloquence, and gratify yourself by reading it while your temper is still hot. Then put it in your desk, and, as a matter of course, burn it before breakfast the following morning. Believe me that you will then have a double gratification." *Loquitur* the perhaps most widely read, and without a perhaps the most prolific, writer of the day.

When Cœur-de-Lion, in Scott's "Talisman," incensed and mortified at the Templar's tactics, yet foresaw the penalty of giving way to his headlong resentment, with a strong effort he remained silent till he had repeated a pater noster, that being the course which "his confessor had enjoined him to pursue when anger was likely to obtain dominion over him." The familiar "count five-and-twenty, Tattycoram," in one of Mr. Dickens' later stories is but another practical application of the selfsame text.

Gibbon adds to his account of the public penance inflicted by Ambrose on Theodosius, for the massacre of Thessalonica, this remark: "and the edict which interposes a salutary interval of thirty days between the sentence and the execution, may be accepted as the worthy fruits of his [the emperor's] repentance." For it was by a hasty resolve that Theodosius swore in his wrath to expiate the blood of his lieutenant, Botheric, by the blood of a guilty people; his fiery and choleric temper being impatient of the dilatory forms of a judicial inquiry. In hot haste he despatched the messengers of death; but attempted, when it was too late, to prevent the execution of his own orders. Avenging furiously in haste, he had to repent at leisure; and he did repent.

It is impossible, perhaps, observed Dean Swift, for the best and wisest among us to keep so constant a guard upon our temper but that we may at some time or other lie open to the strokes of fortune. Incensed on one occasion, "it was natural for me to have immediate recourse to my pen and ink; but before I would offer to make use of them, I resolved deliberately to tell over a hundred; and when I came to the end of that sum, I found it more advisable to defer drawing up my intended remonstrance till I had slept soundly on my resentments." We are told of the celebrated Macklin, that although so particular in drilling the performers at rehearsals, he was scrupulous in keeping his temper down, the irritability of which he knew too well; and that on one occasion he interposed an hour by his stop-watch, all retiring together from the stage to the green-room, at the end of which time all were in good humour again, and the rehearsal was resumed. "When the evil effects of hasty anger approach, the consequences of which may be irretrievable,"—thus moralizes a fellow-craftsman, John O'Keeffe,—"it would be no harm if all of us could suppress our own feelings, even for Macklin's green-room hour." His mighty master, Shakspeare, would have supplied him with a precedent, in the case of good Duke Humphrey, who says as he re-enters,—

> "Now, lords, my choler being overblown
> With walking once about the quadrangle,
> I come to talk of commonwealth affairs."

Sir Thomas Fowell Buxton's secretary, Mr. Nixon, on his own showing, could not refrain from blurting out just what he felt at the moment, when differences arose between the two. This used to vex Sir Thomas, who however would say nothing till the next day, and then, when the secretary thought that the whole matter had passed off (having perhaps received great kindness in the meantime), the remonstrance would come out, "What a silly fellow you were, Nixon, to put yourself in such a passion yesterday! If I had spoken then, we should most probably have parted. Make it a rule never to speak when you are in a passion, but wait till the next day." And we are assured that, if at any time he happened to transgress this rule himself, he was seriously vexed and grieved, and could not rest till he had in some way made amends for his want of self-restraint.

Molière's Arnolphe propounds the prophylactic rule with emphasis and discretion :

> "Un certain Grec disait à l'empereur Auguste,
> Comme une instruction utile autant que juste,
> Que lorsqu'une aventure en colére nous met,
> Nous devons, avant tout, dire notre alphabet,
> Afin que dans ce temps la bile se tempère,
> Et qu'on ne fasse rien que l'on ne doive faire."

——o——

EVANESCENCE OF THE EARLY DEW.

HOSEA vi. 3.

BY the word of the prophet Hosea, the Divine reproach fell on Ephraim and on Judah, that their goodness was as a morning cloud, and that as the early dew it passed away. Bright was the promise of innocent dawn, but the promise was unfulfilled. A stern moral application lies in the words of Dante:

> ". . . The will in man
> Bears goodly blossoms; but its ruddy promise
> Is, by the dripping of perpetual rain,
> Made mere abortion: faith and innocence
> Are met with but in babes; each taking leave
> Ere cheeks with down are sprinkled."

Adam Smith observes, in his "Theory of Moral Sentiment," that, in the eye of nature, it would seem, a child is a more important object than an old man, and excites a much more lively, as well as a much more universal sympathy. "It ought to do so," he adds. "Everything may be expected, or at least hoped, from the child. In ordinary cases, very little can be either expected or hoped from the old man." It is regretful, remorseful eld that is supposed to utter the lament, in gazing on childish faces and forms, heaven-encompassed infancy,—

> "O little souls! as pure and white
> And crystalline as rays of light
> Direct from heaven, their source divine;
> Refracted through the mist of years,
> How red my setting sun appears,
> How lurid looks this soul of mine!"

Mrs. Trench writes to the poet of the "Pleasures of Memory," and with direct reference to that poem, "In looking back, the only days I earnestly desire to recall, are those which glided away while I was 'girt with growing infancy,' and read in the eyes and the smiles of my children, who were affectionate and beautiful, a promise of happiness, such as this world can never fulfil." A more vigorous poet than Samuel Rogers, has a vigorous but gloomy stanza on the kindling emotions of young motherhood, when the wife—

> "Blest into mother, in the innocent look,
> Or even the piping cry of lips that brook
> No pain and small suspense, a joy perceives
> Man knows not, when from out its cradled nook

She sees her little bud put forth its leaves—
What may the fruits be yet?—I know not—Cain was Eve's."

The fallen young mother in Mrs. Gaskell's story hails in her child a new, pure, beautiful, innocent life, which she fondly imagines, in the early passion of maternal love, she can guard from every touch of corrupting sin by ever watchful and most tender care. "And *her* mother had thought the same, most probably; and thousands of others think the same, and pray to God to purify and cleanse their souls, that they may be fit guardians for their little children."

Juvenal asks, "what morn's so holy but its sun betrays theft, perfidy, and fraud." The thief, the betrayer, the cheat, was once a child. Ovid urges the dissimilitude between such a man and such a child: *dissimiles hic vir, et ille puer.* The Abbé Delille expatiates on the attractions of each Spring-tide, and, by affinity, of each new-born Day, as consisting in its refreshing redolence of promise—"*qui ne nous fait que des promesses.*" Fraught with feeling in every line is the following sonnet addressed by the late Baron Alderson to one of his children on her second birthday:

"Sweet is the fragrance of the morning hour,
Sweet is the sun's first radiance, sweet the year,
In the spring's early promise, sweet the flower,
Seen in its buds, ere yet its leaves appear—
But sweeter far, my angel babe, to me
Is that blue eye that speaks thy opening mind,
That beams with new quick thoughts, yet undefined,
That tell of what is now and what may be.
O may the God who taught us that, like thee,
We should be pure and spotless, bless thee still;
Lay on thy infant head His hand, to free
Thine heart from sin, and form thee to His will,
Cleanse thee from aught that's evil or defiled,
And keep thee as thou art, my darling child."

George Eliot somewhere speaks of a promise void, like so many other sweet, illusory promises of our childhood; void as promises made in Eden before the seasons were divided, and when the starry blossoms grew side by side with the ripening peach—impossible to be fulfilled when the golden gates had been passed. Mr. Dickens says of the faint image of Eden which is stamped upon our hearts in childhood, that it "chafes and rubs in our rough struggles with the world, and soon wears away; too often to leave nothing but a mournful blank remaining." Elia, the essay writer, is no way backward to own the demerits and even delinquencies of himself as Elia, the middle aged man; but for the child Elia, that "other me," there, in the background,—he must take leave to cherish the remembrance of that young master—with as little reference, he protests, to this stupid changeling of five-and-forty, as if it had been a child of some other house, and not *his* father's son. "I know how it shrank from any the least colour of falsehood. God help thee, Elia, how art thou changed! Thou art sophisticated. I know how honest, how courageous (for a weakling) it was—how religious, how imaginative, how hopeful. From what have I not fallen, if the child I remember was indeed myself!"

Stupid changelings of forty-five, their name is Legion, for they are indeed many. Glance with Shenstone at the shiny row of plump promissory faces in the dame school:—

"Even now sagacious foresight points to show
A little bench of heedless bishops here,
And there a chancellor in embryo,
Or bard sublime, if bard may e'er be so,
As Milton, Shakspeare, names that ne'er shall die!"

So, to apply the words of Hazlitt, if we look back to past generations (as far as eye can reach), we see the same fears, hopes, wishes, followed by the same disappointments, throbbing in the human heart; and so we may ever see them (if we look forward) rising up for ever, and disappearing like vapourish bubbles. Capable of application even are Joanna Baillie's lines assimilating the stupid changelings aforesaid to a dull cat in contrast with its sprightly, mercurial kittenhood:—

"Ah! many a lightly sportive child,
Who hath like thee our wits beguiled,
To dull and sober manhood grown,
With strange recoil our hearts disown."

Il y a en chacun de nous, writes Sainte-Beuve, *un être primitif, idéal, que la nature a dessiné de sa main la plus maternelle, mais que l'homme trop souvent étoffe ou corrompt.* Mr. Kingsley, in a touching reflection—literally reflection, looking back—on the "long lost might-have been," adverts to that personal idea which every soul brings with it into the world, which shines dim and potential in the face of every sleeping babe, before it has been scarred, and distorted, and encrusted in the long tragedy of life. Dr. Caird has said of the birthday of the worst of men, that although it ushered a new agent of evil into existence, and was a day fraught with more disastrous results to the world than the day in which the pestilence began to creep over the nations, or the blight to fasten on the food of man, or any other physical evil to enter on a career of world-wide devastation,—yet might this day, when the vilest of humanity first saw the light, be in some aspects of it regarded as better (despite Solomon's text) than the day of his death. "For, to take only one view of it, when life commenced, the problem of good or evil, to which death has brought so terrible a solution, was, in his case, as yet unsolved. The page of human history which he was to write was yet unwritten, and to that day belonged, at all events, the advantage of the uncertainty whether it was to be blurred and blotted, or written fair and clean." Life, even in the most unfavourable circumstances, it is urged, has ever some faint gleams of hope to brighten its outset. The preacher owns that the simplicity, the tenderness, the unconscious refinement that more or less characterize infancy, even among the lowest and rudest, soon indeed pass away, and give place to the coarseness of an unideal, if not the animal repulsiveness of a sensual or sinful life. But he insists that at least at the beginning, for a little while, there is something in the seeming innocency, the brightness, the unworldliness, the unworn freshness of childhood, that gives hope room to work. Is there not, he asks, for every child, not in the dreams of parental fondness only, but in reality, and in God's idea, the possibility of a noble future? "The history of each new-born soul is surely in God's plan and intention a bright and blessed one. For the vilest miscreant that was ever hounded out of life in dishonour and wretchedness, there was, in the mind of the All-Good, a Divine ideal, a glorious possibility of excellence, which might have been made a reality." The most hardened ruffian, the most obdurate criminal, the most impenetrable reprobate, was once a child.

If it be a philosophical truth that the child is father of the man—all that is now broadly emblazoned in the man having been once latent—seen or not seen—as a vernal bud in the child; it is not therefore true universally, as Mr. de Quincey points out, that all which pre-exists in the child finds its development in the man. "Rudiments and tendencies, which *might* have found, sometimes by accident, *do* not find, sometimes under the killing frost of counter forces, *cannot* find, their natural evolution." Most of what he has, the grown-up man is shown to inherit from his infant self; but it does not follow that he always enters upon the whole of his natural inheritance. Childhood has been passionately apostrophized as

> " . . . thou vindication
> Of God—thou living witness against all men
> Who have been babes—thou everlasting promise
> Which no man keeps!"

——o——

EARS TO HEAR.

St. Luke viii. 8.

"HE that hath ears to hear, let him hear." These words cried Jesus, at the close of His parable of the Sower. And He went on to say that to some, to the many, He spake in parables, that seeing they might not see—not having eyes to see; and that hearing they might not understand—not having ears to hear in the Gospel sense. Nor in the Old Testament sense; for these very words are cited from Isaiah; in Deuteronomy too we read of those to whom the Lord hath not given ears to hear; and in both Jeremiah and Ezekiel, of those who have ears to hear, and hear not. One apostle laments the destiny of those to whom God hath given the spirit of slumber, eyes that they should not see, and ears that they should not hear. And to another was entrusted the appeal, "He that hath an ear, let him hear what the Spirit saith unto the churches." For only the ear of the wise seeketh knowledge. The unwise is like the deaf adder that stoppeth her ear. The hearing ear, and the seeing eye, the Lord hath made even both of them.

Give but interest in the theme, and the listener's ear fulfils its natural function, that of hearing. "Mine ears hast Thou opened." Intensify the interest, and the listener is all ears, all ear. Milton pictures a time—

> "when, Adam first of men,
> To first of women, Eve thus moving speech,
> Turn'd him, all ear."

So again the attendant spirit in his "Comus":—

> " . . . I was all ear,
> And took in strains that might create a soul
> Under the ribs of Death."

Webster's ill-starred Duchess of Malfi assures her brother, "I will plant my soul in my ears to hear you." *Je t'écoute sans cligner la paupière*, exclaims Marillac, in "Gerfaut," *dût ta narration durer sept jours et sept nuits.* "Alarmed nature starts up in my heart, and opens a thousand ears to listen," cries Colonel Talbot in an old play. Perplexed in the extreme, and cut to the heart, by a revelation of household treachery and wrong, an incredulous husband is described in a modern romance, with his hands clasped together, and with his head bent to catch every syllable of the harrowing news,—listening "as if his whole being were resolved into that one sense of hearing." That reads like a literal translation of Balzac's description of one whose whole *vie se concentra dans le seul sens de l'ouïe.* On another page he is not forgetful of *certains hommes* who *se bouchent les oreilles pour ne plus rien entendre.* None so deaf as those who will not hear. Next to them may rank those who do not care to. The familiar narrative of "Eyes and No Eyes" might easily have its pendent and parallel, point by point, and paragraph by paragraph, in one to be called *Ears and No Ears.*

It is with hearing as with seeing. The eye is not satisfied with seeing, nor the ear filled with hearing. Mendelssohn, in one of his letters from abroad, rapturous with gazing on his "favourite Titian," declares that one "might well wish for a dozen more eyes to look one's fill at such a picture. "Had I three ears I 'd hear thee!" exclaims Macbeth, when summoned to attend by the apparition of an Armed Head, in the witches' cave. Just as one of Plato's epigrams expresses a wish for the thousand eyes of the starry sky, that he might gaze his fill on the star of his life :

εἴθε γενοίμην
Οὐρανὸς, ὡς πολλοῖς ὄμμασιν ἐις σὲ βλέπω.

Horace uses the expressive phrase, *bibit aure,* in one of his odes—literally, "drink in with the ear"—a phrase admired by the commentators for its lyric boldness. "I was all fixed to listen," says Dante, in the tenth gulf of *l' Inferno.* "O speak your counsel now, for Saturn's ear is all a-hungered," entreats the Titan, in Keats's *Hyperion.* D'Artagnan, in the ante-chamber of M. de Treville, is described as looking with all his eyes and listening with all his ears, stretching his five senses so as to lose nothing. The same author tells how Mazarin listened, dying as he was, to Anne of Austria, as ten living men could not have listened. "Will you listen?" asks a prince in the same story; and is answered, "Can you ask me? You speak of a matter of life or death to me, and then ask if I will listen."

When Falstaff asks the prince, "Dost thou hear me, Hal?" "Ay, and mark thee too," is the reply; and that there is a difference between hearing and marking, between lending one ear and giving both, Falstaff knew as well as most men. And could practise what he knew, if occasion prompted. Witness his wilful deafness when taken to task by the Lord Chief Justice. "Boy, tell him I 'm deaf," he bids his page say. So, "You must speak louder, my master's deaf," says the boy. "I am sure he is, to the hearing of anything good," rejoins the

Chief Justice. And when, anon, his lordship taxes the incorrigible knight with being deaf to what he is saying, Sir John assures him, with that consummate assurance of his, that he hears him very well: "Rather, an't please you, it is the disease of not listening, the malady of not marking, that I am troubled withal." Quite capable is that witty profligate of entering into the import of each phrase in the collect on the Holy Scriptures, which prays that we may in such wise hear them, as to mark and learn, and inwardly digest them.

A late divine, treating of "animal men" in the "animal" sense of St. Paul, as those who cannot discern spiritual things, but are absorbed in animalism as their being's end and aim, affirmed that unavailing as it seems to be to talk to them of religion, it avails no more talking of poetry, and art, or speculative science, or the nobler things of the soul: "How can such men discern the things of the Spirit? They understand Tennyson as little as they understand St. Paul." Having ears they hear not anything so far away as the music of the spheres. Of *that*, and such as that, the animal man might say, by self-application of a couplet of Cowper's,

> "For which, alas! my destiny severe,
> Though ears she gave me two, gave me no ear."

——o——

NOT ALONE IN THE VALLEY OF SHADOWS.

PSALM xxiii. 4.

NO good thing will He, from whom cometh every good gift, withhold from them that love Him, and that walk uprightly; least of all then His presence when most that presence is indispensable,—as a *very* present help in trouble. And when so indispensable as in the valley of the shadow of death—darkening more and more unto the perfect night? We must die alone. It is a truism, in its natural sense. But in what the devout mind refuses to call or consider a non-natural sense, the righteous hath companionship as well as hope in his death. He who can say, The Lord is my shepherd, I shall not want, confines not his reliance to the range of green pastures and still waters, but extends it to the glooms of the grave and the swellings of Jordan. Not alone at the last, for the Good Shepherd knoweth His sheep, and is known of them. And how known? For one that will not let them want. "Yea, though I walk through the valley of the shadow of death I will fear no evil; for Thou art with me; Thy rod and Thy staff they comfort me."

Pascal said that the solitude of death was the bitterest pang of humanity; and because one must die alone, the end of life is its heaviest trial. Some Frenchmen and Frenchwomen, very French, have essayed, in their peculiar fashion, to elude the disaster, simply by dying in public. People in Paris died in public in the seventeenth century. Death, as Mr. Herman Merivale puts it, was but the last scene of the play, to be performed with a theatrical bow and exit. He shows us the young beauty, perishing of dissipation, who made her adieux to the world in appropriate costume and sentiments; and the worn-out statesman, who might not turn his face to the wall in peace, but was surrounded by a whole court in full dress, and talked on till his husky accents could no longer convey the last of his smart sayings to the listeners.* With all his fribbles and frivolities Horace Walpole was not quite Frenchified enough to willingly face death in a French hotel, with all its noise and excitement, "and, what would be still worse, exposed to receive all visits; for the French, you know," he writes to Conway, "are never more in public than in the act of death. I am like animals, and love to hide myself when I am dying" —which refers to his periodical, and prolonged, and always perilous attacks of gout. "If," says the author of "Life in the Sick-room," "I could not trust my friends to save me from

* "See the well-known print of Mazarin's death-bed, surrounded by ladies at cards. According to Grimm, the Maréchale de Luxembourg and two of her friends played at loto by that of Madame du Deffand till she expired. But at that time the proceeding was at least thought singular."—"Historical Studies," by Herman Merivale.

involuntary encroachment at the last, I had rather scoop myself a hole in the sand of the desert, and die alone, than be tended by the gentlest hands, and soothed by the most loving voices in the choicest chamber." Wordsworth's Marmaduke exclaims,—

> "Give me a reason why the wisest thing
> That the earth knows shall never choose to die,
> But some one must be near to count his groans.
> The wounded deer retires to solitude,
> And dies in solitude: all things but man,
> All die in solitude."

Special note has been taken of the exceptional characteristic in the altogether exceptional career of the prophet Elijah, that, in his last hour, when he was on his way to a strange and unprecedented departure from this world—when the whirlwind and flame chariot were ready, he asked for no human companionship. "The bravest men are pardoned if one lingering feeling of human weakness clings to them at the last, and they desire a human eye resting on them—a human hand in theirs—a human presence. But Elijah would have rejected all. In harmony with the rest of his lonely severe character, he desired to meet his Creator alone." One hears of such preferences now and then, in oddly constituted natures. Sir Walter Scott, in a letter to his sister-in-law, appears to indicate a disposition of this kind as prevalent in his father's family. "Poor aunt Curle," he tells her, "died like a Roman, or rather like one of the Sandy-Knowe bairns, the most stoical race I ever knew. She turned every one out of the room, and drew her last breath alone. So did my uncle, Captain Robert Scott, and several others of that family." Affectation was so inherent in Chateaubriand's confessions and professions, that one knows not how far genuine may have been his plea for what he calls the "necessity of isolation," and its advantages in death as in life. "Any hand is good enough to reach us the glass of water that we call for in the fever of death. Ah! may that hand not be too dear to us!" The "necessity of isolation" reminds us of Keble's query:—

"Why should we faint and fear to live alone,
Since all alone, so Heaven has will'd, we die,
Nor even the tenderest heart, and next our own,
Knows half the reasons why we smile and sigh?"

And that again reminds us, with a difference—the difference between Madame de Staël and the sweet singer of the "Christian Year,"—of Corinne on her death-bed, saying to Castel Forte: "But for you, I should die alone. There is no help for such a moment; friends can but follow us to the brink; there begin thoughts too deep, too troublous, to be confided." *Mon sort est de mourir seul,* writes Rousseau's bereaved Solitaire; *et la seule Providence me fermera les yeux.* Scott was not of mere imagination all compact when he made Edie Ochiltree say, in the cave that forms the old mendicant's favourite retreat, "I hae had mony a thought, that when I found myself auld and forfairn, and no able to enjoy God's blessed air ony langer, I wad e'en streek mysell out here, and abide my removal, like an auld dog that trails its useless ugsome carcass into some bush or bracken." Montaigne says that, might he have his choice, he thought he should like best to die out of his own house, and away from his own people. The Emperor Marcus Aurelius, on the seventh day of his last illness, admitted none but his unworthy son (Commodus) to his chamber, and after a few words dismissed him, "covered his head for sleep, and"—in Dean Merivale's words—"passed away alone and untended." Epigrammatic historians love to tell of Catherine the Great, who had reigned over five hundred and forty towns, over forty-two governments, over a multitude of isles of the sea from Kamschatka to Japan, and over eighty millions of slaves, that she died alone, entirely alone, without a single slave at hand to support her drooping head. The picture is meant to be sensational, and as written in French and for the French, it may be telling enough. It tells, for instance, upon such a nature as Madame Sophie Gay, who used to promise her friends to come and die among them, when it was her turn and her time; adding, in her very French style, "Je ne veux pas que cette demoiselle"—meaning *la mort*

—"me trouve seule." Upon others, the grand climax of supreme solitude fails of effect. "It has always been my wish," writes Southey, for example, "to die far from my friends, to crawl like a dog into some corner and expire unseen. I would neither give nor receive unavailing pain." When death overtook St. Francis Xavier, he was on board of a vessel bound for Siam, and at his own request he was removed to the shore, that he might die with the greater composure. Stretched on the naked beach, with the cold blasts of a Chinese winter aggravating his pains—thus Sir James Stephen describes his last moments—he contended alone with the agonies of the fever which wasted his vital power. "It was an agony and a solitude for which the happiest of the sons of men might well have exchanged the dearest society, and the purest of the joys of life. . . . It was a solitude thronged by blessed ministers of peace and consolation, visible in all their bright and lovely aspects to the now unclouded eye of faith; and audible to the dying martyr through the yielding bars of his mortal prison-house, in strains of exulting joy till then unheard and unimagined."

"Thou must go forth alone, my soul, thou must go forth alone,—
To other scenes, to other worlds, that mortal hath not known,
Thou must go forth alone, my soul, to tread the narrow vale;
But He, whose word is sure, hath said His comforts shall not fail.
His rod and staff shall comfort thee across the dreary road,
Till thou shalt join the blessed ones, in Heaven's serene abode."

Mr. de Quincey has finely said of solitude, that, although it may be silent as light, it is, like light, the mightiest of agencies; for solitude is essential to man. "All men come into this world *alone;* all leave it *alone.* Even a little child has a dread, whispering consciousness, that, if he should be summoned to travel into God's presence, no gentle nurse will be allowed to lead him by the hand, nor mother to carry him in her arms, nor little sister to share his trepidations." King and priest, we are further reminded, warrior and maiden, philosopher and child, all must walk those mighty galleries alone. The solitude, therefore, which this author describes as in this world appalling or fascinating a child's heart,* is but the echo of a far deeper solitude, through which already he has passed, and of another solitude, deeper still, through which he *has* to pass: reflex of one solitude—prefiguration of another.

Crabbe says of man that, feeling his weakness, it is his habit to run to society, to numbers,—

> "Himself to strengthen, or himself to shun;
> But though to this our weakness may be prone,
> Let's learn to live, for we must die, alone."

Among the pangs which belong to death is emphatically reckoned by F. W. Robertson, in his sermon on Victory over it, the sensation of loneliness which attaches to that transit through the valley of shadows. Have we ever, he asks, seen a ship preparing to sail with its load of pauper emigrants to a distant colony? for that is keenly suggestive of the desolation which comes from feeling unfriended on a new and untried excursion. He dilates on all beyond the seas being to the ignorant poor man a strange land—away from the helps and friendships and companionships of life, scarcely knowing what is before him; and it is in such a moment, when a man stands upon a deck, taking his last look of his fatherland, that there comes upon him what the preacher calls "a sensation new, strange, and inexpressibly miserable—the feeling of being alone in the world. Brethren, with all the bitterness of such a moment, it is but a feeble image when placed by the side of the loneliness of death. We die alone. We go on our dark mysterious journey for the first time in all our existence, without one to accompany us. Friends are beside our bed, they must stay behind. Grant that a Christian has something like familiarity with the Most High, *that* breaks this solitary feeling; but what is it with the mass of men? It is a question full of loneliness to them." Says the elder Humboldt (Wilhelm), in

* "God speaks to children, also, in dreams, and by the oracles that lurk in darkness. But in solitude, above all things, . . . God holds with children 'communion undisturbed.'"—"Autobiographic Sketches," by Thomas de Quincey, i. 24.

one of his letters: "However many companions a man may have in the active sympathising world, he must ever make the journey which leads across the boundaries of earthly things alone; no one may accompany him." Not but that in some moods, and in some sense, this contemplative philosopher might have assented to the protest of Paul Flemming, that had we spiritual organs, to see and hear things now invisible and inaudible to us, we should behold the air thronged with the departing souls of that vast multitude which every moment dies. For, "truly the soul departs not alone on its last journey, but spirits of its kind attend it, when not ministering angels; and they go in families to the unknown land. Neither in life nor in death are we alone." But then as we have *not* the spiritual organs in question, the fact of conscious isolation *in articulo mortis* is not affected; and their character, after all, pertains rather to spiritualism than to spirituality.

A latter-day Christian lyrist expatiates on the sense of loneliness one has at midnight, in the dread calmness of the dark, —or again, on pathless hills, when the sun is set, and the ear listens in vain for some social sound from afar. But,—

> "If this be solitude, while life retains her healthful tone,
> How shall I feel when, faint with pain,—I die alone?
>
> "Of all the happy things that live in ocean, earth, or air,
> Not one with kindred sympathy my lonely lot shall share.
> My friend shall vainly scan the glance that speaks no language now;
> My dog shall lick the languid hand that falters on his brow:
> But none shall venture forth with me, to meet the dread unknown,
> And I between two living worlds—must die alone!"

Je mourrai seul. Pascal's words are continually cited, though only to be forgotten. Mrs. Browning feelingly and earnestly expands into a sonnet what she entitles "A Thought for a Lonely Death-bed. Inscribed to my friend E. C."

> "If God compel thee to this destiny,
> To die alone,—with none beside thy bed
> To ruffle round with sobs thy last word said,
> And mark with tears the pulses ebb from thee,—
> Then pray alone—'O Christ, come tenderly!

By Thy forsaken Sonship in the red
Drear wine-press,—by the wilderness outspread,—
And the lone garden where Thine agony
Fell bloody from Thy brow,—by all of those
Permitted desolations, comfort mine!
No earthly friend being near me, interpose
No deathly angel 'twixt my face and Thine,
But stoop Thyself to gather my life's rose,
And smile away my mortal to Divine.'"

One can hardly quit this subject without recalling the awful significance of a cry that once expressed, if one may say it, inexpressible anguish,—anguish indescribable, incommunicable, —"My God, my God, why hast Thou forsaken Me!" Penultimate words, these were; and appalling in their suggestiveness of uttermost desolation. But not the last words of all. He was not alone, consciously not alone, at the very last. Later than these, and triumphant over these—however subdued and serene the triumph—came those other words, Divinely calm, as became the Speaker,—"Father, into Thy hands I commend my spirit." And it was when He had *this* said, that He gave up the ghost.

INDEX.

Butler & Tanner, The Selwood Printing Works, Frome, and London

LONDON, *October*, 1870.

HODDER & STOUGHTON'S

WORKS IN THEOLOGY & RELIGIOUS LITERATURE.

The Church of the Restoration. By JOHN STOUGHTON, D.D. Forming the Third and Fourth Volumes of "The Ecclesiastical History of England." 2 vols. 8vo, 25*s.*

The Church of the Civil Wars and the Church of the Commonwealth. Being the First and Second Volumes of "The Ecclesiastical History of England." By the same author. 2 vols. 8vo, 28*s.*

Secular Annotations on Scripture Texts. By the Rev. FRANCIS JACOX. Crown 8vo, 6*s.*

Ecclesia: Church Problems considered in a Series of Essays. Edited by HENRY ROBERT REYNOLDS, D.D. Second Thousand. 8vo, 14*s.*, cloth.

Christus Consolator; or, The Pulpit in Relation to Social Life. By ALEXANDER MACLEOD, D.D. Crown 8vo, 5*s.* *Contents:*—The Social Mission of the Pulpit; The Preacher as an Elevator—Poverty and the Poor; The Preacher as a Healer—Restoration of the Fallen; The Preacher as a Reconciler—Employers and Employed; The Preacher as an Educator—National Education; The Preacher as a Liberator—The Crushed Classes; The Preacher as a Regenerator—the Renewal of Life; Some Results of Preaching; Secrets of Failure; Range of Preaching; Detraction; Preachers and Sermons.

Rain upon the Mown Grass, and other Sermons. By the Rev. SAMUEL MARTIN, of Westminster Chapel. 8vo, 10*s.* 6*d.*

Life Problems answered in Christ. Six Sermons. By LEIGH MANN. With Preface by Rev. A. MACLAREN, B.A. Crown 8vo, 4*s.* 6*d.*

The Life and Times of the Rev. John Wesley, M.A., Founder of the Methodists. By the Rev. LUKE TYERMAN. Vol. I., 8vo, 12*s.* To be completed in Three Vols., 8vo, with Portraits, price 12*s.* each. Vol. II. will appear in December, and Vol. III. in March.

One Thousand Gems from the Rev. Henry Ward Beecher. Compiled (with Mr. Beecher's sanction) by the Rev. G. D. EVANS. Crown 8vo, 5*s.*, with Portrait.

BY REV. T. BINNEY.

1. **The Practical Power of Faith.** An Exposition of part of the Eleventh Chapter of Hebrews. Fourth edition. With New Preface. Crown 8vo, 5*s.*, cloth.
2. **Money: a Popular Exposition in Rough Notes.** With Remarks on Stewardship and Systematic Beneficence. Third Edition. Crown 8vo, 5*s.*, cloth.

3. **Micah the Priest-Maker.** A Handbook on Ritualism. Second Edition, enlarged. Post 8vo, 5*s.*, cloth.

Lectures on the First and Second Epistles of Peter. By JOHN LILLIE, D.D., author of "Lectures on the Epistles of St. Paul to the Thessalonians," &c. With a Preface by PHILIP SCHAFF, D.D. In 8vo, price 12*s.*, cloth.

Beacons and Patterns: A Book for Young Men. By the Rev. W. LANDELS, D.D., author of "The Young Man in the Battle of Life," &c. 3*s.* 6*d.*

Bible Lore; or, Brief Studies on Subjects relating to the Holy Scriptures. By Rev. J. COMPER GRAY, author of "Topics for Teachers." 3*s.* 6*d.*

WORKS BY DR. PRESSENSÉ.

1. **The Early Years of Christianity.** A Sequel to "Jesus Christ: His Times, Life, and Work." 8vo, 12*s.*, cloth.
2. **The Martyrs and Apologists.** Being the Second Volume of "The Early Years of Christianity." 8vo. [In the press.]
3. **Jesus Christ: His Times, Life, and Work.** Third and Cheaper Edition. Crown 8vo, 9*s.*, cloth.
4. **The Mystery of Suffering, and Other Discourses.** New Edition. Crown 8vo, 3*s.* 6*d.*, cloth.
5. **The Land of the Gospel: Notes of a Journey in the** East. In crown 8vo, 5*s.*, cloth.
6. **The Church and the French Revolution.** A History of the Relations of Church and State from 1789 to 1802. In crown 8vo, 9*s.*

Human Power in the Divine Life; or, The Active Powers of the Mind in Relation to Religion. By the Rev. NICHOLAS BISHOP, M.A. Crown 8vo, 6*s.*

BY J. BALDWIN BROWN, B.A.

1. **The First Principles of Ecclesiastical Truth.** 8vo, 10*s.* 6*d.*
2. **The Divine Mysteries; the Divine Treatment of Sin, and** the Divine Mystery of Peace. New Edition. Crown 8vo, 7*s.* 6*d.*, cloth.
3. **Misread Passages of Scripture.** New Edition. 3*s.* 6*d.*, cloth.
4. **Misread Passages of Scripture.** Second Series, crown 8vo, 3*s.* 6*d.*
5. **Idolatries, Old and New: Their Cause and Cure.** 5*s.*
6. **The Divine Life in Man.** Second Edition. 7*s.* 6*d.*, cloth.
7. **The Doctrine of the Divine Fatherhood in Relation to** the Atonement. 1*s.* 6*d.*, cloth.

BY REV. CHARLES STANFORD.

1. **Symbols of Christ.** Second Edition. 3*s.* 6*d.* Small crown 8vo, cloth.
2 **Central Truths.** Third Edition. Small crown 8vo, price 3*s.* 6*d.*, cloth

3. **Power in Weakness: Memorials of the Rev. William** Rhodes. New Edition. 3*s.* 6*d.*, cloth.

4. **Instrumental Strength: Thoughts for Students and** Pastors. Crown 8vo, price 1*s.*, cloth.

5. **Joseph Alleine: His Companions and Times.** Second Thousand. Crown 8vo, 4*s.* 6*d.*

The Prophecies of Our Lord and His Apostles. A Series of Discourses delivered in the Cathedral Church of Berlin. By W. HOFFMANN, D.D., Chaplain-in-Ordinary to the King of Prussia. Crown 8vo, 7*s.* 6*d.*, cloth.

Incidents in the Life of Edward Wright. Including Reference to his Work among the Thieves of London. By EDWARD LEACH, author of "Sketches of Christian Work among the Lowly." Crown 8vo, 5*s.*, with Portrait.

Christian Work on the Battle Field. Being incidents of the Labours of the United States' Christian Commission. With an Historical Essay on the Influence of Christianity in Alleviating the Horrors of War. Eight full-page Illustrations. Crown 8vo, 6*s.*

The History of the Church in the Eighteenth and Nineteenth Centuries. By K. R. HAGENBACH, D.D., Professor of Theology in the University of Basle, author of "German Rationalism." Translated by JOHN F. HURST, D.D. In 2 vols., 8vo, 24*s.* cloth.

Masterpieces of Pulpit Eloquence. Ancient and Modern, with Historical Sketches of Preaching in the Different Countries represented, and Biographical and Critical Notices of the several Preachers and their Discourses. By HENRY C. FISH, D.D. In 2 vols. 8vo, cloth, 21*s.*

BY JOSEPH PARKER, D.D.

1. **Ad Clerum: Advices to a Young Preacher.** Crown 8vo, 5*s.*

2. **The City Temple: Sermons Preached in the Poultry** Chapel, 1869–70. 8vo, 6*s.*

3. **A Homiletic Analysis of the Gospel according to St.** Matthew. With an Introductory Essay on the Life of Jesus Christ, considered as an appeal to the imagination. In 8vo, price 7*s.* 6*d.*, cloth.

4. **Springdale Abbey: Extracts from the Diaries and Letters** of an English Preacher. 8vo, 7*s.* 6*d.*, cloth.

5. **Ecce Deus: Essays on the Life and Doctrine of Jesus** Christ. Fourth Edition. Crown 8vo, 5*s.*

The Epistle to the Hebrews: a Popular Exposition. By Rev. R. W. DALE, M.A., author of "Week-day Sermons." Second and Cheaper Edition. 6*s.*

Discourses Delivered on Special Occasions. By the same author. Crown 8vo, 6*s.*

BY REV. E. PAXTON HOOD

1. **Dark Sayings on a Harp, and other Sermons on some** of the Dark Questions of Human Life. New Edition. Crown 8vo, 6*s.*

2. **Lamps, Pitchers, and Trumpets: Lectures on the Vocation of the Preacher.** Illustrated by Anecdotes—Biographical, Historical, and Elucidatory—of every order of Pulpit Eloquence, from the Great Preachers of all Ages. Second Thousand. 10*s*. 6*d*., cloth.

3. **The World of Anecdote: An Accumulation of Facts,** Incidents, and Illustrations—Historical and Biographical—from Books and Times, Recent and Remote. Second Thousand. Large crown 8vo, 10*s*. 6*d*., cloth, 700 pp.

4. **The World of Religious Anecdote.** Being a Second Series of "The World of Anecdote." 8vo, 10*s*. 6*d*.

The Pulpit Analyst. Designed for Preachers, Students, and Teachers. Vols. I. to V., price 7*s*. 6*d*. each, handsomely bound in cloth.

The Daily Prayer-Book, for the Use of Families, with additional Prayers for Special Occasions. Edited by JOHN STOUGHTON, D.D. Crown 8vo, 5*s*., cloth; or morocco antique, 10*s*. 6*d*.

The Gospel according to St. Mark. A New Translation, with Critical Notes and Doctrinal Lessons. By JOHN H. GODWIN, author of "A New Translation of St. Matthew's Gospel," etc. 4*s*. 6*d*., cloth.

Remarkable Facts: Illustrative and Confirmatory of Different Portions of Holy Scripture. By the late Rev. J. LEIFCHILD, D.D., with a Preface by his son. New and Cheaper Edition, 3*s*. 6*d*.

Credo. Crown 8vo, 5*s*., cloth.

The State of the Blessed Dead. Advent Sermons. By the Very Rev. HENRY ALFORD, D.D., Dean of Canterbury. Third Thousand. Square 16mo, 1*s*. 6*d*., cloth.

The Coming of the Bridegroom. Advent Sermons. By the same author. Uniform with above. Square 16mo, 1*s*. 6*d*.

The Theology of the New Testament: A Handbook for Bible Students. By the Rev. J. J. VAN OOSTERZEE, D.D. Translated by the Rev. M. J. EVANS, B.A. Crown 8vo, 6*s*., cloth.

The Son of Man: Discourses on the Humanity of Jesus Christ. Delivered at Paris and Geneva. With an Address on the Teaching of Jesus Christ. By FRANK COULIN, D.D. Fcap. 8vo. 5*s*.

The Melody of the Twenty-third Psalm. By ANNA WARNER. Square 16mo, 2*s*., cloth.

The Song of Christ's Flock in the Twenty-third Psalm. Third Edition. Crown 8vo, 3*s*. 6*d*., cloth.

The Heritage of Peace; or, Christ our Life. By T. S. CHILDS, D.D. Square 16mo, 2*s*., cloth.

Ancient Hymns and Poems; chiefly from St. Ephrem, of Syra, Prudentius, Pope Gregory the First, and St. Bernard. Translated and imitated by the Rev. T. G. CRIPPEN. Fcap. 8vo, price 2*s*., cloth, red edges.

www.ingramcontent.com/pod-product-compliance
Lightning Source LLC
LaVergne TN
LVHW020058110826
845151LV00001B/8
9781425545024